*The Chesapeake
in the
Seventeenth Century*

edited by

Thad W. Tate and David L. Ammerman

Published for the
Institute of Early American History and Culture
at Williamsburg, Virginia

The Chesapeake in the Seventeenth Century

Essays on Anglo-American Society

W · W · NORTON & COMPANY · New York · London

W. W. Norton & Company, Inc., 500 Fifth Avenue, New York, N.Y. 10110
W. W. Norton & Company Ltd., 37 Great Russell Street, London WC1B 3NU

Printed in the United States of America
Library of Congress Catalog Card Number 78-31720

Published as a Norton paperback 1979 by arrangement with
The University of North Carolina Press

Published simultaneously in Canada by Stoddart,
a subsidiary of General Publishing Co. Ltd,
Don Mills, Ontario.

Books That Live
*The Norton imprint on a book means that in the publisher's
estimation it is a book not for a single season but for the years.*
W. W. Norton & Company, Inc.

The illustration on the title page is from
Augustin Herrman's map of Virginia and Maryland, 1670
(courtesy of the Library of Congress).

Library of Congress Cataloging in Publication Data

Main entry under title:

The Chesapeake in the seventeenth century.

"Outgrowth of a conference . . . held on November 1 and 2, 1974, at
College Park and St. Mary's, Maryland."
Includes index.
1. Chesapeake Bay region—History—Addresses, essays, lectures.
2. Maryland—History—Colonial period, ca. 1600–1775—Addresses,
essays, lectures. 3. Virginia—History—Colonial period, ca. 1600–1775
—Addresses, essays, lectures. I. Tate, Thaddeus W. II. Ammerman,
David, 1938– III. Institute of Early American History and Culture,
Williamsburg, Va.
    F187.C5C46   975.5'18   78-31720

ISBN 0-393-00956-4

4 5 6 7 8 9 0

Contents

Preface

This volume is the outgrowth of a conference on the seventeenth-century Chesapeake held on November 1 and 2, 1974, at College Park and St. Mary's, Maryland. The idea of holding such a conference came initially from Warren Billings of the University of New Orleans, one of the scholars who were at the time beginning to publish on the early Chesapeake. That group included, of course, a very active component of scholars at work on Maryland, particularly those who were associated with Lois Green Carr at the St. Mary's City Commission. Thus from the first it was apparent that the conference ought to be a joint Maryland-Virginia venture if it were to reflect accurately how much the remarkable renascence of interest in the seventeenth-century Chesapeake involved the history of both colonies. The St. Mary's City Commission and the Department of History at the University of Maryland, College Park, consequently joined the Institute of Early American History and Culture as cosponsors. The University of Maryland generously provided a grant that assisted greatly in underwriting the costs of the conference, and program sessions during the first day met on the university campus at the Center of Adult Education. Those in attendance moved on the second day to St. Mary's for the final meetings. Cary Carson, then coordinator of research for the St. Mary's City Commission, and John J. McCusker of the Maryland history department were especially helpful in planning and organizing the conference, serving on the committee on arrangements and program together with Norman S. Fiering and Thad W. Tate from the Institute.

The program at College Park included discussion of some ten papers in four program sessions, devoted respectively to Problems of Colonization, Marriage and the Family, Politics, and Social Structure, while the activities at St. Mary's included a tour of archaeological sites and a panel discussion on Material Culture and History. Given the continuing flow of new work on the early Chesapeake, it now almost seems as if the conference had taken place a longer time ago than is actually the case, but many of the unexpectedly large number who turned out for it almost certainly will recall the liveliness of the sessions and the amount of discussion that the papers provoked.

Perhaps those present would also have agreed with the program committee that the conference had indeed more than fulfilled its original purposes with or without publication of the results. Yet a number of the papers presented did seem to unite in illuminating two particularly important themes that were clearly emerging in the work on the Chesapeake: the fragile character of early seventeenth-century Chesapeake society and the significant transformation that began late in the century, eventuating by 1720 in the predominance of a native-born social and political leadership, a large-scale plantation economy, and a labor system based on black slavery. Consequently, with the encouragement of Norman Fiering, editor of publications at the Institute, we began to envision a volume that would not attempt to serve as a record of the proceedings of the conference but rather would recognize both the seminal importance of that gathering and the continuing development of scholarship on the Chesapeake as it grew out of the original sessions. Several participants therefore revised and updated their essays and also assisted in the recruitment of some additional contributions to round out the treatment of the two major themes that the essays sought to illustrate.

The result is the present volume. The essayists, above all those whose work dates back to the original conference, have been remarkably patient—or at the least eminently reasonable in their moments of impatience at what must seem a long gestation period for the volume. We hope that its particular nature, that is, as a group of essays that developed out of the conference and required some further definition along the way, will make the time required to bring it to publication somewhat more understandable. We trust, too, that the volume will testify to the continuing growth and vitality of recent scholarship on the seventeenth-century Chesapeake, a process that seems to us still to be at an early stage of development. Finally, we would be remiss if we did not acknowledge the contribution of all those who participated in the 1974 conference by presiding at sessions, serving as commentators, or presenting papers. This volume would not have appeared without the enthusiasm and interest that they helped build.

Thad W. Tate
David L. Ammerman

The Chesapeake
in the
Seventeenth Century

1

The Seventeenth-Century Chesapeake and Its Modern Historians

Thad W. Tate

As the earliest region of permanent English settlement in the New World the seventeenth-century Chesapeake has always received some measure of attention from early American scholars. Yet it is questionable whether its share has, until recently, ever been proportionate to the Chesapeake's historical significance as a major region of the British Empire in North America—the site of the single largest and most populous colony, the source of a significant percentage of the wealth and commerce generated by the empire, and the provider of a remarkably large share of the political leadership of the new American nation. The fact is, of course, that little in the tenuous, troubled beginnings of Maryland and Virginia foreshadowed that later importance. Apart from a certain curiosity about the first successful settlement at Jamestown—as much antiquarian as scholarly in character—it has often seemed more rewarding to move rapidly to the political and social order of the "golden age" of the mid-eighteenth century. The seventeenth was important only for what it might demonstrate about the progression toward the grandeur and order of the eighteenth.[1]

I should like to thank the other contributors to this volume and also Emory G. Evans, Allan Kulikoff, Warren M. Billings, Norman S. Fiering, and Michael L. Nicholls for reading an earlier draft of this essay and providing me with some helpful comments and suggestions.

1. This statement does not entirely apply to an extensive and continuing body of work that treats English discovery and colonization in the New World, including the Roanoke and Virginia voyages and the Jamestown settlement. Much of that work, especially the contributions of David B. Quinn, but also those of Philip L. Barbour, A. L. Rowse, William S. Powell, Louis B. Wright, Wesley Frank Craven, K. R. Andrews, Nicholas Canny, and others, undoubtedly has important implications for the

3

When Wesley Frank Craven came to prepare the "Critical Essay on Authorities" for his *Southern Colonies in the Seventeenth Century*, which was published in 1949, he accurately observed that "when one surveys the secondary literature covering the Southern colonies in the seventeenth century, it is readily apparent that historians of the South have been chiefly interested in recent years in later periods." They had been content, he added, "to leave the story of the earliest years" where historians such as Philip Bruce and Newton Mereness had "left it a half century ago."[2] For another ten to fifteen years after Craven's comments matters did not change greatly, and then by the middle of the 1960s a major revival of interest in the early Chesapeake began that has yet to reach its peak. The current scholarly investigation constitutes such an intense, distinctive, and conspicuous renascence that, even before it has run its course, it invites bibliographical and historiographical analysis that will trace its origins, compare it with past traditions in writing the history of the Chesapeake, and assess its place in the broad field of early American studies generally.

The lack of extensive historical scholarship on the early Chesapeake for much of the twentieth century implies also a comparable absence of historiographical analysis. The subject has simply not invited the seemingly endless scrutiny that historians of, say, Puritanism or of the American Revolution have received from other historians. One of the few recent examples, Marshall Fishwick's provocative and breezy examination of "Clio in Bondage," which appears as an appendix to his *Virginia: A New Look at the Old Dominion*, is in reality more a comment on mythmaking in the popularization of Virginia history

---

early history of the Chesapeake. By making accessible first-hand accounts and other sources for the first years of the Virginia colony or by reinterpreting them perceptively, these scholars have made it far easier to arrive at a characterization of the social and political organization of the Virginia colony at its inception and to determine the degree of influence that the London Company exercised over life at Jamestown. Yet with some exceptions their main achievement has been to illuminate English history, and their work has come more in response to lines of force in the study of the late Tudor and early Stuart periods than those operating on the history of the Chesapeake. The literature of exploration and colonization of the Chesapeake is consequently not systematically examined in this essay.

I should also make it clear that the essay does not attempt to survey the rich, if uneven, body of local and county histories for both colonies but rather refers only to a few such works that seemed to have had an unusually strong impact on the more general study of the Chesapeake.

2. Wesley Frank Craven, *The Southern Colonies in the Seventeenth Century, 1607–1689*, in Wendell Holmes Stephenson and E. Merton Coulter, eds., *A History of the South*, I (Baton Rouge, La., 1949), 426, 427.

than it is an examination of the full range of scholarly work.[3] The best historiographical discussions of the early Chesapeake have generally addressed specific questions. One thinks, for example, of Craven's review of the long debate on the politics of the internal struggle within the London Company in its last years and Wilcomb E. Washburn's account of past writings on Bacon's Rebellion.[4] Both of these were also excellent case studies of Fishwick's mythmaking process, but primarily they demonstrated that most of the interpretative controversies affecting seventeenth-century Virginia—and something of the same thing might no doubt hold for Maryland—were concerned with individual events or episodes, not with broad syntheses.

A somewhat different kind of historiographical attention has been devoted to those historians and chroniclers who themselves lived in the seventeenth century. The considerable number of critical editions of seventeenth-century historians' works and the several extended analyses of this writing, such as those by Richard Dunn and Alden Vaughan, testify to a long-standing interest.[5] That interest is, however, prompted by the need to retrieve the original works in reliable form as source material or else by concern with the intellectual and literary milieu of the seventeenth century itself rather than by questions of the long-term historiography of the Chesapeake.

The relative absence of broader historiographical discussion may be explained not only by the paucity of work on the Chesapeake but also by the cyclical nature of its appearance. Historiographical scrutiny seems most often stimulated by the spectacle of rival schools of interpretation vying directly with each other. Writing on the Chesapeake has tended not to fall into such divisions, except between generations of historians. Nathaniel Bacon may be a democratic folk

3. (New York, 1959), 273–281.
4. Wesley Frank Craven, *Dissolution of the Virginia Company: The Failure of a Colonial Experiment* (New York, 1932), 1–23, and Wilcomb E. Washburn, *The Governor and the Rebel: A History of Bacon's Rebellion in Virginia* (Chapel Hill, N.C., 1957), 1–16. Washburn's discussion is briefly updated in Jane D. Carson, *Bacon's Rebellion, 1676–1696* (Jamestown, Va., 1976). There is also a perceptive characterization of work published on both the 17th- and 18th-century Chesapeake, dealing more with points of substance than with historiography, in Allan Kulikoff, "Economy and Social Structure in the Early Chesapeake: Toward a Synthesis," *Journal of Southern History*, forthcoming.
5. Richard S. Dunn, "Seventeenth-Century Historians of America," in James Morton Smith, ed., *Seventeenth-Century America: Essays in Colonial History* (Chapel Hill, N.C., 1959), 195–225; Alden T. Vaughan, "The Evolution of Virginia History: Early Historians of the First Colony," in Vaughan and George Athan Billias, eds., *Perspectives on Early American History: Essays in Honor of Richard B. Morris* (New York, 1973), 9–39.

hero to one generation and a rabble-rouser to another, but the debate has only occasionally involved direct confrontation between contemporaries. More often Chesapeake scholarship has alternated between periods of intense activity and those of relatively limited production, with the bulk of the work at any given time reflecting a common approach and point of view.

I

The first such modern cycle of activity in the study of the history of the early Chesapeake dates from the very beginning of scholarly, scientific history in the United States. From the 1880s until the eve of World War I scholarship and publication on the Chesapeake flourished as it would not again until the present day.

As the decade of the eighties opened, John T. Scharf's *History of Maryland from the Earliest Period to the Present Day* had just appeared,[6] while the antiquarian Edward Duffield Neill had already published a half-dozen works on Virginia and Maryland between 1867 and 1878. Neill, whose work was distinguished mostly by its inclusion of extensive excerpts from unpublished sources, completed his last two books within the decade. These were *Virginia Vetusta* and *Virginia Carolorum*, the latter being perhaps his best-known volume.[7] In the same ten-year period publication of the *Archives of Maryland* began, and its first editor, William H. Browne, also brought out *Maryland: The History of a Palatinate*.[8] Bradley T. Johnson's *Foundation of Maryland* was also published, and the earliest of the numerous Johns Hopkins Studies in Historical and Political Science that dealt with Chesapeake subjects, such as Jeffrey Brackett's *Negro in Maryland*, began to appear.[9]

During the 1890s two of the last great "gentleman amateurs" of Virginia history, Alexander Brown and Philip Bruce, published some of their major work. Brown's *Genesis of the United States*, a careful

6. Three vols. (Baltimore, 1879).

7. Edward D. Neill, *Virginia Vetusta, during the Reign of James the First* (Albany, N.Y., 1885); Edward D. Neill, *Virginia Carolorum: The Colony under the Rule of Charles the First and Second, A.D. 1625–A.D. 1685* . . . (Albany, N.Y., 1886).

8. William Hand Browne et al., eds., *Archives of Maryland* (Baltimore, 1883–   ); William Hand Browne, *Maryland: The History of a Palatinate*, 2d ed. (Boston, 1884).

9. Bradley T. Johnson, *The Foundation of Maryland and the Origin of the Act concerning Religion of April 21, 1649* (Baltimore, 1883); Jeffrey R. Brackett, *The Negro in Maryland: A Study of the Institution of Slavery*, Johns Hopkins University Studies in Historical and Political Science, ex. vol. VI (Baltimore, 1889).

investigation of the first decade at Jamestown, replete with documentary excerpts, appeared in 1890.[10] Drawn to Virginia history by his growing interest in the extended dispute being carried on by Virginia defenders and New England critics of the reliability of Captain John Smith, Brown worked diligently and widely in the sources, ultimately rejecting John Smith but arguing more for a broader understanding of the founding of the Virginia colony and for a better appreciation of the role that James I and the first officials of the London Company had played in the effort.[11] Then, eight years later Brown largely reversed his point of view in his much more polemical and less reliable First Republic in America, a full-scale attack on the crown and the old leadership of the London Company. These men, Brown charged, had undermined the beginnings of libertarian government in America by bringing about the dissolution of the company after the leadership passed to a faction led by Sir Edwin Sandys.[12] Brown thus revived a view of the colony's first years that had been originally propounded by the eighteenth-century historian William Stith and set in motion its reestablishment as a dominant interpretative thrust in the historical writing of his era.[13] Philip Bruce's Economic History of Virginia in the Seventeenth Century, which had appeared three years earlier than the First Republic, was in another mold, however, setting a high standard for subsequent historians to follow by its detailed research and by its innovative concentration on nonpolitical institutional development.[14]

In the case of Maryland the issue of Catholicism and its overthrow by the political revolution of the years 1689 to 1692 seemed to fill something of the same dominant place in the colony's historiography as the Virginians' concern with the factional struggles of the London Company. The studies of Francis Sparks and Bernard C. Steiner, among others, evidenced this interest.[15] In the beginning years of the

10. Alexander Brown, ed., Genesis of the United States . . . , 2 vols. (Boston and New York, 1890).

11. Craven, Dissolution of the Virginia Company, 12–14.

12. Alexander Brown, First Republic in America . . . (Boston and New York, 1898).

13. Craven, Dissolution of the Virginia Company, 5–11.

14. Philip Alexander Bruce, Economic History of Virginia in the Seventeenth Century: An Inquiry into the Material Condition of the People, Based upon Original and Contemporaneous Records, 2 vols. (New York, 1896). James C. Ballagh exhibited a similar interest in White Servitude in the Colony of Virginia . . . , Johns Hopkins Studies, XIII, nos. 6–7 (Baltimore, 1895), and Introduction to Southern Economic History, American Historical Association, Annual Report . . . 1897 (Washington, D.C., 1898), 99–129.

15. Francis Edgar Sparks, Causes of the Maryland Revolution of 1689, Johns Hopkins

new century Steiner became the most productive of the Maryland historians, publishing in four installments in the Hopkins Studies a history of the colony to 1660 and succeeding as well to the editorship of the *Archives of Maryland*.[16] Newton Mereness's *Maryland as a Proprietary Province*, published in 1901, became the standard one-volume account of the early history of the colony,[17] while Clayton C. Hall completed *The Lords Baltimore and the Maryland Palatinate* in 1902 and edited the Maryland volume for J. Franklin Jameson's Original Narratives Series in 1910.[18]

New work on Virginia was at least equivalent, aided by the results of historical editing on an unprecedented scale for the Old Dominion. Susan M. Kingsbury's edition of *The Records of the Virginia Company of London* began in this period; in 1910 A. G. Bradley brought out a new edition of Edward Arber's compilation of the writings of John Smith; the bulk of surviving seventeenth-century records of the House of Burgesses appeared in two volumes in 1914 and 1915; and both leading Virginia historical journals, the *Virginia Magazine of History and Biography* and the First Series of the *William and Mary Quarterly*, gave heavy emphasis in these years to the presentation of documentary material.[19] Apart from this remarkable increase in more accurately printed sources, Virginia began to draw a larger share of attention in the Hopkins Studies, including accounts of Virginia

---

Studies, XIV, nos. 11–12 (Baltimore, 1896); Bernard C. Steiner, *The Protestant Revolution in Maryland*, A.H.A., *Annual Report . . . 1897* (Washington, D.C., 1898), 279–353. See also Daniel R. Randall, *A Puritan Colony in Maryland*, Johns Hopkins Studies, IV, no. 6 (Baltimore, 1886), and George Petrie, *Church and State in Early Maryland*, Johns Hopkins Studies, X, no. 4 (Baltimore, 1892).

16. *Beginnings of Maryland, 1631–1639* (Baltimore, 1903); *Maryland during the English Civil Wars* (Baltimore, 1906–1907); *Maryland under the Commonwealth: A Chronicle of the Years 1649–1658* (Baltimore, 1911). They appeared in the Johns Hopkins Studies, XXI, nos. 8–10, XXIV, nos. 11–12, XXV, nos. 4–5, and XXIX, no. 1. He also published *Descriptions of Maryland* (Baltimore, 1904) in XXII, nos. 11–12, and had shorter essays on the first Lord Baltimore and the first courts of the colony in the A.H.A. *Annual Report* for 1901 and for 1905.

17. (New York, 1901).

18. (Baltimore, 1902); *Narratives of Early Maryland, 1633–1684*, Original Narratives of Early American History (New York, 1910).

19. Susan Myra Kingsbury, ed., *The Records of the Virginia Company of London*, 4 vols. (Washington, D.C., 1906–1935); Edward Arber and A. G. Bradley, eds., *Travels and Works of Captain John Smith, President of Virginia, and Admiral of New England, 1580–1631*, 2 vols. (Edinburgh, 1910); H. R. McIlwaine and John Pendleton Kennedy, eds., *Journals of the House of Burgesses of Virginia, 1619–1776*, 13 vols. (Richmond, Va., 1905–1915). Clarence Walworth Alvord and Lee Bidgood, eds., *The First Explorations of the Trans-Allegheny Region by the Virginians, 1650–1674* (Cleveland, Ohio, 1912) also dates from this period.

blacks, slave and free, by James C. Ballagh and John Russell, and Oliver P. Chitwood's *Justice in Colonial Virginia*.[20] The Jamestown Exposition of 1907, a large-scale national commemoration of the three-hundredth anniversary of the first settlement, in the predictable manner of many such celebrations appeared to have only a slight impact on serious publication, although Samuel H. Yonge's *Site of Old "James Towne,"* written by an engineer who had directed the seawall project on Jamestown Island, was a pioneer effort at examining the physical setting itself.[21]

In 1910 Philip Bruce completed his second two-volume study, *The Institutional History of Virginia*.[22] Given the depth of his research and the continuing value of the resultant detail in both works, and considering also the author's commitment to an unusually broad definition of history for his day, Bruce would almost certainly be regarded as the most influential of all these early historians of the Chesapeake, had there not also been published in 1910 the first of several works by Thomas J. Wertenbaker. He, perhaps more than anyone else, deserves recognition for the lasting impact of his work. His *Patrician and Plebeian* of 1910 was followed quickly by *Virginia under the Stuarts* in 1914 and soon after the close of the period under discussion by a third work, *The Planters of Colonial Virginia*.[23] Wertenbaker continued, of course, to be a prolific scholar for another half century into the post-World War II era, but after the 1920s he ranged more widely over early American history, except for two later works on seventeenth-century Virginia, *Torchbearer of Revolution* and *Give Me Liberty*. These studies tended more to exaggerate, even distort, certain interpretations in his earlier work than to add additional evidence or alter his judgments.[24]

20. James Curtis Ballagh, *A History of Slavery in Virginia* (Baltimore, 1902); John H. Russell, *The Free Negro in Virginia* (Baltimore, 1913); Oliver Perry Chitwood, *Justice in Colonial Virginia* (Baltimore, 1905). The three appear in the Johns Hopkins Studies, ex. vol. XXIV, XXXI, no. 3, and XXIII, nos. 7–8, respectively.

21. Samuel H. Yonge, *The Site of Old "James Towne," 1607–1698: A Brief Historical and Topographical Sketch of the First American Metropolis* (Richmond, Va., 1904). A new printing (Richmond, Va., 1907) appeared as a tercentennial edition.

22. *Institutional History of Virginia in the Seventeenth Century: An Inquiry into the Religious, Moral, Educational, Legal, Military, and Political Condition of the People . . . ,* 2 vols. (New York, 1910).

23. *Patrician and Plebeian in Virginia, or, The Origin and Development of the Social Classes of the Old Dominion* (Charlottesville, Va., 1910); *Virginia under the Stuarts, 1607–1688* (Princeton, N.J., 1914); *The Planters of Colonial Virginia* (Princeton, N.J., 1922).

24. *Torchbearer of the Revolution: The Story of Bacon's Rebellion and Its Leader* (Princeton, N.J., 1940); *Give Me Liberty: The Struggle for Self-Government in Virginia*, Memoirs of the American Philosophical Society, XLVI (Philadelphia, 1958).

It was, however, a further recognition of the force and influence of his three earliest books that they were reissued in 1958 as a single volume entitled *The Shaping of Colonial Virginia*.[25]

Wertenbaker, to be sure, displayed a traditional concern with the rise of representative government and political liberty in Virginia, which accounted for his harsh judgment of the Stuart monarchs and his easy exaltation of Nathaniel Bacon to the status of democratic hero. Yet he also exhibited an unusual degree of interest in the full spectrum of the society of seventeenth-century Virginia and in the kinds of essentially nonpolitical evidence that one might use to get at the subject. Wertenbaker concluded that in its first century Virginia had been essentially a yeoman democracy of small landowners, but that this political order was undermined by an increase in slave labor promoted mainly by the class of large planters that emerged late in the century. Thus the small independent farmer had been crushed "beneath the black tide." Revisionist in his view that the large planters had emerged only very late in the history of the colony and did not necessarily exemplify the finest flowering of Chesapeake society, Wertenbaker in the end proved to be no less preoccupied than the earlier historians with the history of Virginia as the history of political liberty. He also displayed more than a little bias against the hapless black as the agent of the degradation of the independent yeoman. Yet there remains the undoubted record of Wertenbaker's concern with taxable wealth, size of landholdings, and slave ownership as indexes of social and economic status. In that sense he—and to some extent Bruce as well—demonstrated a conception of the historical process and of the nature of evidence that was far ahead of most of their contemporaries, both the new Ph.D's, who were still largely confining their work to legal and political institutional studies, and the older generation of learned antiquarians.

That Wertenbaker was a direct bridge to the future, and should almost be regarded as representing a second generation of Chesapeake historians, ought not, however, to diminish the impact of that entire group of early scholars and writers. They left a remarkably large body of writing at a time when publication was a fraction of what it is today. Several considerations may account for the durability of their influence. Their work represented to an unusual degree a

25. (New York, 1958).

confluence of informed amateurs and some of the earliest trained professionals. Out of that combined effort came both major general histories of the two colonies in the seventeenth century and some of the first monographs. The secondary scholarship they produced was, in turn, reinforced by an equally strong current of documentary editing.

At the same time it is no denigration of their accomplishment to note some of the defects that, as American historical study advanced, later scholars increasingly perceived in that early body of work. The tendency of the writing before 1922 was to provide a scholarly, better-documented confirmation of the traditional themes that had long dominated the historiography of both colonies. Hence one finds a strong preoccupation with the religious struggle or the character of proprietary rule in Maryland, and with the nature of the leadership of the London Company in Virginia, the ultimate objective being, in all these cases, to trace the process by which popular government triumphed over authoritarian forces. Despite the examples of Wertenbaker and Bruce, the history of the Chesapeake tended to remain firmly rooted in the study of formal laws and political institutions judged from a Whig perspective.

It is also important to note that the "Chesapeake" historians of the era, given their concern with the political forms of one colony that remained under proprietary rule (except for a brief interlude at the end of the century) and another that quickly became a royal colony, had little chance of conceiving of the coastal Chesapeake as a single social and economic entity. Few wrote on both colonies, and those who did, primarily Edward Neill and Herbert L. Osgood, whose general colonial history began to appear in 1904, nonetheless saw the two as distinct.[26] Similarly, John Latané's 1895 study of early relations between the two colonies and Lewis Whealton's 1904 study of boundary controversies tended to regard Maryland and Virginia as mini-states, separated by disagreements that were the source of endless haggling and quasi-diplomatic negotiations.[27]

Such limitations, however, could be perceived only by hindsight. It

26. Herbert L. Osgood, *The American Colonies in the Seventeenth Century*, 3 vols. (New York, 1904–1907).

27. Louis N. Whealton, *The Maryland and Virginia Boundary Controversy (1668–1894)* (New York, 1904); John H. Latané, *The Early Relations between Maryland and Virginia*, Johns Hopkins Studies, XIII, nos. 3–4 (Baltimore, 1895).

is more compelling to ask why such a remarkable outpouring of work on the Chesapeake occurred in those years and why it reflected its particular point of view. Where the gentlemen scholars are concerned, one can sense a certain regional pride, even a counterattack in the aftermath of the Reconstruction era, although the caliber of the scholarship often transcended such initial purposes. So far as the new professionals were concerned, the emergence of Johns Hopkins in this region as an early center of graduate work, heavily influenced by Herbert B. Adams's interest in institutional studies, was no doubt significant. At a time when Puritanism had not yet come to dominate early American studies—or when the early American field was still largely regionalized—there was a greater awareness, too, of James-town's priority as the first English settlement. And in a pre-Turnerian age, strongly influenced by the idea that early American history must be essentially the study of the transit of English and European civili-zation to America, as Adams's view attests, the colonies to which Old World institutions were presumably exported in their established form may have seemed a more compelling subject than those in which the institutions and forms of government were erected by religious and political dissidents. One would not want to push the point too far, but there do seem to have been affinities between the kind of questions that arose about American beginnings in the Chesapeake and the intellectual world of a Theodore Roosevelt or a Woodrow Wilson.

II

It is also true that the nation had passed through the Progressive era and that by the 1920s the age of Progressive history had begun to come into its own. Much about Wertenbaker's first work seemed a harbinger of that trend, above all his idealization of a democratic Chesapeake world of yeoman farmers who were uncorrupted by excessive wealth or by lordship over dependent laborers.[28] Indeed Wertenbaker's most finished statement of this view came in 1922 in his *Planters of Colonial Virginia*. In the same vein in 1937 William E. Dodd, a professor at the University of Chicago until 1933 and then

28. For an extended discussion of Wertenbaker as a prototypical Progressive his-torian, based on his treatment of Puritanism in *The Puritan Oligarchy: The Founding of American Civilization* (New York, 1947), see Gene Wise, "Implicit Irony in Perry Miller's *New England Mind*," *Journal of the History of Ideas*, XXIX (1968), 579–600.

ambassador to Germany, published his now largely overlooked *The Old South: Struggles for Democracy*, a ringing affirmation, as its title indicates, of the notion that the seventeenth-century South was an early hotbed of the pursuit of liberty by a socially conscious small-farmer class.[29]

Nevertheless, it is more striking to observe how impervious the historiography of the early Chesapeake in fact was to Progressive political history. Wertenbaker and Dodd were nearly isolated examples.[30] After the appearance of Wertenbaker's *Planters* virtually no further book-length publications about the area appeared during the 1920s, apart from Avery Craven's *Soil Exhaustion as a Factor in the Agricultural History of Virginia and Maryland, 1606–1860*, which located the origins of the rapid exhaustion of Chesapeake soil in the earliest tobacco cultivation and traced the economic and social effects of that condition in the subsequent history of the antebellum South.[31]

The 1930s produced a steadier flow of work, although not in the same quantity as during the first decades of the century. It was an era when publication on any subject in the early American field was not plentiful. The period nonetheless included a number of studies of continuing influence that either opened up new lines of inquiry or revised older interpretations. The attention that Avery Craven's study had already drawn to tobacco cultivation as a major determinant of life in the Chesapeake received much more broad-gauged treatment in the opening sections of Lewis C. Gray's *History of Agriculture in the Southern United States*.[32] Several articles by Vertrees J. Wyckoff, one in collaboration with Stanley Gray, and Wyckoff's book-length study of tobacco regulation explored some aspects of Maryland agriculture in more depth.[33] Richard Shryock's classic article con-

29. (New York, 1937).

30. A good example of the failure of Progressive history to influence work on Virginia is Thomas Perkins Abernethy, *Three Virginia Frontiers* (Baton Rouge, La., 1940). Chapter 1 provided an overview of the 17th-century tidewater frontier in which Abernethy argued that a high degree of social stratification existed without serious social conflict or economic competition.

31. University of Illinois Studies in the Social Sciences, XIII, no. 1 (Urbana, Ill., 1926).

32. Lewis Cecil Gray, *History of Agriculture in the Southern United States to 1860*, 2 vols. (Washington, D.C., 1933).

33. *Tobacco Regulation in Colonial Maryland*, Johns Hopkins Studies, ex. vol., N.S., no. 22 (Baltimore, 1936); "The Sizes of Plantations in Seventeenth-Century Maryland," *Maryland Historical Magazine*, XXXII (1937), 331–339; "Seventeenth-Century Maryland Prices," *Agricultural History*, XII (1938), 229–310; "Ships and Shipping of Seventeenth

trasting British and German agricultural traditions raised additional
questions about the effects of agricultural methods in the Chesapeake.[34] Thus there developed an expanded attention to economic
history and its social consequences, though couched more in the
technical terms of agricultural and marketing methods than in the
language of class or economic divisions within society that characterized Progressive history.[35]

The continued flow of work also forced some significant recon-
siderations of more traditional concerns with the political order of the
region. Cyrus H. Karraker's *Seventeenth-Century Sheriff: A Comparative
Study of the Sheriff in England and the Chesapeake Colonies, 1607–1689*, if
it continued the preoccupation of an earlier generation with political
institutions, began like Craven's study of soil exhaustion to treat the
Chesapeake as a unit.[36] Then, in 1932, Wesley Frank Craven's *Dissolution of the Virginia Company: The Failure of a Colonial Experiment*
literally turned around the tradition of interpretation that went back
to William Stith in the eighteenth century, that of treating the Sandys
faction in the London Company as the founders of representative
government in America and their opponents as agents of Stuart
tyranny. Craven's careful, detailed, and clearly reasoned study, if
it never entirely displaced the old idea as a popular conception, made
it impossible for historians ever again to see the evolution of the
Virginia political order in morally simplistic terms. Craven brought
out, as had not been done before, the enormous complexity of the
political and economic situation of the London Company, the difficulty that English government faced in trying to sort out the tangled
affairs of the company, and the absence of grand political designs
in the minds of principal actors on either side. When Charles M.

Century Maryland," *Md. Hist. Mag.*, XXXIII (1938), 334–341, XXXIV (1939), 46–63,
270–283, 349–361; Gray and Wyckoff, "The International Tobacco Trade in the Seventeenth Century," *Southern Economic Journal*, VII (1940–1941), 1–26.

34. "British versus German Traditions in Colonial Agriculture," *Mississippi Valley
Historical Review*, XXVI (1939–1940), 39–54.

35. There was also an increasing interest in land policy and land distribution in
the two colonies, as evidenced in the work of Wyckoff and Lewis Gray but also in Man-
ning C. Voorhis, "The Land Grant Policy of Colonial Virginia, 1607–1774" (Ph.D. diss.,
University of Virginia, 1940). Donnell MacClure Owings's list of Maryland manorial
grants, *Md. Hist. Mag.*, XXXIII (1938), 307–334, and Nell Marion Nugent, comp.,
Cavaliers and Pioneers: Abstracts of Virginia Land Patents and Grants, 1623–1800, I [to 1666]
(Richmond, Va., 1934) were also important digests of documentary evidence.

36. (Chapel Hill, N.C., 1930).

Andrews's comprehensive history of the American colonies began to appear in 1934, it performed a similar function for the relationship of the Chesapeake colonies in their first years to the growing imperial system: the weakness of the colonies and their dependence upon England sharply circumscribed any show of political resistance to imperial authority.[37]

Other studies demonstrated a degree of understanding that the legal and administrative records of the two colonies were valuable sources for illuminating more than the development of legal institutions alone. Among these were A. P. Scott's investigation of criminal law in Virginia and Raphael Semmes's account of crime and punishment in Maryland.[38] Susie M. Ames's *Studies of the Virginia Eastern Shore in the Seventeenth Century*, which appeared just at the end of the decade in 1940, exhibited a similar awareness of the immense potential of the county records of the Chesapeake at a time when most scholars were still largely concerned with provincial and imperial sources.[39] These scholars were not writing genuine social history as the term is understood today, but in some of the questions they asked and in the kind of evidence they employed, they pointed in such a direction in a way that few of their predecessors had done.

There were other indications as well of a broadening conception of the history of the Chesapeake. Louis B. Wright's *First Gentlemen of Virginia* was an early effort to survey the intellectual history of colonial Virginia through an examination of the cultural interests and libraries of selected members of the ruling class.[40] In the opening chapters Wright also essayed an influential revision of Wertenbaker's account of the rise of that elite. Examining the accumulation of wealth and land that made the ownership of libraries possible and afforded the leisure to use them, Wright argued for a much earlier appearance of a well-defined elite, certainly by not long after the middle of the seventeenth century. If the controversy was neither prolonged nor fully developed, it remained for a long time one of the few points of

37. *The Colonial Period of American History*, 4 vols. (New Haven, Conn., 1934–1938).

38. Arthur P. Scott, *Criminal Law in Colonial Virginia* (Chicago, 1930); Raphael Semmes, *Crime and Punishment in Early Maryland* (Baltimore, 1938).

39. (Richmond, Va., 1940). Clayton Torrence, *Old Somerset on the Eastern Shore of Maryland* (Richmond, Va., 1935), should also be noted.

40. Louis B. Wright, *The First Gentlemen of Virginia: Intellectual Qualities of the Early Colonial Ruling Class* (San Marino, Calif., 1940).

departure for investigating the origins of the Virginia gentry. In a somewhat different vein Henry Chandlee Forman's *Jamestown and St. Mary's: Buried Cities of Romance* was not at all what its fanciful title might suggest but offered instead a serious, if controversial, view of the architecture of the two early Chesapeake capitals that succeeded in treating their buildings as revealing social and cultural documents.[41] Also in 1930 Wyndham B. Blanton had published *Medicine in Virginia in the Seventeenth Century*, which has remained a standard treatment of the subject, although historians would now dispute the author's conclusion that colonists in the Chesapeake did not suffer from malaria.[42]

None of this, to be sure, amounted to a full-scale "new" history of the Chesapeake. Indeed if historical writing on the early Chesapeake showed any common characteristics in the twenties and thirties, it was the avoidance of broad syntheses of any sort in favor of the specific and detailed. Yet, in the aggregate, the work had established a number of lines of approach for future research. Students of the political order would be far less able to conceive that those who settled the Chesapeake operated solely on the basis of preconceived programs for tyranny or political liberty. Nor would they be able to overlook the complexity of the forces at work both within the emerging empire and within the colonies themselves that shaped the governmental structure and the response of the colonists to political issues. The significance of tobacco cultivation not only as the economic base of the two colonies but also as a vital determinant of their social order was now more readily apparent. Important questions about the shape of that social order had been raised. The range of sources that scholars might expect to examine profitably had been expanded, not in this instance by documentary editing or new discovery so much as by demonstration of the variety of uses to which their content might be put. If the early history of the Chesapeake, judged by the volume of publication, seemed a less popular subject on the eve of World War II than it had been as World War I began, it nonetheless offered a richer, broader inquiry into the human past to those who cared to look for it.

41. (Baltimore, 1938).
42. (Richmond, Va., 1930).

III

Although World War II effected a major interruption in the pursuit of historical scholarship, that break may have obscured an element of continuity in the historiography of the Chesapeake. Even as the war ended and before the early American field experienced the major revival that took place in the 1950s and 1960s, there was a flurry of work on the Chesapeake, rather akin to that in the last, prewar decade and in some cases by the same authors. For example, the first two books published by the new Institute of Early American History and Culture in 1947 were Louis B. Wright's edition of Robert Beverley's *History and Present State of Virginia* and Abbot Emerson Smith's *Colonists in Bondage*, a general study of white servitude in colonial America. Beverley, although a member of the second rather than the first generation of the Virginia gentry, exemplified the nature of the intellectual interests that Wright had already found among the group—historical and political more than literary and belletristic, and marked by a touch of the practical. Smith had published a few articles in the 1930s anticipating the larger work, including one on servitude and land speculation in seventeenth-century Maryland, and his book, although extremely broad in its coverage, devoted some attention to the Chesapeake.[43] Compelled, moreover, in so general a treatment to rely heavily on printed British and provincial sources, and to deal extensively with recruitment of servants in England, Smith was nonetheless able in the last third of the book to begin to examine the lot of servants within the colonies and in an appendix to investigate briefly their number and distribution in the colonies. If the findings were at times sketchy, no one else had faced questions of patterns of emigration, working conditions, and opportunity for freed servants as seriously, or provided better initial generalizations on which to base more detailed investigations.

In 1945 one of the early issues of the Third Series of the *William and Mary Quarterly* featured a pioneering excursion into early American

43. Robert Beverley, *The History and Present State of Virginia*, ed. Louis B. Wright (Chapel Hill, N.C., 1947 [orig. publ. London, 1705, 1722]); Abbot Emerson Smith, *Colonists in Bondage: White Servitude and Convict Labor in America* (Chapel Hill, N.C., 1947); Smith, "The Indentured Servant and Land Speculation in Seventeenth Century Maryland," *American Historical Review*, XL (1934–1935), 467–472.

demography, Herbert Moller's study of sex composition in the colonies.[44] The article, a spin-off from the author's work on European
population, established, among other things, the general dimensions
of the sexual imbalance of males over females in seventeenth-century
Virginia and posed the question of the social effects of such a sex
ratio. Again a path had been opened up to a significant determinant
of life in the early Chesapeake.

The work of the thirties and the forties received what might be
regarded as an appropriate and timely synthesis—and integration
with what was most durable in the older work—with the publication
in 1949 of Wesley Frank Craven's *Southern Colonies in the Seventeenth
Century*. Craven's focus remained essentially political, but he applied to the whole sweep of events through 1689 the same kind of
understanding that he had already demonstrated in his study of the
London Company years at Jamestown. Craven emphasized not ab-
stract preconceptions but the actual conditions in the colonies and
the elemental concerns of the settlers out of which a political order
emerged. It seems in particular scarcely possible to improve upon his
account of political developments in Virginia from the mid-1620s to
the Commonwealth, that era when the uncertainties following upon
the dissolution of the London Company were resolved and the key
institutions of local government were formed. The same thing might
be said of his treatment of the background to Bacon's Rebellion. Nor
did the similarities of equivalent developments in Maryland escape
him. In his hands the process may at times seem a little smoother and
more orderly than our current understanding of the turbulence of
Chesapeake society would allow, but none of the more recent work
alters the main features of his account.

Then, as the general field of early American studies commenced its
full flowering, study of the seventeenth-century Chesapeake went
into an almost inexplicable decline. From 1950 through 1956 not a
single major study appeared, nor apparently were any relevant doctoral dissertations completed. The 350th anniversary of the Jamestown settlement in 1957 helped to foster the publication of a limited
amount of new work of importance, plus the reissue of Wertenbaker's
trilogy. The Jamestown celebration, strongly supported by the Commonwealth of Virginia, was directly responsible for a group of twenty-

44. "Sex Composition and Correlated Culture Patterns of Colonial America,"
WMQ, 3d Ser., II (1945), 113–153.

three historical pamphlets and for the inauguration of the Virginia
Colonial Records microfilm project, which ultimately made extensive
quantities of British public and private manuscripts relating to Virginia accessible at three major libraries in the state. The Colonial
Records Project, although the larger share of its contents concerned
the eighteenth century, included important seventeenth-century materials and must be accounted an important stimulus to the study of
colonial Virginia in subsequent decades.[45] The pamphlet series, while
intended for a popular audience, included contributions from a number of well-known Virginia scholars and reflected an admirable concern with almost every aspect of Virginia's past: agriculture, education,
medicine, domestic life, architecture, Indians—though not blacks—
as well as political history, although many of the nonpolitical topics
demonstrated as much as anything else how extremely little reliable
and penetrating work there was to draw upon.[46] While it was not
formally designated as a special issue, the January 1957 number of the
Virginia Magazine of History and Biography published several articles
and documentary notes on the seventeenth century, including Charles
E. Hatch, Jr.'s, important treatment of early sericulture.[47]

A volume of essays on *Seventeenth-Century America*, edited by James
Morton Smith, also emerged from a scholarly conference organized
for the 1957 observance by the Institute of Early American History
and Culture. Not all of its contents concerned Virginia, but among
those essays that did were three—by Nancy Lurie, Mildred Campbell,
and Bernard Bailyn—that have been the most influential and probably
among the most lasting in their impact of all the work completed in
the fities and sixties.[48]

Both the Campbell and Bailyn essays, the former by reexamining
the social origins of some Virginia settlers and the latter by positing

45. Julian P. Boyd, "A New Guide to the Indispensable Sources of Virginia History," *WMQ*, 3d Ser., XV (1958), 3–13, is a good overview of the Colonial Records
Project. A more detailed guide to major portions of the collection is Virginia Committee
on Colonial Records, *The British Public Records Office* . . . , Virginia State Library Publications, no. 12 (Richmond, Va., 1960). Annie Lash Jester, comp. and ed., in collaboration with Martha Woodroof Hiden, *Adventurers of Purse and Person: Virginia, 1607–1625*
(Princeton, N.J., 1956), has also proved to be an important brief documentary compilation, particularly because of its accurate transcription of the 1624/25 muster in Virginia.
46. Earl Gregg Swem, ed., *The Jamestown 350th Anniversary Booklets* (Williamsburg,
Va., 1957).
47. Charles E. Hatch, Jr., "Mulberry Trees and Silkworms: Sericulture in Early
Virginia," *Virginia Magazine of History and Biography*, LXV (1957), 3–61.
48. *Seventeenth-Century America: Essays in Colonial History* (Chapel Hill, N.C., 1959).

an extremely suggestive analysis of the kind of social process Bacon's Rebellion seemed to represent—a definition of the position and functions of two levels of the elite, the powerful provincial leaders and the emerging county gentry—carried the examination of Chesapeake society a step further than it had yet gone. Bailyn thereby qualified the older simplistic, democratic interpretation of the rebellion, though Wilcomb Washburn's full-scale study of the episode, when it appeared in 1957, had already carried that demythologizing process about as far as it could go.[49] Washburn seemed to some, in fact, to have come close to erecting a countermyth of an altogether benevolent, if admittedly aging and testy, William Berkeley. Certainly he implicitly denied even the sort of social adjustment rather than genuine upheaval that Bailyn had found to be a feature of the rebellion.

Another reflection of the growing concern with the social process in the work of the fifties was Sigmund Diamond's 1958 article extending the analysis of Chesapeake society back to its very beginning in the London Company period.[50] Diamond traced its origins, in effect, to a breakdown of status based solely on one's position and rank in a company "table of organization" and the substitution of a variety of determinants of status, particularly landholding, that marked the beginning of a more genuine social order.

The more limited amount of published work on Maryland that appeared during the late fifties exhibited something of the same tendency to open up questions of social history, though certainly less comprehensively than in studies of the Old Dominion. The clearest example was William A. Reavis's article on the Maryland gentry and social mobility, which concluded that most seventeenth-century gentlemen were commoners who advanced in rank after entering the colony, most likely as a consequence of officeholding rather than of wealth alone.[51] In a book-length study of the offices of profit in proprietary Maryland, Donnell Owings had four years earlier demonstrated that such offices were capable of providing an impor-

49. Washburn, *The Governor and the Rebel*. There is also an important amplification of Washburn's conclusions about the effects of the rebellion in his "The Effect of Bacon's Rebellion on Government in England and Virginia," paper 17 in *United States National Museum Bulletin 225* (Washington, D.C., 1962), 135–152.

50. Sigmund Diamond, "From Organization to Society: Virginia in the Seventeenth Century," *American Journal of Sociology*, LXIII (1957–1958), 457–475.

51. "The Maryland Gentry and Social Mobility, 1637–1676," *WMQ*, 3d Ser., XIV (1957), 418–428.

tant part of the material base needed to support a provincial gentry, albeit at a high cost for government.[52] Arthur E. Karinen also provided an early and still useful analysis of Maryland population before 1730.[53]

In the fifties several articles and at least one dissertation also appeared that do not seem to fit into any clear interpretative trend, although they added some detail to our understanding of several subjects, among them imperial relations and aspects of the economy.[54] Indeed in a sense the work from the late fifties—Bailyn's and one or two of the other essays from *Seventeenth-Century America* excepted—has not influenced subsequent work as much as that of the pre-World War II years. Diamond's essay was provocative at the time and remains an apt characterization of the social organization, or lack of it, that marked the beginning of the Jamestown settlement, but his definition of the appearance of a more indigenous social order has somehow been largely overlooked in more recent studies. Perhaps the process, as he described it, implied a certain opening up of opportunity that was illusory, given the close correlation that it now appears existed between high company rank and the early control of land and labor for personal gain—in other words, the company table of organization may have been applied to bigger and better things rather than having been overwhelmed from the bottom. Nor can any historian ignore the force of Washburn's argument on Bacon's Rebel-

52. Donnell MacClure Owings, *His Lordship's Patronage: Offices of Profit in Colonial Maryland*, Studies in Maryland History, no. 1 (Baltimore, 1953). See also John A. Kinnaman, "The Public Levy in Colonial Maryland to 1689," *Md. Hist. Mag.*, LIII (1958), 253–274.

53. Arthur E. Karinen, "Maryland Population, 1631–1730: Numerical and Distributional Aspects," *Md. Hist. Mag.*, LIV (1959), 365–407, which was drawn from his "Numerical and Distributional Aspects of Maryland Population, 1631–1840" (Ph.D. diss., University of Maryland, 1958).

54. On economic matters see Manfred Jonas, "Wages in Early Colonial Maryland," *Md. Hist. Mag.*, LI (1956), 27–38; Wesley N. Laing, "Cattle in Seventeenth-Century Virginia," *VMHB*, LXVII (1959), 143–163; and Neville Williams, "England's Tobacco Trade in the Reign of Charles I," *ibid.*, LXV (1957), 403–449. On imperial questions and the Chesapeake see especially James W. Vardaman, "The Baltimore Proprietary and the Growth of English Colonial Policy, 1630–1691" (Ph.D. diss., Vanderbilt University, 1958). There is also very brief mention of Maryland in Philip S. Haffenden, "The Crown and the Colonial Charters, 1675–1688: Part I," *WMQ*, 3d Ser., XV (1958), 297–311. In a series of articles drawn from his dissertation Erich Isaac treated the place of Kent Island in the early history of the Chesapeake ("Kent Island . . . ," *Md. Hist. Mag.*, LII [1957], 93–119, 210–224, 225–232). See also on Virginia, Wyndham B. Blanton, "Epidemics, Real and Imaginary, and Other Factors Influencing Seventeenth Century Virginia's Population," *Bulletin of the History of Medicine*, XXXI (1957), 454–462.

lion, and one must by all odds reckon with his characterization of
Bacon himself and with the limited relationship of Bacon to whatever
reforms were instituted by the assemblies of the period. Nevertheless, an increasing concern in recent years with Chesapeake society
and its instability has restored a social character to Bacon's Rebellion
in the judgment of most Chesapeake scholars and has given Bailyn's
essay perhaps the greater staying power.

It was symbolic of what was happening to the study of the Chesapeake that when in 1959 Darrett Rutman completed his dissertation,
"A Militant New World," he turned aside from Virginia to Puritan
New England for the bulk of his major work before his interest
shifted back at a later time to the social history of Virginia.[55] The
impression of an apparent break in the flow of work is heightened by
a lack of new books in the first half of the sixties. An important
exception was, of course, Richard L. Morton's comprehensive *Colonial
Virginia*, which devotes the first volume to the years 1607 to 1710.[56]
Morton's work is difficult to classify. He himself always reacted in a
testy manner to the attempts of some reviewers to classify the study
as latter-day Whig history. He had, moreover, carried out his research
and writing over many years, and the end result was not a product of
a particular time period, above all not of the 1960s. *Colonial Virginia*
can perhaps best be regarded as magisterial narrative history, drawing on fresh research and representing the finest scholarly achievement of that sort in many years, in fact, more akin in the best sense to
the great body of work of the early twentieth century than to much
that has been published since that time.

A few other articles or books appeared between 1960 and 1966 that
touched in some manner upon the early Chesapeake. Michael Kammen's two articles, one on the causes of the revolution of 1689 in
Maryland and the other, a documentary note on James Blair's and
John Locke's appraisal of Virginia at the end of the century, constituted an important reappraisal of the politics of the two colonies; but

55. "A Militant New World, 1607–1640: America's First Generation, Its Martial
Spirit, Its Traditions of Arms, Its Military Organization, Its Wars" (Ph.D. diss., University of Virginia, 1959). Rutman published two essays based on material related to the
dissertation: "The Historian and the Marshal: A Note on the Background of Sir Thomas
Dale," *VMHB*, LXVIII (1960), 284–294, and "The Virginia Company and Its Military
Regime," in Rutman, ed., *The Old Dominion: Essays for Thomas Perkins Abernethy* (Charlottesville, Va., 1964), 1–20.
56. Two vols. (Chapel Hill, N.C., 1960).

as with the pertinent sections of Michael Hall's *Edmund Randolph and the American Colonies* and a documentary history of the Glorious Revolution jointly edited by Kammen, Hall, and Lawrence Leder, discussion of the Chesapeake primarily represented one aspect of the authors' broader concern with an emerging imperial policy.[57] More exclusively concerned with the Chesapeake were an article by Gordon W. Jones on the important but often neglected problem of health and disease in early Virginia and one by Manfred Jonas on the Claiborne-Calvert controversy in Maryland.[58]

Perhaps the fifteen-year period after 1950 will in retrospect seem more influential on Chesapeake history than the foregoing remarks have allowed. It had produced, after all, a major narrative history, two or three monographs of high quality, and a number of essays that pointed toward an increasing concern with the social history of the region. Moreover, in concentrating so exclusively on the seventeenth century one has to be reminded that the eighteenth-century Chesapeake shared fully in the comparative boom in early American studies during the period. An important reexamination of eighteenth-century political structure perhaps seemed to predominate, but several scholars, among them Jacob M. Price, Aubrey C. Land, and Arthur Pierce Middleton, also launched a significant investigation of the Chesapeake economy. While most of the political history looked ahead to a logical culmination in the American Revolution, the study of the economy inevitably touched in part on the seventeenth-century origins of commerce in tobacco and has been remarkably influential on more recent work on the early Chesapeake.[59]

57. Michael G. Kammen, "The Causes of the Maryland Revolution of 1689," *Md. Hist. Mag.*, LV (1960), 293–333; Michael G. Kammen, ed., "Virginia at the Close of the Seventeenth Century: An Appraisal by James Blair and John Locke," *VMHB*, LXXIV (1966), 141–169; Michael Garibaldi Hall, *Edward Randolph and the American Colonies, 1676–1703* (Chapel Hill, N.C., 1960); Michael G. Hall, Lawrence H. Leder, and Michael G. Kammen, eds., *The Glorious Revolution in America: Documents on the Colonial Crisis of 1689* (Chapel Hill, N.C., 1964).

58. "The First Epidemic in English America," *VMHB*, LXXI (1963), 3–10; "The Claiborne-Calvert Controversy: An Episode in the Colonization of North America," *Jahrbuch für Amerikastudien*, XI (1966), 241–250.

59. Jacob M. Price's work has been particularly extensive, but see esp. "The Economic Growth of the Chesapeake and the European Market, 1697–1775," *Journal of Economic History*, XXIV (1964), 496–511, and *The Tobacco Adventure to Russia: Enterprise, Politics, and Diplomacy in the Quest for a Northern Market for English Colonial Tobacco*, American Philosophical Society, *Transactions*, N.S., LI, Pt. i (Philadelphia, 1961). Perhaps the most influential of Aubrey C. Land's work, both in understanding the Chesapeake economy and in initiating the systematic study of probate inventories,

Still, the collective influence of historical writing from the fifties and early sixties—with these important exceptions—has not been as much as one might have anticipated. Too, it is striking how much of the best new work came either from those primarily concerned with the eighteenth century or as a onetime venture from scholars whose main interests lay outside the Chesapeake. Lurie, an anthropologist, and Diamond, a sociologist, turned to the Chesapeake for case studies that might test more general social theories; Campbell was a specialist in English history; Washburn came to Bacon's Rebellion out of his concern with Indian relations and subsequently turned back in that direction; and Bailyn's essay essentially set the stage for his subsequent work on eighteenth-century political ideology. Thus no new scholar with a primary commitment to the seventeenth-century Chesapeake emerged over these years, an impression that gains additional support from the near absence of dissertations in the field.

It requires no elaborate examination of the important areas of early American scholarship where there *was* intense activity in these same years to discover the cause of this indifference. It was, after all, a time in which intellectual history, especially intellectual history with a high religious or theological content—or its secular alternative, political history with a high ideological content—were the dominant concerns of many early American historians. Puritanism and the American Revolution were understandably preferred subjects. If elements of both themes were not entirely missing from the early Chesapeake, they were scarcely present in a way to make them easy organizing principles for studying the region. Every new incursion into the politics of the early Chesapeake seemed to reveal that the numerous political controversies there were even less principled or ideological than had been assumed, and to suggest that politics in such a time and place had to be conceived rather differently than on the eve of the American Revolution. And Perry Miller's effort in the late 1940s to remake the founding of Virginia into a Puritan quest, while not

---

has been "Economic Base and Social Structure: The Northern Chesapeake in the Eighteenth Century," *Jour. Econ. Hist.*, XXV (1965), 639–654, and "Economic Behavior in a Planting Society: The Eighteenth-Century Chesapeake," *Jour. So. Hist.*, XXXIII (1967), 469–485. See also Arthur Pierce Middleton, *Tobacco Coast: A Maritime History of the Chesapeake Bay in the Colonial Era* (Newport News, Va., 1953).

The present group of social and economic historians of the 17th-century Chesapeake are very explicit in acknowledging the critical influence of the work of this group of historians. See, e.g., Russell R. Menard to author, July 31, 1978.

without its insights into an age in which one wing of Puritanism remained comfortable within the confines of Anglicanism, somehow seemed to leave more questions unanswered than answered.[60]

IV

Perry Miller's article is a reminder, however, that there were continuing efforts to treat intellectual and cultural dimensions of the seventeenth-century Chesapeake. However much one questioned Miller's argument, it commanded attention in the light of both the author's reputation and of the growing emphasis on intellectual history among early American scholars. At about the same time Howard Mumford Jones had published *The Literature of Virginia in the Seventeenth Century*, in which he viewed that literature as composed largely of personal correspondence, of travel accounts and descriptions of the country, and—near the end of the century—of discussions of politics and economic concerns. It was, in sum, not a formal literature at all, but it was nonetheless a body of writing that revealed much about the attitudes and values of the first white Virginians. In his conclusion Jones called it a "literature lacking in introspection, in philosophic and moral meditation," "a secular literature," and "a pragmatic literature . . . content with worldly values and worldly content."[61] Louis Wright, whose *First Gentlemen of Virginia* had already extensively treated the reading habits and libraries of late seventeenth-century Virginians, also added an essay on "Literature of the Colonial South" in 1947.[62] Finally, two major scholars of early Southern literature, Richard Beale Davis and Jay B. Hubbell, had already made a significant start on the extensive work in the field that they would accomplish in succeeding decades.[63]

60. "The Religious Impulse in the Founding of Virginia: Religion and Society in the Early Literature," *WMQ*, 3d Ser., V (1948), 492–522, VI (1949), 24–41. The two elements of the title are reversed in the second installment.
61. *The Literature of Virginia in the Seventeenth Century*, Memoirs of the American Academy of Arts and Sciences (Boston, 1946). The second edition (Charlottesville, Va., 1968) is in some respects preferable. The quotations are from pp. 121–122 of that edition.
62. *Huntington Library Quarterly*, X (1946–1947), 297–315.
63. See, e.g., Davis, "America in George Sandys' 'Ovid,'" *WMQ*, 3d Ser., IV (1947), 297–304. Hubbell had earlier published "John and Ann Cotton, of 'Queen's Creek,' Virginia," *American Literature*, X (1938–1939), 179–201. See also Bertha Monica Stearns, "The Literary Treatment of Bacon's Rebellion in Virginia," *VMHB*, LII (1944), 163–179.

Thus a case might well be made that study of the early Chesapeake was touched more strongly by the new wave of intellectual history than its historians have sometimes been willing to concede. Nor did that attention lessen in the fifties and sixties, as is attested by the publication of Hubbell's major study of *The South in American Literature*; of Davis's account of George Sandys's literary activities at Jamestown and his edition of the letters of William Fitzhugh; of S. G. Culliford's biography of William Strachey, who ranks second only to John Smith among Jamestown's chroniclers; and of a second, revised edition of Howard Mumford Jones's study.[64] Yet in the end neither Miller's insistence that religious impulses operated as powerfully perhaps in the colonization of Virginia as in the colonization of Massachusetts nor Davis's conviction that the Chesapeake from the beginning possessed a culture capable of producing a respectable body of literature found as much acceptance among historians as did a point of view more akin to that of Howard Mumford Jones. In a word, the prevalent intellectual system of the seventeenth-century Chesapeake, in the eyes of its historians, was not to have a system at all.

That conclusion can, however, be qualified in several important respects. For one thing, in matters of religion, social attitudes, and political values historians have found that, especially as the century wore on and a more established elite appeared, early Virginians and Marylanders tended to accept and to act upon prevailing English modes of thought.[65] Scholars have generally recognized, too, a certain vigor of style in, and the possibility of recovering valuable intellectual and literary perceptions of America from, the best narratives of exploration and settlement, those by Smith, Strachey, George Percy, and others.[66] Still, this body of writing essentially reflected the

64. Jay B. Hubbell, *The South in American Literature, 1607–1900* (Durham, N.C., 1954); Richard Beale Davis, *George Sandys: Poet-Adventurer: A Study in Anglo-American Culture in the Seventeenth Century* (New York, 1955); Richard Beale Davis, ed., *William Fitzhugh and His Chesapeake World, 1676–1701: The Fitzhugh Letters and Other Documents* (Chapel Hill, N.C., 1963); S. G. Culliford, *William Strachey, 1572–1621* (Charlottesville, Va., 1965).

65. No one has dealt systematically with this point, apart from Wright, *First Gentlemen of Virginia*, chap. 1, but it seems to be reflected in much of the work on the emergence of a more permanent elite in the late 17th century.

66. In addition to Davis, "America in George Sandys' 'Ovid,'" and Jones, *Literature of Virginia in the Seventeenth Century*, see Edwin C. Rozwenc, "Captain John Smith's Image of America," *WMQ*, 3d Ser., XVI (1959), 27–36; Jay B. Hubbell, "The Smith-Pocahontas Story in Literature," *VMHB*, LXV (1957), 275–300; and Philip L. Barbour,

process of colonization and confrontation with what Europeans chose to regard as the American wilderness. It was primarily a response of the European mind to the New World, and it has taken us only a little way toward understanding the outlook of those who made up Chesapeake society later in the century.

Miller succeeded in reminding historians that neither the hardness of life in the Chesapeake nor the rampant pursuit of material gain could take away the conventional piety of the age and that religion, even the faith of establishment Anglicanism, was a force in the lives of Virginia colonists—a point reinforced by the number of Anglican devotional writings Louis Wright had found in Virginia libraries.[67] Nevertheless, no substantial development of religious themes in Virginia's early history occurred after the appearance in 1947 of George McLaren Brydon's detailed, if uncritical, *Virginia's Mother Church and the Conditions under Which It Grew*.[68] Of the work that was completed, William H. Seiler's essay in *Seventeenth-Century America* and James Kimbrough Owen's promising dissertation (which remained unpublished as a result of the author's untimely death) seemed to establish the direction of most work on Virginia Anglicanism, namely, toward a study of the development of the parish vestry as an important social and political institution rather than toward an investigation of religious thought and practice.[69] On the other hand, that early Virginia had also possessed a tradition of dissent did not pass entirely unnoticed, thanks to the work of Babette Levy on Puritanism and Kenneth L. Carroll on the Quakers.[70]

Maryland had, of course, an even more complex religious history

---

The Three Worlds of Captain John Smith (Boston, 1964), Part II. Although it deals with the New World at large and not exclusively with the Chesapeake, Howard Mumford Jones, *O Strange New World; American Culture: The Formative Years* (New York, 1964) is also important.

67. Wright, *First Gentlemen of Virginia*, esp. chap. 5.

68. Vol. I (Richmond, Va., 1947).

69. William H. Seiler, "The Anglican Parish in Virginia," in Smith, ed., *Seventeenth-Century America*, 119–142; James Kimbrough Owen, "The Virginia Vestry: A Study in the Decline of a Ruling Class" (Ph.D. diss., Princeton University, 1947). Also useful are Henry Culverwell Porter, "Alexander Whitaker: Cambridge Apostle to Virginia," *WMQ*, 3d Ser., XIV (1957), 317–343, and Richard Beale Davis, ed., "A Sermon Preached at James City in Virginia The 23d of April 1686 . . . by Deuel Pead," *ibid.*, XVII (1960), 371–394. Seiler had also previously published "The Church of England as the Established Church in Seventeenth-Century Virginia," *Jour. So. Hist.*, XV (1949), 478–508.

70. Babette M. Levy, "Early Puritanism in the Southern and Island Colonies," *American Antiquarian Society, Proceedings*, LXX (1960), 69–348; Kenneth L. Carroll, "Quakers on the Eastern Shore of Virginia," *VMHB*, LXXIV (1966), 170–189.

in its first century, given the presence of greater diversity and conflict than in Virginia. Thus earlier historical writing on Maryland had already paid much attention to religious themes, although focusing largely on the political consequences of religious conflict. That emphasis did not markedly change in the new work, of which there was in any event not a great deal, apart from Kenneth L. Carroll's extensive studies of Maryland Quakers.[71] Chesapeake religious history remained, then, in large part an extension of political history.

As the sixties drew to a close one could, in sum, point to a surprisingly large body of writing on cultural, intellectual, and literary topics concerning the early Chesapeake, though not to a commanding work on a large theme. Certainly there had been no reconstruction of "the Chesapeake mind." Indeed at times one scarcely found a recognition from historians that it had existed.

V

It is almost unnecessary to point out that another important strand in American historical writing since the late 1940s has concerned the black presence in American life. Nor was it to be expected that early American historians would neglect the subject, above all when they were dealing with the geographic area and the time in which blacks first reached the English mainland colonies and fell, as they had elsewhere in the Americas, under the institution of slavery. The subject had, moreover, never been altogether neglected in the older work on the Chesapeake: at the beginning of the century various works in the Hopkins Studies had treated the legal status of blacks, free and slave, in both Maryland and Virginia, while historians of the 1920s had given more attention to the social and economic aspects of

71. Work on Maryland church history included Nelson Waite Rightmyer, *Maryland's Established Church* (Baltimore, 1956), George B. Scriven, "Religious Affiliation in Seventeenth Century Maryland," *Historical Magazine of the Protestant Episcopal Church*, XXV (1956), 220–229, and Edwin Warfield Beitzell, *The Jesuit Missions of St. Mary's County, Maryland* ([Abell, Md.], 1960). Kenneth L. Carroll's studies on Quakers include "Maryland Quakers in the Seventeenth Century," *Md. Hist. Mag.*, XLVII (1952), 297–313; "Persecution of Quakers in Early Maryland, 1658–1660," *Quaker History*, LIII (1964), 67–80; "The Anatomy of a Separation: The Lynam Controversy," *ibid.*, LV (1966), 67–78; "Elizabeth Harris, The Founder of American Quakerism," *ibid.*, LVII (1968), 96–111; see also n. 98 and n. 114 below for his later work. Also, see J. Reaney Kelly, *Quakers in the Founding of Anne Arundel County, Maryland* (Baltimore, 1963). Gerald Eugene Hartdagen, "The Anglican Vestry in Colonial Maryland" (Ph.D. diss., Northwestern University, 1965), provided a counterpart to the earlier studies of the Virginia vestry system.

slavery. Yet attention to blacks in the colonial period developed somewhat slowly and did not much involve those major scholars in Afro-American history whose primary interests were the nineteenth and twentieth centuries.

A widely read article by Oscar and Mary F. Handlin, published in 1948, served more than anything else to reopen the examination of slavery in the seventeenth-century Chesapeake.[72] Asking why and how the legally defined status of lifetime slavery had developed and what relationship racial feeling by whites bore to the process, the Handlins suggested that slavery as a well-defined legal institution had developed relatively slowly and only after a number of years when blacks, like whites, were able to gain their freedom by serving brief terms as indentured servants. Only gradually did blacks become permanently enslaved, largely because they lacked bargaining power in a situation in which there was an intense demand for labor. The Handlins concluded that the idea of black inferiority came not from deep-seated racial antipathy so much as from whites observing that only blacks lived in the debased status of slaves and could therefore be perceived as unequal. The authors thus added a sociological gloss to James Ballagh's argument, first made in 1902, that the Virginia laws had not initially recognized slavery, an argument to which John H. Russell had added further support in 1913.[73]

Almost at the same time but apparently without an opportunity to examine the Handlins' article, Wesley Frank Craven, persuaded by Susie M. Ames's criticisms of Ballagh and Russell in *Studies of the Virginia Eastern Shore*, addressed the question of slavery in the Chesapeake. Although recognizing that the blacks' status was "a debatable question on which the records do not always speak clearly," Craven concluded that evidence from almost the earliest date showed the colonists making a clear distinction between blacks and whites. In the end, however, he seemed still to think that it was the economic advantage of slave labor on larger plantations rather than racial attitudes that did the most to create slavery.[74] The counterproposition to that of the Handlins—that a strong current of patently racial feeling against blacks had been an important precondition of slavery— was more strongly asserted by Carl N. Degler in his 1959 essay

72. "Origins of the Southern Labor System," *WMQ*, 3d Ser., VII (1950), 199–222.
73. Ballagh, *Slavery in Virginia*, 27–90; Russell, *Free Negro in Virginia*, 23ff.
74. Craven, *Southern Colonies in the Seventeenth Century*, 217–219, 401–403.

"Slavery and the Genesis of American Race Prejudice."[75] It then remained only for Winthrop D. Jordan to propound the middle position that slavery and prejudice developed simultaneously, mutually reinforcing each other, in a 1962 article, "Modern Tensions and the Origins of American Slavery."[76] In the context of his larger study, White over Black, it appears that Jordan did not intend to downplay the force of racial feeling in American history but simply to keep in perspective the complexity of the circumstances in which a pervasive institution such as slavery developed.[77]

Given the force of the debate over the nature of slavery that occurred in American historical writing during these years, it is perhaps surprising that the question of the origins of slavery in the seventeenth-century Chesapeake did not receive greater attention. The debate, if it could be called that, was carried on primarily in three or four key articles.[78] The discussion had, however, served to shift the emphasis in the study of the origins of slavery from statutory law alone to the wider question of how custom and psychological attitudes related to the law. Most historians now agreed that while the advent of slavery as a legal institution owed a great deal to a conscious calculation by planters of its economic advantages, racial attitudes had certainly reinforced its development.

In the case of the Chesapeake's other significant ethnic minority, the native American Indians, historians still seemed content to leave the subject, especially in its cultural aspects, largely in the hands of the anthropologists and ethnologists. To the work of earlier anthropologists on the Indians of the Chesapeake—scholars such as Frank Speck, James Mooney, Charles Willoughby, and David I. Bushnell— were now added the contributions of Maurice Mook, Bernard Hoff-

75. Comparative Studies in Society and History, II (1959–1960), 49–66; see also his Out of Our Past: The Forces That Shaped Modern America (New York, 1959), 26–39.

76. Jour. So. Hist., XXVIII (1962), 18–30.

77. White over Black: American Attitudes toward the Negro, 1550–1812 (Chapel Hill, N.C., 1968), 71–82.

78. Other than the articles by the Handlins, Degler, and Jordan that have already been mentioned, see Paul C. Palmer, "Servant into Slave: The Evolution of the Legal Status of the Negro Laborer in Colonial Virginia," South Atlantic Quarterly, LXV (1966), 355–370, which recapitulates the body of legal evidence from which it is necessary to work but does not greatly alter the terms of the debate. Also pertinent is a paper by Robert D. Ronsheim at the 1956 meeting of the Southern Historical Association that emphasized the relationship of plantation size to labor force and the determination of when large plantations directly affected the labor system as important influences on the development of slavery. The paper is summarized in Jour. So. Hist., XXIII (1957), 79.

man, Christian Feest, John R. Swanton, Theodore Stern, and Lewis R. Binford.[79] Clearly the single study of Virginia Indians that had the greatest impact on Chesapeake historians was Nancy Lurie's investigation of Indian cultural adjustment to European civilization, which, although written by an anthropologist, appeared in a volume of historical essays.[80] It was almost the only piece of work that explicitly opened up for historians the possibilities of dealing with the significant cultural interrelationships of whites and Indians in the Chesapeake, although the Paul Hulton and David B. Quinn edition of *The American Drawings of John White, 1577–1590*, also offered important evidence on Carolina Indians of a very similar culture.[81] When historians themselves addressed the subject, as they did occasionally, they were often more concerned either with questions of official relations with the Virginia tribes, especially in the aftermath of the major wars of 1622 and 1644, or with educational and missionary efforts among the Indians.[82] Such matters of public policy were, of

79. References to most of this work appearing before the mid-1950s can be found in William N. Fenton *et al.*, *American Indian and White Relations to 1830: Needs and Opportunities for Study* (Chapel Hill, N.C., 1957), Nancy Oestreich Lurie, "Indian Cultural Adjustment to European Civilization," in Smith, ed., *Seventeenth-Century America*, 33–60, or Ben C. McCary, *Indians in Seventeenth-Century Virginia*, Jamestown 350th Anniversary Historical Booklet 18 (Williamsburg, Va., 1957), 86–89.

For Binford, see "Archaeological and Ethnohistorical Investigation of Cultural Diversity and Progressive Development among Aboriginal Cultures of Coastal Virginia and North Carolina" (Ph.D. diss., University of Michigan, 1964), and "An Ethnohistory of the Nottoway, Meherrin, and Weanok Indians of Southeastern Virginia," *Ethnohistory*, XIV (1967), 103–218; for Hoffman, see *Observations on Certain Ancient Tribes of the Northern Appalachian Province*, Smithsonian Institution, Bureau of American Ethnology, Bulletin 191 (Washington, D.C., 1964), and "Ancient Tribes Revisited: A Summary of Indian Distribution and Movement in the Northeastern United States from 1534 to 1779," *Ethnohistory*, XIV (1967), 1–46; for Feest, see "Powhatan: A Study in Political Organization," *Wiener Völkerkundliche Mitteilungen*, VII (1966), 69–83, "Virginia Indian Miscellany," *Archiv für Völkerkunde*, XX (1966), 1–7, XXI (1967), 5–25, "Seventeenth Century Virginia Algonquian Population Estimates," Archaeological Society of Virginia, *Quarterly Bulletin*, XXVIII (1973), 66–79, "Another French Account of Virginia Indians by John Lederer," *VMHB*, LXXXIII (1975), 150–159. See also Randolph Turner, "A New Population Estimate for the Powhatan Chiefdom of the Coastal Plain of Virginia," Arch. Soc. of Va., *Qtly. Bull.*, XXVIII (1973), 57–65.

80. Lurie, "Indian Cultural Adjustment," in Smith, ed., *Seventeenth-Century America*, 33–60.

81. Paul Hulton and David Beers Quinn, eds., *The American Drawings of John White, 1577–1590, with Drawings of European and Oriental Subjects*, 2 vols. (Chapel Hill, N.C., 1964).

82. On Indian policy, see Wesley Frank Craven, "Indian Policy in Early Virginia," *WMQ*, 3d Ser., I (1944), 65–82, and William S. Powell, "Aftermath of the Massacre: The First Indian War, 1622–1632," *VMHB*, LXVI (1958), 44–75. On missionary efforts, see Miller, "Religious Impulse in the Founding of Virginia," 498–503; Porter, "Alexander

course, important, but they represented only one aspect of Indian-white relations. Even this small output amounted perhaps to a larger body of work than that which appeared on blacks in Virginia from the mid-forties through the late sixties, but for the moment black history remained the more overriding concern among Chesapeake historians.

VI

If there is any merit in the proposition that somehow the nature of the history of the seventeenth-century Chesapeake was not altogether compatible with the principal interests of historians in the fifties and early sixties, a remarkable turnaround has occurred within the last ten or twelve years—one that has yet to achieve its full momentum. Obviously, given the extent to which much of the new Chesapeake work draws on the methodology of quantitative history, it is tempting to conclude that the Chesapeake, an uninviting terrain for intellectual or ideologically dominated political history, offers a particularly rich and heretofore uncultivated ground for the new social history. Certainly the chronology of the developing interest would support that conclusion. Although the current enthusiasm for social history among early American scholars arose with a widely recognized group of New England town studies, it soon shifted southward. Historians were not long in determining that both the course of development in the early Chesapeake and the strength of its surviving records would support a similar investigation.

Yet the revival of interest in the Chesapeake has wider dimensions, involving still other scholars and other kinds of history, and its origins may, in fact, be more varied. For one thing, a rapid increase in completed dissertations began to occur by the late 1960s, somewhat too soon and on too diverse a group of topics to be entirely a response to the new social history. In contrast to the handful that had appeared

---

Whitaker," *WMQ*, 3d Ser., XIV (1957), 319–320, 336–339; W. Stitt Robinson, Jr., "Indian Education and Missions in Colonial Virginia," *Jour. So. Hist.*, XVIII (1952), 152–168; and, on earlier Spanish efforts, Clifford M. Lewis and Albert J. Loomie, *The Spanish Jesuit Mission in Virginia, 1570–1572* (Chapel Hill, N.C., 1953). Wilcomb E. Washburn touched briefly on dispossession of Indian land by the Virginia Company in "The Moral and Legal Justification for Dispossessing the Indians," in Smith, ed., *Seventeenth-Century America*, 19–22. Keith Glenn, "Captain John Smith and the Indians," *VMHB*, LII (1944), 228–248, is a defense of Smith's Indian policy. See also Stanley Pargellis, ed., "An Account of the Indians in Virginia," *WMQ*, 3d Ser., XVI (1959), 228–243, which reprints a late 17th-century description, probably by the Rev. John Clayton.

in the preceding fifteen or twenty years, one can count a dozen or more in a matter of five or six years. Those of John M. Hemphill II, David Jordan, Lois Green Carr, Warren Billings, Irene Hecht, Martin Quitt, and John Rainbolt have perhaps had the greatest impact, either because of fairly rapid publication or because of their frequent citation by other scholars, but they do not exhaust the list. The "first generation" of new work still concerned itself largely with political or economic history—more strictly speaking, with the exception of Hemphill, economic policy—rather than social history, but the best of the work demonstrated concern with the social context in which political and economic developments occurred.[83] Since that time, a second group of dissertations has approached the social history of the region more directly: by separate county or even parish studies, as in the case of Kevin Kelly, Carville Earle, Lorena Walsh, and Robert Wheeler; by the examination of particular categories of records, as in Gloria Main's analysis of probate records; and by the systematic investigation of an entire colony, as in Russell Menard's study of seventeenth-century Maryland.[84] Although social history appears to

83. All of the following are Ph.D. dissertations: Frederick S. Aldridge, "Organization and Administration of the Militia System of Colonial Virginia" (American University, 1964); Warren M. Billings, "'Virginia's Deploured Condition,' 1660–1676: The Coming of Bacon's Rebellion" (Northern Illinois University, 1968); James LaVerne Anderson, "The Governors' Councils of Colonial America: A Study of Pennsylvania and Virginia, 1660–1676" (University of Virginia, 1967); Lois Green Carr, "County Government in Maryland, 1689–1709" (Harvard University, 1968); Michael David DeMichele, "The Glorious Revolution in Maryland: A Study of the Provincial Revolution of 1689" (Pennsylvania State University, 1967); Irene W. D. Hecht, "The Virginia Colony, 1607–1640: A Study in Frontier Growth" (University of Washington, 1969); John M. Hemphill II, "Virginia and the English Commercial System, 1689–1733: Studies in the Development and Fluctuations of a Colonial Economy under Imperial Control" (Princeton University, 1964); David W. Jordan, "The Royal Period of Colonial Maryland 1689–1715" (Princeton University, 1966); Martin H. Quitt, "The Virginia House of Burgesses, 1660–1706: The Social, Educational and Economic Bases of Political Power" (Washington University, 1970).

84. All of the following are Ph.D. dissertations: Raphael Cassimere, Jr., "The Origins and Early Development of Slavery in Maryland, 1633 to 1715" (Lehigh University, 1971); Kevin P. Kelly, "Economic and Social Development of Seventeenth-Century Surry County, Virginia" (University of Washington, 1972); Gloria L. Main, "Personal Wealth in Colonial America: Explorations in the Use of Probate Records from Maryland and Massachusetts, 1650–1720" (Columbia University, 1972); Russell R. Menard, "Economy and Society in Early Colonial Maryland" (University of Iowa, 1975); Lorena S. Walsh, "Charles County, Maryland, 1658–1705: A Study of Chesapeake Social and Political Structure" (Michigan State University, 1977); Robert A. Wheeler, "Lancaster County, Virginia, 1650–1750: The Counties during the Seventeenth Century" (Brown University, 1972). Paul G. E. Clemens, "From Tobacco to Grain: Economic Development on Maryland's Eastern Shore, 1660–1750" (University of Wisconsin, 1974), also belongs with this group of dissertations. There have, of course, also been

be the strongest line of inquiry now in progress, other new dissertations have pursued more exclusively political topics or subjects dealing with aspects of imperial or English history that impinge directly
on the Chesapeake.[85] Too, the first dissertation in many years by
a historian on relations between Indians and whites in the early
Chesapeake has been completed.[86]

The number of dissertations is not in itself so striking or their focus
so unmistakably clear as is the case with a remarkable group of essays
and articles, largely published since 1970.[87] There is neither space nor
time to undertake a full analysis of this body of work in the present
essay, but even a rough classification of the articles strikingly confirms
the movement toward social and economic concerns.[88] Fully a third
of them deal largely with such questions as immigration patterns,
mortality, population growth, social mobility, sex ratios, and family
structure. It is this group of articles that has done so much to establish

---

a number of important dissertations on the social history of the 18th-century Chesapeake, but they are not examined here.

85. Robert Paul Brenner, "Commercial Change and Political Conflict: The Merchant Community in Civil War London" (Princeton University, 1970), which is of
particular importance; Steven D. Crow, "'Left at Libertie': The Effects of the English
Civil War and Interregnum on the American Colonies, 1640–1660" (University of
Wisconsin, 1974); Susan R. Falb, "Advice and Ascent: The Development of the Maryland Assembly, 1635–1689" (Georgetown University, 1976); John D. Krugler, "Puritan
and Papist: Politics and Religion in Massachusetts and Maryland before the Restoration of Charles" (University of Illinois, Urbana-Champaign, 1971); William Lee Shea,
"To Defend Virginia: The Evolution of the First Colonial Militia, 1607–1677" (Rice
University, 1975); Susan E. Hillier, "The Trade of the Virginia Colony, 1606–1660"
(University of Liverpool, 1971).

86. J. Frederick Fausz, "The Powhatan Uprising of 1622: A Historical Study of
Ethnocentrism and Cultural Conflict" (Ph.D. diss., College of William and Mary,
1977). See also Helen C. Rountree, "Indian Land Loss in Virginia: A Prototype of
Federal Indian Policy" (Ph.D. diss., University of Wisconsin-Milwaukee, 1973).

87. The present discussion rests on an examination of approximately seventy
articles, concentrated particularly in the *Maryland Historical Magazine* and the *William
and Mary Quarterly*, but also including the essays with significant 17th-century content
that appeared in the proceedings of a conference held at the Maryland Hall of Records
in June 1974. See Aubrey C. Land, Lois Green Carr, and Edward C. Papenfuse, eds.,
Law, Society, and Politics in Early Maryland, Proceedings of the First Conference on
Maryland History, June 14–15, 1974 (Baltimore, 1977).

88. The succeeding references make no claim to completeness, but they attempt to
take note of as many of the articles as possible that had been published by mid-1978.
Also helpful for Maryland is Dorothy M. Brown and Richard R. Duncan, comps., "A
Selected Bibliography of Articles on Maryland History in Other Journals," *Md. Hist.
Mag.*, LXIX (1974), 300–316. An annual listing of all writings on Maryland history,
compiled by Richard J. Cox, appeared annually thereafter (*ibid.*, LXX [1975], 211–223,
LXXI [1976], 449–464, and LXXII [1977], 288–314). See also Warren M. Billings, "Towards
the Rewriting of Seventeenth-Century Virginia History: A Review Article," *VMHB*,
LXXXIII (1975), 184–189.

the now widely accepted conclusion that a high death rate and a very low ratio of females to males persisted in the Chesapeake through a large part of the seventeenth century. The extent to which these unusual demographic circumstances produced a sense of uncertainty and impermanence in the life of the Chesapeake is now clear, although the research also suggests how desperately some survivors struggled to create greater order and security both in their personal lives and in the fragile social and political institutions of the two colonies.[89]

Perhaps the next largest group of articles explores prices, wealth distribution, and other aspects of economic development that relate closely to the social order. For the earlier part of the century—until perhaps 1660 or even a bit later—the predominant theme is the degree of opportunity that the growing tobacco economy offered those who managed to survive and acquire control of at least some land and labor.[90] Thereafter the emphasis falls increasingly on an important socioeconomic transformation occasioned by a cycle of

89. Irene W. D. Hecht, "The Virginia Muster of 1624/5 As a Source of Demographic History," *WMQ*, 3d Ser., XXX (1973), 65–92; Russell R. Menard, "Immigration to the Chesapeake Colonies in the Seventeenth Century: A Review Essay," *Md. Hist. Mag.*, LXVIII (1973), 323–329; Lorena S. Walsh and Russell R. Menard, "Death in the Chesapeake: Two Life Tables for Men in Early Colonial Maryland," *Md. Hist. Mag.*, LXIX (1974), 211–227; Darrett B. and Anita H. Rutman, "Of Agues and Fevers: Malaria in the Early Chesapeake," *WMQ*, 3d Ser., XXXIII (1976), 31–60; Russell R. Menard, "Immigrants and Their Increase: The Process of Population Growth in Early Colonial Maryland," in Land, Carr, and Papenfuse, eds., *Law, Society, and Politics in Early Maryland*, 88–110; Lois Green Carr and Lorena S. Walsh, "The Planter's Wife: The Experience of White Women in Seventeenth-Century Maryland," *WMQ*, 3d Ser., XXXIV (1977), 542–571; and Daniel Blake Smith, "Mortality and Family in the Colonial Chesapeake," *Journal of Interdisciplinary History*, VIII (1977–1978), 403–427. On social aspects of immigration from England, see Peter Wilson Coldham, "The 'Spiriting' of London Children to Virginia, 1648–1685," *VMHB*, LXXXIII (1975), 280–287, and David W. Galenson, "'Middling People' or 'Common Sort'?: The Social Origins of Some Early Americans Reexamined," *WMQ*, 3d Ser., XXXV (1978), 499–524. Virginia Bernhard, "Poverty and the Social Order in Seventeenth-Century Virginia," *VMHB*, LXXXV (1977), 141–155, argues for the existence of a high degree of social concern for the poor from very early in the century.

90. Edmund S. Morgan's two articles, "The Labor Problem at Jamestown, 1607–18," *AHR*, LXXVI (1971), 595–611, and "The First American Boom: Virginia, 1618 to 1630," *WMQ*, 3d Ser., XXVIII (1971), 169–198, emphasize that the profits of the tobacco boom accrued principally to a few men who possessed the power and the drive to gain control of labor and that labor itself was significantly degraded in the process. Menard puts more emphasis on the relative opportunities that he thinks also opened up for freed servants ("From Servant to Freeholder: Status Mobility and Property Accumulation in Seventeenth-Century Maryland," *WMQ*, 3d Ser., XXX [1973], 37–64). See also, for tobacco prices in the first part of the century, Menard, "A Note on Chesapeake Tobacco Prices, 1618–1660," *VMHB*, LXXXIV (1976), 401–410.

depression, a shift in the labor force from white servants to black slaves, and the emergence of larger-scale tobacco plantations.[91] Obviously related to this same development is a somewhat smaller group of articles that deal with blacks at the end of the century, exploring the effects of the rapid growth of a slave population in the last decade or two of the century on black-white relations and in the lives of blacks themselves.[92] For the most part, the new work displays little concern with the question that had commanded so much attention a few years earlier, that of the development of slavery as a legal institution before 1680. The implication seems to be that blacks were neither numerically significant nor an important component of the labor force until almost the end of the century and that the black presence and slavery were among those influences that altered rather than helped form seventeenth-century society.

91. Menard, "From Servants to Slaves: The Transformation of the Chesapeake Labor System, 1680–1710," *Southern Studies*, XVI (1977), 355–390, and "The Tobacco Industry in the Chesapeake Colonies, 1617–1730: An Interpretation," *Research in Economic History*, V (1979), forthcoming, are important overviews of the economic and social changes that occurred in the Chesapeake. Gloria L. Main, "Maryland and the Chesapeake Economy, 1670–1720," in Land, Carr, and Papenfuse, eds., *Law, Society, and Politics in Early Maryland*, 134–152, is particularly effective in explaining the process by which larger-scale plantations based on slave labor emerged from the transition despite a period of long-run depression in the tobacco economy. Useful for more localized manifestations of the transition are Paul G. E. Clemens, "The Settlement and Growth of Maryland's Eastern Shore during the English Restoration," *Maryland Historian*, V (1974), 63–78; Paul G. E. Clemens, "Economy and Society on Maryland's Eastern Shore, 1689–1733," in Land, Carr, and Papenfuse, eds., *Law, Society, and Politics in Early Maryland*, 153–170; Russell R. Menard, P. M. G. Harris, and Lois Green Carr, "Opportunity and Inequality: The Distribution of Wealth on the Lower Western Shore of Maryland, 1638–1705," *Md. Hist. Mag.*, LXIX (1974), 169–184; and Lorena S. Walsh, "Servitude and Opportunity in Charles County, Maryland, 1658–1705," in Land, Carr, and Papenfuse, eds., *Law, Society, and Politics in Early Maryland*, 111–133. On Maryland tobacco prices, see Russell R. Menard, "Farm Prices of Maryland Tobacco, 1659–1710," *Md. Hist. Mag.*, LXVIII (1973), 80–85. See also Tommy R. Thompson, "Debtors, Creditors, and the General Assembly in Colonial Maryland," *ibid.*, LXXII (1977), 59–77.

92. Richard R. Beeman, "Labor Forces and Race Relations: A Comparative View of the Colonization of Brazil and Virginia," *Political Science Quarterly*, LXXXVI (1971), 609–636; T. H. Breen, "A Changing Labor Force and Race Relations in Virginia, 1660–1710," *Journal of Social History*, VII (1973–1974), 3–25; Russell R. Menard, "The Maryland Slave Population, 1658 to 1730: A Demographic Profile of Blacks in Four Counties," *WMQ*, 3d Ser., XXXIII (1975), 29–54; and Ross M. Kimmel, "Free Blacks in Seventeenth-Century Maryland," *Md. Hist. Mag.*, LXXI (1976), 19–25. Although its emphasis falls after 1700, Allan Kulikoff, "The Origins of Afro-American Society in Tidewater Maryland and Virginia, 1700 to 1790," *WMQ*, 3d Ser., XXXV (1978), esp. 226–240, is of fundamental importance for understanding the position of blacks in the Chesapeake at the end of the 17th century. See also Peter H. Wood, " 'I Did the Best I Could for My Day': The Study of Early Black History during the Second Reconstruction, 1960 to 1976," *WMQ*, 3d Ser., XXXV (1978), 185–225.

There are, as well, a large number of articles that treat political subjects. Several important discussions of English imperial developments serve to remind us that the development of the Chesapeake, social and economic no less than political, took place in an imperial context that was sometimes crucial.[93] Most of these articles, however, are largely concerned with internal political turmoil and the shift in the character of local and provincial political leadership that the two colonies experienced late in the century and that were closely related to major social and economic changes.[94] Indeed, if the tremendous instability arising out of "demographic failure" is the great theme of Chesapeake history in its first half century, then the pervasive transformation of society, economy, and government that occurred between 1660 and the first decade or two of the eighteenth century constitutes the overriding concern of most of the recent scholarship on the second half century.

93. John C. Rainbolt, "A New Look at Stuart 'Tyranny': The Crown's Attack on the Virginia Assembly, 1676–1689," *VMHB*, LXXV (1967), 387–406; Sister Joan de Lourdes Leonard, "Operation Checkmate: The Birth and Death of a Virginia Blueprint for Progress, 1660–1676," *WMQ*, 3d Ser., XXIV (1967), 44–74; David Alan Williams, "Anglo-Virginia Politics, 1690–1735," in Alison G. Olson and Richard M. Brown, eds., *Anglo-American Political Relations, 1675–1775* (New Brunswick, N.J., 1970), 76–91; Robert Brenner, "The Civil War Politics of London's Merchant Community," *Past and Present*, no. 58 (Feb. 1973), 53–107; John D. Krugler, "Sir George Calvert's Resignation as Secretary of State and the Founding of Maryland," *Md. Hist. Mag.*, LXVIII (1973), 239–254; and Stephen Saunders Webb, "Army and Empire: English Garrison Government in Britain and America, 1569 to 1763," *WMQ*, 3d Ser., XXXIV (1977), 1–31. John C. Rainbolt, "The Absence of Towns in Seventeenth-Century Virginia," *Jour. So. Hist.*, XXXV (1969), 343–360, touches on both economic and political themes but is more than anything else an examination of imperial relations.

94. The only recent article examining a political controversy early in the century is J. Mills Thornton III, "The Thrusting Out of Governor Harvey: A Seventeenth-Century Rebellion," *VMHB*, LXXVI (1968), 11–26. Articles that emphasize interconnections between society and the developing Chesapeake political order include Warren M. Billings, "The Causes of Bacon's Rebellion: Some Suggestions," *VMHB*, LXXVIII (1970), 409–435; Billings, "The Growth of Political Institutions in Virginia, 1634 to 1676," *WMQ*, 3d Ser., XXXI (1974), 225–242; David W. Jordan, "Maryland's Privy Council, 1637–1715," in Land, Carr, and Papenfuse, eds., *Law, Society, and Politics in Early Maryland*, 65–87; and John C. Rainbolt, "The Alteration in the Relationship between Leadership and Constituents in Virginia, 1660 to 1720," *WMQ*, 3d Ser., XXVII (1970), 411–434. Wesley Frank Craven, "'. . . And So the Form of Government Became Perfect,'" *VMHB*, LXXVII (1969), 131–145, is a graceful restatement of the clearheaded conception of 17th-century political development in Virginia that has characterized all of the author's work. See also David W. Jordan, "John Coode, Perennial Rebel," *Md. Hist. Mag.*, LXX (1975), 1–28. More traditional in their approach to the political transition in Maryland are Richard A. Gleissner's two articles, "Religious Causes of the Glorious Revolution in Maryland," *ibid.*, LXIV (1969), 327–341, and "The Revolutionary Settlement of 1691 in Maryland," *ibid.*, LXVI (1971), 405–419.

A few other currents of work also share some concern with aspects of the development of Chesapeake society. A number of recent articles on legal history, for example, seem inspired in some part by the value of legal records as sources for social history.[95] At the same time, new work by historians on Chesapeake Indians, although slow to appear, is beginning to exhibit less interest in questions of public policy toward the Indians than in the significance of intercultural contacts between Indians and whites.[96]

Inevitably there is a scattering of material—sometimes more than that—on other topics,[97] but the above categories, nearly all to one degree or another having social or economic implications, account for a good four-fifths of the total number of recently published articles and essays.

Anyone who surveys the recent work on the early Chesapeake becomes quickly aware that it remains in large part a periodical literature. The number of book-length studies, though growing, is still limited, in part because the recent revival of the field has not afforded

95. Joseph H. Smith, "The Foundations of Law in Maryland: 1634–1715," in George Athan Billias, ed., *Selected Essays: Law and Authority in Colonial America* (Barre, Mass., 1965), 92–115; James W. Deen, Jr., "Patterns of Testation: Four Tidewater Counties in Colonial Virginia," *American Journal of Legal History*, XVI (1972), 154–176; Alan F. Day, "Lawyers in Colonial Maryland, 1660–1715," *ibid.*, XVII (1973), 145–165; Peter G. Yackel, "Benefit of Clergy in Colonial Maryland," *Md. Hist. Mag.*, LXIX (1974), 383–397; Gloria L. Main, "Probate Records as a Source for Early American History," *WMQ*, 3d Ser., XXXII (1975), 89–99; Lois Green Carr, "The Development of the Maryland Orphans' Court, 1654–1715," in Land, Carr, and Papenfuse, eds., *Law, Society, and Politics in Early Maryland*, 41–62; George B. Curtis, "The Colonial County Court, Social Forum and Legislative Precedent: Accomack County, Virginia, 1633–1639," *VMHB*, LXXXV (1977), 274–288; and Clara Ann Bowler, "Carted Whores and White Shrouded Apologies: Slander in the County Courts of Seventeenth-Century Virginia," *ibid.*, 411–426.

96. Gary B. Nash, "The Image of the Indian in the Southern Colonial Mind," *WMQ*, 3d Ser., XXIX (1972), 197–230; Alden T. Vaughan, "'Expulsion of the Savages': English Policy and the Virginia Massacre of 1622," *WMQ*, 3d Ser., XXXV (1978), 57–84, deals in large part with matters of public policy but ends on a note of the irreconcilable cultural conflict between Indian and white. J. Frederick Fausz's dissertation, "The Powhatan Uprising of 1622," is also especially relevant here.

97. Among recent articles not otherwise noted are Robert C. Johnson, "The Lotteries of the Virginia Company, 1612–1621," *VMHB*, LXXIV (1966), 259–292; Kenneth L. Carroll, "Quaker Opposition to the Establishment of a State Church in Maryland," *Md. Hist. Mag.*, LXV (1970), 149–170; and Lindley S. Butler, "The Early Settlement of Carolina: Virginia's Southern Frontier," *VMHB*, LXXIX (1971), 20–28. Also, Gerald E. Hartdagen published a series of articles derived from his dissertation on the Maryland colonial vestry: *Md. Hist. Mag.*, LXIII (1968), 360–398, LXVII (1972), 363–388; *Historical Magazine of the Protestant Episcopal Church*, XXXVII (1968), 371–396, XXXVIII (1969), 349–360, XL (1971), 315–355, 461–479. Several articles and essays on literary topics are discussed in another context, below, pp. 42–43.

many young scholars the time to revise their dissertations for publication but also because the detailed work, much of it quantitative, demanded in such sources as county records is time-consuming. Two dissertations, and portions of two others, have appeared so far in book form. John C. Rainbolt's posthumously published *From Prescription to Persuasion*, which preceded much of the work in social history, relies on provincial and imperial sources to make a broad interpretation of efforts by Virginia provincial leaders to achieve a more diverse economy in the late seventeenth century. According to Rainbolt, that policy ultimately moved the political order toward greater reliance on consent and representation.[98] Lois Green Carr and David Jordan's *Maryland's Revolution of Government, 1689–1692*, which combines some material from their respective dissertations with a much larger body of new work, departs from past studies of the overthrow of the proprietary by drawing extensively on local records to fix the characteristics of the old and new ruling elite in the colony and to assess changes in the Maryland political system more precisely than had previously been done.[99] Carville Earle's study of the settlement system of All Hallow's Parish, Maryland, from 1650 to 1783, the work of a historical geographer, treats its subject with sufficient scope to comprehend the effect of patterns of settlement on social organization.[100] None of the three is obviously a full-scale social history, yet all contribute significantly to an understanding of the transformation of the social order of the Chesapeake that occurred at the end of the century.

It has remained for two, more senior scholars to essay the first efforts at a broader synthesis of some of the most important features of seventeenth-century society, in both instances for the Virginia colony rather than for the entire Chesapeake. Wesley Frank Craven's *White, Red, and Black*—the earlier and briefer of the two studies—constitutes, as the title suggests, a discussion of the three ethnic groups in the colony and their interrelationships, concentrating in the case of the whites and blacks on assessing patterns of immigration to

98. John C. Rainbolt, *From Prescription to Persuasion: Manipulation of Eighteenth [i.e., Seventeenth] Century Virginia Economy* (Port Washington , N.Y., 1974).

99. Lois Green Carr and David William Jordan, *Maryland's Revolution of Government, 1689–1692* (Ithaca, N.Y., 1974).

100. Carville V. Earle, *The Evolution of a Tidewater Settlement System: All Hallow's Parish, Maryland, 1650–1783*, University of Chicago Department of Geography, Research Paper No. 170 (Chicago, 1975).

the colony.[101] Craven's conclusions, deriving from a close study of the records of lands patented under the headright system, do not stop with simply estimating the extent and timing of immigration but are equally concerned with how immigration broadly affected society and politics in Virginia. Although Craven completed his book before the first examples of more detailed work from the county records were available, and although his own calculations of the timing of immigration from the dates of the patenting of headrights have been challenged, his was the first study to pose some of the larger generalizations about population, sex ratio, and immigration on which much of the new work is grounded.[102]

But by far the most comprehensive work that has yet appeared in the seventies is Edmund S. Morgan's *American Slavery, American Freedom*.[103] Although the climax of the book is a brief concluding section analyzing the paradoxical relationship between black slavery and white freedom that developed in Virginia by the eighteenth century and in the author's judgment has permeated all of American history, the key forces that produced the paradox derived from what had happened in seventeenth-century Virginia. All but the final two or three chapters are therefore a detailed account of that first century, focusing particularly on the evolution of its labor system, which was clearly a principal determinant of the characteristics of the social and political order of colonial Virginia, whether one ultimately accepts the slavery-freedom paradox in its entirety or not. Consequently *American Slavery, American Freedom* has quickly emerged not necessarily as an unchallenged overview of the early Chesapeake but certainly as the standard against which all other generalizations are tested. By all odds it is one of the most important books on the early Chesapeake in decades.

Two other volumes—one a new study of the London Company years at Jamestown by Alden Vaughan and the other a documentary history of Virginia to 1689 edited by Warren M. Billings—appeared in

101. Wesley Frank Craven, *White, Red, and Black: The Seventeenth-Century Virginian* (Charlottesville, Va., 1971).

102. See Edmund S. Morgan, "Headrights and Head Counts: A Review Article," *VMHB*, LXXX (1972), 361–371, and Menard, "Immigration to the Chesapeake Colonies in the Seventeenth Century," *Md. Hist. Mag.*, LXVIII (1973), 323–329.

103. Edmund S. Morgan, *American Slavery, American Freedom: The Ordeal of Colonial Virginia* (New York, 1975).

1975.[104] Apart from its careful narrative, centered around a balanced appraisal of Smith's role in establishing the colony, Vaughan's account stresses how far events had moved toward giving permanent shape to Chesapeake society by the time of Smith's death. To some extent he seems implicitly to disagree with many social historians' stronger emphasis on the continued instability of society long after the 1620s. Billings's documentary collection illustrates very well how much the revival of the history of the early Chesapeake and its concentration on social history has required, if not a rediscovery, at least a close reexamination of local records—deeds, wills and inventories of estates, court orders, tax lists, and parish records—of Maryland and Virginia. Billings's contribution in surveying and focusing attention on the Virginia records, both in the volume and elsewhere, has been extensive.[105] Although its topical arrangement may at times make it a little more difficult to appreciate the interaction between social conditions, economic considerations, politics, and other aspects of life in the colony, his volume presents a useful sampling of the kinds of evidence available that would otherwise be difficult to communicate as effectively.

There does not at the moment seem much likelihood, however, that the new emphasis on the early Chesapeake will produce large-scale editorial projects; the nature of the research being done demands consultation of such an extensive range of materials and in such depth that collecting and eventually making accessible to other scholars summary data from the records probably seems more productive than would extensive editorial preparation. That is not to say, however, that there have not been a number of important documentary volumes published during the sixties and early seventies, including a five-year segment of the Accomack-Northampton, Virginia county court records; the letters of John Pory, a major figure in

104. Warren M. Billings, ed., *The Old Dominion in the Seventeenth Century: A Documentary History of Virginia, 1606–1689* (Chapel Hill, N.C., 1975), and Alden T. Vaughan, *American Genesis: Captain John Smith and the Founding of Virginia*, Library of American Biography (Boston, 1975).
105. See, e.g., Warren M. Billings, "The Cases of Fernando and Elizabeth Key: A Note on the Status of Blacks in Seventeenth-Century Virginia," *WMQ*, 3d Ser., XXX (1973), 467–474; Billings, "Some Acts Not in Hening's *Statutes*: The Acts of Assembly, April 1652, November 1652, and July 1653," *VMHB*, LXXXIII (1975), 22–76; Billings, ed., "A Quaker in Seventeenth-Century Virginia: Four Remonstrances by George Wilson," *WMQ*, 3d Ser., XXXIII (1976), 127–140.

the early years at Jamestown; and the papers of Virginia's two pre-eminent seventeenth-century scientists, John Banister and the Reverend John Clayton.[106]

The documentary collections on Pory, Banister, and Clayton form a part of the extensive new work on literary and cultural topics by scholars in both history and literature—something the preponderance of social history may lead one to overlook. Everett H. Emerson has provided a fresh literary treatment of John Smith.[107] Bacon's Rebellion, as a literary event both in its own day and later, has continued to attract interest.[108] J. A. Leo Lemay's *Men of Letters in Colonial Maryland* has fully examined three major seventeenth-century Maryland writers, Andrew White, John Hammond, and George Alsop.[109] Richard Beale Davis, the dean of the scholars of Southern colonial literature, has added to his already distinguished record a volume of collected shorter writings, which includes several pieces on seventeenth-century Virginia, and his magnum opus, *Intellectual Life in the Colonial South, 1585–1763*.[110] In the history of the arts

106. Susie M. Ames, ed., *County Court Records of Accomack-Northampton, Virginia, 1640–1645*, Virginia Historical Society, *Documents*, X (Charlottesville, Va., 1973); William S. Powell, *John Pory, 1572–1636: The Life and Letters of a Man of Many Parts* (Chapel Hill, N.C., 1977); Joseph and Nesta Ewan, *John Banister and His Natural History of Virginia, 1678–1692* (Urbana, Ill., 1970); Edmund and Dorothy Smith Berkeley, eds., *The Reverend John Clayton, a Parson with a Scientific Mind: His Scientific Writings and Other Related Papers*, Virginia Historical Society, *Documents*, VI (Charlottesville, Va., 1965). Philip L. Barbour's new edition of the writings of Captain John Smith is also in progress. Several useful individual documents or descriptions of documentary materials have also been recently published, among them T. H. Breen, ed., "George Donne's 'Virginia Reviewed': A 1638 Plan to Reform Colonial Society," *WMQ*, 3d Ser., XXX (1973), 449–466; J. Frederick Fausz and Jon Kukla, eds., "A Letter of Advice to the Governor of Virginia, 1624," *WMQ*, 3d Ser., XXXIV (1977), 104–129; Lawrence J. Friedman and Arthur H. Shaffer, "The Conway Robinson Notes and Seventeenth-Century Virginia," *VMHB*, LXXVIII (1970), 259–267; Jan Kupp, "Dutch Notarial Acts Relating to the Tobacco Trade of Virginia, 1608–1653," *WMQ*, 3d Ser., XXX (1973), 653–655; and Alden T. Vaughan, "Blacks in Virginia: A Note on the First Decade," *WMQ*, 3d Ser., XXIX (1972), 469–478.

107. Everett H. Emerson, *Captain John Smith*, Twayne's United States Authors Series, 177 (New York, 1971). There is also a group of essays by Emerson, Lewis Leary, Philip Barbour, and Leota Hirsch on Smith and several other authors of early accounts of Virginia in J. A. Leo Lemay, ed., *Essays in Early Virginia Literature Honoring Richard Beale Davis* (New York, 1977). See also Philip L. Barbour, "The Honorable George Percy, Premier Chronicler of the First Virginia Voyage," *Early American Literature*, VI, no. 1 (Spring, 1971), 7–17.

108. Carson, *Bacon's Rebellion, 1676–1696*; Wilber Henry Ward III, "Bacon's Rebellion in Literature to 1861" (Ph.D. diss., University of Tennessee, 1971).

109. (Knoxville, Tenn., 1972).

110. Richard Beale Davis, *Literature and Society in Early Virginia, 1608–1840* (Baton Rouge, La., 1973), esp. chaps. 1–4; Davis, *Intellectual Life in the Colonial South, 1585–1763*, 3 vols. (Knoxville, Tenn., 1978).

the early chapters of John W. Reps's *Tidewater Towns* provide important evidence, both visual and literary, on the difficult process of town development in the seventeenth-century Chesapeake.[111] If the career of Virginia's influential first commissary seems more political than clerical, Parke Rouse's biography of James Blair nonetheless gives due attention to his educational and ecclesiastical activities at the close of the seventeenth century soon after he had arrived in the colony.[112] Another full-length study that clearly focuses on religious history and carries forward his large body of previous work is Kenneth L. Carroll's *Quakerism on the Eastern Shore*.[113]

Still, it cannot be said, one must concede, that there has as yet occurred much integration of the recent social history with the kind of cultural history of the Chesapeake that these works represent. The emphases of the social historians all but explicitly deny much opportunity for a culture in a more formal sense—as opposed to the material culture of the region—to have developed in the seventeenth century. Nevertheless, the output of the literary and cultural historians is so extensive that some more effective synthesis of the two strands of work seems imperative.

VII

When we are reminded once again that the foregoing survey examines only dissertations completed within the past ten or twelve years and for the most part published work appearing since 1970, the extent of the revival of interest in the early Chesapeake seems all the more remarkable. If the historians of that revival perhaps owe their largest debt to those who worked in Chesapeake history in the 1920s and 1930s, they may invite a closer comparison with the generation of pre-World War I scholars in the sheer amount of work they seem likely to produce and in their responsibility for one of the "up" cycles in historical study of the Chesapeake.

For all the variety of subject matter reflected in the dissertations, books, and published articles, the thrust of the work in the mainstream, as noted, has been increasingly social, though it has by no

111. John W. Reps, *Tidewater Towns: City Planning in Colonial Virginia and Maryland* (Charlottesville, Va., 1972).

112. Parke Rouse, Jr., *James Blair of Virginia* (Chapel Hill, N.C., 1971).

113. (Baltimore, 1970). Its elaborate detail on individual Quakers also gives it a good bit of relevance for the new social historians.

means excluded important economic influences on the social order or political consequences of its character. Yet there is a certain spontaneity about the manner in which the field has grown so rapidly and moved in such a uniform direction. It has brought together a remarkable range of scholars: senior historians long active in the field, those who had made their initial reputation in other areas of early American history, and recent Ph.D.'s who have immediately adopted the field as their own. It has attracted not only historians with a variety of methodological inclinations but also literature scholars, biologists with an interest in history, and others. Nor were there in the beginning major centers of work. The younger scholars received their graduate training at a variety of institutions throughout the country, often under dissertation directors who were themselves not immediately interested in the Chesapeake. Indeed, if there was any distinguishing feature about the graduate training, it was the small extent to which the universities of the Chesapeake region, where the bulk of the earlier dissertations in the field had been completed, initially shared in the new wave of activity.

Yet the younger scholars, at least, have increasingly taken on the appearance of a "school," with established centers of activity and with what may at times seem an unusual amount of interchange and interdependence in their work. So far as those who have worked primarily in Maryland history are concerned, the centralization of Maryland records and the excellence of their management at the Hall of Records has played a part in the process. The St. Mary's City Commission, established to undertake an extensive and broadly defined study of Maryland's first capital, has generated extensive research by its own staff and has also emerged, along with the Hall of Records, where the commission's historians are based, as a center for the Chesapeake scholars. If the situation in Virginia, where research and archival activity is somewhat more dispersed and where there is a more numerous and older group of preservation agencies, has not been quite so concentrated, the Colonial Records Project, the opening of the extensive microform collections of the Colonial Williamsburg Foundation to visiting scholars, and the work of several important projects in historical archaeology, among other things, have nonetheless supplied something of the same focus for the work on that colony. Most Chesapeake historians would probably recognize, too, that the all too often unrewarding scholarly conference has been and continues to be for them an unusually effective rallying point, as is attested by the present volume, another growing out of the 1974 Maryland Hall of Records conference, and an even more recent publication of the proceedings of a conference at the Regional Economic History Center at the Eleutherian Mills-Hagley Foundation.[114] If one can legitimately separate the scholarly and the academic, one might conclude that not only has the onset of a revival of interest in the seventeenth-century Chesapeake been sudden, the results extensive, and the concentration in one historical direction marked, but also that the work is going on to an unusual degree from a base outside the university. In that sense the current Chesapeake historiography could reflect the "new" history in more ways than in its focus upon social questions.

So rapid a survey of an important body of scholarship can hardly expect to do full justice to its content. It can at best indicate only in a general way the scope and significance of that work. Too, its juxtaposition of the active period of writing on the Chesapeake at the beginning of the twentieth century, the relative inactivity of the period between the two world wars (though the important contributions of that era should not be lost sight of), and the new wave of activity in the last decade will perhaps convey an impression of the proportions of the remarkable renascence that we have been witnessing.

VIII

Obviously to understand fully this renascence there is no shortcut to extensive reading in the more recent literature. The essays that follow provide another addition to that literature, one that perhaps may illuminate the most significant aspects of the development of Anglo-American society in the Chesapeake, bring investigation of Maryland and Virginia together in a single volume more successfully than has yet been achieved, and testify to the continuing vitality of the study of the seventeenth-century Chesapeake.

Initially the new work that has already been published sought to explore the extent of the "demographic failure" of the early Chesapeake and all of its ramifications on population, social structure, and

114. Glenn Porter and William H. Mulligan, Jr., eds., *Economic Change in the Chesapeake Colonies*, Working Papers from the Regional Economic History Center, I, no. 3 (1978).

family life. At least three of the essays in the present volume add depth and precision to our understanding of that phenomenon. Obviously one critical determinant of the instability of life in the Chesapeake was the high death rate; yet there have still been only a few attempts to explain in detail why colonists died in such incredible numbers in an essentially temperate climate. In particular, Anita and Darrett Rutman's 1976 article, "Of Agues and Fevers," has already restored the significance of malaria, not so much as a primary killer but as a disease that weakened colonists and left them susceptible to other, more fatal illnesses.[115] Carville Earle's essay now employs scientific studies of estuaries such as the James River to demonstrate how bad water infected the first Jamestown settlers with still other illnesses. In asserting the primacy of disease over starvation in accounting for high mortality in the first years of the Virginia colony, he provides a dramatic example of another problem: how little the first colonists seemed to understand the environment into which they had come.[116]

At the same time, the end purpose of the study of early Chesapeake demography was from the beginning more than simply to fix precisely the rate of mortality, the unusually large predominance of the young among the total population, or the exceptionally high preponderance of men over women. Rather the intention has been to trace the effects of these unusual demographic characteristics on traditional social bonds and family structure. Darrett and Anita Rutman explore this question in depth for the Virginia county of Middlesex (and thereby provide an early glimpse into their much more comprehensive study of that county which is in progress), while Lorena Walsh provides a similar and somewhat broader investigation for the whole Maryland colony. Although the Rutman's discussion of the methodology they have applied to the Middlesex sources and the unusual female mortality curve that they establish may prove of particular interest to social historians, a much wider group of readers should find that both essays provide a very clear and specific picture of the disruption of family life and the breakdown of social restraints that occurred. These readers will no doubt see the pattern of frequent

115. Rutman and Rutman, "Of Agues and Fevers," *WMQ*, 3d Ser., XXXIII (1976), 31–60.
116. "Environment, Disease, and Mortality in Early Virginia," pp. 96–125.

and rapid remarriage and the resultant complicated family relationships within the same household as equally informative.[117]

A second major theme in the recent scholarship has been the transformation of Chesapeake society from the instability and uncertainty of the early seventeenth century to the relative order and stability that came to prevail by the second decade of the eighteenth century. No one doubts the difficulty of explaining that transformation, marked as it was by the extremely complex interaction of a declining death rate among white colonists, an apparent lessening of economic opportunity for freed servants, and the virtual disappearance of white servant immigrants and their replacement by African slaves. The transformation takes on added complexity from having occurred at a time of political turmoil and economic depression in both colonies. Nor was one key element of the transformation—the dramatic shift in the labor base of the Chesapeake from white servitude to black slavery—necessarily in the exclusive control of the Chesapeake colonists themselves. Economic and demographic circumstances in England, as well as the founding of new colonies that also required settlers, may well have affected the supply of white servants, while slave labor almost certainly became available in significant quantities only when changing economic conditions made the Chesapeake as attractive a market for traders as the West Indies and South America.

There is, of course, a well-formulated account of the manner in which the transformation progressed in Edmund Morgan's *American Slavery, American Freedom*.[118] The process, as he describes it, was one in which the increasing survival rate of settlers by 1660 markedly reduced economic opportunities for those who had completed indentures; a volatile, rebellious class of landless freedmen began in turn to appear; and larger landowners turned toward blacks, who were in any event becoming a better investment as a consequence of the same improved longevity that had started the lot of the freedman on its downward spiral. Thus, the changes in Chesapeake society appear largely to have been generated within the region itself, although Morgan by no means entirely dismisses such external in-

117. " 'Now-Wives and Sons-in-Law': Parental Death in a Seventeenth-Century Virginia County," pp. 153–182; " 'Till Death Us Do Part': Marriage and Family in Seventeenth-Century Maryland," pp. 126–152.
118. Morgan, *American Slavery, American Freedom*, chaps. 11, 16.

fluences on the labor supply as conditions in the Atlantic slave trade or in the English economy.

A few previously published essays, for the most part more limited in their focus and more confined to Maryland, view the extent of opportunity for freed servants a little more optimistically or assign somewhat more weight to outside forces in effecting the conversion to slave labor. It would be a mistake, however, to try to make a full-scale debate of the matter, although admittedly it is necessary, if one is to account for the displacement of servitude by slavery, to strike some balance between internal influences—particularly the degree to which freedmen began to despair of their prospects—and those forces arising outside the Chesapeake.

For the moment, however, there seems to be a greater need to explore the whole process of change in the late seventeenth century as thoroughly as possible than to take hard and fast positions. Three of the essays in this volume examine aspects of this large question in such a spirit. James Horn's discussion of seventeenth-century immigration to the Chesapeake is, to be sure, concerned with far more than the decline of that immigration near the end of the century.[119] Nevertheless, in reopening the broad subject of the character of that immigration and the preconditions that underlay it in England, above all the extensive internal migration that preceded overseas emigration, he reminds us how much patterns of immigration to the Chesapeake were shaped from the first by what was happening in England. Yet those who migrated to the Chesapeake after mid-century clearly did find themselves in a society that was changing rapidly. Whatever the exact nature of their economic situation, there seems a good bit of evidence that as the century moved on, freed servants and other lesser men were likely, if they became landowners, to do so by spending some time as free laborers or tenants and by eventually acquiring less advantageously located lands—a process that Kevin P. Kelly spells out very explicitly in his study of settlement patterns in one such area, the interior sections of Surry County, Virginia.[120]

The third essay, by Lois Green Carr and Russell R. Menard, faces in broad terms the pivotal question of changing economic opportunity

119. "Servant Emigration to the Chesapeake in the Seventeenth Century," pp. 51–95.
120. "'In dispers'd Country Plantations': Settlement Patterns in Seventeenth-Century Surry County, Virginia," pp. 183–205.

for freedmen, making the case more strongly than previously that freedmen had a good chance of realizing their ambitions in the older areas of settlement in Maryland, at least until about 1680, and that even thereafter they possessed other alternatives such as migration to newer areas of settlement.[121] Since they conclude, in effect, that reasonable opportunities persisted past the time when a really adequate supply of English immigrants was available, one implication of their essay is to give more importance to those external conditions that governed the flow of labor as a determinant of the social and economic transformation of the Chesapeake.

However one explains the actual process of change in the Chesapeake labor force, everyone agrees on the end result, namely that the appearance of a large black population held in permanent bondage had a critical influence on the character of eighteenth-century Chesapeake society. There is an equivalent consensus about another element in the transformation, the growth for the first time of a large native-born white population. That change, too, helped shape the society of the eighteenth century, among other things by producing a very different leadership from that of the seventeenth century—a group who by virtue of their native birth came to feel more secure, to have a distinctive sense of their identity, and to govern with a greater degree of responsiveness to their constituents.

That, too, was a change of great magnitude, one that was not accomplished without a long and sometimes stormy sequence of events, as major late-century rebellions in both Virginia and Maryland would suggest. In the long run, however, the slower process by which the character of the elite changed and its members altered their perception of their situation may have been more influential than the sporadic and inconclusive periods of unrest that have so far received the greater amount of attention. The two final essays in the volume address that longer-range development. David W. Jordan explains how and at what rate a native-born elite emerged in Maryland between 1660 and 1715, succeeding at the same time in giving a good bit of attention to similar developments in Virginia.[122] Comparing the English-born generation that still controlled Virginia in the 1680s with

121. "Immigration and Opportunity: The Freedman in Early Colonial Maryland," pp. 206–242.
122. "Political Stability and the Emergence of a Native Elite in Maryland, 1660–1715," pp. 243–273.

the native group that had come to power by the turn of the century, Carole Shammas finds "new kinds of responses to the problems which arose from living far from the national center of authority and culture," "a new receptivity toward building up colonial institutions," and "a new commitment to colonial politics."[123]

Nothing perhaps more clearly indicated the arrival of a new era in the Chesapeake than the appearance of this now entrenched, sometimes self-conscious elite—unless, of course, it was the parallel alteration of the labor force from servant to slave. In combination, then, these essays provide an insight into both the difficult conditions under which a social order was forged in the early Chesapeake and the most important changes that it had experienced by the end of its first century.

123. "English-Born and Creole Elites in Turn-of-the-Century Virginia," pp. 274–296.

2

Servant Emigration to the Chesapeake in the Seventeenth Century

James Horn

I

One of the most important factors influencing the social and economic development of Chesapeake society in the seventeenth century was the prolonged influx of English immigrants. Unlike New England, where most settlers arrived within the span of a single decade, Virginia and Maryland continued to receive large numbers of immigrants throughout most of the century.[1] These newcomers fulfilled two vital functions: they provided the labor necessary for the production of the colonies' staple, tobacco, and they replenished a declining population that was unable to reproduce itself by natural means until the last quarter of the century.[2] Without sustained immigration the Chesapeake colonies would have failed.

1. Carl Bridenbaugh, *Vexed and Troubled Englishmen, 1590–1642* (New York, 1968), chap. 12; N.C.P. Tyack, "Migration from East Anglia to New England before 1660" (Ph.D. diss., University of London, 1951); Charles M. Andrews, *The Colonial Period of American History*, I (New Haven, Conn., 1934), chap. 18; T. H. Breen and Stephen Foster, "Moving to the New World: The Character of Early Massachusetts Immigration," *William and Mary Quarterly*, 3d Ser., XXX (1973), 189–222; John J. Waters, "Hingham, Massachusetts, 1631–1661: An East Anglian Oligarchy in the New World," *Journal of Social History*, I (1967–1968), 351–370.

No reliable figure for total immigration to the Chesapeake during the 17th century has been worked out. Wesley Frank Craven has suggested that over 82,000 people entered Virginia between 1635 and 1699, while Russell Menard has recently estimated that about 32,000 arrived in Maryland between 1634 and 1681. Combining these two figures and allowing for immigration outside of the years covered by these estimates, we attain an overall total of approximately 130,000 to 150,000 for the whole of the 17th century. It should be kept in mind that this is only a rough estimate, but in the absence of more precise data it serves to give some idea of the magnitude of emigration from England. See Craven, *White, Red, and Black: The Seventeenth-Century Virginian* (Charlottesville, Va., 1971), 16; and Menard, "Economy and Society in Early Colonial Maryland" (Ph.D. diss., University of Iowa, 1975), 176.

2. Menard, "Economy and Society," 174–205; Craven, *White, Red, and Black*, 1–37; Lorena S. Walsh and Russell R. Menard, "Death in the Chesapeake: Two Life Tables for Men in Early Colonial Maryland," *Maryland Historical Magazine*, LXIX (1974), 211–227.

Considering the importance of immigrants in shaping Chesapeake society, it is surprising that so little is known about them. Who were the tens of thousands of men and women who made the long journey across the Atlantic to settle in Virginia and Maryland? Where did they come from? What induced them to leave their hometowns and villages? And how did they set about emigrating? This essay seeks to answer these questions by the detailed analysis of lists of indentured servants who left England for the Chesapeake between 1654 and 1707.[3] Although these lists have been known to historians for many years, their full potential for establishing the social and economic background of servants has not yet been realized.[4] Previous studies of immigration to Virginia and Maryland have concentrated either on the numbers and rate at which servants entered the colonies or on their social characteristics.[5] The perspective has been an American

3. The Bristol list is contained in four manuscript volumes: "Servants to forraign plantations, 1654–1663," Bristol Record Office (hereafter cited as B.R.O.) 04220 (1); "Servants to forraign plantacons, 1663–1679," B.R.O. 04220 (2); "Actions and Apprentices," B.R.O. 04355 (6); "Actions and Apprentices," B.R.O. 04356 (1). The list has been partially transcribed by N. Dermott Harding and R. Hargreaves-Mawdsley, eds., *Bristol and America: A Record of the First Settlers in the Colonies of North America, 1654–1685* (London, 1929). A more recent and accurate transcript has been made by Noel Currer-Briggs, ed., "Indentured Servants from Bristol to America, 1654–1686" (unpubl. MS). The London list of servants of 1682–1692 may be found in the Lord Mayor's Waiting Books, vols. XIII–XV, in the Guildhall Library, London. They have been transcribed by Michael Ghirelli, *A List of Emigrants from England to America, 1682–1692* (Baltimore, 1968). The original indentures of the servants who left London between 1683 and 1684 are in the Greater London Record Office. A transcript has been made by C.D.P. Nicholson, "Some Early Emigrants to America," *Genealogists' Magazine*, XII, Nos. 1–16 (1955–1958), XIII, Nos. 1–8 (1959–1961); and by John Wareing, "Some Early Emigrants to America, 1683–4; A Supplementary List," *ibid.*, XVIII (1975–1976), 239–246. The Liverpool list has been transcribed by Elizabeth French, "List of Emigrants to America from Liverpool, 1697–1707," *New England Historical and Genealogical Register*, LXIV (1910) and LXV (1911). Finally, a list of over 2,000 emigrants who went to Virginia in 1635 may be found in John Camden Hotten, ed., *The Original Lists of Persons of Quality . . . and others who went from Great Britain to the American Plantations, 1600–1700* (London, 1874), 35–138.

4. As can be seen from n. 3, the Bristol and Liverpool lists were first transcribed 50 years ago. Abbot Emerson Smith discussed three of the four main lists used in this study, but made no attempt to analyze them; see *Colonists in Bondage: White Servitude and Convict Labor in America, 1607–1776* (Chapel Hill, N.C., 1947), appendix, 308–310. The Bristol list and one of the London records were used by Mildred Campbell in her seminal work, "Social Origins of Some Early Americans," in James Morton Smith, ed., *Seventeenth-Century America: Essays in Colonial History* (Chapel Hill, N.C., 1959), 63–89.

5. Craven, in *White, Red, and Black*, was more concerned with measuring the pace and magnitude of immigration than with describing in detail the social and economic backgrounds of the colonists. His generalizations about the origins of servants are based on the work of Mildred Campbell mentioned above. Campbell was the first historian to recognize the value of the Bristol and London lists for assessing the social character of emigrants. However, she did not attempt a rigorous quantitative analysis

one: what impact these newcomers had upon the developing societies. Little attention has been given to the English origins of servants.[6] The emigrant is here studied in the context of English social and economic development in the seventeenth century. I have made no attempt to follow the fortunes of servants in the New World, since this has been done by other historians.[7] In sum, the object of this study is threefold: first, to describe who the emigrants were, in terms of age, sex, status, and occupation in order to evaluate their relative positions in English society; second, to ascertain the sorts of communities they came from —village, market town, provincial town, or city—and the type of economy that prevailed in these areas; and, finally, to speculate about why and how they emigrated.

The most important source used in this paper is a list of over ten thousand indentured servants who left Bristol for America between 1654 and 1686.[8] Entries that contain full information—name, occupation, and place of origin of the servant—are restricted to the first six years and the final two years of the list. Places of destination are given (or can be inferred) in all but a few cases, and usually the name, occupation, and place of origin of the master to whom the servant was bound is supplied.[9] Approximately five thousand servants emigrated to the Chesapeake during the period covered by the list, but the core of the following analysis involves the 829 men and women whose place of origin and occupation or status are known.

Other lists of indentured servants are less extensive. In the Lord

of the data and did not examine closely the places from which servants came. More recently Russell Menard has studied the sorts of people who immigrated to the Chesapeake in terms of age and sex, but the English origins of servants were not discussed; see Menard, "Economy and Society," 153–173.

6. A notable exception is Campbell's article cited above, but as stated earlier the English origins of servants are dealt with only in general terms and relate to emigration to America as a whole.

7. Besides the essays in this book, see Russell R. Menard, "From Servant to Freeholder: Status Mobility and Property Accumulation in Seventeenth-Century Maryland," *WMQ*, 3d Ser., XXX (1973), 37–64; Lorena S. Walsh, "Servitude and Opportunity in Charles County, Maryland, 1658–1705," in Aubrey C. Land, Lois Green Carr, and Edward C. Papenfuse, eds., *Law, Society, and Politics in Early Maryland* (Baltimore and London, 1977), 111–133; Edmund S. Morgan, *American Slavery, American Freedom: The Ordeal of Colonial Virginia* (New York, 1975); Menard, "Economy and Society"; Smith, *Colonists in Bondage*, 221–306.

8. See n. 3 above.

9. For the degree of non-registration of information during the first six years of the records, see David Souden, "'To Forraign Plantacons': Indentured Servant Emigration, c. 1650–1660" (B.A. diss., Cambridge University, 1976), table 2:1, 13. I would like to thank David Souden for permitting me to read his paper.

Mayor of London's Waiting Books, volumes thirteen to fifteen, there is a list of 390 servants who left London for Virginia and Maryland between 1682 and 1686. These records give the name, place of origin, occupation, and age of the emigrant.[10] Similar information is given for a further 483 servants who were enrolled before the Middlesex Sessions Court in 1683 and 1684.[11] Finally, the names of thirteen hundred servants who left Liverpool for the Chesapeake between 1697 and 1707 are to be found in the records of the Corporation of Liverpool. These entries were apparently kept unofficially and in many cases are incomplete.[12] In all, the names, ages, occupations, places of origin, and sex of over three thousand seventeenth-century emigrants to the Chesapeake have been abstracted and analyzed.[13]

Using lists of indentured servants to study emigration introduces various problems that need to be recognized from the outset. The most obvious of these is that they leave out entirely the question of free emigration, for, apart from genealogical material, there are no comprehensive sources for the study of free emigrants.[14] Since between 70 and 85 percent of emigrants to the Chesapeake in the seventeenth century arrived as servants, this limitation does not seriously distort the main arguments developed below.[15] Nevertheless, it is probable that there were systematic differences between the two types of settler, free and non-free, that have yet to be defined. One cannot simply assume that both types were of similar socioeconomic origins. In all likelihood, free settlers were of higher social standing than servants and markedly different from the point of view of age, marital status, occupation, and wealth. The amount of capital that a free emigrant was able to take with him and the presence or absence of political and

10. See n. 3 above.

11. *Ibid*.

12. *Ibid*.

13. This figure comprises about 2 or 3% of the total number of emigrants to the Chesapeake in the 17th century. Despite the small size of the sample there is evidence to suggest that it is representative of the whole of servant emigration. The remarkable uniformity in the age of servants and the diversity of their occupational backgrounds confirm this. However, problems involved in the use of lists are discussed below; see also, Souden, " 'To Forraign Plantacons,' " 8–12, and David W. Galenson, " 'Middling People' or 'Common Sort'?: The Social Origins of Some Early Americans Reexamined," *WMQ*, 3d Ser., XXXV (1978), 499–524 *passim*.

14. I have not used genealogical material because of the difficulty of checking its accuracy. The whole issue of free emigration to the Chesapeake deserves more attention but is outside the scope of this article.

15. Craven, *White, Red, and Black*, 5; Menard, "Economy and Society," 162.

economic connections in the Chesapeake were critical to his future success or failure, giving him a distinct advantage over the servant, who probably lacked these resources.[16] Such connections may have been forged in England via kinship, friendship, or business relationships. Until more research has been completed on the origins of free settlers, however, few generalizations can be made with any certainty.

Another problem involved in the use of these lists concerns the number of people registered. There is no way of knowing how many servants were kidnapped, or spirited away, to use the contemporary phrase, thereby going unrecorded in the lists. A good deal of legislation passed by the government in the seventeenth century was aimed at stopping this abuse.[17] A look at emigration over the whole period, however, shows how unlikely it is that servants taken forcibly from England made up more than a tiny fraction of the total.[18] A more serious problem relates to the sorts of emigrants enrolled. Only those servants who had indentures are recorded in the Bristol, London, and Liverpool records, but many servants arrived in the Chesapeake without contracts and served according to the custom of the country.[19] They were younger, less often skilled, more likely to be illiterate,

16. See, for example, Bernard Bailyn, "Politics and Social Structure in Virginia," in Smith, ed., *Seventeenth-Century America*, 90–115; Richard S. Dunn, *Sugar and Slaves: The Rise of the Planter Class in the English West Indies, 1642–1713* (Chapel Hill, N.C., 1972), chaps. 2–3; Menard, "From Servant to Freeholder," *WMQ*, 3d Ser., XXX (1973), 37–64; Menard, "Economy and Society," chaps. 2–5; Walsh, "Servitude and Opportunity," in Land, Carr, and Papenfuse, eds., *Law, Society, and Politics*; Peter Laslett, "The Gentry of Kent, 1640," *Cambridge Historical Journal*, IX (1948), 148–174.

17. The first ordinance passed by Parliament to prevent kidnapping was in 1645. Ten years later the city of Bristol passed its own legislation requiring all servants to be registered before transportation: the Bristol list is the result of this municipal ordinance. During the early years of the Restoration another attempt was made by the government to stop "spiriting," as the abduction of innocent men and women came to be called. All ports trading with America were to record the age of servants, where they were born, and where they last resided. In 1664 an official registry office was created by the Council of Foreign Plantations, and placed under the supervision of one Roger Whitley. No records of this office survive, but, like earlier efforts, it proved unsuccessful in stopping kidnapping. In 1682 another act was passed by Parliament whereby servants were to be taken before a magistrate who witnessed the indenture. The clerk of the peace was to keep a fair book and a file was to be made to aid finding individuals in the records. Despite all these injunctions spiriting continued unabated into the 18th century. See Smith, *Colonists in Bondage*, 71–80.

18. *Ibid.*, 86.

19. Walsh, "Servitude and Opportunity," in Land, Carr, and Papenfuse, eds., *Law, Society, and Politics*, suggests that as many as 40% of servants entering Charles County, Maryland, between 1658 and 1705 did not have indentures. Appendix 2, 129.

and generally of lower social origins than indentured servants.[20] This study deals only with indentured servants, since the origins of those without contracts are unknown.

Despite these lacunae, lists of indentured servants remain the most valuable sources for a thorough analysis of the servant trade in the seventeenth century. No other material approaches the comprehensiveness and detail provided in them. They may be used to study how the trade worked, who the people were who made their livelihood from it, and how the demand for labor from the various colonies periodically rose and fell. Most important of all, they are the only sources that contain extensive information on the thousands of ordinary men and women who left England to make a new start in the Chesapeake: what sorts of people they were, where they came from, and how they ended up in Virginia and Maryland.

II

Public opinion of indentured servants in seventeenth-century England seems to have been generally unfavorable. William Bullock described them as "idle, lazie, simple people . . . such as have professed idlenesse, and will rather beg than work."[21] In 1662 the mayor of Bristol complained: "Among those who repair to Bristol from all parts to be transported for servants to his Majesty's plantations beyond the seas, some are husbands that have forsaken their wives, others wives who have abandoned their husbands; some are children and apprentices run away from their parents and masters; oftentimes unwary and credulous persons have been tempted on board by menstealers, and many that have been pursued by hue-and-cry for robberies, burglaries, or breaking prison, do thereby escape the prosecution of law and justice."[22] Political writers in favor of emigration, and those opposed to it, were agreed that servants were low, base people.[23] Even

20. *Ibid.*, 112.
21. William Bullock, *Virginia Impartially examined* . . . (London, 1649), 14.
22. W. Noel Sainsbury *et al.*, eds., *Calendar of State Papers, Colonial Series* (London, 1860–), *America and West Indies, 1661–1668*, no. 331. Cited by Smith, *Colonists in Bondage*, 82–83.
23. Mildred Campbell, "'Of People Too Few or Many,' The Conflict of Opinion on Population and Its Relation to Emigration," in William Appleton Aiken and Basil Duke Henning, eds., *Conflict in Stuart England: Essays in Honour of Wallace Notestein* (London and New York, 1960), 171–201. For an example of a writer in favor of emigration who held servants in low esteem, see Sir Josiah Child, *A New Discourse of Trade* . . . (London, 1693), 170.

promotional tracts such as those of John Hammond and George Alsop
had a defensive tone, refuting the "abusive exclamations" made about
the character of servitude.[24]

Owing to the absence of other evidence, this unflattering contemporary attitude toward servants led previous historians to construct
a familiar model of the seventeenth-century indentured servant.[25]
Marcus Jernegan believed them to have been "convicts, paupers, and
dissolute persons of every type," while Abbot E. Smith described
them as "rogues, whores, vagabonds, cheats and rabble of all descriptions, raked from the gutter and kicked out of the country."[26] This
interpretation was first challenged nearly twenty years ago by Mildred
Campbell.[27] Following an analysis of the occupations of indentured
servants who sailed from Bristol to America between 1654 and 1662,
and from London in 1683 and 1684, she concluded that rather than
being drawn from England's "riff-raff," servants came predominantly
from "the middling classes: farmers and skilled workers, the productive groups in England's working population."[28] This theory, based
on quantifiable data rather than literary evidence, has now been accepted by most historians.[29]

To assess the validity of these two conflicting interpretations, a
detailed analysis of the occupations of servants who emigrated from
Bristol and London to the Chesapeake was undertaken and is presented below in table 1. Only male occupations are included, since
those of women servants will be examined later.

The most obvious feature of the Bristol list is that a large proportion

24. "Leah and Rachel, Or, the Two Fruitfull Sisters Virginia and Mary-land, by
John Hammond, 1656," in Clayton Colman Hall, ed., *Narratives of Early Maryland,
1633–1684* (New York, 1910), 284–285; "A Character of the Province of Maryland, by
George Alsop, 1666," *ibid.*, 357.

25. Marcus Wilson Jernegan, *Laboring and Dependent Classes in Colonial America,
1607–1783: Studies of the Economic, Educational, and Social Significance of Slaves, Servants,
Apprentices, and Poor Folk* (Chicago, 1931), 45–47, 52; Marcus Lee Hansen, *The Atlantic
Migration, 1607–1860: A History of the Continuing Settlement of the United States* (Cambridge, Mass., 1940), 34, 37; Thomas Jefferson Wertenbaker, *The First Americans, 1607–
1690* (New York, 1927), 25, 63; Smith, *Colonists in Bondage*, 3, 7.

26. Jernegan, *Laboring and Dependent Classes*, 45; Smith, *Colonists in Bondage*, 3.

27. Campbell, "Social Origins," in Smith, ed., *Seventeenth-Century America*, 63–89.

28. *Ibid.*, 76.

29. See Craven, *White, Red, and Black*, 8–9; Menard, "Economy and Society,"
172–173; Menard, "From Servant to Freeholder," *WMQ*, 3d Ser., XXX (1973), 47; Lois
Green Carr and Russell R. Menard, "Immigration and Opportunity: Servants and
Freedmen in Early Colonial Maryland" (paper presented at 32d Conference in Early
American History, College Park, Maryland, 1974), 5.

TABLE 1. Occupations of Male Indentured Servants Who Emigrated
from Bristol and London to the Chesapeake, 1654–1686

	Bristol Servants, 1654–1686				London Servants, 1683–1684			
Occupational	Chesapeake		All Colonies		Chesapeake		All Colonies	
Categories	No.	%	No.	%	No.	%	No.	%
Agriculture	252	46.9	910	48.0	31	23.7	59	23.2
Food, Drink, and Supplies	15	2.8	55	2.9	3	2.3	10	3.9
Clothing/Textiles and Allied Trades	78	14.5	282	14.9	19	14.5	36	14.2
Leather Trades	26	4.8	101	5.3	10	7.6	14	5.5
Building/Woodwork	29	5.4	125	6.6	10	7.6	22	8.7
Metalwork	14	2.6	62	3.3	2	1.5	17	6.7
Gentry and Professional	9	1.7	44	2.3	16	12.2	28	11.0
Semiskilled and Unskilled	112	20.9	310	16.4	37	28.2	59	23.2
Miscellaneous	2	0.4	6	0.3	3	2.3	9	3.5
Total	537	100.0	1,895	100.0	131	99.9	254	99.9

Sources:
  Bristol servants, 1654–1686: "Servants to forraign plantations, 1654–1663," Bristol
Record Office 04220 (1); "Servants to forraign plantacons, 1663–1679," B.R.O. 04220
(2); "Actions and Apprentices," B.R.O. 04355 (6); "Actions and Apprentices," B.R.O.
04356 (1); Noel Currer-Briggs, ed., "Indentured Servants from Bristol to America,
1654–1686" (unpublished MS).
  London servants, 1683–1684: C. D. P. Nicholson, "Some Early Emigrants to America,"
Genealogists' Magazine, XII, Nos. 1–16 (1955–1958), XIII, Nos. 1–8 (1959–1961); John
Wareing, "Some Early Emigrants to America, 1683–4; A Supplementary List," *ibid.*,
XVIII, No. 5 (1975–1976), 239–246.

of servants came from agricultural backgrounds. Of males with designated occupations, 44 percent described themselves as yeomen.[30]
The next largest group of men came from the semiskilled and unskilled
category, of which laborers formed the majority. Of those men leaving
Bristol between 1654 and 1686, 102 were laborers, composing 19 percent of the total. The only other numerically significant group was

  30. The other occupations in this category are as follows: 14 husbandmen, 1
gardener, and 1 planter. The total number of yeomen was 236.

engaged in the clothing and textile trades, which made up 14.5 percent of male occupations recorded.[31] Thus, according to these figures, twice as many yeomen as laborers emigrated to Virginia and Maryland in this period, and agricultural occupations in general outnumbered those of clothing and textile trades by a ratio of three to one.

The London list of 1683–1684 shows a slightly more even distribution of occupations. Semiskilled and unskilled workers were the largest category, with 28 percent of the total, followed by males from agricultural backgrounds with 24 percent.[32] As was the case with the Bristol group, clothing and textile workers made up 14.5 percent of all occupations, but unlike the Bristol figures a much larger proportion of London men came from professional trades such as accounting and clerical work. Variations in the occupational structure of servants from Bristol and London are attributable to the different origins of the two groups. London servants more often came from urban backgrounds than those who emigrated from Bristol, so agricultural occupations are relatively less important. On the other hand, clerks, accountants, grooms, and laborers are to be found in greater numbers from the metropolis.[33]

An overwhelming impression gained from the two lists is that of the sheer diversity of occupations. Sixty-six different trades are represented by the Bristol servants, and thirty-four by the London group. They ranged from buttonmould makers to hemp dressers and barber-surgeons. An important point is that there was no difference in the sorts of people going to the various colonies. Just as many yeomen went to the Chesapeake as to the West Indies, and this was the case with other trades. It appears that the former occupation of a servant played no part in determining where he went in the colonies.[34]

31. The percentages differ from those of Campbell in "Social Origins," in Smith, ed., *Seventeenth-Century America*, 71, because my figures include servants until 1686, and because I have not dealt with women's occupations in this table.

32. The first category is composed of 21 grooms and 16 laborers; agricultural occupations include 20 husbandmen, 7 gardeners, 3 ploughmen, and 1 farmer.

33. The occupations of the fathers of 129 servants who left London for the Chesapeake between 1682 and 1686 show this urban/rural dichotomy even more conclusively. Only 11.6% of the sample were from agricultural occupations, while 17.8% were engaged in food, drink, and distributive trades, and 18.6% in the clothing and textile industry. Nearly a quarter of the fathers were unskilled laborers of various kinds. Ghirelli, *List of Emigrants*.

34. Skilled men such as carpenters, coopers, masons, and blacksmiths were in more demand than unskilled men. But, in general, the former occupation of a servant had no bearing on his eventual destination.

The argument so far seems to support Campbell's theory that servants were drawn mainly from the middling classes. However, a caveat should be made at this point. Both the figures presented above and those used by Campbell are based on the registered occupations of servants only and do not take into account the large number of men (between 30 and 60 percent of the total) whose occupations were not recorded.[35] In the Bristol list, for example, the number of laborers registered between 1655 and 1659 fell dramatically from 37 percent of all occupations to 1 percent. During the same period men from agricultural occupations rose from 10 percent to 31 percent. It is possible that shifts occurred from time to time in the occupational background of servants, but not to this degree. A more likely explanation is that after 1655 laborers were recorded less frequently by the clerks than were other occupations. The reason for this apparent change in the registration procedure is unknown. Possibly as the volume of work increased for the clerks after 1655 they began to abbreviate entries by omitting the occupations of unskilled men.[36] This being the case, it should be borne in mind that the figures in table 1 greatly underestimate the number of unskilled laborers and youths who had no specific trade. David Galenson has suggested that about half the servants emigrating from Bristol were composed of these two groups, and it seems probable that a similar proportion, if not larger, prevailed among the London emigrants.[37]

The problem with analyzing occupations in this way is that, at best, they provide only a rough guide to social status. A person's occupation can tell us about his particular social and economic origins, and whether or not he had acquired a skill. It is possible to argue that those men with skills were of higher social standing than those who were unskilled. By placing too much emphasis on occupational structure, however, one runs the danger of forgetting other crucial factors for evaluating what sort of people servants were: age, experience, and the gradual accumulation of wealth. Just as the analysis of oc-

35. Only 36% of men from London, 1683–1684, had their former occupations recorded. Bristol registration was generally higher: 64.5% between 1654 and 1660, but within these years fluctuations are severe. See Galenson, "'Middling People' or 'Common Sort'?," WMQ, 3d Ser., XXXV (1978), 499–524 passim; Souden, "'To Forraign Plantacons,'" 8–12.

36. Galenson, "'Middling People' or 'Common Sort'?," WMQ, 3d Ser., XXXV (1978), table II, 501, 502.

37. Ibid., 506–507.

cupations places servants into broad social and economic categories, so the age of servants indicates their social standing within those groups.

Unfortunately, the ages of Bristol servants were not registered, but from the London and Liverpool lists we can deduce that the most likely time for men and women to emigrate was between the ages of fifteen and twenty-four (see table 2), with twenty and twenty-one predominating.[38] At this stage in his life it is unlikely that a servant would have acquired much property. If he had, surely he would have paid his own passage. He might recently have finished an apprenticeship but would have had little independent experience and would yet have earned little capital from the exercise of his skills. If he was from an agrarian background it is doubtful that he had possessed land of his own; in all likelihood he had worked for his father or for others. Almost certainly, he would have been single, or, to put it another way, a non-householder.[39] In short, the age of indentured servants indicates that they had little stake in society, little "substance" of their own. Though about half the servants, by virtue of their parents' occupations or their own acquired skills, came from the broad middle ranks of English society, they were not yet established members within it. Experience in their trade or occupation might allow them to move up the social ladder, but until that time we must assume that they occupied a position at the bottom of the middle ranks: below their older and wealthier contemporaries, but above the poor laborers, vagrants, and the destitute who formed the lowest level of English society.[40]

38. The length of a servant's period of servitude gives a rough idea of his age. The usual term given to adults was four or five years, while children were given longer terms and served until they reached majority. On this basis, 84% of servants leaving Bristol between 1654 and 1660 were over the age of 21; see Souden, " 'To Forraign Plantacons,' " table 3:2, 24.

Three London lists were used: those of 1682–1692 and 1683–1684, and a list of over 2,000 emigrants who sailed to Virginia in 1635. The Liverpool list of 1697–1707 also gives the ages of servants.

39. Peter Laslett, *The World We Have Lost* (London and New York, 1965), 85.

40. By the term "middle ranks" I am referring to that section of English society which Harold Perkin described as stretching from the "gentry and nobility" to the "labouring poor"; see *The Origins of Modern English Society, 1780–1880* (London, 1969), 23. For further discussion of the composition of preindustrial society, see Laslett, *World We Have Lost*, chap. 2; B. A. Holderness, *Pre-Industrial England: Economy and Society, 1500–1750* (London, 1976), chap. 2; Charles Wilson, *England's Apprenticeship, 1603–1763* (London and New York, 1965), 16–17; Lawrence Stone, "Social Mobility in England, 1500–1700," *Past and Present*, No. 33 (Apr. 1966), 17–22; Christopher Hill, *Change and*

TABLE 2. Age of Indentured Servants Who Emigrated from London and Liverpool to the Chesapeake, 1635–1707 (in Percentages)

Age Categories	London Servants, 1635		London Servants, 1682–1686 & 1683–1684		Liverpool Servants, 1697–1707	
(Years)	Males (N 1,740)	Females (N 271)	Males (N 414)	Females (N 159)	Males (N 518)	Females (N 284)
Under 15	3.8	3.0	6.5	1.9	23.0	4.2
15–19	27.4	30.0	21.0	25.8	32.0	30.6
20–24	39.9	48.1	51.0	57.2	26.8	46.5
25–29	14.2	11.1	12.6	11.9	9.5	13.6
30–34	8.5	4.1	8.0	2.5	5.4	3.5
35–39	3.2	1.5	0.2	0.6	1.9	1.4
40–44	1.6	0.7	0.2	—	1.0	0.4
45 & over	1.4	1.5	0.5	—	0.4	—
Total	100.0	100.0	100.0	99.9	100.0	100.0

Sources:
   London servants, 1635: John Camden Hotten, ed., *The Original Lists of Persons of Quality . . . and others who went from Great Britain to the American Plantations, 1600–1700* (London, 1874), 35–138.
   London servants, 1682–1686 and 1683–1684: Michael Ghirelli, *A List of Emigrants from England to America, 1682–1692* (Baltimore, 1968), *passim;* C. D. P. Nicholson, "Some Early Emigrants to America," *Genealogists' Magazine,* XII, Nos. 1–16 (1955–1958), XIII, Nos. 1–8 (1959–1961); John Wareing, "Some Early Emigrants to America, 1683–4; A Supplementary List," *ibid.,* XVIII, No. 5 (1975–1976), 239–246.
   Liverpool servants, 1697–1707: Elizabeth French, "List of Emigrants to America from Liverpool, 1697–1707," *New England Historical and Genealogical Register,* LXIV (1910), LXV (1911).

Finally, what sort of women emigrated to the Chesapeake? As can be seen from table 3 far fewer women emigrated than men. For every female servant who left London for Virginia in 1635, there were six males. The Bristol group provides a ratio of three men for every woman between 1654 and 1686, while the London and Liverpool lists, toward the end of the century, show a ratio of two and a half to one. The number of women emigrating to Virginia and Maryland increased sharply between the 1630s and 1650s, but grew slowly thereafter.[41]

The reason for this preponderance of males is clear. Men and boy servants were more attractive to merchants and planters because their

Continuity in Seventeenth-Century England (London, 1974), chaps. 8 and 9; Hill, *Reformation to Industrial Revolution: The Making of Modern English Society, Vol. I, 1530–1780* (New York, 1967), 54.
   41. Menard, "Economy and Society," 193–195.

TABLE 3. Sex Ratios of Servants Who Emigrated to the Chesapeake, 1635–1707

London Servants, 1635[a] (N 2,011)	642.1
Maryland Headright Sample, 1646–1657[b] (N 99)	312.5
Virginia Headright Sample, 1648–1666[c] (N 4,272)	341.8
Bristol Servants, 1654–1686[d] (N 5,065)	308.1
Servants in Maryland Inventories, 1658–1679[e] (N 584)	320.1
Maryland Headright Sample, 1658–1681[b] (N 625)	257.1
Servants in Maryland Inventories, 1680–1705[e] (N 960)	295.1
London Servants, 1682–1686[f] (N 873)	245.7
Virginia Headright Sample, 1695–1699[g] (N 1,094)	296.4
Liverpool Servants, 1697–1707[h] (N 1,325)	236.0

Note:
This table is adapted from Russell R. Menard, "Economy and Society in Early Colonial Maryland" (Ph.D. diss., University of Iowa, 1975), 194.

Sources:
[a]John Camden Hotten, ed., *The Original Lists of Persons of Quality . . . and others who went from Great Britain to the American Plantations, 1600–1700* (London, 1874), 35–138.

[b]Russell R. Menard, "Economy and Society in Early Colonial Maryland" (Ph.D. diss., University of Iowa, 1975), 156, 217–221.

[c]Wesley Frank Craven, *White, Red, and Black: The Seventeenth-Century Virginian* (Charlottesville, Va., 1971), 27.

[d]Herbert Moller, "Sex Composition and Correlated Culture Patterns of Colonial America," *William and Mary Quarterly*, 3d Ser., II (1945), 117–118.

[e]St. Mary's City Commission, "Social Stratification in Maryland, 1658–1705" (National Science Foundation Grant, GS-32272).

[f]Michael Ghirelli, *A List of Emigrants from England to America, 1682–1692* (Baltimore, 1968); C. D. P. Nicholson, "Some Early Emigrants to America," *Genealogists' Magazine*, XII, Nos. 1–16 (1955–1958), XIII, Nos. 1–8 (1959–1961); John Wareing, "Some Early Emigrants to America, 1683–4; A Supplementary List," *ibid.*, XVIII, No. 5 (1975–1976), 239–246.

[g]Edmund S. Morgan, "Slavery and Freedom: The American Paradox," *Journal of American History*, LIX (1972–1973), 27.

[h]Elizabeth French, "List of Emigrants to America from Liverpool, 1697–1707," *New England Historical and Genealogical Register*, LXIV (1910), LXV (1911).

labor potential was greater than that of women.[42] Recent research has suggested that sometimes women were put to work in the fields alongside the men, but it is unlikely that a woman could have consistently produced as much tobacco as a man.[43] The skewed sex ratio had an immense influence on the development of early Chesapeake society. Combined with high rates of mortality and morbidity, the lack of women retarded Virginia and Maryland's ability to sustain their populations by natural reproduction.[44] This in turn led to instability in all spheres of life—political, economic, and social.[45] Not until the last quarter of the seventeenth century did the population grow by natural means, and not until the eighteenth century did the Chesapeake enjoy a prolonged period of stability.

Little is known about the occupational background of women servants. Of the 226 women who left Bristol between 1654 and 1686, and whose occupation or status was registered, 214 are described simply as spinsters, 10 were widows, and 2 were wives of men servants. The London records reveal little about the occupations of women, but occasionally the clerks recorded slightly more information about them than was usual.[46] Mary Read, for example, was formerly a servant of

42. See Bullock, *Virginia Impartially examined*, 52, 60–62; *A Relation of Maryland; Together, With A Map of the Countrey, The Conditions of Plantation, His Majesties Charter to the Lord Baltemore*, translated into English (London, 1635), 52. Possibly women were in shorter supply than men, but this seems unlikely. Smith, *Colonists in Bondage*, 65, quotes a ship's master engaging servants for transportation from Ireland to Barbados who stated that women "are now Reddear to goe then men, whereof we ar furnished with as many as we have Rome." Similarly, William Tracy had little trouble recruiting women for service on Berkeley plantation, Virginia, in 1620. See Susan Myra Kingsbury, ed., *The Records of the Virginia Company of London* . . . (Washington, D.C., 1906–1935), III, 266.

43. Lois Green Carr and Lorena S. Walsh, "The Planter's Wife: The Experience of White Women in Seventeenth-Century Maryland," *WMQ*, 3d Ser., XXXIV (1977), 542–571. Some women stipulated in their indentures that they would not work in the fields. Margaret Prou was bound to Richard Bray to serve four years in Virginia, "Working in the Ground excepted." Mary Goldsmith from Southwark, who sailed for Maryland in 1684, was "To serve on Howsholdworke." Nicholson, "Early Emigrants," *Genealogists' Mag.*, XIII, Nos. 1–8 (1959–1961), 177, 49.

44. Menard, "Economy and Society," 174–205; Craven, *White, Red, and Black*, 25; Walsh and Menard, "Death in the Chesapeake," *Md. Hist. Mag.*, LXIX (1974), 211–227.

45. Menard, "Economy and Society," 205, 422. All the following essays were delivered at the 32d Conference in Early American History, College Park, Maryland, 1974: Darrett B. and Anita H. Rutman, "'Now-Wives and Sons-in-Law': Parental Death in a Seventeenth-Century Virginia County"; Lorena S. Walsh, "'Till Death Us Do Part': Marriage and Family in Maryland in the Seventeenth Century"; Carole Shammas, "English-Born and Creole Elites in Turn-of-the Century Virginia"; David W. Jordan, "Political Stability and the Emergence of a Native Elite in Maryland, 1660–1715"; and Carr and Menard, "Immigration and Opportunity."

46. Only 32 women of the 120 who left London for the Chesapeake, 1683–1684,

Jane Corfield. She had been committed to Bridewell for "pilfering" two chickens from the shop of her master, John Corfield. We may surmise that this was why her mistress had consented "freely to part with her." Probably one reason that led Hester Speed to emigrate to Virginia in 1685 was that her husband had been "slaine in the rebellion in the West"—a reference to Monmouth's rebellion.[47]

Like most male servants, the majority of women emigrated between the ages of fifteen and twenty-four. However, relatively more women than men came from this category, and fewer were from the older age ranges (see table 2). Throughout the seventeenth century approximately 30 percent of women servants left England when under twenty years of age, and a further 50 percent below twenty-five years. Given that the average age of first marriage for women was twenty-four, it appears that the great majority of female servants were not old maids who went to the Chesapeake in search of husbands. Most women emigrants left England when they were at or below marrying age.[48]

From the above analysis it is possible to sketch a general picture of the sorts of people who emigrated to the Chesapeake in the seventeenth century. They were predominantly young adults from a broad cross section of English society. Probably about half of them were either minors or unskilled workers of various types, while the rest came from agricultural occupations and a miscellany of crafts and trades that defies any simple classification. Their youthfulness indicates that within their respective occupations they were of relatively low social standing. They were mainly non-householders and had acquired little personal wealth. They came from the middle and lower echelons of that section of society that contemporaries labeled "the Commons": the ordinary people who made up the vast majority of England's population and who were obliged to work with their hands to earn a living.

---

had their occupations or status recorded: 28 were spinsters, 2 were dairymaids, 1 was a widow, and the other a wife.

47. Ghirelli, *List of Emigrants*, 69, 76.

48. For the average age of women at first marriage see Laslett, *World We Have Lost*, 85–86. The idea that old maids could find husbands in the colonies was popular even in the 17th century. George Alsop described women's opportunities in Maryland as follows: "The Women that go over into this Province as Servants, have the best luck here as in any place of the world besides; for they are no sooner on shoar, but are courted into a Copulative Matrimony, which some of them (for aught I know) had they not come to such a Market with their Virginity, might have kept it by them untill it had been mouldy." "Province of Maryland," in Hall, ed., *Narratives of Early Maryland*, 358.

III

Servants who emigrated to the Chesapeake came from towns and villages all over England. The southeastern part of the country, particularly London and the Home Counties, provided the bulk of emigrants in the seventeenth century. During the first four decades of colonization between 80 and 90 percent of servants sailed from London.[49] In the second half of the century London's share of the servant trade dropped to about 60 percent owing to the rise in importance of other tobacco ports such as Bristol and Liverpool. Up to the 1680s Bristol, together with its surrounding counties and parts of South Wales, was the second most important source of servants with 20 percent of the trade. In the last two decades of the century Liverpool's growing share of the tobacco market made the Northwest and North Wales an important area for those engaged in recruiting servants.[50]

The Bristol list provides the best evidence for locating the geographical origins of servants. Figure 1 shows the spatial distribution of their places of origin (or previous residence) and the different kinds of communities from which they came.[51] As can be seen from the map, the majority of emigrants were from the area around Bristol. If one drew a circle with a radius of forty miles from the city, over 60 percent would fall within its circumference (see table 4). The city itself pro-

49. Carr and Menard, "Immigration and Opportunity," 3–4; Laslett, "Gentry of Kent," *Cam. Hist. Jour.*, IX (1948), 148–174.

50. Carr and Menard, "Immigration and Opportunity," 3–4, including table 1. It should be stressed that these figures are rough estimates based on a suggested relationship between the number of servants exported from a particular port and its share of the tobacco trade. Such a link may be closer than at first appears. A port's prosperity would directly influence the number of ships sailing per year to the Chesapeake. The greater the number of ships making the crossing would also mean the greater the numbers of servants transported. The figures for the second half of the century, particularly the period between 1668 and 1681, are based on more reliable data in the form of headright claims.

51. Functional rather than numerical criteria have been employed here to categorize communities. See John Patten, "Village and Town: An Occupational Study," *Agricultural History Review*, XX (1972), 8–9; Peter Clark and Paul Slack, eds., *Crisis and Order in English Towns, 1500–1700: Essays in Urban History* (London, 1972), 1–56; Peter Clark and Paul Slack, *English Towns in Transition, 1500–1700* (London, 1976); Gideon Sjoberg, *The Pre-Industrial City: Past and Present* (New York, 1960); Fernand Braudel, *Capitalism and Material Life, 1400–1800*, trans. Miriam Kochan (London, 1974 [orig. publ. Paris, 1967]), chap. 8. Villages and market towns were defined on the basis of descriptions supplied by John Adams in his *Index Villaris: or an Exact Register, alphabetically digested, of all the cities, market-towns, parishes . . .* (London, 1690). County towns and provincial capitals or cities were distinguished from market towns because the former had more complex functions, being the political and administrative centers of regions as well as markets.

FIGURE 1. Places of Origin of Servants Who Emigrated from Bristol to the Chesapeake, 1654–1686

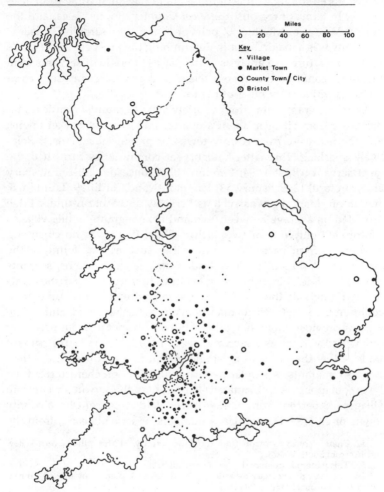

Sources:
  "Servants to forraign plantations, 1654–1663," Bristol Record Office 04220 (1); "Servants to forraign plantacons, 1663–1679," B.R.O. 04220 (2); "Actions and Apprentices," B.R.O. 04355 (6); "Actions and Apprentices," B.R.O. 04356 (1); Noel Currer-Briggs, ed., "Indentured Servants from Bristol to America, 1654–1686," unpublished manuscript.

vided ninety-four servants, or 13 percent of all those whose origins can be traced, though some of these might have first come from elsewhere. In terms of regions, the West Country, South Wales, and the Severn Valley contributed 87 percent of the total sample.[52] Clearly, proximity was a major factor in determining the prospective servant's port of departure. An analysis of the places of origin of servants from Liverpool confirms this theory. Nearly 70 percent came from communities within forty miles of the town.[53]

Bristol emigrants came from a variety of backgrounds. A little under half were from villages; about a quarter had lived in market towns; and the rest were from county towns or provincial capitals.[54] Relatively speaking, this latter category of communities furnished the most servants: Bristol, 94; London, 19; Gloucester, 13; Shrewsbury and Hereford, 12; Salisbury, 11; Monmouth and Cardiff, 9; Taunton, 8; and so on. Market towns such as Berkeley and Wotton-under-Edge provided on average between two and six emigrants, while villages contributed only one or two each.[55] Thus, there was no clustering of servants from particular communities such as was found in the case of the Puritan migration. Aside from the larger towns, servants traveled to Bristol in ones and twos from hundreds of parishes scattered throughout the West. To be sure, more servants came from communities near to Bristol than from places further afield, and certain regions provided more than others, but one cannot pick out particular towns and villages as major and regular contributors to the servant trade. Other than Bristol, no single community produced more than twenty emigrants. A similar pattern of distribution characterized the Liverpool group. Approximately 45 percent of the servants were from villages, 38 percent from market towns, and 17 percent from county towns or cities.[56] Though large numbers of servants came from the

52. There were 237 servants from the West Country, 317 from the Severn Valley, and 167 from South Wales.

53. This pattern is examined in greater detail below.

54. The exact percentages are as follows: villages 44.4, market towns 26.0, county towns and provincial capitals 29.6.

55. Of those places that could be identified, 231 servants came from 31 county towns and provincial capitals, giving an average of 7.6 servants per county town. Excluding Bristol, the average dropped to 4.7. Two hundred and seven emigrants came from 97 market towns providing an average of 2.1. Finally, 258 servants came from 207 villages, giving an average of 1.25 servants per village.

56. The exact proportions were 45.4% from villages, 37.6% from market towns, and 17% from county towns and provincial capitals. Of the servants whose place of origin could be traced, 161 came from 31 county towns and cities providing an average

TABLE 4. Distances Traveled to Bristol, Liverpool, and London, 1654–1707, by Servants Emigrating to the Chesapeake

Distance Traveled (Miles)	Bristol, 1654–1686		Liverpool, 1697–1707		London, 1682–1686	
	No.	%	No.	%	No.	%
0–9	140	20.0	51	6.5	185	52.3
10–19	105	15.0	122	15.6	9	2.5
20–39	188	26.8	375	47.8	14	4.0
40–59	138	19.7	80	10.2	31	8.8
60–79	39	5.6	39	5.0	10	2.8
80–99	21	3.0	14	1.8	19	5.4
100–149	45	6.4	38	4.9	40	11.3
150–199	13	1.9	52	6.6	26	7.3
200–249	11	1.5	7	0.9	9	2.5
250 and over	1	0.1	6	0.8	11	3.1
Total	701	100.0	784	100.0	354	99.9

Sources:

Bristol, 1654–1686: "Servants to forraign plantations, 1654–1663," Bristol Record Office 04220 (1); "Servants to forraign plantacons, 1663–1679," B.R.O. 04220 (2); "Actions and Apprentices," B.R.O. 04355 (6); "Actions and Apprentices," B.R.O. 04356 (1).

Liverpool, 1697–1707: Elizabeth French, "List of Emigrants to America from Liverpool, 1697–1707," *New England Historical and Genealogical Register,* LXIV (1910), LXV (1911).

London, 1682–1686: Michael Ghirelli, *A List of Emigrants from England to America, 1682–1692* (Baltimore, 1968), *passim;* C. D. P. Nicholson, "Some Early Emigrants to America," *Genealogists' Magazine,* XII, Nos. 1–16 (1955–1958), XIII, Nos. 1–8 (1959–1961); John Wareing, "Some Early Emigrants to America, 1683–4; A Supplementary List," *ibid.,* XVIII, No. 5 (1975–1976), 239–246.

area surrounding Manchester, the overwhelming impression one gets is of the scattered nature of their places of origin.

Urban backgrounds figure largely in the socioeconomic origins of servants. At a time when about four-fifths of England's population lived in the countryside, only half that proportion of servants came from rural communities.[57] One must be careful, however, not to make too many distinctions between rural and urban life in preindustrial England. As Peter Clark and Paul Slack have pointed out, "the urban community was permeated by the countryside: gardens and or-

---

of 4.9 servants per county town. A total of 334 emigrants came from 87 market towns, giving an average of 3.8, and 289 people migrated from villages, providing an average of 1.7.

57. Clark and Slack, eds., *Crisis and Order,* 6.

chards, oast-houses, pigs and poultry flourished within the limits of
the largest towns, while the countryside crept to the back-door of
houses on the High Street of the smaller centre."[58] A study of the
occupations of Bristol servants from towns shows that while more
men were engaged in food and drink trades and various crafts than
their counterparts in the country, over 60 percent of yeomen came
from "urban" as distinguished from "rural" communities.

Nonetheless, the differences between town life and country life
cannot be ignored. In the larger towns there was a greater variety of
occupations that had their own systems of manufacture and distribution, markedly different from those of rural trades. The greater density
of population brought with it more heterogeneity, since town people
were more likely to have come from diverse social backgrounds.[59]
Market days would bring an influx of men and women from the
neighboring countryside to sell their produce and to buy essential
goods that only the town provided. These occasions provided an
opportunity not only to exchange goods but also to trade local news
and gossip. Markets and fairs must have played an essential role in
the dissemination of information from one locality to another, a factor
of some importance with regard to the motivation for migration.[60]

The distribution of the places of origin of servants who emigrated to
the Chesapeake from London was significantly different from that of
either the Bristol or the Liverpool groups. Over half of them came from
the city itself, but as figure 2 shows, the rest came from communities
all over England. The majority were from urban backgrounds; only 29
percent came from villages.[61]

Almost all the servants who came from London had lived on the pe-
riphery of the city or in the suburbs. In all, 94 servants gave the exact
location of their former place of residence in London. Of these, 28 were
from the West End; 21 from the south bank of the Thames; 27 from

58. *Ibid*. John Patten states that "in pre-industrial England the relations of rural
and urban settlements to one another and their individual characteristics are often far
from clear." "Village and Town," *Ag. Hist. Rev.*, XX (1972), 1; see also Patten, "Rural-
Urban Migration in Pre-Industrial England," *Research Paper No. 6* (School of Geography,
University of Oxford, 1973), 24.

59. Clark and Slack, *English Towns*, 14–15.

60. This theme will be developed below.

61. Of servants who emigrated from London, 185 or 52.3% came from the city,
though, as with the Bristol group, many of these were probably born elsewhere. Only
2% were from county towns or provincial capitals; 16.6% came from market towns;
and 29.1% were from villages.

FIGURE 2. Places of Origin of Servants Who Emigrated from London to the Chesapeake, 1682–1686

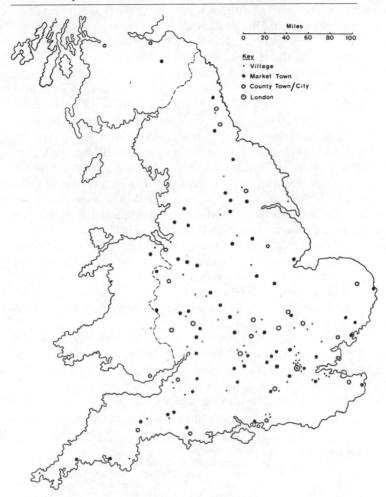

Sources:
    Michael Ghirelli, *A List of Emigrants from England to America, 1682–1692* (Balti-more, 1968); C. D. P. Nicholson, "Some Early Emigrants to America," *Genealo-gists' Magazine*, XII, Nos. 1–16 (1955–1958), XIII, Nos. 1–8 (1959–1961); John Wareing, "Some Early Emigrants to America, 1683–4; A Supplementary List," *ibid.*, XVIII (1975–1976), 239–246.

the East End; 14 from the edges of the inner city (Aldgate, Aldersgate, Cripplegate, Bishopsgate, and Newgate); 2 from the north; and 2 from the inner city.[62] The districts surrounding the inner city together with the outlying suburbs contained the greatest concentrations of poor people. Demographically, they were the fastest growing areas of the metropolis in the seventeenth century. By 1700 their population exceeded 200,000, composing about a third of the total population of London. The East End in 1550, for example, had been a rural area with only patches of urban development. A century and a half later it was characterized by high density low-class housing and the development of important shipbuilding and textile industries.[63]

The growth of London during the seventeenth century was phenomenal: its population rose from approximately 200,000 at the beginning of the century to 575,000 by 1700, at which time it was the largest city in Europe. Given the excess of deaths over births, the whole of this increase may be attributed to immigration. E. A. Wrigley has estimated that to sustain its rate of growth London must have absorbed at least 8,000 persons a year throughout the latter half of the century. Put another way, at certain times half the natural increase of provincial England fueled the rapidly expanding metropolis.[64] "The most apparent and important single population movement in pre-industrial England," John Patten concludes, "was thus the tremendous flow of people into London."[65]

Long-distance migrants accounted for much of this movement. Of the deponents from Stepney in the East End who came before the archdeaconal courts of the Diocese of London between 1580 and 1640, 74 percent were born outside of London and the Home Counties. Only 13 percent were born in the city itself.[66] A study of the geographic origins of a group of young men who began apprenticeships

62. London is here defined as the City and Liberties together with Westminster, the riverside parishes to the east, and Southwark to the south.
63. Clark and Slack, *English Towns*, 63; M. J. Power, "East London Housing in the Seventeenth Century," in Clark and Slack, eds., *Crisis and Order*, 237–262; Norman G. Brett-James, *The Growth of Stuart London* (London, 1935); John Stow, *A Survay of London* . . . (London, 1598); M. Dorothy George, *London Life in the XVIIIth Century* (London and New York, 1925).
64. E. A. Wrigley, "A Simple Model of London's Importance in Changing English Society and Economy, 1650–1750," *Past and Present*, No. 37 (July 1967), 44–49.
65. Patten, "Rural-Urban Migration," 27.
66. David Cressey, "Occupations, Migration and Literacy in East London, 1580–1640," *Local Population Studies*, No. 5 (1970), table 2, 58.

in the city during the middle decades of the seventeenth century demonstrated that only between a third and a half came from the metropolis and its neighboring counties. There was considerable variation from company to company, but in no case was the proportion of apprentices from London higher than 25 percent.[67] Thus, London attracted people from all parts of the country; it was "the node, the great centraliser of the Kingdom."[68]

It would appear, therefore, that the number of servants who emigrated from London and who gave their place of origin as the city is exaggerated. At least half of them had probably been born elsewhere and lived in the capital a few months or years before moving to the Chesapeake. Yet, if we look beyond London, the pattern of migration displayed by servants is similar to that of other migrant groups who moved to the city. Outside of the concentration of emigrants from the metropolis and the Home Counties, they came from communities all over England in roughly equal numbers. The high proportion of servants from urban backgrounds suggests that individuals had first moved from their home parishes to the local town.[69] Finding little or no work there, or simply following the lure of the capital, they migrated to London.[70]

The significance of this conclusion is that it places emigration to the Chesapeake within the broader context of migratory patterns in preindustrial England. Men and women who eventually ended up as indentured servants in Virginia and Maryland migrated to London with thousands of their contemporaries who, for one reason or another, had chosen to work and live in the nation's capital. For those people who found the living conditions harsh in London, the prospect of regular work, food, and shelter, albeit overseas, was no doubt

67. S. R. Smith, "The Social and Geographic Origins of the London Apprentices, 1630–1640," *Guildhall Miscellany*, IV, part 3 (1973), 204. See also D. V. Glass, "Socio-Economic Status and Occupations in the City of London at the End of the Seventeenth Century," in A.E.J. Hollaender and William Kellaway, eds., *Studies in London History Presented to Philip Edmund Jones* (London, 1969), 373–389.

68. Patten, "Rural-Urban Migration," 25.

69. Mr. Malcolm Kitch of Sussex University has informed me that it was significantly higher than he would have expected for apprentices (private correspondence).

70. For the attraction of the city, or "great centres of commerce," see E. G. Ravenstein, "The Laws of Migration," *Journal of the Royal Statistical Society*, XLVIII (1885), 198–199. See also William Petersen, "A General Typology of Migration," *American Sociological Review*, XXIII (1958), 259–260; and Paul A. Slack, "Vagrants and Vagrancy in England, 1598–1664," *Economic History Review*, 2d Ser., XXVII (1974–1975), 360–379.

tempting. Thus, the decision to emigrate came not when a person left his home village or town but after he had arrived in one of the country's principal towns and ports.

This theory is supported by evidence from the Bristol and Liverpool records. The majority of Bristol servants came from places within forty miles of the city, thereby conforming to general conclusions about migration fields in early modern England that have stressed the essentially short-range nature of mobility.[71] However, nearly 40 percent, a very considerable minority, came from outside this limit (see table 4). Bristol attracted immigrants from regions far beyond its own commercial hinterland. As the third largest city in England and a major seaport, Bristol was, like London, "a super-receptor of immigrants."[72] The magnetic attraction of Liverpool was a good deal less powerful than that of Bristol or London, reflecting John Patten's theory that the geographical extent of a community's migration field is proportional to its size.[73] Nevertheless, 30 percent of Liverpool servants were from places over forty miles from the port, as far away as Plymouth in Devon or Aberdeen in Scotland.

This analysis of the places of origin of servants suggests that emigrants to the Chesapeake should be viewed as a subset of a much larger group of young and single people who moved from town to town in search of greater opportunities than were to be had at home. After arriving in cities and ports such as London, Bristol, and Liverpool they found there were plenty of people like themselves looking for work, and precious little to be found. Some eked out a living; others moved elsewhere or returned home; still others decided to try their luck in a new setting and embarked for Virginia or Maryland.[74]

71. Thus, most movement appears to have taken place within a radius of between 20 and 40 miles. See J. Cornwall, "Evidence of Population Mobility in the Seventeenth Century," *Bulletin of the Institute of Historical Research*, XL (1967), 143–152; E. J. Buckatzsch, "Places of Origin of a Group of Immigrants into Sheffield, 1624–1799," *Econ. Hist. Rev.*, 2d Ser., II (1949–1950), 303–306; A. J. Willis and A. L. Merson, comp. and ed., *A Calendar of Southampton Apprenticeship Registers, 1609–1740*, Southampton Records Series, 12 (Southampton, 1968), xix–xx; Peter Laslett and John Harrison, "Clayworth and Cogenhoe," in H. E. Bell and R. L. Ollard, eds., *Historical Essays, 1600–1750, Presented to David Ogg* (London, 1963), 157–184.

72. Souden, "'To Forraign Plantacons,'" 27. For an interesting discussion of the pattern of servant migration to Bristol compared to apprentice migration, see Souden, "'Rogues, Whores, and Vagabonds?' Emigrants to North America, Internal Migrants, and the Case of Mid-Seventeenth Century Bristol," *Social History*, No. 7 (Jan. 1978).

73. Patten, "Rural-Urban Migration," 45.

74. Needless to say, this explanation does not assume that all emigrants left

IV

Perhaps the most intriguing questions relating to emigration to the Chesapeake are why and how people emigrated. Unfortunately, these questions are also the most elusive. From the outset we must recognize that for the vast majority of servants we will never know the precise reasons that led them to leave England. The best we can do is look at the social and economic origins of servants in the aggregate and hypothesize about general reasons for emigration.

Nationwide factors that might have induced people to emigrate have been described by other historians.[75] English society in the sixteenth and early seventeenth centuries was marked by a sharp population increase that furnished the raw material for colonization: people. It was a period that experienced a long and steep rise in the general level of prices and a steady decline in the purchasing power of wages. The poorer sections of society were therefore most adversely affected. On the basis of increasing wheat prices, Peter Bowden has suggested that "the third, fourth, and fifth decades of the seventeenth century witnessed extreme hardship in England, and were probably among the most terrible years through which the country has ever passed. It is probably no coincidence that the first real beginnings of colonization of America date from this period."[76]

At the same time that both population and prices were rising, the number of unemployed also increased. Employment in the agrarian sector fell throughout the century, despite a rise in the amount of land under cultivation. Enclosures, engrossing, and the growing specialization of products from particular areas led to the creation of larger farming units, and, consequently, fewer people were able to work on

---

England in this way. Doubtless, there were many who had relatives or friends in the Chesapeake and who decided to join them. Others might have had specific political or economic reasons for leaving the mother country. But I would argue that for the vast majority of emigrants the decision to leave England came after a period of migration within the country, usually ending in cities such as Bristol and London.

75. Craven, *White, Red, and Black*, 18–21; Campbell, "Social Origins," in Smith, ed., *Seventeenth-Century America*, 84–89.

76. H. P. R. Finberg, ed., *The Agrarian History of England and Wales* (Cambridge, 1967–), Joan Thirsk, ed., IV, *1500–1640*, 621. The argument presented in this paragraph is crystallized by Peter Bowden in the above volume, 601–621. See also E. H. Phelps Brown and Sheila V. Hopkins, "Seven Centuries of the Prices of Consumables, Compared with Builders' Wage-rates," *Economica*, N.S., XXIII (1956), figure 1; W. G. Hoskins, "Harvest Fluctuations and English Economic History, 1620–1759," *Ag. Hist. Rev.*, XVI (1968), 15–31.

the land.[77] Manufacturing industry could not have employed more than 20 percent of the surplus labor and was itself suffering from a disastrous slump in the cloth trade during the first half of the century.[78]

Assessing the impact of the Civil War on the local economies of various parts of the country is extremely difficult. One can hazard a guess, however, that the area around Bristol was especially hard hit. Owing to the obvious importance of the city, it early became the objective of Royalist and Parliamentarian forces alike and was successively occupied by both armies. The war probably hastened the decline of cloth production, causing widespread unemployment in the clothing towns of Wiltshire, Somerset, and Gloucestershire. The dislocation of trade and destruction of crops may have ruined many small-scale clothiers and farmers of the region. Religious and political persecution during the Commonwealth and Restoration years also led large numbers of people to emigrate, as is shown by the five hundred Quakers who left Bristol between 1654 and 1662.[79]

To test the validity of these general theories about the causes of emigration, a detailed analysis of the socioeconomic backgrounds of servants who left Bristol and London for the Chesapeake was undertaken. By examining the local economies of regions that produced large numbers of servants, it should be possible to speculate with more assurance about the reasons that led people to emigrate.

The spatial distribution of the places of origin of the Bristol servants reveals that many communities were clustered in a linear pattern along the roads and rivers or were concentrated near the coast. This pattern is unsurprising. Roads and rivers were the trade routes that linked Bristol to its hinterland: northwards via the Severn Valley to the Midlands and the Border Counties; west across the Bristol Channel to the Vale of Glamorgan and the South Wales coastal plain; southwest along the coast to the Cornish peninsula; and east to London. All

77. Finberg, ed., *Agrarian History of England and Wales*, Thirsk, ed., IV, *1500–1640*, 598, 398–399.

78. B. E. Supple, *Commercial Crisis and Change in England, 1600–1642: A Study in the Instability of a Mercantile Economy* (Cambridge, 1959); J. de L. Mann, *The Cloth Industry in the West of England from 1640 to 1880* (Oxford, 1971), xiii–xviii; G. D. Ramsay, *The Wiltshire Woollen Industry in the Sixteenth and Seventeenth Centuries* (London, 1943), 71–84, 111–114, 124–125; David Underdown, *Somerset in the Civil War and Interregnum* (Newton Abbot, 1973), 14, 43.

79. Campbell, "Social Origins," in Smith, ed., *Seventeenth-Century America*, 84; Mann, *Cloth Industry*, 3–7; Ramsay, *Wiltshire Woollen Industry*, 111–114; Underdown, *Somerset*, 43.

these regions had strong trading connections with Bristol in the seventeenth century, and from the towns and villages that lay between them came large numbers of migrants. Roads and rivers were also major lines of communication. Besides being the axes along which much coming and going took place, they served to disseminate local news. Fairs and markets provided forums for the passing on of information that would then be carried home along the roads. Trade and news followed the same routes. It is possible that such gossip told of the greater opportunities to be had in the larger towns and, in particular, Bristol. Thus, "the decision to move cannot have been random: greater information and traffic along the main routes helped form the streams and counterstreams in which most migratory movements took place."[80]

Figure 3 shows clearly that most servants came from the lowland areas surrounding Bristol, which may be divided into three regions: the Severn Valley, the South Wales coastal plain, and the low-lying districts of Somerset. These regions were mainly woodland and pastoral areas, in this period devoted to dairy farming, stock rearing, and the cultivation of a variety of crops. Dairying was especially common in the Severn Valley, the Vale of Glamorgan, and eastern Somerset. The heavy clay soils of the Vales of Berkeley and Gloucester were unsuitable for extensive tillage, and most farmers grew only a limited amount of crops. Like the dairying districts of the wood-pasture region of eastern Somerset, the basic unit of production was the family farm. Along the coast of Somerset agriculture was more mixed. Farmers raised cattle and sheep for market, engaged in dairying, and produced a number of crops including barley, beans, oats, and wheat, of which the latter was the most important. Throughout the entire region there was small-scale pig rearing and horse breeding, while in the fen country of the Somerset Levels fowling and fishing supplemented stock raising. These lowland regions were also characterized by a good deal of rural industry, particularly spinning and weaving in the Severn Valley and eastern Somerset, which was an extremely important aspect of the local economy. Heavier industries, such as iron ore

80. D. Hollis, ed., "Calendar of the Bristol Apprentice Book, 1532–1565," part 1, 1532–1542, *Bristol Record Society*, XIV (1949), 15–16, 197; Slack, "Vagrants and Vagrancy," *Econ. Hist. Rev.*, 2d Ser., XXVII (1974–1975), 373–374; Peter Clark, "The Migrant in Kentish Towns, 1580–1640," in Clark and Slack, eds., *Crisis and Order*, 123; Finberg, ed., *Agrarian History of England and Wales*, Thirsk, ed., IV, *1500–1640*, 466–592; Souden, "'To Forraign Plantacons,'" 34.

FIGURE 3. Detail of Places of Origin of Bristol Servants to the Chesapeake, Showing Topography and the Number of Servants from Each Community

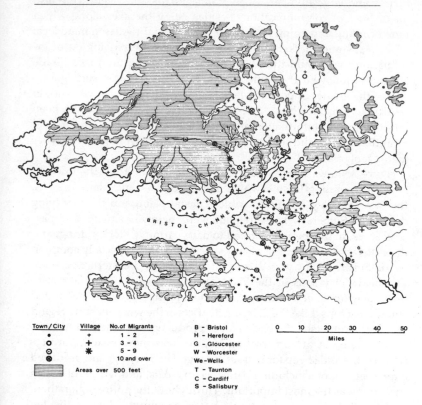

Town / City	Village	No.of Migrants
●	+	1 - 2
○	+	3 - 4
◎	✳	5 - 9
⊛		10 and over
▓ Areas over 500 feet		

B - Bristol
H - Hereford
G - Gloucester
W - Worcester
We - Wells

T - Taunton
C - Cardiff
S - Salisbury

0   10   20   30   40   50
Miles

Sources:
"Servants to forraign plantations, 1654–1663," Bristol Record Office 04220 (1); "Servants to forraign plantacons, 1663–1679," B.R.O. 04220 (2); "Actions and Apprentices," B.R.O. 04355 (6); "Actions and Apprentices," B.R.O. 04356 (1); Noel Currer-Briggs, ed., "Indentured Servants from Bristol to America, 1654–1686," unpublished manuscript.

extraction and coal mining, in the Forests of Dean and Kingswood respectively, also contributed to the prosperity of the area.[81]

In comparison with upland regions, pastoral and woodland areas tended to be very populous. Eastern Somerset had been the most thickly populated part of the county since Domesday times, while to the west the Vale of Glamorgan had one of the highest population densities in Wales.[82] During the middle decades of the seventeenth century, however, partly as a result of the growing numbers of people (both through natural increase and immigration) and partly due to changes in the structure of the local economy, it appears that lowland areas were finding it progressively difficult to support their populations. One reason for this was the slow conversion of arable to pasture farming. "In general," Giles Harrison has pointed out, "there was a gradual but continual contraction of the arable in many areas of the south-west as more land was put to meadow and pasture. The increasing importance of pasture farming represented a positive shift towards specialization in that branch of agriculture to which the south-west was best suited, and which the dawning of a national economy increasingly allowed it to pursue."[83]

This shift in the local economy was by no means universal, and certain areas were affected more than others. It was a process of attrition, rather than radical change, which slowly undermined the economic position of the small farmer. In the Vale of Berkeley, for example, specialization in the production of milk, cheese, and butter led to the concentration of land in the hands of the big landowners. Fewer people owned land in 1700 than fifty years previously. Small farmers were driven out by the economies made possible by large-scale production, conversions to pasture, and technical improvements.[84] In the densely populated northeastern part of Somerset the introduction of artificial grasses began to take over from arable farming after 1640,

81. This discussion is based on Dr. Joan Thirsk's analysis of farming regions. Finberg, ed., *Agrarian History of England and Wales*, Thirsk, ed., IV, *1500–1640*, 4–109. See also Thirsk, "Seventeenth-Century Agriculture and Social Change," *Ag. Hist. Rev.*, XVIII (1970), 148–175.

82. Finberg, ed., *Agrarian History of England and Wales*, Thirsk, ed., IV, *1500–1640*, 72, 144–145.

83. Giles Harrison, "The South West," *ibid.*, V, *1640–1750*. I am grateful to Mr. Harrison and to Dr. Joan Thirsk for allowing me to see this essay.

84. This conclusion is based on my research of landholding in the Vale of Berkeley between 1634 and 1712. See also Thirsk, "Seventeenth-Century Agriculture," *Ag. Hist. Rev.*, XVIII (1970), 157.

while in other areas the cultivation of orchards gradually replaced the production of more traditional crops.[85] The effect of these changes is clear: they produced rural unemployment with the relative contraction of the labor-intensive arable sector. How much influence rural unemployment (or underemployment) had upon making people leave the land and migrate to the towns and cities is impossible to determine. It seems likely, however, that the high proportion of men from agricultural backgrounds who emigrated from Bristol can be partially explained by lack of work and shrinking opportunity in the countryside.

An integral part of the local economies of Gloucestershire and Somerset in the seventeenth century was cloth production. The most important cloth-producing region stretched in a wide arc from Ilminster, in southern Somerset, through Yeovil, Shepton Mallet, Frome, and Bath, to Wotton-under-Edge and Stroud in Gloucestershire. Along with parts of Wiltshire, Lancashire, Yorkshire, and East Anglia it was one of the main centers of manufacture in the country. All these regions suffered a sharp fall in production during the first half of the century owing to a series of setbacks from which the industry never fully recovered. The failure of Alderman Cokayne's attempt to export finished cloth to the Continent in place of the traditional undressed broadcloth, the rise in demand for new, lighter materials produced in Holland, and the disruption of trade and loss of markets caused by the Thirty Years' War and the English Civil War led to a severe recession in cloth production with concomitant hardship for those who made their living from it. Exports, which had averaged about sixty thousand pieces of cloth at the beginning of the century, had been halved by 1640.[86]

The depression was particularly severe in the West. Many small farmers of eastern Somerset engaged in cloth making to supplement their income from farming and to sustain members of their families who would not otherwise have been fully employed.[87] Some areas had attracted large numbers of poor people because of the expected opportunity for work in the industry. The Somerset-Wiltshire border was described in 1623 as being "forest and woodlands, and the rest very barren of corn . . . the people of the country (for the most part)

85. Harrison, "South West," in Finberg, ed., *Agrarian History of England and Wales*, Thirsk, ed., V, *1640–1750*.
   86. See n. 79.
   87. Finberg, ed., *Agrarian History of England and Wales*, Thirsk, ed., IV, *1500–1640*, 79.

being occupied about the trade of cloth-making, spinning, weaving, and tucking. Also we find that by reason of the trade of cloth-making, and the increase of people working about that trade, there have been many cottages erected . . . for them to work in, which have no means of living but about that trade."[88] The depression was equally severe in the towns, which accounts for the large number of servants who came from cloth-producing centers such as Wells, Frome, Bradford-upon-Avon, Bath, and Malmesbury. Many people in the Bristol area, therefore, were partly or entirely dependent on cloth making for their livelihood. This vulnerability to fluctuations of the trade produced periodic and sometimes prolonged unemployment, and forced many people to move in search of work.[89]

Certain lowland areas were notable for the number of poor people they supported. In the Vale of Tewkesbury, Winchcombe was locally renowned for its numbers of poor, who had flocked to the town following the introduction of tobacco growing in the area after 1621. According to the overseers of the poor, at one time there were twenty households begging for alms from every household able to bestow them.[90] Further south, the expansive commons and wasteland of Slimbridge also attracted poor people. They were encouraged by the opportunity to squat on the commons without fear of interference from neighboring landowners. Commenting on the parish in 1639, John Smyth complained that "the more large the wast grounds of a manor are, the poorer are the inhabitants; such common grounds, commons, or wast grounds, used commonly as they are . . . drawe many poor people from other places, burden the township with beggerly Cotages, Inmates, and Alehouses, and idle people; where the greater part spend most of their daies in a lazy idlenes and petite theeveries, and few or none in profitable labour."[91]

Forests and woodlands were traditional havens for the poor and indigent. The Forests of Dean and Kingswood in Gloucestershire, and Frome-Selwood in Somerset, all produced numbers of emigrants.[92] Frome and its neighborhood were especially susceptible to harvest

88. *Ibid.*, 80.
89. Slack, "Vagrants and Vagrancy," *Econ. Hist. Rev.*, 2d Ser., XXVII (1974–1975), 375; Campbell, "Social Origins," in Smith, ed., *Seventeenth-Century America*, 84–85.
90. Thirsk, "Seventeenth-Century Agriculture," *Ag. Hist. Rev.*, XVIII (1970), 165–166.
91. John Smyth, *The Berkeley Manuscripts*, ed. Sir John Maclean, III (Gloucester, 1885), 51.
92. Souden, " 'To Forraign Plantacons,' " 38–39.

failures and were well known for poverty. In 1631 the justices of the town complained about an invasion of poor cottagers who had congregated in Frome and the nearby forest.[93] Forest dwellers in general seem to have been disliked by their contemporaries. A petition about the poor inhabitants of the Forest of Dean described them as "people of very lewd lives and conversations, leaving their own and other countries, and taking this place for a shelter and cloak to their villanies." Their numbers had so increased by 1640 that it was feared that "the poor people there would impoverish the richer sort."[94]

Heath and woodland parishes were attractive to the poor because of the relative ease with which they could establish homes while avoiding paying rent to the local landlord, and because of the opportunity for work on nearby farms or in local industries. If no work was available they could abandon their temporary refuge and move elsewhere. Thus, these parishes had a relatively free and open society that was characterized by a high degree of mobility. In contrast to the more static population of the surrounding champion country, where stronger manorial control and a less diverse economy prevailed, there was constant movement in and out of the marginal lowland areas around Bristol, and it is probable that many poor people moved from these regions to the city at one time or another. Perhaps more significant is that woodland areas were under attack in the mid-seventeenth century as the increase in demand for food led to the internal colonization of commons, wastelands, and royal forests. The disafforestation of Frome-Selwood and Neroche in Somerset, for example, removed an important shelter for poor people and led to rioting during the Civil War. With the erosion of these woodland areas some people may have had no other option but to move to the towns in the hope of finding work and a place to stay.[95]

Servants who emigrated to the Chesapeake from Bristol, therefore, were from a variety of backgrounds. Some came from pastoral regions, others from clothing towns, and some from marginal areas. What characterizes them all is declining opportunity and the contraction of the labor market. Two especially important factors in this process

93. Finberg, ed., *Agrarian History of England and Wales*, Thirsk, ed., IV, *1500–1640*, 80; Slack, "Vagrants and Vagrancy," *Econ. Hist. Rev.*, 2d Ser., XXVII (1974–1975), 375.

94. William Bradford Willcox, *Gloucestershire: A Study in Local Government, 1590–1640* (New Haven, Conn., 1940), 157n.

95. Harrison, "South West," in Finberg, ed., *Agrarian History of England and Wales*, Thirsk, ed., V, *1640–1750*; *ibid.*, IV, *1500–1640*, 409–412, 462–464.

were, first, the slow but continual conversion of arable to pasture farming and, second, the decay of the cloth industry on which many people, particularly in the towns, were dependent for their sole means of support.

So much for emigration from Bristol. Unfortunately, unlike the Bristol data, the spatial patterns of the places of origin of servants who went from London to the Chesapeake reveal little about the servants' reasons for emigrating. Leaving London aside, there were no significant concentrations of people from particular localities that could be linked to specific social and economic conditions in those areas. The high proportion of migrants from towns suggests that the long-distance journey to the city might have been preceded by a shorter move to the local market town. What occasioned this original move is unknown.

Information concerning emigrants recorded in the London lists, however, provides some valuable clues to why people went to America. Loss of economic support owing to the death of a parent appears to have been a powerful inducement. Of servants under twenty-one years of age who left London between 1682 and 1686, 63 percent had lost one or both parents through death.[96] Thomas Martin, for example, who was born in Morpeth, Northumberland, was only eight years old when his father died. He moved to Newcastle with his mother, and when she died two years later he was supported by the parish. At the age of sixteen he traveled to London and decided to go from there to Maryland.[97] John Browne, an orphan from Essex, was "desired by the parish to be sent to sea," while James Rither, who sailed for Virginia in 1685 at the age of thirteen, was described as "having no friends."[98] For those families who had few kin or friends to help

96. Ghirelli, *List of Emigrants*, *passim*. This figure is probably a conservative estimate since I only counted as deceased the fathers who were specifically mentioned as dead. There were numerous entries where either the mother or other kin had a child indentured with no mention of what had happened to the father. A more likely figure for the number of orphans is about 70%. Establishing age-specific mortality for parents throughout 17th-century England in general is very difficult. Of 386 bridegrooms who were married in Manchester between 1653 and 1660, 48% had lost their fathers; see Peter Laslett, "Parental Deprivation in the Past: A Note on the History of Orphans in England," *Local Pop. Studies*, No. 13 (1974), 18. It is probable that mortality rates of parents varied from time to time and from place to place, but if we accept 50% as an approximate figure for the whole country then the number of servants who had lost their mothers and fathers was considerably higher than the national average.

97. Nicholson, "Early Emigrants," *Genealogists' Mag.*, XIII, Nos. 1–8 (1959–1961), 12.

98. *Ibid.*, 13; Lord Mayor's Waiting Books, XIV, fol. 459.

them, the death of the father was an economic disaster of the first magnitude. Though the mother might be able to earn enough to support herself and the younger members of the family, it seems likely that the older children would be expected to fend for themselves. Evidently some of them considered laboring in the Chesapeake as a way of earning a living.

Probably the most common reason for emigration from London was the difficulty of finding regular work in the capital: preindustrial London was said to have been the best recruiting ground in the country for the army and the American colonies. A report of the mid-eighteenth century commented that if newcomers "cannot get such employment as they expected or chuse to follow, many of them will not go home to be laughed at . . . but enlist for soldiers, go to the plantations Etc. if they are well inclined; otherwise they probably commence thieves or pickpockets."[99] The problem of unemployment was compounded by gross overcrowding in certain parts of the city. The suburbs, which provided the majority of servants of London origins, were particularly bad off in this respect. During the seventeenth century the population of the East End rose by four and a half times. M. J. Power has suggested that decades such as the 1600s, 1620s, and 1680s stand out as periods of especially high emigration. It may be no coincidence that the latter two periods were also years of marked emigration to the colonies.[100]

Examining the areas from which servants came allows us to speculate about the reasons that may have led people to emigrate, but this approach does not account for temporal fluctuations in the numbers of people who left England for America in the seventeenth century. Unfortunately, the London and Liverpool records are not comprehensive enough to allow this kind of analysis. Only the Bristol list covers a period sufficiently long to reveal significant shifts in the number of registrations over time.

Figure 4 shows the destinations and annual totals of servants who left Bristol between 1654 and 1680. As can be seen, the total number of servants emigrating increased steadily during the first five years of the records and reached a peak in 1659. A slight fall occurred in 1660, but another peak was attained in 1662. Thereafter numbers fell sharply

99. George, *London Life*, 347 n. 2.
100. Patten, "Rural-Urban Migration," 31; Power, "East London Housing," in Clark and Slack, eds., *Crisis and Order*, 237.

FIGURE 4. Destinations and Annual Totals of Servants Who Emigrated from Bristol to America, 1654–1680

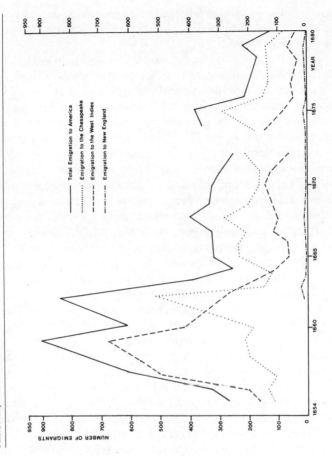

Source:
Noel Currer-Briggs, ed., "Indentured Servants from Bristol to America, 1654–1686," unpublished manuscript.

to a low in 1664, which was followed by a gradual rise in registrations up to 1668 and then by another slump. This pattern was repeated between 1669 and 1680.

Several factors have been suggested by historians to explain these fluctuations. Mildred Campbell has stressed religious reasons, such as the persecution of Quakers and the Restoration statutes passed against dissenters in 1662.[101] Wesley Frank Craven, while recognizing political and religious motivations for emigration, has given more weight to social and economic difficulties caused by a series of bad harvests in the third quarter of the century.[102]

From this analysis it appears that Craven has the better argument. In the first eight years of recorded emigration from Bristol, the West experienced no less than six years of bad or deficient harvests. After 1662 there was a succession of average to good harvests, but in 1668, another year of high emigration, there was again deficiency in the West. Two years of good harvests in the early 1670s were marked by a decline in the numbers of servants leaving Bristol, but during the middle and latter years of the decade, when harvests once again failed, this trend was reversed. The correlation is by no means exact, but it is sufficiently close to suggest that the "heartbeat of the English economy," as W. G. Hoskins calls the rise and fall of wheat production, was a crucial factor in forcing people to migrate.[103]

Evidence of harvest failure in the Bristol region in the mid-seventeenth century is widespread. In Somerset, during the late 1640s and 1650s, the Assizes passed various measures to mitigate the effects of dearth caused by a series of bad harvests. The "great scarcity of corne" led justices in 1658 to "take such course for the surpressinge the multiplicity of those maltsters and the supplying the occasions of these poore as shalbe agreeable to law and justice."[104] Pastoral areas and woodlands, with their high population densities, were particularly vulnerable to harvest failures, as were the towns that were dependent on supplies of corn from the countryside. Poor farm laborers and artisans, who subsisted on their wages, were hardest hit by the

101. Campbell, "Social Origins," in Smith, ed., *Seventeenth-Century America*, 86–87.
102. Craven, *White, Red, and Black*, 19–20.
103. Hoskins, "Harvest Fluctuations," *Ag. Hist. Rev.*, XVI (1968), 17, 29. See also Petersen, "General Typology," *Am. Soc. Rev.*, XXIII (1958), 260.
104. J. S. Cockburn, ed., "Somerset Assize Orders, 1640–1659," *Somerset Record Society*, LXXI, *passim*, esp. 45. Cited by Souden, " 'To Forraign Plantacons,' " 46.

short-term effects of famine. While the price of bread rocketed, their wages rose little, if at all.[105]

In sum, a number of reasons, both general and local, were responsible for causing people to migrate. The contraction of the labor market in the agrarian sector, the decline of the cloth trade, personal tragedy, harvest failures, the lack of work in towns and cities, or simply the attraction of the large ports encouraged people to move to Bristol and London. But what happened when they got there? What circumstances transformed an English migrant into an indentured servant bound for America? The next section examines the role of the merchant community in the servant trade and attempts to explain how the trade operated.

V

An analysis of the masters to whom servants were bound in Bristol and London reveals a remarkable number of individuals involved in the trade and a high degree of diversity in their backgrounds. Over a thousand masters transported servants to America from Bristol between 1654 and 1660, of whom four hundred traded with Virginia and Maryland. Slightly over a third of the Chesapeake masters described themselves as mariners, a fifth were merchants, and just under 10 percent were planters (see table 5). The rest came from a wide range of trades, from pump makers to soap-boilers. Forty-two occupations were represented in all, confirming Roger North's observation that in Bristol "all men that are dealers, even in shop trades, launch into adventures by sea."[106] Clearly, the trade in servants was not monopolized by a minority of wealthy merchants as has been previously suggested; the whole trading community of the city was involved.[107]

Table 6 shows the large number of small-scale masters engaged in the Bristol servant trade. Of the 401 masters in the sample, over 70 percent transported either one or two servants, while only 4 percent exported more than ten. Put in a different way, only a fifth of

105. For the decline in purchasing power of wages in the 17th century, see n. 76. See also Hill, *Reformation to Industrial Revolution*, 45.

106. Cited by Patrick McGrath, "Merchant Shipping in the Seventeenth Century: The Evidence of the Bristol *Deposition Books*," part 2, *Mariner's Mirror*, XLI (1955), 29.

107. Smith, *Colonists in Bondage*, 43–86; Wilcomb E. Washburn, *Virginia under Charles I and Cromwell, 1625–1660* (Williamsburg, Va., 1957), 14.

TABLE 5. Occupations of Masters Transporting Servants to the Chesapeake, 1654–1660

Occupation of Masters	Number of Masters	Percentage of Masters
Mariners	142	35.4
Merchants	84	20.9
Planters	37	9.2
Grocers	8	2.0
Surgeons	8	2.0
Coopers	7	1.7
Shipwrights	6	1.5
Soap-boilers	5	1.2
Clothiers	3	0.7
Gentlemen	3	0.7
Mercers	3	0.7
Barber-surgeons	2	0.5
Blacksmiths	2	0.5
Clerks	2	0.5
Shoemakers	2	0.5
Vintners	2	0.5
Widows	2	0.5
Yeomen	2	0.5
Apothecary	1	0.2
Clothier's wife	1	0.2
Cordwainer	1	0.2
Draper	1	0.2
Farrier	1	0.2
Gentleman-Merchant	1	0.2
Hosier	1	0.2
Innkeeper	1	0.2
Innkeeper's wife	1	0.2
Ironmonger	1	0.2
Mariner's wife	1	0.2
Milliner	1	0.2
Pinmaker	1	0.2
Planter's wife	1	0.2
Pumpmaker	1	0.2
Ropemaker	1	0.2
Sailmaker	1	0.2
Spinster	1	0.2
Tailor	1	0.2
Turner	1	0.2
Victualer	1	0.2
Victualer's wife	1	0.2
Upholsterer	1	0.2

TABLE 5. continued

Occupation of Masters	Number of Masters	Percentage of Masters
Wooldraper	1	0.2
Unknown	57	14.2
Total	401	98.5

Note:
The percentage total has been rounded up.

Source:
Tabulated from David Souden, ''List of Masters Trading to America from Bristol, 1654–1660'' (unpublished notes).

TABLE 6. Number of Servants Transported per Master from Bristol to the Chesapeake, 1654–1660

Number of Servants Transported per Master	Number of Masters		Number of Servants	
	No.	%	No.	%
1	202	50.4	202	19.3
2	85	21.2	170	16.3
3	35	8.7	105	10.0
4	27	6.7	108	10.3
5	12	3.0	60	5.7
6	10	2.5	60	5.7
7	3	0.7	21	2.0
8	6	1.5	48	4.6
9	6	1.5	54	5.2
10–19	13	3.2	165	15.8
20 & over	2	0.5	52	5.0
Total	401	99.9	1,045	99.9

Source:
Tabulated from David Souden, ''List of Masters Trading to America from Bristol, 1654–1660'' (unpublished notes).

the servants were bound to masters who transported ten or more individuals. The vast majority (nearly 80 percent) were contracted by small merchants and traders who sent between one and nine servants.[108]

108. Patrick McGrath, ''Merchants and Merchandise in Seventeenth-Century Bristol,'' *Bristol Record Society*, XIX (1955), ix–x. I am grateful to David Souden for allowing me to use his unpublished data on servant emigration from Bristol.

The trade in servants to the Chesapeake from Bristol appears to have been on a smaller scale than that of the West Indies. A third of the servants who went to the island plantations were indentured to masters transporting over ten individuals, half as many again as Chesapeake servants bound to big operators. There may also have been a qualitative difference in the sorts of people trading to the American colonies. As David Souden has noted, "Mariners, particularly on Virginia voyages, would often take over one or two servants, in order to make a quick profit on the side." On the other hand, "merchants were more often connected with Barbados, since trade with the West Indies had to be more organized, given the more capitalist-intensive nature of sugar production and trade."[109]

Evidence about masters from the London records is more difficult to interpret. There was less variety in occupational backgrounds than in the Bristol group. As many as 72 percent of the masters who transported servants between 1683 and 1684 were described as mariners or merchants, and only seven other occupations were recorded. Again, the number of small merchants involved in the trade is striking. Well over three-quarters of masters transported only one or two servants (see table 7). Owing to the availability of capital, stronger trade connections, and greater resources in general, one might have expected to see indications of larger-scale servant transportations than was the case with Bristol. This was borne out by an analysis of the 1683–1684 list, where 43.9 percent of the servants were sent to the Chesapeake by men exporting ten or more individuals. John Bright, a merchant of London, bound fifty-six servants in a three-month period between June and August 1684. He was by far the biggest operator in the city at that time. What should be emphasized once more, however, is that for every large trader there were innumerable smaller ones. The Bristol and London records both testify to the widespread involvement in the servant trade of merchants, mariners, and tradesmen of all types.[110]

109. Souden, " 'Rogues, Whores, and Vagabonds,' " *Social Hist.*, No. 7 (Jan. 1978), 18–19.

110. Between 1606 and 1660, 1,304 merchants engaged in trade with Virginia from London and the outports. Of these, 81.4% (1,062) were involved in only one voyage. See Susan E. Hillier, "The Trade of the Virginia Colony, 1606–1660" (Ph.D. diss., University of Liverpool, 1971), 26, 27. The large number of small-scale operators involved in the servant trade from London to the Chesapeake is confirmed by the list of

TABLE 7. Number of Servants Transported per Master from London, 1682–1686

Number of Servants Transported per Master	London, 1682–1686				London, 1683–1684			
	Number of Masters		Number of Servants		Number of Masters		Number of Servants	
	No.	%	No.	%	No.	%	No.	%
1	115	66.5	115	29.9	86	57.3	86	17.9
2	22	12.7	44	11.4	26	17.3	52	10.8
3	13	7.5	39	10.1	10	6.7	30	6.2
4	7	4.0	28	7.3	8	5.3	32	6.7
5	4	2.3	20	5.2	2	1.3	10	2.1
6	2	1.2	12	3.1	1	0.7	6	1.2
7	2	1.2	14	3.6	4	2.7	28	5.8
8	2	1.2	16	4.2	1	0.7	8	1.7
9	—	—	—	—	2	1.3	18	3.7
10–19	6	3.5	97	25.2	6	4.0	83	17.3
20 and over	—	—	—	—	4	2.7	128	26.6
Total	173	100.1	385	100.0	150	100.0	481	100.0

Sources:
London, 1682–1686: Michael Ghirelli, *A List of Emigrants from England to America, 1682–1692* (Baltimore, 1968).
London, 1683–1684: C. D. P. Nicholson, "Some Early Emigrants to America," *Genealogists' Magazine*, XII, Nos. 1–16 (1955–1958), XIII, Nos. 1–8 (1959–1961); John Wareing, "Some Early Emigrants to America, 1683–4; A Supplementary List," *ibid.*, XVIII, No. 5 (1975–1976), 239–246.

How was the trade organized? Servants who emigrated to Virginia and Maryland were usually indentured between July and September and would sail a month or two later. This timing fitted neatly with the annual rhythm of the tobacco trade. "The ordinary time of going," explained William Bullock in 1649, "is about September, or October, which times Ships have made choice of, in respect the Crop of Tobacco, will be ready for their homeward fraught, which is always in, or about December, and so they lade, and return in February, March, or April."[111]

Whether the servant went to the Chesapeake or to the West Indies largely depended on the demand for labor in these colonies. Judging by the Bristol records, the demand for servants in the West Indies, par-

---

1682–1686. Only a quarter of the 385 servants transported were contracted by merchants sending 10 or more individuals, while over 40% were exported by merchants who sent either one or two servants (see table 7).
111. Bullock, *Virginia Impartially examined*, 46.

ticularly Barbados, was high until 1659, but thereafter fell dramatically, possibly as a result of the greater reliance placed upon slave labor. As the demand for servants from the island plantations dropped, so the numbers of servants transported to Virginia and Maryland steadily increased (see figure 4). Russell Menard has suggested a correlation between the rate of emigration to the Chesapeake and the price of tobacco. "When the price of tobacco was high, merchants actively recruited servants and produced a boom in immigration; when tobacco was low they were reluctant to invest in labor and the rate of immigration declined."[112] The tendency of servant migration to rise and fall with tobacco prices supports this theory. Thus, the servant's individual desires played little part in determining where he eventually ended up. Instead, it was the trading community that was responsible for directing and regulating emigration in response to the needs of the colonies. The hundreds of mariners, merchants, and small traders involved in the servant trade provided the crucial link between the Chesapeake and England. They were the middlemen between the planter on the one hand and the prospective servant on the other, the men who had the connections, resources, and motivation to take up such English men and women as they could find and ship them to the colonies.

Very little is known about how servants were recruited by masters or their agents. Some Chesapeake planters either acquired their servants themselves when in England, or requested relatives, friends, or business associates to send them over.[113] Others engaged agents, such as Richard Smith, a small planter from Charles County, Maryland, who was employed by Captain William Batten, also of Maryland, to "procure servants in England to be transported into this province."[114] A more common practice was to solicit the aid of the local mercantile community in recruiting. Valentine Price and Edward Lapselly of Bristol were engaged by Nicholas Dangerfield of St. Christopher to provide twenty "men servants or boy servants apparelled

112. Menard, "Economy and Society," 164.
113. Thirty-four Virginia planters acquired servants in Bristol between 1654 and 1660. For an example of a planter sending to England for servants, see Richard Beale Davis, ed., *William Fitzhugh and His Chesapeake World, 1676–1701: The Fitzhugh Letters and Other Documents* (Chapel Hill, N.C., 1963), 82, 91–92, 127, 193, 268, 308.
114. William Hand Browne *et al.*, eds., *Archives of Maryland* (Baltimore, 1883–), XLI, 363, 369–370. I am indebted to Lorena Walsh for drawing my attention to this reference.

to serve the said Nicholas in the Islands aforesaid."[115] In a similar fashion, five part shareowners of the ship *Anne* of Bristol were asked to acquire twenty servants from Kinsale in Ireland for transportation to the West Indies.[116] Though both these examples refer to St. Christopher, it seems likely that a similar method of recruiting was followed by Chesapeake masters.

How servants were "procured" is unknown. Seventeenth-century literature emphasizes the role of spirits and kidnappers.[117] The Bristol list of servants, for example, was begun in an attempt to stop the "Inveigling, purloining, carrying and Stealing away [of] Boys, Maides and other persons and transporting them beyond the Seas and there selling or otherwise disposeing them for private gaine and profitte."[118] While it is impossible to deny that such practices went on, it is likely that only a tiny fraction of servants went to America in this way.[119] A more probable method of recruitment is that merchants had contacts (or employed agents) who knew where the poor people lived and who toured these sections of the port persuading all those who had the inclination to try their luck in the Chesapeake.[120] Possibly word of mouth or billboards informed some prospective emigrants that a ship bound for Virginia was taking on servants, and so they might have presented themselves at the dockside looking for a master to pay the cost of their passage.[121] The population of a city such as Bristol, or the

115. "Recognizances for the Peace, 1643–1649," *Gloucester Corporation Records, 1456–1576*, fol. 36. This, and a similar volume of a slightly later date, are incorrectly described in W. H. Stevenson, comp., *Calendar of the Records of the Corporation of Gloucester* (Gloucester, 1893), 465, as "Recognizances for the Peace." In fact, they contain lists of mercantile bonds dealing with a wide range of goods shipped from Bristol to overseas. Entries supply the name, occupation, and, in some cases, the place of residence of those involved in the bond. The sum of money in question is always recorded, and sometimes an outline of the venture itself is described.

116. "Recognizances for the Peace," *Gloucester Corporation Records*, fol. 16.

117. Smith, *Colonists in Bondage*, chaps. 3 and 4.

118. "Servants to forraign plantations, 1654–1663," B.R.O. 04220 (1). This citation is from the city ordinance of Sept. 29, 1654, which appears at the beginning of the volume.

119. Smith, *Colonists in Bondage*, 86.

120. For an account of the methods by which servants were recruited in London during the second half of the 18th century, see William Eddis, *Letters from America*, ed. Aubrey C. Land (Cambridge, Mass., 1969), 37.

121. See C. M. MacInnes, *A Gateway of Empire* (New York, 1968 [orig. publ. Bristol, Eng., 1939]), 160. In 1726 and 1727 advertisements were placed in the local newspaper of Bristol encouraging people to enroll as servants for transportation to Virginia and Pennsylvania. Possibly, in earlier times, billboards or posters were used to attract attention. If individuals did go to the dockside seeking someone to pay their

riverside parishes of London, though large by the standards of the day, was yet small enough to be dominated by the pervasive influence of the mercantile community and was therefore in constant contact with the demands of the trade.

The bulk of the servant trade was based on the principle of supplying servants to the Chesapeake in much the same manner as any other marketable commodity. Small traders procured servants by various means and, at the risk of £6 invested for their passage, shipped them to the Chesapeake in the expectation of a handsome profit. John Pope and Henry Gough, merchants of Bristol, informed their factor, Henry Barkwell, in 1661, that they had placed £249 worth of goods upon the *Providence* for sale in Virginia. After receiving detailed instructions he was told, "You are Alsoe to take note of one Servant that is aboard and to dispose [of him] there to our best Advantage for which we have paid his passage."[122]

For many merchants and small traders who had an interest in the transatlantic trade, the transportation of servants was simply one aspect of the main business of importing tobacco and exporting their own merchandise. When demand for servants was high they devoted more of their resources to shipping servants to the Chesapeake, but this was always a small part of a much wider sphere of mercantile activity. The demand for servants was too haphazard, and the return too uncertain, for a total commitment to the trade.

VI

On the whole, indentured servants present a less colorful image than previous studies have led us to believe. They were neither rogues, whores, and vagabonds nor the scions of the middle classes. Instead, they came from a variety of backgrounds covering the whole range of social rank below the peerage. From quasi-criminal elements and unskilled workers to the sons of gentlemen, servants who emigrated to the Chesapeake compose a representative cross section of the ordinary working men and women of England.

Many reasons induced a person to emigrate—general, local, and individual—but one of the most common factors that uprooted people

---

passage to America, this may explain the large number of mariners engaged in the trade. This, however, is pure speculation.

122. Westmoreland County, Virginia, Deeds, Wills, Etc., 1661–1662, Virginia State Library, Richmond, 34.

was lack of work. In town and countryside alike, lack of work forced the young especially to move from place to place in search of opportunity.[123] Previous studies have suggested, implicitly or explicitly, that prospective servants left their home parishes and traveled to the country's principal ports with the preconceived plan of emigrating. This does not appear to have been the case. Emigrants to the Chesapeake were part of a general movement of people who migrated to cities and ports such as Bristol, London, and Liverpool in the expectation of finding work. They had little idea that the journey to a city would eventually lead them to America.

In this latter respect the merchants were the crucial link between England and the Chesapeake. They found and persuaded young people to emigrate. They provided the cost of the passage and arranged for the servant to be transported. Responding to the ebb and flow of the tobacco trade, they recruited as many men and women as possible when demand for servants was high and transported fewer when demand was low. During the seventeenth century, mariners, merchants, and small traders involved in the servant trade were responsible for supplying Virginia and Maryland with their most valuable import: people.

123. "In any population it is normally the young and single who migrate most readily." Wrigley, "A Simple Model," *Past and Present*, No. 37 (July 1967), 47.

3

Environment, Disease, and Mortality in Early Virginia

Carville V. Earle

Disease was one of the principal causes of death in early Virginia, and Jamestown was the locus of mortality. This association between disease and place has long been observed, but seldom understood. A geographic model of disease mortality, however, can account for the spatial, seasonal, and annual mortality variations in Jamestown and the James River estuary between 1607 and 1624. This model, derived from the first year in Jamestown, suggests the probable causes of disease-related deaths and offers a logical and consistent account of the pathogenic organisms; the sources of infection; the incidence of infection, morbidity, and mortality; and the recurrence of epidemics. This essay presents the derivation of the model, based on the first year at Jamestown; examines the application and testing of the model for the years 1608 to 1624; discusses the colonists' and the Virginia Company's inability to lower mortality rates; and, last, offers some speculation on the causes of declining death rates in Virginia after 1624.

The first year in Virginia portended the dreadful mortality that ravaged the colony until 1624. Initially things went well. The expedition of three vessels and 144 persons left England in December 1606, headed south and west to the West Indies, and then veered north to the Chesapeake Bay, entering it on April 26, 1607. Shortly thereafter, the colonists established Jamestown on the north side of the James River, nearly fifty miles from its mouth.[1] The Virginia spring was

The final version of this paper has been improved by the comments and criticisms of Daniel Doeppers, James Knox, Allan Kulikoff, and Russell Menard. Map credits go to the Cartographic Laboratory of the University of Wisconsin-Madison and Cartographic Services of the University of Maryland, Baltimore County.

1. "Observations by Master George Percy, 1607," in Lyon Gardiner Tyler, ed.,

FIGURE 1. The James River, 1607–1624

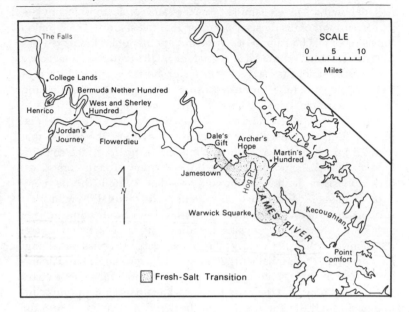

beneficent, and when Captain Newport departed on June 22, he left 104 healthy colonists. But soon the colony took on a somber attitude. On July 6 George Percy's journal mentioned John Asbie's death by the "bloudie Flixe." Three days later George Flowre died of the "swelling." In the space of a month 21 colonists died, causing Percy to lament that "our men were destroyed with cruell diseases, as Swellings, Flixes, Burning Fevers, and by warres, and some departed suddenly, but for the most part they died of meere famine."[2] By the end of September, 46 were dead, and in January when the first supply ship arrived in Virginia, just 38 of 104 colonists were barely alive.[3]

Narratives of Early Virginia, 1606–1625, Original Narratives of Early American History (New York, 1907), 5–23. On the selection of Jamestown, see Carville V. Earle, "The First English Towns of North America," *Geographical Review*, LXVII (1977), 34–50.

2. "Observations by Percy," Tyler, ed., *Narratives of Early Virginia*, 20–21. "The Proceedings of the English Colony" (1607) claims 105 colonists. Edward Arber and A. G. Bradley, eds., *Travels and Works of Captain John Smith, President of Virginia, and Admiral of New England, 1580–1631* (Edinburgh, 1910), I, 94.

3. Arber and Bradley, eds., *Travels and Works of Captain John Smith*, I, lxxvi, 9, 95; Alexander Brown, *The First Republic in America, An Account of the Origin of This Nation,*

The abundance of death demanded an explanation. But Percy's speculation that "meere famine" was the cause of death is unconvincing. In support of his thesis we can say that the colonists' daily ration consisted of just half a pint of wheat and another of barley, mixed in a gruel that yielded roughly half the caloric intake required for an active man of the colonists' stature.[4] But we should not hastily accept Percy's "meere famine," if only because of the political disputes and intrigues rending the first colony. Percy may have had an axe to grind. The selection of Jamestown over the Archer's Hope site displeased him, and conceivably he chose to support the faction that accused President Edward Maria Wingfield of hoarding the colony's food and drink for presidential favorites. Whatever Percy's motives, his emphasis on famine spotlighted President Wingfield. The president, of course, denied such allegations.[5] His rebuttal drew indirect support from one of his enemies, Captain John Smith. Smith made little of the shortage of provisions, stating matter-of-factly on several occasions that the colony still had many weeks of supplies remaining. He knew that the annual sturgeon run would provide a supplementary source of food. Thousands of these fish entered the James estuary in April and May, and their run to freshwater spawning grounds continued through the summer, when the big fish came in. "From the later end of May till the end of June," wrote Smith, "are taken few, but young Sturgeons of 2 foot or a yard long. From thence till the midst of September, them of 2 or three yards long and fewe others. And in 4 or 5 houres with one nette were ordinarily taken 7 or 8: often more."[6] A few years later John Rolfe related that two men in a few hours had axed forty sizable sturgeon.[7] Since the Atlantic sturgeon averages over one hundred pounds, the output of two axe-wielding men would have totaled four thousand pounds, or nearly forty pounds

Written from the Records Then (1624) Concealed by the Council, Rather than from the Histories Then Licensed by the Crown (Boston and New York, 1898), 55.

4. Herbert Renardo Cederberg, Jr., "An Economic Analysis of English Settlement in North America, 1583–1635" (Ph.D. diss., University of California, Berkeley, 1968), 144; Arber and Bradley, eds., *Travels and Works of Captain John Smith,* II, 391–392.

5. "A Discourse of Virginia per: Ed: Ma: Wingfield," in Arber and Bradley, eds., *Travels and Works of Captain John Smith*, I, lxxiv–xci.

6. *Ibid.,* 8–9, 51.

7. Philip Alexander Bruce, *Economic History of Virginia in the Seventeenth Century: An Inquiry into the Material Condition of the People, Based upon Original and Contemporaneous Records* (New York, 1896), I, 112.

per colonist per day.[8] A daily intake of two pounds of sturgeon, some crabs, and the wheat-barley gruel was more than adequate for the colonists' metabolic needs. Furthermore, two pounds of fish daily would have provided 90 percent of the daily thiamine requirement, and would thus have thwarted the outbreak of beriberi that has been postulated by the medical historian Wyndham Blanton.[9]

The food supply during Jamestown's first summer, though unappealing, provided sufficient nourishment to ward off starvation and vitamin deficiency diseases. Starvation was not the principal cause of death at Jamestown, but the possibility was constantly feared by the colonists. By mid-September they perceived that starvation was imminent. Newport had left them supplies for thirteen or fourteen weeks, and even though the death of 50 colonists had reduced the drain on the supplies, by September they had only enough for four to eight weeks and did not expect additional supplies until October at the earliest. Moreover, the sturgeon run fell off.

Although Percy blamed famine, his list of clinical symptoms brings us closer to the actual causes of death—typhoid, dysentery, and perhaps salt poisoning. Medical historians generally agree that Percy's "flixes" or "bloudie Flixes" describe dysentery, and "Burning Fevers" are symptomatic of typhoid fever.[10] The "Swellings," though perhaps associated with dysentery, could also result from salt intoxication from the salty river water.[11] These three diseases are also indicated by the incidence and rapidity of death, as chronicled by Percy. Typhoid fever progresses rapidly after infection by the bacterium *Salmonella*

8. Edward C. Raney, "Freshwater Fishes," in *The James River Basin, Past, Present, and Future*, Virginia Academy of Science, James River Project Committee (Richmond, Va., 1950), 154. James Wharton, *The Bounty of the Chesapeake: Fishing in Colonial Virginia*, Jamestown 350th Anniversary Historical Booklets, no. 13 (Williamsburg, Va., 1957).

9. H.L.A. Tarr, "Changes in Nutritive Value Through Handling and Processing Procedures," in Georg Bergstrom, *Fish as Food* (New York, 1961–1965), II, 248. Wyndham B. Blanton, "Epidemics, Real and Imaginary, and Other Factors Influencing Seventeenth Century Virginia's Population," *Bulletin of the History of Medicine*, XXXI (1957), 454–462.

10. Very useful are John Duffy, *Epidemics in Colonial America* (Baton Rouge, La., 1953); Wyndham B. Blanton, *Medicine in Virginia in the Seventeenth Century* (Richmond, Va., 1930), 3–77; Thomas P. Hughes, *Medicine in Virginia, 1607–1699*, Jamestown 350th Anniversary Historical Booklets, no. 21 (Williamsburg, Va., 1957); and Richard Harrison Shryock, *Medicine and Society in America, 1660–1860* (New York, 1960), 82–116.

11. Hans G. Keitel, *The Pathophysiology and Treatment of Body Fluid Disturbances* (New York, 1962), 162–164; John Hardesty Bland, "Clinical Physiology and Four Avenues of Loss and Gain," in Bland, ed., *Clinical Metabolism of Body Water and Electrolytes* (Philadelphia, 1963), 133–164.

typhosa. The first week may be symptomless, as the organisms spread through the bowel wall and into the lymphatic glands. In the second week the organism enters the bloodstream, causing a rapid rise in body temperature, recognized by colonists as the "Burning Fever." The illness peaks in the third week, and death may result. Before the use of antibiotics, it is estimated that 15 to 20 percent of infected persons died.[12] Dysentery, caused by amoebic parasites, produced the "bloudie Flixe." While several types of amoebic parasites reside in the human intestinal tract, most are harmless commensals or organisms that may cause diarrhea or mild dysentery. More dangerous is *Endamoeba histolytica*; it may invade the bowel wall, causing ulceration and the bloody stools that gave the disease its seventeenth-century name. More serious complications result when these parasites bore into a large blood vessel, causing massive hemorrhage, or when the amoeba get into the bloodstream and travel to other organs. Dysentery is often fatal, especially when populations are weakened by other illnesses or undernourishment. Pre-antibiotic mortality rates of 12 to 25 percent have been recorded.[13] Like typhoid, dysentery can act quickly, though the rates of incubation vary with the individual. Controlled experiments with human volunteers have shown "that the prepatent period, i.e., from exposure until the amoebas appeared in the stools, averaged nine days, varying from one to 44 days in the 17 of 20 exposed individuals who became infected."[14] Clinical symptoms usually appear within one to four weeks, but the range may be from a few days to several months.

12. The fever lasts 21 days usually and occasionally up to 33 days. Frederick P. Gay, *Typhoid Fever Considered as a Problem of Scientific Medicine* (New York, 1918), 13–24; William Budd, *Typhoid Fever: Its Nature, Mode of Spreading, and Prevention* (New York, 1931); Jacques Meyer May, *The Ecology of Human Disease* (New York, 1958), 171–188. Gay shows 15 to 27 percent mortality for the London Fever Hospital, 1848 to 1870. In general I agree with Jones that typhoid killed numerous Virginians in 1607. I disagree with him on the following points: (1) that typhoid, aided by beriberi, was the principal killer; (2) that typhoid was probably introduced by Reverend Robert Hunt; and (3) that the Jamestown environment was essentially passive in the typhoid epidemic. Gordon W. Jones, "The First Epidemic in English America," *Virginia Magazine of History and Biography*, LXXI (1963), 3–10.

13. Ernest Carroll Faust, *Amebiasis*, American Lecture Series, no. 191, American Lectures in Internal Medicine (Springfield, Ill., 1954); Martin D. Young, "Parasitism in Southeastern United States: A Symposium," *Public Health Reports*, LXX (1955), 957–975; Blanton, *Medicine in Virginia*, 63; Arthur L. Bloomfield, "A Bibliography of Internal Medicine: Amoebic Dysentery," *Journal of Chronic Diseases*, V (1957), 235–252; May, *Ecology of Human Disease*, 189–215.

14. Faust, *Amebiasis*, 58.

An epidemic of typhoid fever and dysentery is consonant with Percy's description of death and sickness at Jamestown. Percy first noted disease-related deaths on July 6, and sickness and death continued "for the space of six weekes"—a time span in keeping with the progression of typhoid fever and dysentery. Furthermore, 50 of the 104 colonists had perished by mid-September. The actual mortality rate of 48 percent just slightly exceeds the sum of expected pre-antibiotic mortality rates for typhoid (15 to 20 percent) and dysentery (12 to 25 percent), or a total rate of 27 to 45 percent. Our estimated rate of mortality may be criticized as too high on the grounds that some colonists died of both pathogens, and therefore the separate rates are not additive. The evidence does not permit an estimate of multiple causes of death. On the other hand, my guess is that the correct estimate of disease mortality probably lies in the 27 to 45 percent range and near the upper end. This supposition is based on several factors. First, the Jamestown population was probably under thirty years of age, and hence included the most susceptible age groups for typhoid (15 to 25 years) and dysentery (26 to 30 years).[15] Furthermore, the concentrated and confined population facilitated the spread and incidence of these diseases and perhaps their virulence as they passed rapidly from one infected colonist to another (via the feces and ingestion).[16]

The role of typhoid and dysentery may be further clarified by identifying the disease agents, the process of introduction, and the sources of human exposure. The introduction of these two diseases is not problematic. The colony contained numerous carriers of both diseases. According to modern laboratory diagnostic surveys, *Endamoeba histolytica* is carried by 40 percent of the population from 26 to 30 years old, with a decreasing incidence away from that peak.[17] And typhoid bacilli are carried by 2 to 30 percent of the general population.[18] In both diseases carriers may be symptomless and therefore almost

15. *Ibid.*, 28. About 50 percent of all typhoid cases occur between the ages of 15 and 25. Gay, *Typhoid Fever*, 13.

16. Faust, *Amebiasis*, 26. Modern surveys for *Endamoeba histolytica* in the southeastern United States average 11 percent positive in the general population, but among the concentrated populations of a mental hospital and an orphanage, the positives rose to 40 and 55.5 percent respectively. Willard H. Wright, "Parasitism in Southeastern United States: Current Status of Parasitic Diseases," *Public Health Reports*, LXX (1955), 966–975; Gay, *Typhoid Fever*, 14–15, 43–45.

17. Faust, *Amebiasis*, 28.

18. Gay, *Typhoid Fever*, 43.

impossible to detect in the absence of laboratory diagnoses. The Jamestown carriers passed millions of disease organisms in their feces and also their urine in the case of typhoid. The diseases were then transmitted, in all probability, through a contaminated water supply.

But what was the water supply, and why was it contaminated in July and August and not earlier or later? The colonists drank river water. In spring the water was safe. With river discharge at a maximum—owing to high precipitation, low evaporation, and high runoff —the fresh running water swirled around Jamestown Island and flushed disease organisms downstream. But the water supply became contaminated as summer set in. River discharge fell, water levels receded some ten to fifteen feet, and Jamestown Island became a peninsula attached to the mainland.[19] Pools of standing water and stagnant marshes rimming the mainland side of the island created a wetland environment ideal for the retention of *Salmonella typhosa* and *Endamoeba histolytica*. Even more deadly was the summer contamination of the river water with salt, sediment, and fecal material. As freshwater discharge fell, saltwater invaded some thirty miles up the James estuary from Hog Point in the spring to Jamestown by mid-summer. And along the landward-moving freshwater-saltwater boundary, sediments and organic wastes were trapped by the salt plug—particularly on the north side of the James, owing to the rightward deflection of the marine incursion by the earth's rotation.[20] Percy put it succinctly: "Our drinke [was] cold water taken out of the River, which was

19. The normal regime of Chesapeake estuaries is described here. Discharge, however, will depart from the norm of spring highs and summer lows under atypical meteorological conditions, e.g., prolonged drought or excessive rainfall, variable evapotranspiration, variable snow-melt water. Virginia, Virginia Conservation Commission, Division of Water Resources, *Surface Water Supply of Virginia: James River Basin*, nos. 5, 13, 17, 25 (Charlottesville and Richmond, Va., 1944–1961). As the James rose in spring and receded in summer, Jamestown occupied alternately an island and a peninsula attached to the mainland. C. A. Browne, "Reverend Dr. John Clayton and His Early Map of Jamestown, Virginia," *William and Mary Quarterly*, 2d Ser., XIX (1939), 5–6. The recession in river depth is estimated from depths of the main channel at Jamestown. Percy gives 6 fathoms (36 feet) in spring; an English pilot, interrogated by the Spanish in 1611, put the depth at 3½ fathoms (21 feet) at the least. The river's annual range is 15 feet. "Observations by Master George Percy," in Tyler, ed., *Narratives of Early Virginia*, 15; Alexander Brown, *The Genesis of the United States, A Narrative of the Movement in England, 1605–1616, Which Resulted in the Plantation of North America by Englishmen, . . . Set Forth Through a Series of Historical Manuscripts . . .* (Boston and New York, 1890), 519; Samuel H. Yonge, *The Site of Old "James Towne," 1609–1698 . . .* (Richmond, Va., 1904).

20. An excellent survey of the James is Maynard M. Nichols, "Sediments of the James River Estuary, Virginia," *Geological Society of America*, Memoir 133 (1972), 169–212.

at a floud verie salt, at low tide full of slime and filth, which was the destruction of many of our men."[21] At flood tide the colonists drank water containing salinity concentrations of over five parts per thousand—far above the recommended standard for constant daily usage of one part per thousand. The colonists suffered from salt poisoning, with its characteristic symptoms of "swellings" (edema), lassitude, and irritability. The idle, lazy, and factious behavior of early Virginians was, in part, the result of a steady summer diet of salty water.[22] The ebb tide, though less saline, was very turbid, organically polluted, and deadly. The trapped pathogens of typhoid and dysentery, thus floated back and forth past Jamestown with the summer tide. The danger from contaminated water faded in September. River discharge increased, pushing the salt incursion and its deadly associates downstream toward Hog Point.

The 1607 epidemic of typhoid and dysentery was the first of many summer epidemics in early Virginia. Fevers, fluxes, sickness, and death visited the colony recurrently between 1607 and 1624. One decisive factor underlying these repeated epidemics is the limited immunity conferred by the diseases themselves. Dysentery survivors acquire no immunity to subsequent attacks. Severe dysentery attacks do invoke a limited antibody response for two weeks after the infection, but thereafter the survivor is again susceptible to infection.[23] Typhoid attacks confer slightly more immunity. Typhoid recurrence is usually put at .75 to 4.2 percent; however, the recurrence rate rises to 8 to 15 percent in especially virulent and massive infections, like those in Jamestown.[24] Thus, the survivors of dysentery and of typhoid epidemics at Jamestown were only slightly less susceptible to these diseases than newly arrived immigrants. Survivors of a Virginia sum-

21. "Observations by Master George Percy," in Tyler, ed., *Narratives of Early Virginia*, 21–22.
22. Drinking water preferably should contain not more than 0.5 parts per thousand salt content; however, some contemporary municipal water supplies use two parts per thousand without public complaint. Thomas R. Camp and Robert L. Meserve, *Water and Its Impurities*, 2d ed. (Stroudsburg, Pa., 1974), 2; Keitel, *Pathophysiology and Treatment of Body Fluid Disturbances*, 162–164, 209–210; Bland, "Clinical Physiology and Four Avenues of Loss and Gain," in Bland, ed., *Clinical Metabolism*, 133–164. A composite of early Virginians' behavior would include irritability, laziness, short tempers, factiousness, and hyperbolic perceptions. The extremity of their situation accounts for some of these behaviors; salt poisoning accounts for them all. On idleness in early Virginia, see Edmund S. Morgan, "The Labor Problem at Jamestown, 1607–1618," *American Historical Review*, LXXVI (1971), 595–611.
23. Faust, *Amebiasis*, 30–32.
24. Gay, *Typhoid Fever*, 148.

mer did become "seasoned" to a new disease environment, but they were not particularly immune to future epidemics of typhoid, dysentery, or salt poisoning. These epidemics recurred for another reason —the annual summer invasion of saltwater up the James that contaminated the Jamestown water supply.

This close relationship between environment, disease, and mortality in 1607 Jamestown may be stated more generally for all Chesapeake estuaries. For our purposes, an estuary is an ecological unit wherein freshwater from the land is mixed with encroaching water from the sea, producing three salinity zones: a zone of freshwater, with salinity less than .5 parts per thousand; a zone of freshwater-saltwater transition (the oligohaline), with salinities of .5 to 3 parts per thousand; and a zone of salty water, with salinity above 3 parts per thousand (includes the mesohaline, polyhaline, and marine).[25] Sediment and fecal material entering an estuary are flushed out of its freshwater portion, temporarily trapped or plugged up by the salt incursion in the oligohaline until a large portion is eventually flushed downstream into the saltier water. Thus, pathogenic river-borne organisms are least common in the freshwater zone, maximum in the oligohaline zone, and intermediate in the mesohaline and polyhaline zones near the estuary mouth. Contamination also varies by bank side. Left bank contamination exceeds that of the right bank owing to the deflection of the salt incursion by the earth's rotation. This geographic distribution of estuarine contamination is, in turn, directly correlated with human exposure, infection, and mortality from the pathogens of typhoid and dysentery.[26] Mortality also varies seasonally

25. Chesapeake estuaries are moderately stratified, i.e., turbulence by tidal action mixes underlying salty water and overriding freshwater, thus bringing salt to the water surface. The variety of estuaries is discussed in a massive compendium: George H. Lauff, ed., *Estuaries*, American Association for the Advancement of Science, no. 83 (Washington, D.C., 1967). Several articles therein are pertinent: Donald W. Pritchard, "What Is an Estuary: Physical Viewpoint," 3–5; and his "Observation of Circulation in Coastal Plain Estuaries," 37–44; M. M. Nichols and R. L. Ellison, "Sedimentary Patterns of Microfauna in a Coastal Plain Estuary," 283–288; and J. L. McHugh, "Estuarine Nekton," 581–620, which contains the salinity classification. Also see D. W. Pritchard, "Salinity Distribution and Circulation in the Chesapeake Bay Estuaries System," *Journal of Marine Resources*, XI (1952), 106–123.

26. The distribution of disease organisms within an estuary depends on their point of entry, the circulation and flushing time of the estuary, and the life expectancy of the disease organisms. Laboratory experiments show that coliform bacteria, an indicator of disease contaminants, die off rapidly to one-tenth their original population in a period of one half to two or three days. The extent of downstream contamination increases when river circulation is rapid and the pollutants are flushed downstream before

with the migrations of the salt incursion. In the oligohaline zone the probability of infection increases when the saltwater-freshwater boundary passes by; clinical symptoms and mortality lag behind during the incubation period, with a normal lag of about one week to one month. The location of this deadly boundary zone migrates with river discharge. In the Chesapeake estuaries low discharge usually occurs in summer, and the saltwater invades the estuary to its landward maximum; on the James it penetrates thirty miles to the vicinity of Jamestown, where as a result seventeenth-century mortality rates should have peaked in July and August. Highest discharge customarily comes in the spring, and pushes the saltwater to its seaward maximum; on the James the retreat is to Hog Point, where mortality rates should have peaked in April and May. Within the saltwater zone, mortality rates should have risen slightly in spring because of the proximity of the salt trap; however, this zone would have received tidal flows of fecal material throughout the summer, thus assuring summer sickness and death. Recurrent epidemics were possible when population occupied the freshwater-saltwater and saltwater zones.[27]

Having put forward a geographic model of mortality, I hastily remind the reader of its crudity. The model coarsely subdivides estuaries into three salinity zones and hypothesizes their variable mortality. A more refined model might specify the precise concentrations of contaminants, as a function of estuarine flushing and of the transport and the life expectancies of pathogens, and the expected levels of infection and mortality. The hydrologic information for early Virginia hardly warrants such refinements.

---

death. Bostwick H. Ketchum, "Distribution of Coliform Bacteria and Other Pollutants in Tidal Estuaries," *Sewage and Industrial Wastes*, XXVII (1955), 1288–1296; Clarence J. Velz, *Applied Stream Sanitation* (New York, 1970), 339–379; *Wastes Management Concepts for the Coastal Zone: Requirements for Research and Investigation*, Committee on Oceanography and Committee on Ocean Engineering, National Academy of Engineering (Washington, D.C., 1970).

27. The expected timing and location of disease morbidity and mortality rest on the assumption of "average" climatic conditions and "normal" estuarine circulation, i.e., peak discharge and salt retreat in spring, and low discharge and salt incursion in late summer. Atypical weather conditions could alter the timing and location of disease incidence. The timing of epidemics is affected also by physiological factors. The increased incidence of typhoid and dysentery in later summer may have to do with increased human output of pathogens at that time. Counts of coliform bacteria in the Detroit River rose steadily in spring, reaching a peak in August; the reasons underlying this increased productivity are incompletely understood. For our purposes, this increased summer output should produce higher mortality in the landward edge of the oligohaline than on the seaward edge. Velz, *Applied Stream Sanitation*, 239–242.

The data for early Virginia afford several opportunities of testing the geographic model of mortality. For the period from 1607 to 1624, deaths may be estimated from contemporary statistics and estimates of population and immigration, which must be handled with circumspection. Figures can lie, and early Virginians regularly juggled population estimates to suit their purposes. The most probable causes of death are deduced from colonists' descriptions of the timing and symptoms of death and the reasonableness of their explanations as to the causes of death. The locations of population and of mortality derive from contemporary accounts. Particularly useful is the geographic census of the living and dead for 1623–1624.

The first question at issue is the relationship of mortality and the location of population in early Virginia. A chronological survey of the period from 1608 to 1624 reveals the recurrent deadliness of Jamestown summers. When population was concentrated in the town, mortality rates invariably rose above 30 percent; and when the population dispersed, death rates declined sharply.

The first two summers in Virginia were disastrous; the third offered the first glimmer of hope. As of October 1608 perhaps 244 colonists had come to Jamestown, and 144 of them had subsequently died.[28] But the death rate fell abruptly between October 1608 and the summer of 1609, when by the most liberal estimates just 21 of 130 persons died, including eleven by drowning. This anomaly of survival deserves comment.[29] Captain John Smith claimed credit for this success, and rightly so. Smith, though a vainglorious man, was also a sensitive ethnographer.[30] He carefully recorded the Indians' seminomadic

28. In December 1606, 144 colonists went to Virginia; 104 were left by Newport in June 1607; 38 to 40 survived in January 1608; 100 to 120 immigrants arrived between January and September 1608; and 60 were alive in October 1608. The mortality rate in the text is from Irene W. D. Hecht, "The Virginia Colony, 1607–1640: A Study in Frontier Growth" (Ph.D. diss., University of Washington, 1969), 68; Brown, First Republic in America, 55, 58–59, 68. Brown's population and immigration figures are usually accurate, and I rely on them frequently. However, his friendliness toward the Sandys administration from 1619 to 1624 and its "democratic" character leads him to minimize the mortality problem then, while he is excessively critical of mortality under the crown and under Thomas Smythe.

29. Friends of Smith claimed that only 7 or 8 died out of 200. Brown shows 130 alive in October 1608; 11 drowned in mid-January, and not more than 109 survived. Arber and Bradley, eds., Travels and Works of Captain John Smith, I, 154–157; Brown, The First Republic in America, 70–71; Philip L. Barbour, The Jamestown Voyages under the First Charter, 1606–1609, Hakluyt Society Publications, 2d Ser., CXXVII (Cambridge, 1969), II, 411.

30. The full story of Smith's ecological and ethnographic sensitivity and his application of this knowledge remains untold. Arber and Bradley, eds., Travels and Works of

economy and undoubtedly understood its survival value. In the spring the Indians congregated along the James estuary, subsisting on marine life while they planted their crops of corn, pumpkins, beans, and so forth. As summer approached, the tribes dispersed into smaller groups, residing usually on a hill with a fresh water spring, yet near the river where they gathered fish, oysters, and crabs. By dispersing, the Indian bands avoided the deadly estuarine zone, while exploiting scattered edible plants and animals during this leanest of seasons. But survival had its price. The scattered bands were politically and militarily weak. They sniped at their vulnerable, sick, and weak English enemies, but a summer war of attrition was impossible. As this flux in Indian power eluded most Virginians, they were terrified by late summer. Percy fully expected annihilation in 1607, and he marveled that God had saved them by putting "a terrour in the Savages hearts."[31] Smith saw things more clearly; the Indians were almost as vulnerable as the whites. In 1609 he dispersed his men with impunity. Smith also understood the Indians' generosity in the fall. Then they reassembled, harvested their crops, and gorged themselves. Their full bellies made them charitable, and they brought "Bread, Corne, Fish and Flesh in great plentie" to the confounded colonists.[32] With the onset of winter, the Indians once again fragmented into small bands and migrated upland into their piedmont hunting grounds, where they stalked deer, bear, and other game animals. Smith's genius was in placing the puzzling Indian behavior and subsistence strategies into a coherent ecological whole. He realized that the colony's survival, no less than the Indians', depended on seminomadism, at least during the deadly summer season.

In late May 1609 President Smith scattered the Jamestown settlers into the surrounding countryside. His scheme infuriated Captain Gabriel Archer, who described more than he understood: "Howbeit when Captaine Argoll came in [about July 10, 1609], they were in such distresse, for many were dispersed in the Sauages townes,

---

Captain John Smith, I, 61–70; Maurice A. Mook, "Virginia Ethnology from an Early Relation," *WMQ*, 2d Ser., XXIII (1943), 101–129; Philip L. Barbour, *The Three Worlds of Captain John Smith* (Boston, 1964), 243–276. Smith can be eulogized too much. While others died in Jamestown, he explored the healthier reaches of the Chesapeake. In 1608 Smith returned to Jamestown long enough to see the summer sickness, and then he was off again. Brown, *First Republic in America*, 60.

31. "Observations by Master George Percy," in Tyler, ed., *Narratives of Early Virginia*, 22.

32. *Ibid.*

living upon their almes for an ounce of Copper a day; and fourescore
lived twenty miles from the Fort and fed upon nothing but oysters
eight weekes Space."[33] Smith's scheme of dispersal, though repug-
nant to Argall, was the wisest to date. But the scheme encountered
opposition in August with the arrival of between 185 and 270 immigrants. Smith was able to dispatch a third of the colonists to Nansemond on the south side of the river in the saltwater zone and another
third to the freshwater zone at the falls near the head of the James.
But the rest stayed in Jamestown, assuredly against Smith's better
judgment. Predictably, sickness ravaged 100 Jamestown colonists,
and 50 died by October. Yet at Nansemond and at the falls, few
sickened and none died.[34] Indian behavior had given Smith the key
to life in the James estuary, but this precious knowledge was soon
lost. He was relieved of the presidency in October and returned to
England; with him went the schemes of seminomadism and summer
dispersal. The colony once again clustered at Jamestown, and death
hung heavy over the settlement.

Between Smith's departure and Thomas Gates's arrival in May
1610, the colony experienced the infamous "starving time." The accounts of hundreds starving, of cannibalism and other inhumanities,
have proved irresistible. But these accounts are biased, sensational-
ized, and exaggerated. They have warped the death rate and its
causes out of all proportion and have diverted attention from the
summer epidemics. In the first place, the death toll in the winter of
1609–1610 was much less than is usually assumed. The most common
error has been the belief that 490 to 500 immigrants came to Virginia
in October, with just 50 to 60 surviving when Gates arrived in May
1610—meaning that over 400 died.[35] In fact the Virginia population
in October stood at 250 or less, and after Smith departed with 30

33. Arber and Bradley, eds., *Travels and Works of Captain John Smith*, I, xcvi.

34. Staying in Jamestown during August was inconsistent with Smith's strategy,
and so I conclude that his opponents were responsible for the return to the town. By
summer's end 1609 the population stood at 250. Louis B. Wright, ed., *A Voyage to
Virginia in 1609: Two Narratives, Strachey's "True Reportory" and Jourdain's Discovery of the
Bermudas* (Charlottesville, Va., 1964), 83.

35. The "starving" time is embedded in Virginia's historical lore, embracing every-
thing from AAA Guide Books to Edmund Morgan's sophisticated research. Yet another
and less dramatic explanation may be suggested. Proponents of the starving time err in
assuming that 490 to 500 immigrants reached Virginia before the winter of 1609–1610;
only 185 to 270 arrived, finding about 109 survivors, making a total of 294 to 379. As it
fits Strachey's estimate, 300 sounds about right; 50 of them died at Jamestown in
August 1609 (Brown, *First Republic in America*, 97, 109, 112–113). When Gates arrived in
May 1610, 100 were alive. Wright, ed., *Voyage to Virginia: Two Narratives*, 82–83, 115.

unruly youths, 220 colonists remained. At least 15 of them were killed by Indians, and 25 to 30 others returned to England, leaving 180 in the colony.[36] When Gates arrived in May, he found 40 men in good health, along with President Percy, at Point Comfort near the mouth of the James. And at Jamestown 60 ragged men dragged out to meet Gates.[37] In other words, 100 survived the winter, 15 were killed by the Indians, and 80 died from other causes.

Was starvation the cause of death? Enemies of the company and of Sir Thomas Smythe's administration placed the blame on starvation resulting from inadequate provisions. Purportedly, "famine compelled us wholly to devour those Hoggs, Dogges and horses that weare then in the Collony," along with vermin and human flesh.[38] Yet there are serious inconsistencies surrounding the "starving time." Gates reported that 600 hogs were destroyed, which at conservative dressweights of 50 pounds per hog amounted to 30,000 pounds for 200 colonists or less—or about 150 pounds per capita during the seven months.[39] And supplemented by 500 chickens, seven horses, dogs, rats, snakes, and other vermin, the colonists' diet seems sufficient to have warded off starvation—even without human flesh.[40] Gates offered a different interpretation. He noted that Powhatan stepped up hostilities, confining the colonists to Jamestown between October and May. Some of the colonists were murdered, others fled, "and most by drinking of the brackish water of James Fort weakened and endangered, famine and sickness by all these means increased."[41] Brackish water, probably contaminated with typhoid and dysentery, is implicated once again, but this time in winter. One source of salty

36. Brown, *First Republic in America*, 97, 109, 112–113. Despite his careful analysis of mortality, Brown is anxious to blame Captain Smith and the company and so he accepts the thesis of starvation promulgated in " 'A Trewe Relaycon': Virginia from 1609 to 1612," *Tyler's Quarterly Historical and Genealogical Magazine*, III (1922), 264–270; "A Briefe Declaration of the Plantation of Virginia duringe the first Twelve Yeares . . . ," *Colonial Records of Virginia* (Richmond, Va., 1874), 70–73; William Stith, *The History of the First Discovery and Settlement of Virginia, being an essay towards a general history of this colony* (New York, 1969; orig. publ. 1747), 108–117.

37. Percy's abandonment of Jamestown for the healthier Point Comfort site was pragmatic, but not the most heroic of gestures. Wright, ed., *Voyage to Virginia: Two Narratives*, 62–63.

38. "A Briefe Declaration," *Colonial Records of Virginia*, 71.

39. Gates's comments are excerpted in Wright, ed., *Voyage to Virginia: Two Narratives*, 99; also, Strachey's remarks, *ibid.*, 86–87.

40. Gates's hog estimate was confirmed by Smith. *Ibid.*; Arber and Bradley, eds., *Travels and Works of Captain John Smith*, I, 167.

41. The tragedy was also blamed on "idleness," perhaps the result of salt intoxication. Wright, ed., *Voyage to Virginia: Two Narratives*, 98–99.

water was, of course, shallow wells, tapping brackish aquifers contaminated by pathogens percolated downward into the ground water.
Another possible source of bad water was the river, contaminated
during the severely cold winter of 1609–1610. Climatologists have
observed that cold temperatures and subsiding air depress rainfall. A
cold, dry winter—common in many parts of the mid-latitudes during
the late fifteenth and early sixteenth centuries—would have lowered
river discharge and delayed the retreat of the estuarine salt incursion,
fecal material, and sediment from Jamestown.[42]

We cannot say conclusively that typhoid, dysentery, and salt poisoning were the principal causes of death in that winter; however, we
can suggest that the case for massive starvation is far from proven.
For instance, the mortality rate of 44.4 percent is much lower than the
rate usually suggested by proponents of the "starving time." Starvation appears dubious given the livestock available to be consumed in
the winter. Moreover, the mortality rate is very similar to expected
and observed rates of death from typhoid and dysentery for 1607 and
1608. Finally, winter mortality in early Virginia was rare except in
extremely severe winters (for example, 1607–1608 and 1609–1610).[43]
Cold, dry winters and estuarine hydraulics could have produced a
contaminated water supply and epidemic typhoid and dysentery in
the so-called starving time.

With the arrival of Lord De la Warr in June of 1610, Jamestown was
retained as the colony's center. In mid-June 350 people were alive,
the sickness began one month later, and 150 (43 percent) had died by

42. For 17th-century climate, see H. H. Lamb, "The History of Our Climate:
Wales," in James Taylor, ed., *Climatic Change with Special Reference to Wales and Its Agriculture*, Memorandum no. 8, University College of Wales, Aberystwyth (1965), 1–18.
C.E.P. Brooks, *Climate Through the Ages: A Study of the Climatic Factors and Their Variations*,
2d rev. ed. (New York, 1970), 359–378. The extremely cold winter of 1609–1610 is noted
in Brown, *First Republic in America*, 113. Salty water at Jamestown in 1609–1610 would
explain the presence of water too cold to wade in for oysters, yet unfrozen because the
salt incursion lowered the freezing point. "A Briefe Declaration," *Virginia Col. Records*,
71. Twentieth-century records of the James River provide evidence of winter discharge
falling below late summer levels. However, salinity records are too recent and spotty to
indicate a winter saltwater incursion. Virginia Conservation Commission, *Surface Water
Supply*.

43. Arber and Bradley, eds., *Travels and Works of Captain John Smith*, I, 23, 98. Brown
estimates that 57 of 110 colonists died between January and April 1608 and that 25 of 83
died between April and October 1608. The winter mortality of 52 percent exceeds
slightly the 44 percent rate (80/180) for the cold winter of 1609–1610. Brown, *First
Republic in America*, 57; Arber and Bradley, eds., *Travels and Works of Captain John Smith*,
II, 398, 407, 434.

the end of the summer. By April 1611, 50 more died.[44] Colonial leaders strongly suspected the Jamestown water supply as the cause of death. Gates and William Strachey stated as much, and Gates and De la Warr, on their return to England in the fall of 1610, communicated their fears to the Virginia Company leaders.[45] Jamestown's days were numbered, or so it seemed.

The establishment of a healthier town site took time, and meanwhile the summer death continued. Thomas Dale arrived in Virginia on May 22, 1611, with 300 colonists, bringing the colony's strength to 480.[46] By mid-June, Dale had chosen a new town site—the falls at the head of the James—but building did not commence until September. The colonists spent the summer in Jamestown, with the sickness beginning in early July. A few days later Dale instituted martial law, but tough discipline did not thwart disease. At least 240 of the colonists became so sick that they could not work.[47] A death toll of about a third of the population, or 160, would be consistent with summer mortality and with later population estimates. At summer's end in 1611 the colony's population stood as follows: Dale's 320 survivors, plus 300 immigrants brought by Gates in August, all of whom were evacuated to the healthier falls site, and 62 brought by Argall in late September putting the colony total at 682—a figure just slightly below the 700 estimated for early 1612 by a Spanish prisoner at Jamestown.[48]

44. Gates withdrew from Jamestown with 200 in June 1610. The 40 others at Point Comfort probably were not included in this count. The colony thus numbered 200 to 240. De la Warr arrived with 150 men, putting the colony at 350 to 390. The colonists were heartened when De la Warr announced he had provision for 400 men for one year. They would have been less cheerful if De la Warr had brought 200 to 300 immigrants, as is sometimes asserted. Wright, ed., *Voyage to Virginia: Two Narratives*, 85, 115; Brown, *First Republic in America*, 116, 128, 134–139; Richard L. Morton, *Colonial Virginia: The Tidewater Period, 1607–1710* (Chapel Hill, N.C., 1960), I, 27–28; Hecht, "The Virginia Colony, 1607–1640," 330; "'A Trewe Relaycon': Virginia from 1609 to 1612," *Tyler's Quarterly*, 269–270.

45. For Strachey's insights, see Wright, ed., *Voyage to Virginia: Two Narratives*, 82–83; Morton, *Colonial Virginia*, I, 28–29.

46. In March 1610, 150 were alive; 30 arrived soon after, and Dale brought 300 in May 1611—a total of 480. Brown, *First Republic in America*, 138–139, 149; Ralphe Hamor, *A True Discourse of the Present Estate of Virginia, and the successe of the affaires there till the 18 of June. 1614 . . .* (London, 1615), 26.

47. Brown, *First Republic in America*, 149–155; Morton, *Colonial Virginia*, I, 28–31; Brown, *Genesis of the United States*, I, 506–507; Darrett B. Rutman, "The Virginia Company and Its Military Regime," in Darrett B. Rutman, ed., *The Old Dominion: Essays for Thomas Perkins Abernethy* (Charlottesville, Va., 1964), 1–20.

48. Brown, *First Republic in America*, 156, 172; Arber and Bradley, eds., *Travels and*

Rome was not built in a day, nor was Henrico, the new town at the falls. Construction began in the autumn of 1611 and continued through winter. But the schedule was interrupted by spring planting in 1612, and full-scale settlement of the new town awaited the end of the harvest. My guess is that the majority of colonists spent the summer of 1612 at Jamestown. The mortality figures suggest as much. According to the Spanish prisoner Molina, 350 died out of a total population of 700. Molina's report appears accurate; 700 colonists seems about right for the spring of 1612. Molina, however, gives two estimates of the survivors in May 1613—either 305 or 350. The death rate for 1612–1613 was probably 50 percent or more.[49]

With the establishment of Henrico and the general dispersal of population between 1613 and 1616, early Virginia enjoyed its healthiest era. By 1614 Jamestown had dwindled as the colony's center, and the population shifted toward the head of the James River. Rolfe's description of settlement in 1616 revealed that Jamestown contained just 19 percent of the colony population, and just 32.3 percent resided in both the oligohaline (Dale's Gift and Jamestown) and the saltwater (Kecoughtan). The remaining 67.7 percent occupied the freshwater zone at Henrico, Bermuda Nether Hundred, and West Sherley Hundred.[50] Mortality was rarely mentioned in the contemporary correspondence or accounts of these years, and for good reason. The population in May 1613 consisted of 305 to 350 persons, and by May 1616, 45 immigrants had arrived and 351 colonists survived.[51] The mortality rate had declined sharply. Assuming no natural increase,

---

Works of Captain John Smith, II, 509; "Letter of Don Diego de Molina, 1613," in Tyler, ed., Narratives of Early Virginia, 220, 223–224.

49. As late as May 1613, Jamestown contained almost half of the colony's population and Henrico only a third. The pattern surely changed by the summer of 1613. "Letter of Don Diego de Molina, 1613," in Tyler, ed., Narratives of Early Virginia, 223–224; Hamor, A True Discourse, 32. Dale's letter of June 1614 is enlightening. Although his obligation in Virginia was complete, he believed the colony was in "desperate hazard." Abandoning her might reflect on his reputation. Perhaps, too, Dale had to endure another summer to see if the healthy year preceding (1613) resulted from his settlement policies or from dame fortune. Hamor, A True Discourse, 51–59.

50. John Rolfe, A True Relation of the state of Virginia lefte by Sir Thomas Dale, Knight, in May last 1616 (New Haven, Conn., 1951), 33–41; Hamor, A True Discourse, 26–33; Charles E. Hatch, Jr., The First Seventeen Years: Virginia, 1607–1624, Jamestown 350th Anniversary Historical Booklet, no. 6 (Williamsburg, Va., 1957), 32–33.

51. Brown, First Republic in America, 220, 224, 229; Hecht, "The Virginia Colony, 1607–1640," 332. Writing in 1614 about the martial law invoked in 1611, Hamor defended Dale's measures, "for more deserved death in those daies, then do now the least punishment." Healthful conditions had marvelously reformed idle and factious Virginians! Hamor, A True Discourse, 27.

the Virginia population either held steady or declined at a rate of about fifteen deaths per year—an astonishing annual mortality rate of about 3.8 percent.

The marked improvement in mortality rates following the redistribution of population into healthier freshwater environments is consistent with the model used here; however, the causal role of dispersal is clouded by a simultaneous reduction in immigration. The latter explanation for declining mortality is favored by proponents of the "seasoning" thesis. They maintain that mortality rates among immigrants were very high, but fell sharply among the survivors, who were "seasoned" to the Virginia disease environment. The seasoned survivors were less susceptible (immune) to disease in future years. An alternative hypothesis, and the one favored here, maintains that seasoned colonists were nearly as susceptible as newcomers to typhoid, dysentery, and salt poisoning and that their vulnerability can be demonstrated for the period under discussion. Immigration to Virginia came to a virtual standstill in the summer of 1611. The seasoning thesis would posit a sequence of high mortality rates in that summer, the survival of seasoned colonists, and a sharp mortality reduction in the summer of 1612. In fact, we have shown that mortality remained high in both summers. Death rates dropped dramatically in 1613, after the Virginians shifted their settlements into the freshwater zone. Environment and location were the decisive factors lowering mortality between 1613 and 1616; immigration and seasoning were largely irrelevant.[52]

The healthy era, 1613 to 1616, was the product of a lengthy and painful process of environmental learning and adjustment. The three years from 1607 to 1610 were spent enduring death and identifying its

52. Seasoning was at once a well-recognized process in Virginia and a theory of curative medicine, i.e., treatment of individuals. By exposing the individual to infection in a new disease environment, future susceptibility was reduced. The theory worked fine for self-immunizing or debilitating diseases such as malaria, bacillary dysentery, paratyphoid, but curative medicine worked miserably on non-immunizing, virulent diseases. Exposure to these diseases brought death year after year. The only effective remedy against them, at least before vaccines and antibiotics, was the preventive medicine of environmental modification or avoidance. Since Virginians were powerless to change the oligohaline, the best course was to avoid the zone. An excellent discussion of the seasoning process and the role of malaria is Darrett B. Rutman and Anita H. Rutman, "Of Agues and Fevers: Malaria in the Early Chesapeake," *WMQ*, 3d Ser., XXXIII (1976), 31–60. Blanton, *Medicine in Virginia*, 37–41; Colonel P. M. Ashburn, *The Ranks of Death: A Medical History of the Conquest of America*, ed. Frank D. Ashburn (New York, 1947), 118–123, 159–160; Duffy, *Epidemics in Colonial America*, 214–218; May, *Ecology of Human Disease*, 26.

geographic pattern and its causes. By the spring of 1610 colonial leaders had associated death with the water supply and the Jamestown environment. They persuaded the company in London of this pattern by the fall of that year. Implementation of a new settlement distribution consumed the next three years from the winter of 1610–1611 to the fall of 1613. During these years Dale reconnoitered, chose a site, began construction of Henrico, cleared land for crops, and instituted an aggressive Indian campaign. Thus, in seven years the company had perceived the solution to summer mortality, and Dale worked swiftly toward that end. But the resettlement scheme was greatly facilitated by the Indians. Dale's provocative encroachment into Powhatan's territory at the head of the James met little resistance from the chief. Perhaps Powhatan's advanced age and the capture of his daughter Pocahontas tempered his retaliation, but his mysterious behavior suggests intrigue. The chief remained incommunicado from May 1613 to March 1614, and he removed his quarters from the James to the Pamunkey River. Is it not possible that Powhatan had his hands full with the hostile Monacans on his western flank, and until they were subdued, he temporarily conceded Dale the James River head? Whatever Powhatan's motives, the English colony profited from his passivity.[53]

When Dale left Virginia in the spring of 1616, he felt confident that the colony would endure. The mortality problem had been solved by diminishing Jamestown's importance and locating the settlements in healthier zones. With sickness and death on the wane, the healthy colonists produced a surplus of food. Trade relationships altered. Formerly the colonists begged, stole, or traded for Indian food; now the Indians came seeking the colony's corn.[54] Healthy conditions continued through the summer of 1616. There were no reports of widespread mortality, and the colony probably contained 335 to 351 colonists. But with the arrival of a new governor in the spring of 1617, all of Dale's insights were abandoned, to be painfully relearned.

53. Hamor, *A True Discourse*, 54–55; William Strachey, *The Historie of Travell into Virginia Britania*, ed. Louis B. Wright and Virginia Freund, Hakluyt Society Publications, 2d Ser., CIII (London, 1953), 105–106; Nancy Oestrich Lurie, "Indian Cultural Adjustment to European Civilization," in James Morton Smith, ed., *Seventeenth-Century America: Essays in Colonial History* (Chapel Hill, N.C., 1959), 33–60; Wesley Frank Craven, *White, Red, and Black: The Seventeenth-Century Virginian* (Charlottesville, Va., 1971), 46–50.

54. Rolfe, *A True Relation*, 36.

Governor Samuel Argall was not one to learn from his mistakes. This was the same Argall who earlier had condemned Smith's dispersal of colonists in the summer of 1609. As governor in the spring of 1617, Argall was again appalled by the state of the colony and Jamestown where "he found but five or six houses, the Church downe, the Palizado's broken, the Bridge in pieces, the Well of fresh water spoiled; the Store-house they used for the Church; the marketplace, and streets, and all other spare places planted with Tobacco: . . . the Colonie dispersed all about, planting Tobacco."[55] On June 9 Argall wrote the company that he liked "James Town better than Bermudas 40 miles above it, [and] will Strengthen it."[56] Argall must have succeeded in realigning settlement, for that summer a great mortality ensued. Death struck 105 to 115 of the 415 colonists, and suddenly the mortality rate had risen from almost nil to 25 percent.[57]

The realignment of settlement begun by Argall and continued under the Sandys administration was one of the principal causes of death until 1624. The hard-won knowledge of the environment and the adjustments made between 1607 and 1617 were abandoned. Between 1617 and 1623, 36 new settlements dotted the James estuary, and 13 of them occupied the oligohaline and the saltier water.[58] More important, population shifted into the lower estuary, and Jamestown was reaffirmed as chief city and center of government. The extent of realignment is revealed by the census of 1623–1624, and by the records of deaths from the massacre of March 1622, both of which help provide a more accurate picture of population distribution from 1618 to 1622 (see table 1).[59] These sources show that 72 percent of the

55. Arber and Bradley, eds., *Travels and Works of Captain John Smith*, II, 535–536, quotation is on p. 535.

56. Susan Myra Kingsbury, ed., *The Records of the Virginia Company of London*, 4 vols. (Washington, D.C., 1933–1935), III, 73.

57. *Ibid.*, 92. The mortality rate is based on the following: probably 335 (my estimate) were alive in May 1617, plus 80 brought in by Argall, or a total of 415. In May 1618 the colony contained about 400, 90 to 100 of whom had arrived between March and May 1618. Subtracting these from the 400 yields 300 to 310 alive in March 1618. Thus from May 1617 to March 1618, 105 to 115 had died. Arber and Bradley, eds., *Travels and Works of Captain John Smith*, II, 535–536; Brown, *First Republic in America*, 253–256, 260, 277; Hecht, "The Virginia Colony, 1607–1640," 333–334; Evarts B. Greene and Virginia D. Harrington, *American Population before the Federal Census of 1790* (New York, 1932), 135.

58. Hecht, "The Virginia Colony, 1607–1640," 174, 361–363.

59. "Lists of the Livinge and Dead in Virginia, Feb. 16th, 1623[4]," *Colonial Records of Virginia*, 37–60; Kingsbury, ed., *Records of the Virginia Company*, III, 565–571. The census of 1623–1624 alone gives a misleading impression of population distribution

TABLE 1. Population Distribution in 1622–1624 (and the Probable Distribution from 1617 to 1624)

Estuarine Zone	Massacre Deaths	Living, 1623–1624	Dead, 1623–1624	Total	Percentage of Population
Freshwater	209	289	57	555	28.5%
Oligohaline	145	603	211	959	49.3%
Mesohaline, Polyhaline	0	303	101	431	22.2%

Note:
   This table does not include population on the Eastern Shore or on recently arrived vessels.

Virginia colonists resided in the oligohaline and saltwater zones; 28 percent occupied the freshwater—almost a direct reversal of the pattern under Dale, when 68 percent lived in the freshwater zone.

   Increased mortality accompanied the shift in population. Several thousand colonists died between 1618 and 1624, and disease was an important cause. Comments on summer sickness and death increasingly punctuated colonial correspondence. But disease was not the sole killer. Indian attacks, starvation, and plague also contributed. While the surviving evidence precludes a precise bill of mortality, some estimates of disease-related deaths can be made from the census of 1623–1624.

   Here 1623–1624 is used as a benchmark year for estimating the usual mortality rate from typhoid, dysentery, and salt poisoning from 1618 to 1624. Several bits of evidence suggest these diseases as the principal causes of death in 1623–1624: the reports of summer sickness and death in that year; the absence of other reported causes of mortality; an abundant food supply, making starvation an unlikely cause of death; and the census listing of colonists killed, presumably by the Indians, so that these deaths can be excluded from our disease estimate.[60] Typhoid and dysentery are also implicated by the spatial

between 1618 and 1622. Massacre casualties on March 22, 1622, were heaviest upriver from Jamestown, and hence I have included them as a more accurate representation of population geography under the Sandys administration.

   60. Brown, *First Republic in America*, 569–570; Edmund S. Morgan, *American Slavery, American Freedom: The Ordeal of Colonial Virginia* (New York, 1975), 104–105. The year following the massacre of 1622 was very sickly, but the resultant mortality probably antedated the census of 1623–1624. Tyler, ed., *Narratives of Early Virginia*, 438; Morton, *Colonial Virginia*, I, 83–90.

TABLE 2. Estuarine Zones and Mortality Rates, 1623–1624

Settlements	Estuarine Zone	Percentage Dead	
College Lands		0.0% (0/33)	
Neck of Land		9.8% (4/41)	
West & Sherley Hundred		17.9% (10/56)	
Jordan's Journey	Freshwater	16.0% (8/50)	16.7% (50/299)
Flowerdieu Hundred		18.6% (18/63)	
West & Sherley Hundred Island		17.9% (10/56)	
James City & "within the Corporation thereof"		32.7% (89/272)	
"Plantation over against James River"	Oligohaline	45.8% (65/142)	37.1% (207/558)
Hogg Island		8.8% (3/34)	
Martin's Hundred		51.0% (26/51)	
Warwick Squarke		40.7% (24/59)	
Elizabeth City }	Mesohaline, Polyhaline	23.3% (98/420) }	23.3% (98/420)

Note:
   This table includes only those settlements returning lists of dead. "Killed" colonists are not here included among the dead.

pattern of death recorded in the census of 1623–1624. Within those settlements reporting deaths during the year, 16.7 percent died in the freshwater zone; 37.1 percent in the oligohaline; and 23.3 percent in the saltier portion of the James estuary (table 2).[61] The match between reality and our estuarine model is good, but not perfect. Freshwater death rates are higher than expected, perhaps reflecting the severe disruptions in this area caused by the massacre of 1622. Another peculiarity is Hog Island in the oligohaline, where only 8.8 percent died. A safer right-bank location, the removal of pollutants toward the north bank by a river meander, and the small population probably combined to make Hog Island a healthy micro-environment. Otherwise the census pattern points toward death by typhoid and dysentery in the oligohaline and the salty lower James.

   Having isolated these diseases as probable causes of death, we can estimate their usual contribution to Virginia mortality. The annual

   61. "Lists of the Livinge and Dead in Virginia," *Colonial Records of Virginia*, 37–60.

TABLE 3. Estimated Annual Disease Mortality Rates Based on Population
Distribution and Estuarine Zone Mortality Rates, 1618–1624

Estuarine Zone	Percentage of Colony Population (1)	Annual Mortality Rate (2)	Percentage of Total Mortality Rate (1 × 2)
Freshwater	28.5%	16.7%	4.8%
Oligohaline	49.3%	37.1%	18.3%
Mesohaline, Polyhaline	22.2%	23.3%	5.2%
Estimated Annual Disease Mortality Rate for Virginia			28.3%

disease mortality rate (table 3) is estimated as the sum of the products
of the ecological zone death rates (table 2) and the population distribution for 1618–1624 (table 1). A disease mortality rate of 28.3 percent
per year is indicated; for typhoid, dysentery, and salt poisoning
alone, 23.5 percent, with the oligohaline contributing 18.3 percent
and the saltwater 5.2 percent. In the freshwater zone 4.8 percent
died, but the causes are not known.

Argall and the Sandys administration, by redistributing Virginians
into the most deadly zones, share the responsibility for the deaths of
24 to 28 percent in any single year. But the gravity of their offense
worsened with time; epidemics struck year after year, killing immigrants and seasoned colonists alike. Disease claimed considerably
more colonists than 28 percent between 1618 and 1624. The overall
contribution of disease to death is estimated from the several censuses
and immigration figures, and the basic data are given in table 4.[62]
Between December 1618 and February 1624 about 5,145 persons resided in or immigrated to Virginia; 24.8 percent survived in 1624, 49.3
percent died from disease, and 25.9 percent died from other causes or
went back to England. Two of every three deaths resulted from
typhoid, dysentery, and salt poisoning. These diseases were the

62. Population estimates for 1618 to 1622 and 1624 are from: Brown, *First Republic
in America*, 328–329, 375, 381, 415, 462, 464, 466–467, 503–505, 612; Morgan, *American
Slavery, American Freedom*, 412–413; Greene and Harrington, *American Population before
the Federal Census of 1790*, 134–136. Immigration estimates are from Brown, *First Republic
in America*, see above for pages. Hecht, "The Virginia Colony, 1607–1640," 334–345.
The unknown population of April 1623 is estimated by working backwards, i.e.,
population of February 1624 (1,275) minus immigrants between April 1623 and February
1624 (405) plus deaths during this period (371) equals the population as of April 1623
(1,241). "Lists of the Livinge and Dead in Virginia," *Colonial Records of Virginia*, 37–60.

TABLE 4. Disease-Related Death Estimates in Virginia, 1618–1624

Time Period	Population at Beginning	Population at End	Immigrants	Overall Mortality Rate[a]	Disease-Related Deaths[b]	Disease Death/Total
Dec. 1618–Mar. 1620	600	887	814–914	37.3%–41.4% (527–627/ 1,414–1,514)	402–430 (28.3%)	402–430/ 527–627 (68–76%)
Mar. 1620–Mar. 1621	887	843	1,051	56.5% (1,095/1,938)	550(28.3%)	550/1,095 (50.2%)
Mar. 1621–Mar. 1622	843	1,240	1,580	48.8% (1,183/2,423)	688(28.3%)	688/1,183 (58.2%)
Mar. 1622–Apr. 1623	1,240	1,241	695	35.9% (694/1,935)	347(17.9%)[c]	347/694 (50.0%)
Apr. 1623–Feb. 1624	1,241	1,275	405	22.5% (371/1,646)	371(22.5%)[d]	371/371 (100.0%)

Summary:
Population in Feb. 1624--------------1,275
Disease-related deaths, 1618–1624--------2,538
Other causes of death or
    return to England-------------1,332
              Total---5,145

2,538/3,870 (65.6%)

Notes:
[a]Includes deaths from all causes as well as those returning to England alive.
[b]Using estimate of 28.4% per year.
[c]Since 347 known deaths occurred in the massacre, the remainder are assigned to disease.
[d]Overall death rate fell below the disease rate, hence all were assigned to disease.

principal killers in some years, and they were significant contributors in all.[63]

The leaders of the company and the colony tried desperately to reduce summer mortality but failed because of their misconceptions of its causes. Preventive measures were aimed at the immigrants and not at the environment and at population distribution. Guest houses (hospitals) were established, and immigrant arrivals were scheduled for fall after the sickly summer months, all done on the false assumption that seasoned colonists would survive.[64] But seasoned colonists stood little chance of survival in the oligohaline zone, as revealed in the muster of 1625. Then 57 settlers gave arrival dates before 1616; 24 resided in the freshes, 25 in the salt, and just 9 in the oligohaline. Older settlers, those arriving before 1620 of all giving arrival dates, made up about one-fifth of the population in the oligohaline, one-third in the saltwater zone, and two-fifths in the fresh.[65] These spatial and environmental patterns of death went undetected by the company, and that oversight was instrumental in its dissolution.

The demise of the Virginia Company in 1624 signaled a new era in Virginia demography. The old constraints focusing the colony on Jamestown and the oligohaline were relaxed, and mortality fell. Between 1625 and 1634 Virginia's population grew from 1,210 to 4,914,

63. These estimates of annual disease mortality permit an assessment of other causes of death. Morgan, for example, has suggested starvation and malnutrition, occasioned by control of Virginia's food and labor supply by a handful of private capitalists. The most likely years for such crass behavior were 1620 to 1622, when causes *other than* Indian killings and diseases contributed 40 to 50 percent of all deaths. Morgan, *American Slavery, American Freedom*, 92–107. Note, however, that immigration was also heaviest in these years—suggesting Craven's point of inadequate provisioning of the immigrants by the company. Probably both company and private wheeler-dealers were responsible for the increased death rate; in any case, the critical years were 1620–1622. Wesley Frank Craven, *Dissolution of the Virginia Company: The Failure of a Colonial Experiment* (New York, 1932), 152–153.

64. The company believed in the curative medicine of seasoning, rather than the preventive medicine of settlement dispersal. Craven, *Dissolution of the Virginia Company*, 148–175; Kingsbury, ed., *Records of the Virginia Company*, III, 275, 301–302.

65. John Camden Hotten, ed., *The Original Lists of Persons of Quality; and Others Who Went from Great Britain to the American Plantations, 1600–1700* (New York, 1931), 200–265.

66. Morgan, *American Slavery, American Freedom*, 159, estimates 1,000 immigrants per year. Morgan underestimates the magnitude of declining mortality rates after 1624. A lower death rate is not inconsistent with his literary evidence. Ship captains experienced high mortality (42 percent in 1636) precisely because they plied in the oligohaline zone. And 1,800 deaths in 1636, given the population and increased immigration in

TABLE 5. Population Growth, 1625–1634, under Pre-1625 Disease Mortality Rates and a Fitted Mortality Rate

	Pre-1625 Disease Mortality Rate (28.3% per year)		Fitted Mortality Rate (14.2%) for 1625–1634	
Date	Population & Immigrants	Survivors	Population & Immigrants	Survivors
1625–1626	1,210 + 1,000	1,582	1,210 + 1,000	1,896
1626–1627	1,582 + 1,000	1,849	1,896 + 1,000	2,485
1627–1628	1,849 + 1,000	2,040	2,485 + 1,000	2,990
1628–1629	2,040 + 1,000	2,177	2,990 + 1,000	3,423
1629–1630	2,177 + 1,000	2,275	3,423 + 1,000	3,794
1630–1631	2,275 + 1,000	2,344	3,794 + 1,000	4,113
1631–1632	2,344 + 1,000	2,394	4,113 + 1,000	4,387
1632–1633	2,394 + 1,000	2,430	4,387 + 1,000	4,622
1633–1634	2,430 + 1,000	2,456	4,622 + 1,000	4,824
1634–1635	2,456 + 1,000	2,475	4,824 + 1,000	4,997

Note:
The actual population in 1634 was 4,914. The above calculations assume no natural increase. Some children were born in the colony during the period, but the imbalanced sex ratio favoring males, and other evidence suggests that children contributed little to population growth at this time.

while receiving an estimated 9,000 immigrants.[66] Although over half of the population died in the nine-year period, this figure obscures the marked improvement in annual mortality. Had the pre-1625 mortality rate of 28.3 percent per year continued, Virginia in 1634 would have numbered 2,456 instead of 4,914. In effect, annual mortality was cut in half (to about 14.2 percent) during the early royal period (see table 5).[67]

Several factors caused the decline in mortality. By far the most important was the shift in population patterns. By 1634 the deadliest zone along the James, including James City, Warwick, and Warros-

that year, produces a mortality rate in between that of the period 1618 to 1624 (28.3 percent) and our post-1624 estimated rate (14.2 percent).

67. Morgan's 1625 to 1640 estimate of 1,000 immigrants per year has been questioned as too high by Menard. He suggests that immigration varied directly with tobacco prices, and therefore Virginia immigration peaked at about 2,000 in 1635–1636 and in preceding years (1625–1635) immigration generally fell substantially below 1,000 per year. If Menard is correct, then annual mortality for the period 1625 to 1634 falls even lower than the 14.2 percent presented here. Russell R. Menard, "Economy and Society in Early Colonial Maryland" (Ph.D. dissertation, University of Iowa, 1975), 167–170.

quyoake counties, contained 45 percent of the total population. But
population had spread into healthier zones, including the lower York
in the saltwater zone on the south side of the river, the freshwater
zone at the head of the James, the lower James, and the Eastern
Shore.[68] The general dispersal of tobacco plantations within all ecological zones also favored survival. Typhoid and dysentery could not
become epidemic when settlement was scattered. And as population
grew, settlement progressed inland away from the deadliest parts of
the James and onto the hills, ridges, and drainage divides where
fresh springs provided a safe water supply. Dietary habits probably
changed too, with increased consumption of wine, beer, and cider instead of water, and reduced consumption of oysters and clams during
May to August when these bivalves concentrated microorganisms.
As the "new healthiness" of the country took hold, Virginians and
their visitors usually attributed it to climate, improved by forest
clearance. More accurately, the spread and dispersal of settlement
along with certain dietary adjustments were the keys to life.[69]

Frontier expansion and plantation dispersal continued during the
rest of the seventeenth century, with generally beneficial demographic
effects. Although travelers commented on the pallid complexions,
sickness, and frequent death found in the saltwater environments
of the lower estuaries, the population there was generally much
healthier than in the freshwater-saltwater transition zone.[70] When
the frontier expanded into the oligohaline zones of the York, Rappahannock, and Potomac rivers, death rates assuredly rose above those

68. "A List of the number of men, women and children . . . Within the Colony of
Virginia. Anno Dne, 1634," *Colonial Records of Virginia*, 91.
69. On dispersal and tobacco, see Morton, *Colonial Virginia*, I, 122–133; Hecht,
"The Virginia Colony, 1607–1640," 195–207; Craven, *Dissolution of the Virginia Company*,
170–171. In a revealing note, Governor Wyatt in 1623 blamed the colony's ill fortune
on "the intemperate drinking of water." "To plant a colony by water drinkers was an
inexcusable errour in those who laid the first foundation and have made it a received
custome," Kingsbury, ed., *Records of the Virginia Company*, IV, 10–11, 453; Wharton,
Bounty of the Chesapeake, 46; William Ancisz and C. B. Kelly, "Self-Purification of the
Soft Clam Mya arenaria," *Public Health Reports*, LXX (1955), 605–614.
70. Gilbert Chinard, ed., *A Huguenot Exile in Virginia, or Voyages of a Frenchman
Exiled for His Religion with a Description of Virginia and Maryland* (New York, 1934), 130,
174. Recognition of the freshwater-saltwater transition and its dangers is incipient in
Bullock's "flowing of the salt." Clayton thought all saltwater bad, as it impregnated the
air and thus damaged the human body. William Bullock, *Virginia Impartially examined,
and left to publick view, to be considered by all Judicious and honest men* (London, 1649), 4;
Edmund Berkeley and Dorothy Smith Berkeley, eds., *The Reverend John Clayton . . . His
Scientific Writings and Other Related Papers* (Charlottesville, Va., 1965), 54.

in the saltwater zones. While I cannot prove this statement from the available evidence, the oligohaline zone appears to have been more deadly in the eighteenth century. The spatial pattern of mortality can be crudely reconstructed from a 1725–1726 parish census of births and burials (figure 2).[71] For all four Virginia estuaries, the pattern of mortality hypothesized by the estuarine model for early Virginia remains recognizable a century later. The proportion of burials to births generally is least in the freshwater zone, peaks in the oligohaline zone, and drops slightly in the saltwater zone of the lower estuaries. Left bank (north side) proportions are usually higher than the corresponding right bank (south side). The map's subtleties and its several departures from the model—notably the higher-than-expected mortality levels in the upper Rappahannock, lower James, and the Potomac estuary generally—warrant more attention, but to do so would push us beyond the limited scope of this essay.[72] More important is the map's suggestion that typhoid and dysentery caused some

71. The census records births and burials for the year beginning April 15, 1725. I have assumed census recording procedures were uniform among Virginia parishes, but undoubtedly these procedures varied markedly. More thorough studies of Virginian demography may reveal whether the parishes departing from the estuarine-disease model reflect actual differences or recording biases in the census. C.O. 5/1320, f. 74, Public Record Office. Parish boundaries are roughly accurate. The four Henrico County parishes are aggregated on the map. Charles Francis Cocke, *Parish Lines, Diocese of Virginia*, Virginia State Library Publications, no. 28 (Richmond, Va., 1967); George Carrington Mason, *Colonial Churches of Tidewater Virginia* (Richmond, Va., 1945). The freshwater-saltwater transition zones are located according to Nichols, "Sediments of the James River," 171–179. Evon Ruzecki, Virginia Institute of Marine Science, personal communication; H. C. Whaley and T. C. Hopkins, *Atlas of the Salinity and Temperature Distribution of Chesapeake Bay*, Chesapeake Bay Institute, Johns Hopkins University, Graphical Summary Reports, nos. 1–2, Ref. 52–4, 63–1 (Baltimore, 1952, 1963); Chinard, *A Huguenot Exile in Virginia*, 174.

72. This geographical pattern of mortality might be explained by other models, such as the Rutmans' malarial endemicity. According to the Rutmans, malarial "morbidity climbs as endemicity rises, since a greater percentage of infectious bites by *Anopheles* leads to symptomatic malarial attacks. Yet the rate of morbidity will be balanced at some point by the rate of immunities in the population and then will begin to decline until, in a hyperendemic situation, morbidity is largely limited to children, non-immune newcomers to the community, and pregnant women." Put geographically this process of endemicity should move roughly with the frontier of settlement, i.e., old settled areas being hyperendemic, newly settled areas having low but rising morbidity, and middle-aged areas having very high morbidity. If I have reasoned correctly, the entire James River area, as the oldest settled zone, should show similarly low values on our map, followed by very high values in the middle-aged tier of Gloucester, Middlesex, Lancaster, Westmoreland, and Northumberland counties, and low values elsewhere. I do not detect such a pattern, and accordingly favor the three-zone estuarine model of enteric diseases. Rutman and Rutman, "Agues and Fevers," *WMQ*, 3d Ser., XXXIII (1976), 37–39, 44–45.

FIGURE 2. Proportion of Burials to Births, 1725–1726: Virginia Parishes

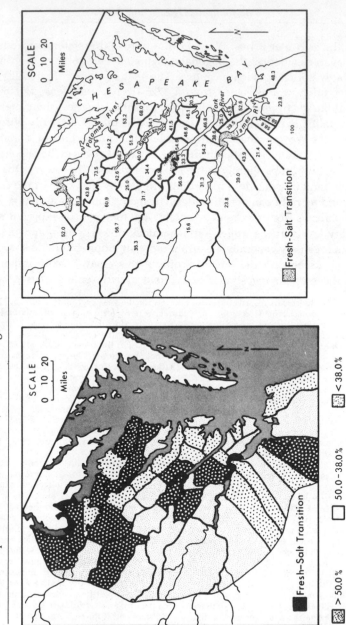

eighteenth-century mortality, perhaps enough to account for the high rates of the oligohaline zone and the intermediate rates in the salt-water zone.

The demographic history of early Virginia is both sad and tragic. Sad because so many died; tragic because they died needlessly. Smith, Dale, and others knew that epidemics of typhoid, dysentery, and salt poisoning were recurrent; they knew that these epidemics were spawned by a contaminated water supply in the vicinity of Jamestown and the freshwater-saltwater transition on the James estuary. They knew that dispersing in the summer or shifting permanently into the freshwater zone were the only ways to save lives. And they knew that scattered settlements required the protection of an aggressive Indian policy. Smith and Dale saved lives, but their insights were abandoned with the arrival of new colonial leaders or a new company administration. Jamestown was reclaimed, mortality rose, and the painful environmental learning process began again at ground level. The Sandys administration never learned. The nexus of environment and mortality confounded and eluded them. They mistakenly believed that the seasoning process would eventually take hold and Virginia's population would grow. But typhoid and dysentery were no respecters of flawed theories of immunity. From a demographic standpoint, the best thing that happened in early Virginia was the dissolution of the company with its fixation on Jamestown.

4

"Till Death Us Do Part": Marriage and Family in Seventeenth-Century Maryland

Lorena S. Walsh

The fabric of family life in seventeenth-century Maryland took on a markedly different texture from that found in either Old or New England. It has been argued that in Elizabethan and Stuart Britain parents had great and long-lasting influence over their children's lives. The head of the household exercised patriarchal authority over other members of the family and especially over his children, who often did not achieve economic independence until well after they reached majority. Paternal control was most evident in the father's dominant role in his children's marriages. In order to marry, a child had to have not only his parents' consent but also their economic support in the form of a marriage settlement. The choice of a mate was not just a matter of individual preference; the parents were the final arbiters of when and whom their children would marry.[1]

Englishmen who immigrated to New England were able to transfer these same patterns of behavior with relatively little disruption. They soon established and then maintained stable families and orderly communities in which fathers retained traditional authority over their children. Late marriages of men and women in strict birth order, delays in the transference of real and personal estates from fathers to sons, and residence of married children on their father's lands were characteristic of many New England families in the seventeenth century and much of the eighteenth.[2]

I would like to thank Lois Green Carr, Russell R. Menard, and James K. Somerville for thoughtful reading and comments on this essay.
    1. Peter Laslett describes this view in *The World We Have Lost* (New York, 1965), 3–4, 18–21, 78–79, 150–151, 173. See also Lawrence Stone, *The Crisis of the Aristocracy, 1558–1641* (Oxford, 1965), chap. 11, and Christopher Hill, *Society and Puritanism in Pre-Revolutionary England* (New York, 1964), chap. 13.
    2. Philip J. Greven, Jr., *Four Generations: Population, Land, and Family in Colonial*

In contrast, immigrants to the Chesapeake experienced an immediate and profound disruption in the patterns of family life, first in the selection of their mates, then in family politics, and finally in relationships with their children. As a result, traditional family arrangements were much less successfully transplanted there in the seventeenth century.

Differing demographic experience in New England and in the Chesapeake was undoubtedly one of the most important causes of the apparent differences in family life. Immigrants to the Puritan settlements included larger numbers of women and children, and they more often arrived in family groups. In addition, a much smaller proportion of the immigrants were bound laborers. Since New Englanders not only had a greater opportunity to marry but also outlived their fellows in Maryland, they raised more children. These larger families, combined with the reduction in immigration after the first decade, allowed the native-born population to dominate New England society much earlier than in Maryland, where families were smaller and significant numbers of immigrants arrived over a longer period of time. Consequently, the northern colonies more rapidly succeeded in recreating the characteristics of a settled community.

The situation in Maryland was different. A majority of the immigrants who ventured their lives in the tobacco colony were young and single, and they married late. Nearly three-quarters of them arrived as indentured servants, and neither men nor women servants were free to marry until their terms were completed. Additional years were often required to accumulate the capital necessary to establish a household. Immigrant women in Maryland usually married in their mid-twenties, and men seldom wed before their late twenties. Perhaps even more significant—since New Englanders were also late to marry—was the lack of women. Because male immigrants outnumbered female by as much as three to one, many men remained single; over one-quarter of the men who left estates in southern Maryland in the second half of the seventeenth century died unmarried.[3]

Andover, Massachusetts (Ithaca, N.Y., 1970), chaps. 4, 6, 8, 9; Daniel Scott Smith, "Parental Power and Marriage Patterns: An Analysis of Historical Trends in Hingham, Massachusetts," *Journal of Marriage and the Family*, XXXV (1973), 419–428.

3. Russell R. Menard, "The Growth of Population in Early Colonial Maryland, 1631–1712," manuscript report, St. Mary's City Commission, Hall of Records, Annapolis, Md., 1972; Menard, "Immigration to the Chesapeake Colonies in the Seventeenth Century: A Review Essay," *Maryland Historical Magazine*, LXVIII (1973), 323–329; Menard, "Immigrants and Their Increase: The Process of Population Growth in Early

Not only did the immigrants marry late, they also died very young. A man who came to Maryland in his early twenties could expect to live only about twenty more years. By age forty-five this man and many of his companions would be dead. Native-born sons fared only slightly better than their fathers. A boy reaching majority in southern Maryland before 1720 had only about twenty-five more years to live. In contrast, men reaching age twenty in the Plymouth Colony in the same period could expect to live an additional forty-eight years.[4]

The life cycle of growing up, marrying, procreating, and dying was compressed within a short span of years in seventeenth-century Maryland. Most marriages were of brief duration. One-half of the unions contracted in one Maryland county in the second half of the century were broken within seven years by the death of at least one of the partners. As a result, families were small; most couples had only two or three children.

This situation did not change significantly until rather late. Although native women married very early—between sixteen and nineteen— and were likely to bear one to two more children than had their immigrant mothers, families remained small. In the first place, immigrants constituted a majority of the population until the end of the century. Moreover, because there continued to be fewer women than men in the colony, most native-born men married only two and a half years earlier than their immigrant fathers. Since women who raised large families usually had two or more husbands, the number of children per couple remained small. Wives were twice as likely to survive their husbands in Charles County, Maryland, between 1658 and 1705 than were husbands to survive their wives. In addition, three widows married again for every widower who remarried.[5]

Colonial Maryland," in Aubrey C. Land, Lois Green Carr, and Edward C. Papenfuse, eds., *Law, Society, and Politics in Early Maryland* (Baltimore, 1977); Lorena S. Walsh, "Charles County, Maryland, 1658–1705: A Study of Chesapeake Social and Political Structure" (Ph.D. diss., Michigan State University, 1977), chap. 2. For a good general discussion of the effects of unbalanced sex ratios, see Roger Thompson, *Women in Stuart England and America: A Comparative Study* (London and Boston, 1974), chap. 2.

4. Lorena S. Walsh and Russell R. Menard, "Death in the Chesapeake: Two Life Tables for Men in Early Colonial Maryland," *Md. Hist. Mag.*, LXIX (1974), 211–227; Maris A. Vinovskis, "Mortality Rates and Trends in Massachusetts before 1860," *Journal of Economic History*, XXXII (1972), 184–213.

5. Menard, "Economy and Society in Early Colonial Maryland" (Ph.D. diss., University of Iowa, 1974), chap. 4; Walsh, "Charles County," chap. 2. The pattern of marriage survivorship in England may have been different. Among the aristocracy between 1558 and 1641 husbands were more than twice as likely to survive their wives. Stone, *Crisis of the Aristocracy*, 619–623.

These various demographic features had far-reaching effects on marriage and family relationships in the Chesapeake. However much the new immigrants may have attempted to recreate traditional procedures and norms, they found it impossible. Old World social structure and institutions were inevitably disordered in the process of transferring them across an ocean, and when combined with extreme demographic disruption, this circumstance forced alterations in the forms of marriage, in sexual mores, and in the kinds and degree of control exercised by the family.

Marriage and Family Politics

Unlike the New England Puritans, whose religious philosophy called for retention of a traditional patriarchal family structure but with a reinterpretation of the character of marriage and divorce, settlers in Maryland demonstrated no desire to reform either the laws or the attitudes about marriage then prevalent in England. Whenever conditions permitted, they followed the five steps indicated by Edmund Morgan as necessary to a proper marriage in England—espousals, publication of banns, execution of the espousal contract at church, celebration, and sexual consummation.[6]

Often, however, the austerity of a recently settled area caused some of the steps to be eliminated. As in England, all marriages were recognized as valid "that had been consummated in sexual union and preceded by a contract, either public or private, with witnesses or without, in the present tense or the future tense."[7] Espousals were probably the first step and were then frequently followed directly by the last, sexual consummation of the marriage.[8] Banns were published only irregularly until after 1696, and, with the scarcity and sometimes complete absence of clergy in a colony that banned public

6. Edmund S. Morgan, *The Puritan Family: Religion and Domestic Relations in Seventeenth-Century New England*, rev. ed. (New York, 1966), 30–32. A study of family life in 17th-century Maryland is severely handicapped by the complete absence of literary sources; one must rely almost entirely on scattered information found in court records. The discussion that follows is based largely on manuscript materials available at the Hall of Records, Annapolis, Md. The series primarily used are the Charles County Land and Court Records for the years 1658 to 1705 and Testamentary Proceedings for the same years. Materials from later volumes of the Testamentary Proceedings, from Wills, from Provincial Court records, and from Provincial Court Papers are also used.

7. Morgan, *Puritan Family*, 31.

8. The binding nature of espousals is illustrated by the fact that an intended marriage gave the surviving partner the right to administer the other's estate and to be guardian of the deceased's children. Testamentary Proceedings, XIIB, 71–73, XIV, 140.

support of religion, very few marriages, especially those of non-Catholics, were solemnized by a minister. Before justices of the peace were authorized to perform marriages, many couples simply married themselves, signifying their union by some customary ceremony such as breaking a piece of silver between them.[9]

Marriage celebrations were apparently uncommon in the seventeenth century; there are almost no records of wedding feasts until after 1700. A marriage in St. Mary's County in 1676 was thus described: "One Charles Fitzgeferis went Over St. Mary's River to St. Inegoes to be married to one Ann Townsend in Company . . . with John Sikes, John Miller, and William Wheret, and . . . they came back againe the same day to the house of the said John Sikes and there Beded as Man and Wife and from that time passed as man and wife."[10]

Giles Tomkinson, a planter, expressed very well the prevailing conception of a marriage when, in November 1665, he came to the Charles County Court to refute the charges of Constable Thomas Gibson, who "Accuseth a woman living at Gils Tomkinsons to bee illegitimately got with child":

The sayd Gils Tomkinson affirmeth in open Court that shee is and was befor the Getting of her with Child his lawfull wiffe and Confeseth himself the father of the Child shee now Goeth with and hear in Open Court alleageth that his marriage was as good as possibly it Coold bee maed by the Protestants hee beeing one because that befor that time and ever since thear hath not bin a protestant minister in the Province and that to matrimony is only

9. William Hand Browne et al., eds., Archives of Maryland . . . (Baltimore, 1883–), XLIX, xxiii, 42–43, 84–85, XLI, 456–457; Charles County Court, E#1, 145; Somerset County Deeds, IKL (Marriage register). Registration of marriages was still uncommon in the middle of the eighteenth century. In 1786 an Anglican minister, Rev. Henry Addison, stated, "If the rule was Established here that no marriage should be deemed valid that had not been registered in the Parish Book it would I am persuaded bastardize nine tenths of the People in the Country." Montgomery County Land Records #3 (C), 330.

10. Provincial Court Deeds, PL#6, 265. This argument from negative evidence seems more valid in the light of, first, abundant evidence about funeral dinners in the 17th century, in contrast to almost none about wedding celebrations, and, second, frequent reference to both in 18th-century sources. In addition, the kinds of evidence presented in court as proof of the validity of a marriage changed. Most 17th- and early 18th-century proofs were similar to the example given in the text; continued cohabitation and community acceptance of the union were the main evidence submitted. See also the discussion above on pp. 139–140. By the mid-18th century, proofs of marriage usually began by describing the wedding ceremony and subsequent celebration. For example see Montgomery County Land Records #3 (C), 326–331. Widows' applications for Revolutionary War pensions contain many such descriptions. See Revolutionary War Pension series, National Archives. The two latter sources were brought to my attention by Allan Kulikoff.

necessary the parties Consent and Publication thereof befor a lawfull Churchman and for their Consents it is Apparent and for the worlds satisfaction they hear publish themselves man and wife till death them doe part.[11]

Maryland colonists of marriageable age were peculiarly lacking in family ties. Most had come as indentured servants, and even among the free immigrants there were few family groups. When the immigrants left Europe, their break with their families was usually complete. Few of them expected ever to return to the Old World, and probably there was little communication with relatives left behind. In addition, when many immigrants came to marry, questions of property were irrelevant. An ex-servant had accumulated through his own hard labor whatever estate he brought to a marriage, and thus he was not obliged to ask anyone's consent to its disposition.

Parental control over native-born men and women in Maryland was not significantly greater than that of the immigrant generation. Because most parents died before their children reached marriageable age, native-born men and women in Maryland also frequently married without parental consent. Stepparents or guardians could prevent their charges from marrying before they were of age but could not control what they did afterwards. Up to the 1690s, most men did not marry until several years after the age of inheritance, at which time their own fathers had often been dead for some years. Thus the wishes of a man's parents infrequently entered into his decision about when and whom to marry.[12]

Somewhat more control was exercised over women, since they married much earlier than men. Because of community distaste for child brides, most guardians refused to allow, or the court instructed them to prevent, girls marrying much below the age of fourteen.[13] Orphaned women, however, generally became free to order their lives when they reached the age of inheritance—sixteen—making relatively short the period in which others could restrict their freedom to marry.[14]

Seventeenth-century marriages were unusual in other ways. Frequent disparity in the age and status of the partners characterized

11. Charles County Court, B#1, 492.
12. Table 1 confirms that one-quarter of men leaving inventories in southern Maryland between 1658 and 1705 died without ever marrying and that, of those who married, at least two-thirds left families in which all the children were under 18.
13. Charles County Court, P#1, 240; Testamentary Proceedings, XVII, 206.
14. Charles County Court, B#1, 355–356; Testamentary Proceedings, XVI, 269, XVII, 51.

many unions. Often, a man marrying for the first time was ten years older than his bride. When widowed, a woman might choose a second husband no older and perhaps younger than herself. Since many unions were broken by the early death of one of the partners, second marriages were frequent. Single men often married widows with a charge of children, and some single girls chose husbands with families by earlier wives. If both husband and wife had previously married, they were each likely to have custody of underaged offspring by their first spouses.[15] Age differences and conflicts arising from the presence of both natural children and stepchildren in the same household must have heightened tensions within a marriage.

Lack of family ties, unsettled New World conditions, and the pressures of the sex ratio all contributed to a milieu of relative sexual freedom in seventeenth-century Maryland. One result was a high rate of bridal pregnancy, especially among immigrants. In a register of marriages and births for seventeenth-century Somerset County, more than a third of the immigrant women whose marriages were recorded were pregnant by the time of the ceremony. Such a high rate of bridal pregnancy—two to three times that of many contemporary English parishes—is testimony to the extent of social disruption. There is little evidence that the community objected to this kind of sexual freedom; no presentments for bridal pregnancy appear in any of the Maryland courts.[16]

Native-born women also shared in this freedom, although to a lesser degree than their mothers. Preliminary research suggests that in the seventeenth century about one out of five Maryland-born brides was pregnant when she married. Lack of parental control was a contributing element. Orphaned girls were apparently particularly vulnerable to premarital conceptions; initial study indicates an even

15. Walsh, "Charles County," chap. 3. For a similar observation (not elaborated) about the structure of 17th-century French families, see Elizabeth Wirth Marvick, "Nature versus Nurture: Patterns and Trends in Seventeenth-Century French Child-Rearing," in Lloyd deMause, ed., *The History of Childhood* (New York, 1974), 288.

16. Russell R. Menard, "The Demography of Somerset County, Maryland: A Preliminary Report" (paper presented at the Conference on Early American Social History, Stony Brook, New York, June 1975), contains the information on bridal pregnancy. The observation on presentments for bridal pregnancy was supplied by Lois Green Carr. For rates of English premarital pregnancy see P.E.H. Hair, "Bridal Pregnancy in Rural England in Earlier Centuries," *Population Studies*, XX (1966–1967), 233–243, and N. L. Tranter, "Demographic Change in Bedfordshire, 1670–1800" (Ph.D. diss., University of Nottingham, 1966), 244, reported in J. D. Chambers, *Population, Economy, and Society in Pre-Industrial England* (London, 1972), 75.

greater frequency of bridal pregnancy among women whose fathers had died during their minority.[17]

While not approved by the community, other kinds of sexual freedom persisted after marriage. Both the lax marriage laws and the freedom of movement to another colony or back to England provided the unscrupulous with opportunity for bigamy.[18] Sarah Younger related that Alexander Younger, "pretending himselfe to bee a person free to marry being a widdower did persuade . . . her to marry him" and then took all her goods, including her children's portions, sold the land, and left for England with the proceeds. Two neighbors testified that they happened to meet Younger in London, where he introduced them to his English wife and maintained that in Maryland, Sarah was "only his Whore."[19]

The large measure of freedom that native-born children enjoyed when marrying in Maryland was as much a result of historical accident as of deliberate policy on the part of parents. In instances where parents survived until their children were of marriageable age, they tried to direct their children's marriages much as parents in New England did. Where substantial amounts of property were involved, it was essential that the prospective couple obtain their parents' consent. Sons and daughters of wealthy families, unlike many of their compatriots, could not simply marry at will. After giving consent, their parents or guardians negotiated the terms of the marriage contract, and dissatisfaction with the share offered by one of the parties could prevent a match.[20]

A surviving parent, whether affluent or of more ordinary circumstances, customarily bestowed a "portion" of his property on his children when they married and also might help the couple by extending them credit with which to buy household goods. Although not many deeds of gift at marriage were recorded, there are other indications that children customarily received their shares of their father's estate at this time. Married children were frequently granted only token bequests in their father's will, often with the notation that

17. Menard, "Demography of Somerset County, Maryland."

18. Morgan, *Puritan Family*, 31.

19. Provincial Court Deeds, WRC#1, 122–123. See also Browne *et al.*, eds., *Archives of Maryland*, XXV, 13, 22–24, 42, 140; Testamentary Proceedings, XIV, 29–30; Provincial Court Papers, St. Mary's County, *Wildman* v. *Wildman*, 1718.

20. Charles County Court, S#1, 111; Z#1, 42–49; Browne *et al.*, eds., *Archives of Maryland*, LIII, 631.

21. Charles County Court, F#1, 182–183; Q#1, 2–3; Testamentary Proceedings, XIII, 331–332; Wills, III, 475, IV, 40, V, 91, VI, 251, VII, 11, XI, 199, 381.

they had already received their due portions; gifts previously made to married offspring often were confirmed but not augmented by the will.[21] Also, in cases where a father died intestate, the county courts were ordered to determine, before apportioning the estate, which orphans had been "advanced by the Dec[ease]d in his Lifetime" and which had yet received nothing.[22] The effect of these practices must have been to give surviving parents considerable influence over their children's choice of mates.

Parents might provide for their own future maintenance as part of the marriage settlements for their children. This was uncommon simply because few parents lived long enough to see their offspring married. One who did was Christopher Kirkly, a joiner, who made over all his estate, including forty acres of land, a house, livestock, household goods, and debts receivable, to his daughter, Susannah, when she married John Vincent in 1705/6. In return he was to have "Meat Drinck washing and apparrell in the same manner and noe worse than the said John Vincent himself his heires Executors or Administrators (according to his or their ability) shall Eate Drinck or Weare." Kirkly reserved for himself one chamber, a bed, a gun, the use of a horse, his workshop and joiner's tools, and all the tobacco and money he could make from carrying on his trade.[23]

Since few parents lived to see their children married, the question of whether or not they tried to control the lives of adult offspring by retaining economic sanctions after children wed is relevant in but a few instances. Surviving parents apparently did not try to maintain such controls. Fathers did not often retain title to lands that constituted an adult son's portion, and in the few cases where land on which a son was already seated was bequeathed by will, it appears that the son had only recently reached twenty-one.[24]

Because the woman was usually younger and her parents thus more likely to be alive when she married, the wife's parents more often gave advice or intervened in a marriage than the husband's.

22. Lois Green Carr, "County Government in Maryland, 1689–1709" (Ph.D. diss., Harvard University, 1968), 352–353.
23. Charles County Court, Z#1, 227–228; K#1, 131–133; Provincial Court Deeds, WRC#1, 211–213.
24. Wills, II, 78, VII, 71, 268; Testamentary Proceedings, VI, 269. For instance, John Lewgar wrote from London in 1663 to promptly assign to his son John a warrant for 1,000 acres, "which land I hear is since layd out for my sone John and hee hath entered upon it." Charles County Court, B#1, 110.

Her family might, for example, look after her and her husband's interests in cases of inheritance. Robert Cager, Jr., was "near 21 and married" when Henry Hyde, the executor of his father's will, made his final account. The account "was first Read unto the said heire and his wifes father and Brothers then present in Court and the same was Immediately delivered unto the said Robert Cager and the heire, and notice given by the Judge heereunto him and his wifes relations . . . that they had liberty to except to the said account." Cager decided to approve the account after deliberation with his father- and brothers-in-law.[25]

Recognizing the likelihood of an early death, parents might attempt to control their children posthumously. Some fathers, prompted by a desire to provide for their widows and to keep their families together, did seek to order their children's futures through their wills. Edward Bowles, for example, gave his son Edward his entire estate, with the proviso that Edward maintain his mother in the family home "with Sufficient meat, drink, and apparrell with one room to herself and a good bed and chest."[26] If one child were of age, the father might require that he allow the younger children to live with him, so long as they remained unmarried and worked. Robert Marston received all his father's land, but with the restrictions that his two younger brothers were to live and work with him and that he would maintain them to age eighteen and his sister Elizabeth to sixteen. He was also to support another sister, Mary, then of age, so long as she was single and kept house for him.[27] A wealthier planter bequeathed his sons substantial acreage on the frontier but stipulated that they not leave their mother to settle on it until they reached age twenty-five.[28]

Restrictions on a child's future freedom of action by his parents through their wills were, however, the exception, not the rule. In the majority of cases, a father sought to give his children as much freedom as possible to order their lives after his decease, apparently feeling that flexibility rather than rigid control would best protect his children's interests in an uncertain future. This emphasis on freedom rather than on regulation was the result of a fear (often well-grounded) of the treatment the children might receive at the hands of subse-

25. Testamentary Proceedings, VI, 323–324.
26. Wills, I, 87.
27. *Ibid.*, VI, 271.
28. *Ibid.*, 241.

quent stepfathers or guardians. Sons were frequently made of age by
will at seventeen or eighteen and sometimes as young as sixteen.
Richard Jones, for example, willed that his son was "to enjoy the
benefit of his Estate in his own hands and to bee free from all
servitude at the age of sixteen either from his mother or any other
person."[29] An arrangement that allowed a measure of both freedom
and regulation was often employed. A father would direct that his
sons could act only with the consent of their guardians until age
twenty-one but that they should work "for themselves" (that is,
enjoy the proceeds of their labor) at age eighteen. In this way, the
length of time a boy labored for someone else would be minimized.
The boy could gain experience at making his own living and begin
adding to his estate, while still enjoying the legal protection and the
advice of a guardian.[30]

Precisely because he could not foresee the future, a man sometimes
maximized his children's future options by providing one or more
alternative arrangements for his family after his death. For instance,
he might will that the children were to remain with their mother
when she remarried, so long as their new stepfather did not mistreat
them, or, in the event that he did, they were to be removed to the
household of a guardian. A way of protecting both widow and child,
if the child was nearly of age, was to bind the child to his mother until
he reached majority or until she died. If the mother lived, she could
look after the child's welfare and in return might be at least partially
supported out of the proceeds of his labor. However, if she should die
before the child reached majority, he would then be free and would
not have to continue working for a stepfather after his mother's
death.[31]

If the threat of early death and resulting disruptions to family life
affected the kinds and amount of control that seventeenth-century
Maryland fathers sought to exercise over their children, these circumstances also influenced the ways in which husbands regarded their
wives. The kinds of provisions that dying husbands made for their
widows must reflect to some degree the position that married women
occupied in family politics. In St. Mary's and Charles counties over
the seventeenth century nearly three-quarters of married male testa-
tors left their widows with more than the dower the law required, a

29. *Ibid.*, 201. See also 177, VII, 320, 393.
30. *Ibid.*, IV, 189, XIII, 157; Charles County Court, X#1, 251.
31. For instance, see Charles County Court, D#1, 99; A#2, 259; Wills, V, 82, 167.

husband frequently giving his wife all or a major part of the estate for her life and usually making her his executor. This is an indication of great trust indeed, considering that the men knew that their widows were highly likely to remarry. By the standards of the time, most Maryland wives received highly favorable property settlements and were accorded an unusually influential role in managing the estate and in bringing up the children.[32]

Because a woman could not legally own property or make any contracts while married, it was essential that before remarrying, a widow safeguard her own and her children's estate while she was still *feme-sole* and free to act. Some prudent widows deeded shares of the deceased husband's estate to their children before remarrying in order to protect the children's inheritance.[33] In other cases, the marriage contract specified in detail what the second husband had to pay to the children of his wife's first marriage as their portions of their father's estate.[34] Such measures were clearly advisable in view of the speed with which remarriage frequently took place. The offspring of less prudent widows often suffered from their mother's failure to safeguard their interests.[35]

It is impossible to determine whether marriages in Maryland in this period were more or less happy than marriages in other periods and locations. That difficulties did occur is clearly demonstrated in the court records. Adultery, continual and violent quarreling, and desertion signaled the factual if not the legal end of a marriage.[36] There is ample evidence as well of other problems that might not end a marriage but that would make living together difficult: disputes over the estates of the respective partners, disagreements about the upbringing of children, and personality conflicts between husband and wife.

In Maryland, as in England, there was no divorce. Separations could be obtained in the event that the marriage contract was broken. When Robert Robins charged his wife with adultery, the couple

32. Lois Green Carr and Lorena S. Walsh, "The Planter's Wife: The Experience of White Women in Seventeenth-Century Maryland," *William and Mary Quarterly*, 3d Ser., XXXIV (1977), 542–571.

33. Testamentary Proceedings, XIV, 14–20, 116–117, XVII, 29–31; Charles County Court, V#1, 160; Provincial Court Deeds, WRC#1, 439.

34. Testamentary Proceedings, VI, 63–65, XVII, 29–31; Charles County Court, A#1, 216–217; B#1, 78; C#1, 270–271; P#1, 180; Q#1, 39.

35. Testamentary Proceedings, XIII, 1–2.

36. See Morgan, *Puritan Family*, chap. 2, and John Demos, *A Little Commonwealth: Family Life in Plymouth Colony* (New York, 1970), chap. 5.

decided to separate. Before the county clerk they "did make this their Particular declaratione": "I Robert Robins doe hearby disclayme my wife Elizabeth Robins for ever to acknowledge her as my wife and I doe hear oblige myself and everie one from mee never to molest or trouble her any further." Elizabeth made the same declaration, with the additional promise that she would not ask Robert "for maintainance or any other necessaries."[37]

Separation with maintenance by the husband might be ordered by the court in cases of extreme and prolonged incompatibility. Suits of this sort were unusual. Most couples resolved their marital difficulties by other means than legal proceedings. Anne Hardy, the wife of a Charles County justice, did resort to the courts. In 1702 she, "upon a difference betweene her and her Husband petitions that shee wth her Children may be Permitted to live upon her Owne Land and to be allowed a Sufficient maintenance to Subsist upon." In this instance two of the justices were appointed to try to compose the couple's differences. The two continued to quarrel, however, disagreeing particularly about the treatment and discipline of Anne's children by a former husband. In 1703 she complained of Hardy's "harsh and ill usage of her Children and desires they may be taken away from him and that they may all be bound out to trades." She finally petitioned in 1706 that "through his harsh and Ill Usage shee is not able to Live and Cohabitt with him and Therefore Desires with the approbation of the Court Shee may Live from him and that the Court would Order her A competency for a Separate Maintenance." Hardy agreed to a separation and "propounds to Allow her fifteen hundred pounds of Tobacco [about £5] Yearly and Every Yeare Dureing her natural Life and Doth promise and Engage to Deliver her her necessary Utencills of Cloathing and as shee is now Possest with According to the Degree of his wife." This "mutual agreement of boath partyes" was approved by the court.[38]

More frequently, unhappy spouses sought to escape unwelcome marriages by simply running away. Anthony Smith, for example, was reported in 1691 as having "absented himselfe from his sd wife Martha and hath left her destitute of any way of releiveing herselfe or to gett her livelyhood." In 1669 Elizabeth Johnson, in desperation, for several months "absented herselfe from Dan: Johnson then her hus-

37. Charles County Court, A#1, 4, 39.
38. *Ibid.*, A#2, 5, 250; B#2, 242–243. See Carr, "County Government," 189.

band and having noe place of Residence or abode Bt wandering from place to place," sought shelter from various neighbors.[39]

In many instances couples turned to relatives and neighbors rather than the courts when they encountered marital problems. Neighbors, for example, intervened on St. Clement's Manor in 1659 when Clove Mace came to the house of his neighbor John Shanks, "beinge bloudy and said that Robin Coop and his wife were both upon Him." Shanks asked another neighbor, John Gee, to go with him to Mace's house. Shanks "asked her [Mrs. Mace] to come to her husband and shee replyed that hee had abused Robin and her and . . . John Shancks gott her consent to come the next morning and Robin up to bee freinds with her . . . husband but hee would not bee freinds with her but the next night following they were freinds."[40] Wives, especially, could probably expect little sympathy from an all-male court that had a special interest in preserving the authority of husbands and fathers. Many women, trapped in unhappy marriages, probably just endured the situation.

From evidence about matches that failed, it can be deduced that colonists considered normal and exclusive sexual union, peaceful cohabitation, and economic support of the wife by the husband the minimal duties that spouses must perform. Testimony about the more positive ingredients of a marriage are more rarely encountered. A 1719 case of contested administration, however, provided an explicit discussion of contemporary attitudes about marriage.

The case involved Kenelm Cheseldyne, a substantial landowner, who died in 1718, naming his wife, Mary, as administratrix of his estate. Cheseldyne had, in fact, never married the woman with whom he had been living. At Mary's request, a number of neighbors testified that they believed that she and Cheseldyne had been man and wife because Cheseldyne had behaved in ways that defined the manner of a husband, not a paramour.[41]

The Cheseldynes' problems arose because, about 1712, they had "Marryed in private," without banns, license, clergyman, justice, or witnesses, after Mary, then the Widow Phippard, was pregnant, and possibly not until after the birth of the child. Although Cheseldyne asserted that "shee was his Lawfull wife" as much as any other

39. Charles County Court, C#1, 80; E#1, 96, 99; R#1, 279–280; Testamentary Proceedings, XIII, 458–462.
40. Browne *et al.*, eds., *Archives of Maryland*, LIII, 628.
41. Testamentary Proceedings, XXIII, 349–377.

man's, proof of Cheseldyne's marriage depended solely on their word and on community acceptance.

John Greaves testified about why he considered the couple married. He related that while he was constable he had gone to arrest Mary Phippard at Cheseldyne's because she had recently borne an illegitimate child. Cheseldyne had forewarned him "from taking her away at his perrill for that he would give his oath that there was not any such person as Mary Phippard," claiming Mary as his wife and declaring the child legitimate. Because Cheseldyne had always acknowledged Mary as his wife and because neighbors had believed they were married, Greaves had also accepted the union.

Sarah Turner, the midwife who had delivered the three children of Kenelm and Mary, testified that they were man and wife because "the said Cheseldyne particularly was at the birth of the second and seemed very fond of the child and [Mary]. . . . Cheseldyne called her his wife and took care of her as such and Owned the Children."

Benjamin Reeder, a neighbor, had inquired of Cheseldyne's kinsman, John Coode, whether or not they were married. Coode had assured him that they had been married in private. Reeder had then believed that they were, and he testified that "afterwards . . . Cheseldyne came with her publickly to Church and helped her off and on her Horse and shewed her the respect due to a wife."

Another neighbor, Thomas Bolt, once went to Cheseldyne's house, and found him "walking in his Hall with one of the Children he had by [Mary] . . . in his Armes and in discours about a certaine Mr. Donaldson who had been [at the house] but a small time before and was angry about [Mary's] . . . giving the said Donaldson's Child Indian Bread in boiled Milk . . . Cheseldyne sayd that he thought his wife knew what was best for children for says he our own Children Eat the same."

The conception of a husband expressed by these neighbors was that he always acknowledged his wife, that he appeared with her in public, that he showed affection and respect for her, and that he supported her in a condition commensurate with his means. A husband also owned the children born of the union, showed affection toward them, and cared for them. In addition, he acknowledged his wife's joint authority in their upbringing.

Bringing up Children

Colonists in seventeenth-century Maryland bore children and brought them up through the early years of life much as they themselves had been born and brought up in the Old World. In later childhood and adolescence, however, familiar patterns often broke down. Because at least one of a child's natural parents so often died early, the community was forced to take on responsibilities for the support, supervision, and education of children that had traditionally been carried out by the family. Not entirely prepared for the role so suddenly thrust upon it, the community was far from completely successful in carrying out these responsibilities.

Babies were born in the home, usually with the help of a midwife.[42] The husband was probably customarily at hand; the explanation of "his wife being neare Delivery" regularly excused men from jury duty and other official business.[43] He might be joined by his nearer neighbors as soon as they heard the delivery was in progress. They apparently went to the house in order to be among the first to view the new arrival and to celebrate the event with a round of drink.[44] When a minister was available, the infant was normally baptized within two months, otherwise baptism would be delayed until a minister arrived in the neighborhood.[45]

Infants were breast-fed, and if for some reason the mother could not nurse, a neighbor with milk to spare was hired to help nourish the baby. One such negotiation was recorded. John Ashbrooke related: "Mr. Arthur Turner came to this Deponent's house on the 25th of October last past hee Sat him downe by the table, and this Deponants wife Sukling her owne Child upon the left breast, the sayd Turner Sitting by Sayd unto this Deponants wife, Roase I see thow hast good Store. I Sir Replyed this Deponants wife. So I have thanke Godd for it wheaupon the sayd Turner Sayd hee had a Child that wanted it to which this deponant Sayd, Sir, if in Case you have I coold wish it had as much as my wife coold Spaer it."[46] Infants were occasionally also nourished by other means. Turner had previously

42. Charles County Court, A#1, 37–39, 225–227, 269; D#1, 4; S#1, 297–298; X#1, 51; Testamentary Proceedings, XXIII, 363.

43. Charles County Court, A#2, 81, 164.

44. *Ibid.*, A#1, 37; Testamentary Proceedings, XXIII, 363.

45. Charles County Court, F#1, 244; K#1, 11–12; P#1, 208, 210, 211; Q#1, 11; Y#1, 143; Testamentary Proceedings, V, 348.

46. Charles County Court, A#1, 35, 38.

approached Marie Dod about nursing the child, and she "answered Shee coold not for Shee thought She was with child herself but if hee woold have it drie nurst she woold doe her best endeavor for it."[47]

For the first two or three years of their lives, children were probably attentively cared for. Petitions for aid from the county levy to help maintain orphan infants attest to "the trouble I have with such an one," and "the Trouble of my hous with 2 small children [twins about a year and a half old] washing Lodgeing Combeing, Pickeing, nurseing and fostering them one whole yeare."[48] Until a child was able to walk well, it was carried in the arms of one of the parents when they went abroad, and very young children were probably frequently picked up and fondled. Women are often recorded as going out "with their infants in their arms," and a father was described as "walking in his Hall with one of the Children . . . in his Armes."[49]

The line between infancy and childhood was crossed at age three. A child was likely to be weaned sometime at the beginning of the second year, and a new baby might be expected by the end of it.[50] One or both of these events apparently signified the transition from the status of infant to that of "little adult." A child's chances of surviving to maturity also improved about the third birthday. This fact was reflected in public policy. The county courts authorized payment from public taxes to persons who cared for orphans without estates until they were two years old. Thereafter orphans, in theory, paid for their maintenance through their own labor. Clearly, a child of three or four would not be able to do much work, so the custom of public payments for early care must have taken into account a high infant death rate. The chances of a baby not living to repay the costs of its care were apparently so great that public compensation was necessary to induce a couple to take charge of an orphaned infant. Conversely, masters were willing to accept the risk for children above age three.[51]

47. *Ibid.*, 38.
48. *Ibid.*, I#1, 230; X#1, 303; Y#1, 13, 130.
49. *Ibid.*, A#1, 4, 32; B#1, 145–150; Testamentary Proceedings, XXIII, 365–366.
50. Demos, *A Little Commonwealth*, 135–136. See also Alan Macfarlane, *The Family Life of Ralph Josselin, A Seventeenth-Century Clergyman: An Essay in Historical Anthropology* (Cambridge, 1970), 87–88, and appendix A, for a similar example of the effect of breast-feeding on birth intervals.
51. Carr, "County Government," 346–347; Charles County Court, A#1, 37; C#1, 244; F#1, 13; H#1, 105, 242; I#1, 124, 230–231; K#1, 84; L#1, 71; Y#1, 143; B#2, 3. A child was able to produce substantial returns by his labor beginning between ages eight and ten. Testamentary Proceedings, XIIB, 238–254; Provincial Court Judgments,

From an examination of period inventories something can be learned about the material conditions in which children were raised. It appears that whatever toys children may have had were homemade and of so little worth that they were never valued. Since most houses were quite small, usually just one or two rooms, children generally slept with their brothers and sisters in the same room as their parents or in a loft above. Most children were provided with but one new suit of clothes and a pair of shoes and stockings per year. They might in addition be given combs, and boys perhaps received pocket knives. There was little in a typical merchant's stock that was designed specifically for the young, aside from clothing, which, except in the case of infants, apparently differed from that of adults merely in size. Probably the single treat that a parent might ever purchase for his children at the store would be a little sugar.[52]

Usually the only valuable thing children possessed was livestock. Frequently a father would register a separate livestock mark for each child, and when his stock gave birth he would present the child with an animal of his own. Grandparents, uncles and aunts, and godparents might also give a favorite child livestock. Gifts of animals were the seventeenth-century equivalent of opening a bank account or purchasing a savings bond for a child today.[53]

The most frightening aspect of childhood in the seventeenth century must have been the genuine uncertainty of the future. Most children could expect that at least one, or perhaps both, of their parents would die before they were old enough to care for themselves. In southern Maryland between 1658 and 1705, 67 percent of married or widowed male decedents left all minor children, while only 6 percent left all adult children.[54] Hence, in the best of circumstances, minor orphans

DSC, 55–56; Charles County Court, E#1, 81. Apparently Englishmen shared similar expectations for children, at least those of the poorer classes. Locke in his *Report for the Reform of the Poor Law* (1697) proposed that "working schools" be set up for poor children between the ages of three and fourteen so that "from their infancy [they] be inured to work. . . . " Quoted in Joseph E. Illick, "Child-Rearing in Seventeenth-Century England and America," in deMause, ed., *History of Childhood*, 341.

52. Testamentary Proceedings, VI, 118–146; Inventories and Accounts, WB#3, 718; XXV, 390, XXII, 99. See Laslett, *World We Have Lost*, 105, for the similar condition of children in England.

53. See, for example, Charles County Court, A#1, 66, 110, 138; B#1, 111, 243; D#1, 5, 6; E#1, 34, 101.

54. "Social Stratification in Maryland, 1658–1705," a study of Maryland inventories conducted by P.M.G. Harris, Russell R. Menard, and Lois Green Carr under the auspices of the St. Mary's City Commission and with funds from the National Science Foundation (GS-32272).

would have to adjust to a new stepparent and subsequently learn to live with stepbrothers and sisters. The potential for conflict was great in situations where children of more than one marriage lived together in a family. Each parent naturally tended to favor his own children and to discriminate against those from a partner's previous marriage. Parental favoritism only heightened conflicts between stepchildren already competing for their parents' attention and affection.

Complaints of ill treatment by stepparents were legion. Margaret O'Daniell protested about her stepfather, Thomas Denton: "Your pet[itione]r after her father's decease, lived with . . . Thomas Denton about 9 yeares as his servant working for him at the Hoe, as hard as any servant, and when hee saw, shee would marry, hee put her off, without any clothes or shift to her back, that was good for anything, soe that her husband was forced to buy her necessaries, and now refuseth to give her anything of her fathers estate or her owne."[55] Stepparents sometimes went so far as to try to rid themselves entirely of stepchildren. Thomas Price was presented in 1696 "by the Information of Hannah Price his wife for selling a child of the sd Hannahs which shee had by another Husband in the Colony of Virginia."[56] Enough suspicion was aroused by the death of Katherine Lee that her stepmother was accused, but later acquitted, of poisoning her.[57]

Although the county court acted to remove children from the custody of patently abusive stepparents, it firmly maintained the stepparent's right to compensation for raising another's offspring. Almost every orphan was expected to work to some degree for his maintenance, since by law only the income from his inheritance—not the principal—could be used for the child's upbringing. In this period few estates were large enough to so support an orphan.[58]

Mothers who were unable to remarry quickly or otherwise support their orphans had no choice but to put the children out. For example, Mary Empson, age four, was given to another family to raise, in return for four cows, because her mother was too poor to keep her

55. Testamentary Proceedings, IX, 512–515.
56. Charles County Court, V#1, 1.
57. *Ibid.*, P#1, 123.
58. *Ibid.*, B#2, 129; F#1, 199; Browne *et al.*, eds., *Archives of Maryland*, LXII, 302; Wills, IV, 313; Carr, "County Government," 340–347. In this period an orphan was defined as a child whose father had died. The mother could be the guardian only if she could give the bond required to ensure payment of the child's portion, and she was accountable to the court for the condition of the child and his property. If she remarried and was then *feme covert*, the new husband was required to give bond, or else the court would appoint other guardians, at least to care for the property.

after her father died. Often, a remarried woman sought to buy back the children she had been forced to bind out after the death of her first husband. Fatherless children were put out to others often while quite young. Their only advantages over other servants were that they could not be sold to other masters and that the mother was sometimes able to mitigate treatment and conditions of labor and to stipulate that they receive some education.

The fate of children who lost both parents might be even worse. Seldom were there surviving relatives to take them in. Unless they had a large estate, the county court bound them out to labor for someone else until they reached majority.[59] The court was responsible for overseeing the treatment of all orphans, and each year a special jury inquired into their welfare. If children were mistreated or their property embezzled, the court was supposed to place them with other masters or guardians.[60]

The experience of the Watts children in St. Mary's County tells much about the standards of care expected as well as about abuses. William Watts died in 1678, two years after his wife, leaving three sons: Charles, eight, William, six, and Edward, four. The children's grandfather protested in 1682 about the treatment accorded them by their acting guardian, Gerrard Slye, the executor of Watts's estate: "I never know any bastard Children in the Province soe used as to victualls and Cloathes and Labour as his Grand Children. . . . They have noe manner of Cloathes but such Raggs and old Clouts that scarce would cover their nakedness and those given them by the charity of others and as to victualls nothing allowed this present year but salt and hominy and half a bull for meate amongst all the family."

A laborer, Richard Craine, added further testimony. Captain Slye had given him the eldest Watts son at age ten to work for half a share. Craine told Slye the boy was not able to perform such labor, as did John Sheppard, the cooper, but Slye replied that their estate would not maintain them and that if Craine would not take the boy, he would put him to another quarter. So Craine worked Charles for two years and for the last year had worked the next youngest at planting

59. Charles County Court, A#1, 145; M#1, 221; V#1, 310; Y#1, 78, 100; A#2, 131, 260; B#2, 141; Testamentary Proceedings, VIII, 355; Carr, "County Government," 345.
60. Charles County Court, I#1, 259. For a discussion of the jurisdiction and functioning of the orphans' court in Maryland, see Lois Green Carr, "The Development of the Maryland Orphans' Court, 1654–1715," in Land, Carr, and Papenfuse, eds., *Law, Society, and Politics.*

corn and suckering tobacco. For clothes, Craine testified, the last year the two eldest had a yard of linen apiece and a pair of shoes and stockings and the youngest only an ozenbuck frock, "so that for the most part of this Last yeare they were almost quite naked only a paire of drawers apice that this deponent made them of Sacking Cloath."

One neighbor swore "that they were putt to unreasonable Labour supposing them to have been bastard Children much more orphants that had an Estate left them." A stranger to the quarter testified that, when he had asked who the naked and ragged children were, a woman had told him that the children were put to hard work, had little or no clothes, "and were saddly beaten and abused by the overseer as tyed up by the hands and whipt." The Chief Judge of Probate agreed that the orphans "have not the Common Care had of them as is usuall for planters to have of their meanest Serv[an]ts or Slaves" and recommended that the county court put them in their grandfather's custody. There were delays, however, and not until two years later were the children finally put in their grandfather's hands.[61]

This sad history shows that the community expected orphans to be at least minimally clothed and fed. Second, it suggests that there was some concept of "children's work." Witnesses stated that expecting a ten-year-old to raise a crop half the size of that grown by an adult was "unreasonable." The older boy must have been performing tasks in the field more laborious than those performed by the younger—planting corn and suckering tobacco. Perhaps these latter jobs were among those regularly assigned to young children. Third, flogging of children was clearly not an accepted method of discipline. Fourth, it was expected that orphans be accorded different treatment depending on the size of the estate left them. Bastard children could expect nothing beyond minimal maintenance. Legitimate children with no estates were accorded a higher status than the illegitimate but probably were given little more in the way of food and clothing and were also expected to work to cover the costs of their care. Orphans with inheritances were supposed to be better maintained and apparently were required to work less. Such children were to "be kept from Idleness," but they were not to be "Kept as Comon Servants" working continually at routine tasks.

61. Testamentary Proceedings, XIIB, 238–254, XIII, 135–139. For similar cases see Testamentary Proceedings, X, 312–313, XVII, 122.

Because of the real uncertainty of a parent's survival, the choice of godparents for his child was an important decision. The practice of naming godparents was probably most common in southern Maryland among Catholic families, who had greater access to the sacrament of baptism, but Protestant couples named them also. The godparent promised to see that the godchild was brought up in the natural parents' religion, and should the child be orphaned, this promise could theoretically include raising and educating the child. Many godparents took these duties very seriously. Frequently they made some gift to their godchildren in their lifetime such as a cow, horse, or sheep; others left livestock or some personal belonging in their wills. In the event that a man had no children of his own, he might will a substantial portion of his estate to his godchildren. When one or both parents died, a child's godparents might provide a home and some education; because of the special interest that godparents might take in orphans, county courts often preferred to bind the children to their godparents rather than to more indifferent masters.[62]

Of course, the lives of all orphans were not so dismal as those in some of the preceding illustrations. Neighbors, family friends, or other relatives might supply kindness and support. Nevertheless, the wicked stepfather and the brutal master of today's "fairy stories" were often real persons in the lives of seventeenth-century Maryland children.

There are suggestions that, among boys at least, something of an adolescent crisis may have occurred. Not all children exhibited the "dutifull behaviour" expected of them. Especially in families where the father had died, teenaged sons argued with their parents, sought to escape from work and from the authority of others, spent their inheritances imprudently, and got into scrapes with the law.

Older men often commented on the lack of industry and self-discipline they saw in younger charges. A father complained that his stepson, age seventeen, "takes to idle company, absents himself from the house and endeavours to get his freedom."[63] Another man described his future stepson as "a young Wilde and dissolute person much given to Company Keeping and of such as are debouched and rude fellows, and that hee is uncapable of managing his own estate

62. *Ibid.*, A#1, 95; E#1, 132; P#1, 195; S#1, 402; V#1, 126; Y#1, 16, 311; Z#1, 160; Testamentary Proceedings, IV, 9–10, XIIB, 71–73, XIV, 21–23; Wills I, 379, II, 102, III, 638, VI, 93, 181, 342, XI, 377.
63. Charles County Court, B#2, 129.

left by his father being Considerable but living up and downe, or to and fro the County one weeke in one place and a fortnight in another letting his estate fall to Ruine and decay for want of Management."[64] William Dent willed that his children have their estates in Maryland delivered to them at age seventeen, but admonished, "I will not have any of the boys to have their Moneys in England till twenty one yeares to the intent that if they Take loose and Idle Courses here which Godd for bidd they may have one after game more to play by which time they may see their former folly and amend."[65] Since girls generally assumed adult roles earlier than their brothers, there was less time for conflict with parents to develop. For a girl, marriage frequently proved an easy escape from an unhappy home situation.

The education that children received was supposed to suit their station, and might be practical or academic or both. Apprenticeship was a common method of educating children in many places, but as practiced in southern Maryland in the seventeenth century, it was mainly a means for teaching trades, including planting, to orphans. Until the late 1690s very few fathers bound out their children; when families were not broken up by the early death of the father, both sons and daughters were kept at home. Rather, it was the widows who insured that their orphaned sons were cared for and taught how to earn a living through apprenticeship and that their orphaned daughters were provided for by binding them out to learn house-keeping.[66] Unlike the New England area, where nonagricultural trades developed, the labor-intensive, staple crop economy of the Chesa-peake offered no rationale for apprenticing children to trades when their labor was needed in the family's fields.

The criterion of an academic education was the ability "to read distinctly in the Bible." Usually it was expected that children could achieve this proficiency with two years of instruction.[67] Literate parents frequently taught their own children to read or perhaps sent them to another relative for instruction. A schoolmaster might then be employed in the home for six months to a year to teach writing or accounting. Generally the latter instruction was reserved for boys. After being taught to read, girls were put to sewing "and Such other

64. Testamentary Proceedings, IX, 174–178.
65. Wills, III, 475–480.
66. Walsh, "Charles County," chap. 3.
67. Charles County Court, A#1, 16–17; Y#1, 209, 311; A#2, 306; B#2, 129, 174; Wills, IV, 201, VI, 93, XI, 199; Inventories and Accounts, XIIIB, 122.

Education as is suitable for Woomen." Less frequently, both boys and girls might also be sent for a season or so to a boarding school. Such an education served two purposes. It conferred an advantage in making a living, and it enabled the child to gain a firsthand knowledge of the Bible.[68]

The age at which children received their education varied widely. Thomas Dickinson's father willed in 1673 that his son, then age sixteen, should have two years' schooling and then be put to work. Robert Cole's five children ranged in age from five to twelve years when they were first instructed. William Hawton directed that his godchild, Richard Smoot, have two years' schooling at age seven or eight. Clearly there was a danger that children who received their education when quite young might "forgett their learning" before they came of age unless parents or guardians saw that their lessons were periodically reviewed.[69]

The paucity of education so often noted in the colonial South was probably as much a result of a short life expectancy as it was of the absence of towns and the low density of settlement. Parents often did not live long enough to oversee their children's education or to teach them whatever they themselves knew. Guardians, stepparents, or masters were not likely to have the same interest in seeing that a child was educated as would his own parents. Toward the end of the century, it was more and more often stipulated in indentures that an orphan receive some education, usually that boys be taught to read and write and that girls learn to read distinctly from the Bible.[70] Unless the mother lived long enough to enforce the contract, however, the children frequently may not have gotten the specified instruction. If an apprentice complained to the courts that he had not received the education to which he was entitled by his indenture, he was frequently awarded monetary compensation instead of remedial instruction.[71]

Even when an orphan could be educated out of the proceeds of his own estate, his guardian might not attend to it. Colonel John Courts

68. Testamentary Proceedings, VI, 118–146; XIIB, 71–73; Charles County Court, A#1, 13–14; G#1, 1; S#1, 430; X#1, 130, 343; Y#1, 16, 176, 311; A#2, 386; B#2, 5; Wills, IV, 189, XII, 14.

69. Wills, I, 182–186, II, 78, XI, 377; Testamentary Proceedings, VI, 118–146.

70. See, for example, Charles County Court, K#1, 209; S#1, 402; V#1, 126, 164, 310, 454; X#1, 130; Y#1, 35, 129, 209, 340.

71. Charles County Court, S#1, 402; V#1, 410; X#1, 50, 375; B#2, 175; Carr, "County Government," 344.

complained about the situation of his godson, John Warren, the orphan of a wealthy Charles County planter and justice of the peace. Warren's father and two subsequent guardians had died during his minority, and he was then in the custody of the widow of the second guardian, who, Courts maintained

is but a woman and I believe has a great deale of business of her owne to mind. . . . [Warren was being] brought up to nothing but idlenesse, swearing and all other ill vices. She hath pretended to put him to schoole to Mr. Potter about 4 months agoe after that shee heard that I did intend to move the Court about him; I will testify that hee has not been att schoole above fifteene days in the four months. . . . [Courts promised to] keepe him close to schoole untill I have learned him to read and write a legible hand and to cast account as farr as the Rule of Three, and after soe done to learn him to know how to gett his living and that hee shall have the same in dyett lodging and apparrell as well as my owne Children or little worse.[72]

Of course, neglect of education was not so serious a matter then as now. Many of those children who received no education at all prospered as adults. Literacy was not necessary for economic success. Nevertheless, in Maryland, as in England, most of those who held positions of real power had at least a minimal education.[73] From the period of first settlement, parents were concerned that their children be "brought up in Civility good litterature and the feare of God," but the struggle just to stay alive often made this goal impossible to achieve.

By the turn of the century, demographic conditions were changing. Immigration to the Chesapeake slowed after 1700, a substantial number of native-born children were coming of age, and many single men were leaving the settled regions of southern Maryland for areas that offered more opportunity. Thus the proportion of men and women was becoming more equal. More men were able to marry, and they often could do so by the time they reached majority. The age at marriage for women remained low, and as a result the birthrate increased and native-born finally outnumbered immigrant in the population. Life expectancy also increased somewhat for those born after 1700.[74]

72. Charles County Court, Y#1, 311–312.
73. Russell R. Menard, "From Servant to Freeholder: Status Mobility and Property Accumulation in Seventeenth-Century Maryland," WMQ, 3d Ser., XXX (1973), 47, 56–57; Laslett, World We Have Lost, 19, 65–66.
74. Walsh, "Charles County," chap. 2; Menard, "Growth of Population." The fall

As a consequence of a longer life span and a more uniformly early age at marriage, many more parents lived to raise their children to maturity and to see them married. In addition, when one or both parents did die before their children were of age, in a society in which the majority were native born, kin were much more often present.[75] Eighteenth-century orphaned minor children usually had uncles, step-uncles, aunts, cousins, older siblings or step-siblings, or other relations under whose oversight they might fall. Previously, many a father, fearing the consequences of his early death for his family, had given his children as much freedom as possible to control their lives after his demise. By the early eighteenth century, parents were more often able to reassert control over the lives of their maturing offspring.

Family life in colonial Maryland throughout the seventeenth century had in contrast been gravely affected by the extreme demographic disruption that occurred in the process of transplanting Old World population and civilization to the New. In concert, unbalanced sex ratios, various economic impediments to early marriage, and short life spans virtually guaranteed that marriages would be brief and that often the futures of the offspring born to these unions would be uncertain. In these circumstances traditional controls over sexual behavior and marriage formation broke down, as did to a great extent patriarchal authority over wives and children. Fathers who survived to see their children become adults often tried to direct their children's lives in a traditional manner, but few lived that long. The majority died while their children were still minors, and while some responded to anxiety about their family's future by attempting to restrict their children's subsequent careers, others reacted by bequeathing their offspring a large measure of freedom. So long as immigrants continued to predominate in the population, family life continued to be brief, soon broken by the early death of one or both of the parents, and usually unreinforced by the presence in Maryland of other kin. Consequently the community had to take on major responsibilities for the support, supervision, and education of a good proportion of the first generation of children born in the colony. In human terms, the initial costs of peopling Maryland had been high indeed.

in age at marriage was dramatic. Men born in the 1670–1679 cohort married at a mean age of 26, while those born in the 1680–1689 cohort married at a mean age of 20. Those born in 1690–1699 married at a mean age of 22. An improvement in life expectancy in the 18th century is demonstrated in the unpublished research of Paul G. E. Clemens of Rutgers University and in Allan Kulikoff, "Tobacco and Slaves: Population, Economy,

TABLE 1. Marital Status and Life Cycle of Southern Maryland Decedents, 1658–1705

Date	Total No. Male Decedents	No. Single	No. Married	No. Widowers	No. Unknown	Life Cycle				
						1	2	3	4	5
1658–1669	158	50	85	21	2	88	15	3	1	3
1670–1679	380	125	209	45	1	197	21	10	4	21
1680–1689	380	111	231	33	5	187	23	18	7	46
1690–1699	459	95	285	50	29	211	46	26	6	97
1700–1705	294	55	170	49	20	105	38	28	5	72
Total	1671	436	980	198	57	788	143	85	23	239

Key to life cycles:
1. has been married, all children under 18
2. has been married, some children under 18, some children over 18
3. has been married, all children over 18
4. not number 1
5. cycle unknown

Source:
A study of Maryland inventories, "Social Stratification in Maryland, 1658–1705," being conducted by P. M. G. Harris, Russell Menard, and Lois Green Carr under the auspices of the St. Mary's City Commission and with funds from the National Science Foundation (GS-32272).

---

and Society in Eighteenth-Century Prince George's County, Maryland" (Ph.D. diss., Brandeis University, 1976), chap. 3.

75. An increase in kin ties is demonstrated in preliminary analysis by the St. Mary's City Commission of early 18th-century St. Mary's County wills and in biographical studies of county decedents who left inventories.

5

"Now-Wives and Sons-in-Law": Parental Death in a Seventeenth-Century Virginia County

Darrett B. and Anita H. Rutman

"In the name of God Amen . . ." With the customary words Maximilian Petty, "planter" and undersheriff of Middlesex County, Virginia, "sick and weake in Body," began his last will and testament in the closing days of 1687. To his God he bequeathed his soul, to the grave his body, and to his wife and children "those Worldly Goods the Lord hath lent me."[1] Within a matter of weeks after writing his will Petty was dead; his wife, Christian, was a young widow; and his two children, Maximilian and Ann, were fatherless. Young Max was just ten, Ann seven and a half.

To us in the twentieth century there is a sadness to such a death. The plight of young widowhood and of fatherless children is enough of an anomaly in our society to give us pause. But there was no such anomaly in late seventeenth–century Virginia. Indeed, few of the children of this time and place reached their majority without losing at least one parent, while over a third lost both. Parental death was a part of the fabric of life.

The extensiveness of parental death in early Virginia shows itself in the course of an in-depth study of community organization and life-

Over the years the larger study of Community Organization and Life Style in Middlesex County, Virginia: 1650–1750—of which this essay is a part—has been supported by the Central University Research Fund of the University of New Hampshire, the American Council of Learned Societies through its Committee for Computer-Oriented Research in the Humanities, and the National Endowment for the Humanities.

1. Middlesex County, Virginia, Wills, Etc., 1675–1798, Pt. 1, p. 54; *The Parish Register of Christ Church, Middlesex County, Va., from 1653 to 1812* (Richmond, Va., 1897), 36. All manuscript county records cited are to be found in the Virginia State Library, Richmond. Dates throughout are given in the original (Julian) form, but the year has been adjusted to make January 1 a consistent New Year's day.

style in one county—Petty's own Middlesex.[2] A long splinter of land
bounded by the Rappahannock River and Chesapeake Bay on the
north and east, the Piankatank River and Dragon Swamp on the
south and west, Middlesex was first settled about mid-century. From
York River and the Eastern Shore, from Northumberland on the
Potomac, and from England, men and women had entered the land,
some simply to take up acreage, resell, then move on, but most to
settle permanently, raising corn and tobacco, cattle and children.
(Richard Perrott, Jr., born in February 1651, was, as the parish register
carefully noted, "the first Man Child that was gott and borne In
Rappahannock River of English parents.")[3] Servants and free laborers
arrived, worked for a time, then moved on or found land in the
county to patent, buy, or rent. Very quickly a permanent, stable
population appeared. By the late 1660s, when both the county and
the coterminous parish of Christ Church had been organized, the
area was home to some 90 families. In 1687 a militia report on the
households of the county capable of supplying horses and arms for
defensive purposes gives indication of 142 families, while a best
estimate places the total population at 1,225.[4] Just over a generation
later (1724) the minister of Christ Church reported to the bishop of
London that there were some 260 white families in his parish, while
the total population can be estimated at 1,560 white men, women,
and children and 820-odd blacks.[5] Names from the earliest days of
the county—Perrott, Wormeley, Kemp, Minor, Tuggle—were still
there one, two, three generations later (some are even still there

2. See appendix for "A Note on the Sources and Method" which underlie this
study. It will be obvious from that note that full citation would be overly extensive and
redundant. The footnotes below will be confined to direct quotations and a few salient
points.

3. *Parish Register of Christ Church*, 41.

4. Tithable List, Nov. 1668, Lancaster County, Orders, Etc., No. 1, 1666–1680,
pp. 86–87, extracting those residing in what would become Middlesex; Militia List,
1687, Middlesex County, Order Book No. 2, 1680–1694, pp. 317–319; for tithable counts
for 1686, 1687, and 1688 see *ibid.*, p. 274, and C. G. Chamberlayne, ed., *The Vestry Book
of Christ Church Parish, Middlesex County, Virginia, 1663–1767* (Richmond, Va., 1927), 51,
57, 60. A crude multiplier to convert from tithables to population (1.9) can be constructed from the count of tithables and untithables forwarded by the county court in
1701 (C.O. 5/1312, 19, 10, Public Record Office). Every test indicates it is a sounder
multiplier for this specific place and time than the general multiplier offered by Evarts B.
Greene and Virginia D. Harrington, *American Population before the Federal Census of 1790*
(New York, 1932), xxiii. The militia list is very inaccurately transcribed in William
Armstrong Crozier, ed., *Virginia Colonial Militia, 1651–1776* (New York, 1905), 98–99.

5. William Wilson Manross, comp., *The Fulham Papers in the Lambeth Palace Library:
American Colonial Section, Calendar and Indexes* (Oxford, 1965), 177.

today). Some names disappeared as surnames but cropped up subsequently as first names, indicative of family memories of family ties.
There are no Eltonhead surnames in the parish register, for example,
but the 1678 entry of the birth of Eltonhead Stanard is in a real sense a
memorial to four Eltonhead sisters who underlie so many Middlesex
families—Agatha, who married first Ralph Wormeley, then Sir Henry
Chicheley; Alice, who married, in order, Rowland Burnham, Henry
Corbin, and Henry Creek; Eleanor, wife of Middlesex's William Bro-
cas, then Lancaster's John Carter (living just across the Rappahannock
on Corotoman Creek); and Martha, who married Edwin Conaway
and was the grandmother of the Eltonhead Stanard of 1678. Marriage
and remarriage was a way of life, and in its complexities one first
senses the magnitude of parental loss.[6]

Mary, the wife of George Keeble, for example: Her parentage is
unknown, but from her gravestone we know that she was born about
1637 and presumably had seven children by Keeble prior to finding
herself widowed at about twenty-nine years of age. At least four of
these children (Walter, Mary, George, and Margaret) were alive when
she married Robert Beverley in 1666, shortly after Keeble's death. By
Beverley she had five more children (Peter, Robert, Harry, John, and
Mary). She died in 1678 at the age of forty-one, and Robert Beverley
almost immediately remarried. His new wife, Katherine, was herself
recently widowed by the death of Major Theophilus Hone. So quick
was the remarriage that Major Hone's personal property was already
in the Beverley house by the time the inventory of it was taken.[7]
Dropping into the Beverley household in 1680, just after this most
recent marriage, we conceivably would have found Keeble children
(those of Mary and George), at least one Hone child (Theophilus, Jr.),
Beverley children by Robert and Mary, and the first of four Beverley
children by Robert and Katherine—William Beverley, born in 1680.

6. Here and there in the literature of Anglo-America one finds allusions to parental
loss. Peter Laslett, *The World We Have Lost: England before the Industrial Age* (New York,
1965), 95–96, refers to the evil stepmother of fairy tales and to his Clayworth study (in
May 1688, 35.5% of all the children alive in Clayworth were orphans) in commenting
upon "the society of the pre-industrial world" being "inured to bereavement and the
shortness of life." Joseph E. Illick in a parenthetical expression in his "Child-Rearing in
Seventeenth-Century England and America," in Lloyd deMause, ed., *The History of
Childhood* (New York, 1974), 321, notes that "the likelihood of both natural parents surviving until a child reached his majority was not high," and cites five autobiographies
and "the popularity of such tales as *Cinderella*" (p. 344). But we have found no systematic study of the extent of such loss or any suggestions as to its ramifications.
7. Middlesex County, Order Book No. 1, 1673–1680, p. 208.

Thomas, Katherine, and Christopher Beverley would follow prior to Robert Beverley's death in 1687. His widow, Katherine, immediately married Christopher Robinson; in the vernacular of genealogists she was now Katherine (Armistead) Hone-Beverley-Robinson.[8] Robinson himself was a widower, having lost his wife Agatha Hobert in 1686 (four of their children survived—Anne, Christopher, Clara, John); Katherine would bear four more children before her death in 1692 (Elizabeth, Clara, another Theophilus—her earlier son by Major Hone having died[9]—and Benjamin). The chain of marriages and remarriages finally broke the next year with the death of Christopher Robinson. In sum, the progeny of six marriages among seven people amounted to twenty-five known children. Not one of these children could have grown to maturity without losing at least one parent and passing through a period under a stepparent.

Such examples could be multiplied. Another Armistead—Elizabeth—married Ralph Wormeley in 1688. Wormeley was at the time a widower with two known children by his first wife, Katherine Luntsford, who herself had been a widow when she married Ralph. Three children are known to have been born to Ralph and Elizabeth. Widowed in 1701, Elizabeth married the widower William Churchill, whose wife Susanna had been a widow with two known children. Churchill and Elizabeth themselves had three known children. In all, five marriages among seven people are known to have produced ten children. Only two of these ten—Susanna Churchill's two children by her first husband—could possibly have grown to maturity without knowing the loss of a parent, and that possibility exists solely because we cannot yet determine with certainty the children's birth dates. Even when the complex skein of marriage and remarriage is not in evidence, reconstituted families exemplify parental loss. Richard Perrott, Jr., Rappahannock River's first English "Man Child," married only once. His fifteen-year-old bride, Sarah (Curtis) Halfhide was already a widow, but presumably her marriage to William Halfhide had been brief and childless. In 1693 both Richard and Sarah died; of the eight known children of their twenty-one-year marriage, the eldest was

8. The assumption that Katherine was an Armistead rests on Christopher Robinson's will printed in *Virginia Magazine of History and Biography*, VII (1899–1900), 17–23. See also the note pertaining to Maj. Theophilus Hone, *ibid.*, iV (1896–1897), 4.

9. The frequent practice of giving subsequent children the same names as earlier children who had died explains other name duplication in this section, but not all. Note Christopher son of Katherine and Robert Beverley, and Christopher son of Agatha and Christopher Robinson.

nineteen at the time of his parents' death, the youngest four, and six in all were under fifteen.

For all the examples of children losing parents, however, there are examples to the contrary. Four of the five known children of Ezekias and Elizabeth Rhodes who survived to maturity were married by the time Ezekias died in January 1717. (His widow lived on until 1727.) The fifth child, William, was eighteen at the time his father died. Peter and Eleanor Brummell's four known children were married before their parents' death. So, too, were the four surviving children of John and Mary Brim. With examples on both sides, the question becomes one of representativeness: Which set of examples best states the main trend?

The answer in part lies in the vital statistics for Middlesex's men and women. At what age did they marry? At what age die? How many of the children of their marriages could they possibly see to maturity? Seventeenth-century observers have left suggestive hints about the demographic situation. A traveler to Virginia in the late 1680s noted that he had "met few old people"; in the same decade John Clayton, Virginia's scientific parson, wrote that "if the English live past 33 they generally live to a good age" but "many die between 30 and 33"; and William Fitzhugh, writing in 1687, when he was thirty-six, looked upon himself as in his "declining age."[10] But this sort of fragmented and subjective information does not give us the precision and the neutral vantage point that are required to answer the questions we have set.

Despite the difficulties, and although our study of Middlesex is not yet definitive, we have been able to make some progress in compiling the vital statistics of the county's population in the seventeenth century. Middlesex's first generation was an immigrant generation; evidence of birth dates—essential to such considerations—is scattered though the records of older counties and in England, and is therefore difficult to recover. Yet enough material on the first and second generations (those born through 1710) has been gathered to allow

10. Gilbert Chinard, ed., *A Huguenot Exile in Virginia: or Voyages of a Frenchman Exiled for His Religion with a Description of Virginia and Maryland* (New York, 1934), 173; "A letter from the Revd Mr: John Clayton . . . in answer to several Querys . . . A.D. 1687," in Edmund and Dorothy Smith Berkeley, eds., *The Reverend John Clayton, A Parson with a Scientific Mind: His Scientific Writings and Other Related Papers* (Charlottesville, Va., 1965), 39; Fitzhugh to Nicholas Hayward, Jan. 30, 1687, in Richard Beale Davis, ed., *William Fitzhugh and His Chesapeake World, 1676–1701: The Fitzhugh Letters and Other Documents* (Chapel Hill, N.C., 1963), 203.

the construction of a tentative table of life expectancies (table 2 below), while an availability sample allows a tentative estimate of the median age of first marriage. On the basis of these figures we can hypothesize Middlesex's median couple, a highly idealized concept, we stress, a couple that does the most improbable of all things—live strictly according to statistical expectations. Presuming that, for both husband and wife, the marriage was a first marriage, he would be just turned 24, she just 20. In the course of their marriage they would have between four and six children, perhaps one of which would die in infancy, in some instances leaving no record but a gap in the progression of recorded births or baptismal dates of children born to the mother. Four or five would survive, however. In the normal course of events, and leaving room for the probability of a fetal death or a child who did not survive, these children would be born when the wife was 21, 24, 30, 34, and 37. The wife of this median marriage could be expected to die at 39, leaving in her husband's care children who were 18, 15, 9, 5, and 1. The husband, 43 at the death of his first wife, would probably remarry almost immediately and have still other children. But he could be expected to die in turn at 48. The children of his first marriage, now orphaned, would be 23, 20, 14, 10, and 6 respectively; any children of his second marriage, losing their father, would be even younger.

The marriage sketched above (and in figure 1) is hypothetical and based on tentative statistics. Yet that, very roughly, it reflects a reality is suggested by a sample of 239 children for whom the requisite data exist as to date of birth and the death dates of parents.[11] The sample indicates that almost a quarter of Middlesex's children suffered the loss of one or both parents by the time of their fifth birthday, and over half by the time of their thirteenth birthday. And 73.2 percent had lost one or both parents by the time they reached twenty-one or married, whichever came first (table 1).[12] To put the results another way: The

11. The subject children were those born to the wives of men listed in the 1687 militia list for whom firm information as to date of birth and parental death dates was available. Given the nature of the list—ranging from older men with many years of marriage behind them to young men newly married, but more of the latter than the former—the distribution of birth dates of the subject children, as expected, concentrated in the period immediately surrounding the date of the list yet spanned a range of years with large enough subsets to allow testing for a trend over time. Of the subject children, 15.2% were born in the years 1655–1679, 49.6% in the years 1680–1694, and 35.2% in 1695–1724.
12. The awkwardness of this last category follows from the ambiguity of the concept of "majority." In law, Virginia girls were of age at 18, boys at 21, but in point of

239 children of the sample were the products of sixty-eight marriages;[13] at the end of sixty-two (91 percent) of these marriages,
minor children were left in the care of the surviving spouse; the subsequent death of the survivor left orphaned minors in forty-one (60
percent) of the cases.

Obviously the society had to accommodate the many children losing
parents. Apprenticeship absorbed some of the children of the poor—
the one fact about orphanhood generally commented upon.[14] Indi-

---

fact marriage endowed maturity regardless of age. The following is a further breakdown of the data of table 1, discriminating between male and female children and
between the loss of a mother or father. Note that of the 83 males known to have
reached maturity (*), 42 had lost their fathers (31 orphaned males plus 11 males who
retained only a mother, ergo lost a father)—50.6%. Although we did not test the
children again (at, say, 25 years of age), the mortality rates are such (table 2) as to
warrant an expectation of 75% or more.

| Achieved Age and Sample Size (N) by Sex | Children with but One Parent at Age | | | | Orphaned Children | |
| | With Father | | With Mother | | | |
	Male	Female	Male	Female	Male	Female
1 M=122 F=117	4	6	3	4	0	0
5 M=117 F=110	15	15	8	9	4	2
9 M=111 F=100	25	19	10	13	10	10
13 M=99 F=95	26	18	7	15	18	20
18 M=88 F=85	22	18	10	12	27	27
* M=83 F=81	17	19	11	14	31	28

---

13. This computes to 3.5 children per marriage, roughly half the rate found in
early New England. See Philip J. Greven, Jr., *Four Generations: Population, Land, and
Family in Colonial Andover, Massachusetts* (Ithaca, N.Y., 1970), 23, and John Demos, *A
Little Commonwealth: Family Life in Plymouth Colony* (New York, 1970), 192—to cite
simply the two most prominent early American studies. But the Middlesex figure
cannot be used to suggest fertility, for only marriages productive of children for whom
specific data were known were entered into the sample. Moreover, a figure for births
per marriage is extremely crude as a comparative index for it does not take into account
potential variation in years per marriage. Stronger, more formal demographic indexes
of fertility are required. We suggest that as this study of Middlesex proceeds and such
indexes are developed they will indicate a relatively high level of fertility.

14. See, for example, Philip Alexander Bruce, *Institutional History of Virginia in the
Seventeenth Century* (New York, 1910), I, 85, 545–546; Arthur W. Calhoun, *A Social*

FIGURE 1. Age Profile of an Idealized
Early Middlesex County, Virginia, Marriage

Husband's Achieved Age	Wife's Achieved Age	Children's Achieved Ages				
		First	Second	Third	Fourth	Fifth
24 (Married)	20					
25	21	Born				
26	22	1				
27	23	2				
28	24	3	Born			
29	25	4	1			
30	26	5	2			
31	27	6	3			
32	28	7	4			
33	29	8	5			
34	30	9	6	Born		
35	31	10	7	1		
36	32	11	8	2		
37	33	12	9	3		
38	34	13	10	4	Born	
39	35	14	11	5	1	
40	36	15	12	6	2	
41	37	16	13	7	3	
42	38	17	14	8	4	Born
43	39	18	15	9	5	1
44	Dead	19	16	10	6	2
45		20	17	11	7	3
46		21	18	12	8	4
47		22	19	13	9	5
48		23	20	14	10	6
Dead						

Source:
Table of life expectancies (table 2 below) and median ages of first marriage for men and women based upon a sample of 184 Middlesex males and 203 females born through 1710. Male: $\bar{X}$ = 24.7; Md = 24.0; Range = 16–39; $\underline{s}$ = 3.9. Female: $\bar{X}$ = 20.6; Md = 20.1; Range = 13–33; $\underline{s}$ = 3.65. The idealization has utilized medians as a reflection of the slight negative skewness displayed in both male and female distributions.

History of the American Family (New York, 1960 [orig. publ. Cleveland, Ohio, 1917]), I, 307–308. Other works—such as Mary Newton Stanard, *Colonial Virginia: Its People and Customs* (Philadelphia, 1917), and Edmund S. Morgan, *Virginians at Home: Family Life in the Eighteenth Century* (Williamsburg, Va., 1952)—do not consider orphans or parental loss at all.

TABLE 1. Parental Loss in Early Middlesex County, Virginia

Achieved Age	Children Known to Survive to Age		Children with Both Parents at Age		Children with but One Parent at Age		Children Orphaned at Age	
1	239	(100%)	222	(92.9%)	17	(7.1%)	0	(0.0%)
5	227	(100%)	174	(76.7%)	47	(20.7%)	6	(2.6%)
9	211	(100%)	124	(58.8%)	67	(31.8%)	20	(9.5%)
13	194	(100%)	90	(46.4%)	66	(34.0%)	38	(19.6%)
18	173	(100%)	57	(32.9%)	62	(35.8%)	54	(31.2%)
*	164	(100%)	44	(26.8%)	61	(37.2%)	59	(36.0%)

*21 or age of marriage, whichever came first.

Source:
   See footnote 11.

gent orphans were bound out by the parish vestry and churchwardens or, much more often, by the county court. Thus James Merritt, whose father's estate was administered by Cuthbert Potter as chief creditor, was, by the court, bound in 1679 "till he comes of Age" to Christopher Robinson.[15] But an indigent widow who, by virtue of age, incapacity, or the paucity of her estate, was not a candidate for remarriage might well apprentice one or more children as well. Mary Gibbs, for example, left a widow with three sons by the death of her husband Gregory in 1683 (and pregnant with a fourth son), that same year bound her ten-year-old eldest to Richard Willis, who contracted "to teach him the art and trade of a shooemaker and to finde him sufficient Diet and Cloathing"; another son was put to apprenticeship four years later. Mary lived on in widowhood until 1726, her third son, John, presumably staying with her. The fourth son, Charles, baptized in September 1684, apparently died young.[16]

Yet apprenticeship absorbed only a few of the children. The children of the affluent, of the "middling sort," even of most of the poor, were expected to stay with the surviving parent, who more often than not remarried, endowing the child with a stepparent. In the case of the remarriage of the surviving wife, the stepfather normally became the guardian of the child. But for good and sufficient reasons—the failure

15. Middlesex County, Order Book No. 1, 1673–1680, p. 177.
16. Middlesex County, Order Book No. 2, 1680–1694, pp. 135, 308.

of the guardian to educate the child as befitting its parentage and estate, for example, or, as in the case of the son of Elizabeth Maguire, abuse by the guardian—the county court could intervene and place the child in the custody of another. And the child itself, at the age of fourteen, had the right to go before the court and request a new guardian, as did Henry, Edwin, and Martha Thacker in 1681, following the remarriage of their mother, Eltonhead, to William Stanard.[17]

Orphanhood, an event for almost 20 percent of the children before their thirteenth birthday and for over 30 percent before their eighteenth, required still other arrangements. The county court had general oversight of the children. On its own, or at the request of a child of fourteen or older, it could specify custody and guardianship. But the wishes of parents expressed in their wills were, by law, paramount. Tobias Mickelburrough provided that his minor son by a first marriage "remain and abide" with his second wife (the child's stepmother) "provided shee deals well and kindly by him," otherwise the designated overseers of the will were to "remove and place him where in their discression they shall See most Convenient"; due care was to be taken for the child's education "that he may be Instructed and taught to read write and Cipher so far that he may be well capable of doing any ordinary Business."[18] Frequently wills designated that orphaned children be put into the charge of an elder brother or stepbrother, sometimes even an elder sister or stepsister. (In half the cases of our sample of marriages where the orphanhood of minors resulted, elder brothers or sisters had already reached majority.) James Dudley, for example, survived three wives and was survived by five children; in writing his will he charged his eldest son (born to Dudley's second wife) with the care of his two youngest children (born of the third marriage), requiring him "to bring them up in the fear of God and to put the[m] to Schoole in Moderation, the girle for to read and the boy for to Read and Rite and Siffer if it be possible he can." Thomas Stiff, leaving two grown children and two minor children (ages nine and seven), named his eldest son executor

17. For the laws see, for example, William W. Hening, comp., *The Statutes at Large: Being a Collection of all the Laws of Virginia from the First Session of the Legislature in 1619* (Richmond, New York, and Philadelphia, 1809–1823), II, 92–94, III, 371–376. The Maguire case is to be found in Middlesex County, Order Book No. 2, 1680–1694, p. 503; that of the Thacker children, *ibid.*, p. 47. The abuse of the Maguire child lay in his not being raised in a Christian manner. Middlesex displays no such abuse as the rape of a minor girl by her stepfather and subsequent infanticide that occurred on the Eastern Shore (*VMHB*, IV [1896–1897], 185–197).

18. Middlesex County, Will Book A, 1698–1713, pp. 139–141.

"and required him to take care" of the two minors. William Daniell survived two wives and was survived by children ranging in age from thirty-four to four; in his will he stipulated that his three youngest daughters remain on the plantation bequeathed to his eldest son, William, "till they are marryed." Thomas Kidd provided that his four "smallest" (ranging in age from eight to eleven) remain upon the plantation left to them and be brought up by his daughters Frances, twenty-two, and Mary, eighteen. Thomas Toseley, in writing his will, assumed that his two minor children would remain with their mother, his second wife, but provided that, should she die, the two sons of his wife's first marriage (in other words, not Toseley's sons at all) "manage and looke after My Children and their Estates." Thomas Tuggle left his children (ranging from Mary, nineteen, to Henry, ten) in the care of their elder half-brother by his wife's first marriage but seems to have anticipated problems: They were all to live together on the plantation left to Tuggle's eldest son, if they could do so "contentedly"; if not, the half-brother was to build a fifteen-foot-square house on the property and live by himself, leaving the children in the main house.[19]

Children were left in the care of uncles as well. When, for example, James Blaze died in February 1701, two young nieces were living with him—Agatha Vause, who had lost her father at age two and remained with her mother through two remarriages before being orphaned, and Mary Osborne, age two when her mother died, twelve at the death of her father. In his will Blaze provided inheritances to maintain the girls and expressed his desire that they "have two yeares Sculeing a pees and then to Returne Home and Learne Houseold work of my wife" Elizabeth.[20] On occasion godparents took their godchildren into their homes, or, as in the case of the widow of minister John Sheppard, the godchild of the deceased spouse: Richard Robinson, minister Sheppard's godson, was thirteen when his mother died, eighteen when his father died, and was living with Mistress Sheppard at age nineteen (1694) when he testified in her behalf in a suit against Francis Dodson.[21] Even simple friends had to be relied upon to care for one's orphans. Anne Chowning, widow of Robert Chowning and mother of seven children ages fifteen through four, made no other

19. *Ibid.*, pp. 245–246, 231, 236–237; Will Book B, 1713–1734, pp. 267–268, 311; Wills, Etc., 1675–1798, Pt. 1, pp. 27–28.
20. Wills, Etc., 1675–1798, Pt. 1, pp. 136–138.
21. Middlesex County, Order Book No. 2, 1680–1694, p. 679. Mrs. Sheppard was also Robinson's distant cousin.

arrangement than to ask friends Richard Allen and Richard Shurley "to Act and doe" for the children "for the best advantage."[22] Such designated overseers seem to have been expected to take the children in and act as guardians in the absence of kin. And in a society in which orphans were so common and where wives and husbands could reasonably expect that their own children might require accommodation, the widow Chowning's trust in her friends seems not undue. Edwin Conaway anticipated no problems when he interceded in behalf of the orphans of Elias Edmonds. Their estate was being rapidly dissipated by bad management (or so he thought); hence he suggested to one of the justices of the court new managerial arrangements. In anticipation of objection he added that "you will say who will keep the Children upon those terms. I answer I will find those that shall keep them and give them better Education than those in whose Custody they are."[23]

Conaway's letter points up a very real problem associated with the death of parents in this society—although not one to be overstated. The children were heirs and heiresses of property and personalty large and small. Partible inheritance was the rule, sons generally sharing realty equally (after deduction of the dower rights of the widow), although the eldest was frequently favored, sometimes with an augmented share, more often by the bequest to him of the improved home property while unimproved realty went to younger sons. (Daughters generally inherited realty only in the absence of sons.) Sons and daughters shared personal property (again after the deduction of the widow's share), the most frequent bequest by a father to a daughter being specific cattle and the increase thereof. The expense of rearing minor children was an appropriate deduction from the income, even at times the capital, of the inheritance. Hence those to whose charge the minors fell—widows and guardians—had the control of inheritances until children came of age or, in the case of a girl, married.[24] To both the father of the children and the society at large the central concern was to effect the transfer of the property from the testator, through the minority of the child (when the inheritance was under the control of others), to the mature adult in as nearly intact a condition as possible. A multi-tiered system by which

22. Middlesex County, Will Book B, 1713–1734, p. 132.

23. Conaway to Toby Smith, Mar. 27, 1654, Lancaster County, Deeds, Etc. [Wills and Settlements of Estates] No. 2, 1654–1702, pp. 1–2.

24. One result was that the law was extremely restrictive regarding the marriage (even the solicitation to marriage) of minor girls. See, for example, Hening, comp., *Statutes at Large*, II, 281, III, 149–151, 441–446.

estates were handled—in some cases fathers named executors and overseers as well as guardians to watch after their children's estates—was a defense mechanism. But beyond that, fathers sought to protect their children's inheritances by prescribing and proscribing, in their wills, the actions of guardians. Thomas Tuggle, for example, charged the potentially troublesome half-brother to preserve the property of the children, removing "no fences . . . nor to sell any timber from the land but to Make use of no more then will serve the plantation." James Blaze stipulated that his wife Elizabeth was to have the use of his plantation during her lifetime, but she was "neither to sell nor Give Aney of the timber," cutting only "for hur owne ocashon to build with." "If she Cannot Keep Hands upon the plantation In the Ingan necke and Keepe the Houseing in Repare Shee may Lease it and Like wise to Keepe the plantation In Repare wheare on I nowe Live." James Dudley required his designated overseers, in the event his wife remarried, to "take good and Sufficient Security for the Money left to my Dear Children and also to see that none of my Lands be cleared which I have given to my Son James nor no timber cut off of it further than what is Necessary for repaireing the houses and for tobo: Caske for the said Plantacon."[25] The gentlemen justices of the county court, for their part, required performance bonds of most guardians and administrators, set aside special court days for "Orphans' Court," when the guardians were to bring in accounts for auditing, and acted promptly to protect the estates of orphans when malfeasance was called to their attention. And in the colony assembly the same sorts of men—fathers and gentlemen justices—passed one after the other general laws to protect and preserve the estates of orphans.

All of this is testimony to the realization that great opportunity existed to despoil the parentless. And, indeed, examples of spoliation or attempted spoliation can be found. In 1664 the children of Oliver Segar and Humphrey Owens sought the assistance of the court against Humphrey Jones, who had assumed their guardianship by virtue of marrying their common mother, Eleanor. In response to their assertion that Jones was claiming (as part of Eleanor's dower) a goodly portion of their estates, the court empaneled "a Jury of the ablest and neerest inhabitants" to make a just division. When, in 1681, Henry, Edwin, and Martha Thacker went to court to obtain a guardian other than their mother's new husband (William Stanard),

25. The Dudley, Blaze, and Tuggle wills are cited above, nn. 19, 20.

it was obviously because the children—or at least Henry, the eldest at eighteen—suspected that their new stepfather would act against their interest. In 1686 Henry, on behalf of himself and the other children, brought suit against Stanard for his mishandling of their estates, and Stanard fled the county. In 1685 the county court acted quickly to preserve the estates of John Gore and George Ransom from the spoliation of John Ascough, who had married the mother of the children and was "about Selling all his [and their] estate" prior to sailing for England. The court ordered that all of Ascough's property, and that of the children, be forestopped "from any Sale or Alienacon untill the Said Orphts. estates be well Secured." And in 1706 the court moved to protect the children of the deceased Richard Stevens. His "considerable personall estate" was "likely to be Imbezelled away" by the "ill Management and Riotous Liveing" of the widow Sarah "and the orphans of the sd. decd. thereby ruined"; hence the court placed the estate in the hands of the county sheriff.[26]

But given the extensiveness of parental loss and the number of children whose estates were vulnerable, the number of assaults upon the estates of orphans seems relatively few. Most men involved with the estates were like Edwin Conaway—scrupulously attentive to the welfare of the Edmonds children when, in 1654, he questioned the management of their estate—or like Robert Carter, one of the five overseers of the estate of Ralph Wormeley a half-century later. Every page of the extant Wormeley estate record testifies to Carter's concern for the young heirs to the largest fortune in Middlesex, in this case particularly vulnerable heirs inasmuch as young Ralph and John were completing their education in England and as the main Wormeley property, called Rosegill, was in the hands of their mother and her new husband, William Churchill. When, in 1706, after five years' oversight of the estate, Carter heard that the boys were to return, he wrote that it was "high time": "Col. Churchills living upon the place [Rosegill] together with his relations have given him the Opportunity to fix himself absolutely in the Government of the Estate, the management whereof is become very much a trouble to all concerned, I believe, to me I am sure it is."[27] One suspects that care and scrupu-

26. Lancaster County, Deeds, Etc. [Wills and Settlements of Estates] No. 2, 1654–1702, p. 307; Middlesex County, Order Book No. 2, 1680–1694, pp. 100, 240; Will Book A, 1698–1713, p. 179.

27. Wormeley Estate Papers, 1701–1716, with Christ Church, Lancaster Processioners' Returns, 1711–1783, Va. State Lib. Extensive extracts are printed with the

losity in such matters were in effect products of the situation: What
men such as Conaway and Carter did for the children of others they
could hope other men would do for theirs.

Parental loss and orphanhood were pervasive in this early Virginia
society. So much is clear. Children from every socioeconomic level
and from every birth-cohort from the earliest period to well into the
eighteenth century were involved. No breakdown of our sample of
children has produced significant deviation from the percentages
cited. Parental loss was a constant over time, as witness the Chowning
family: Robert Chowning, Jr., lost his father at the age of fifteen;
when Robert, Jr., died in 1698 he left seven children ranging in age
from fourteen to two; his eldest son died in 1721, leaving six children
ages fourteen to one. This prevalence of loss, and its pervasiveness,
had great implication in the society, and for our study of it.

Households tended to be mixed and complex affairs. We have
noted the phenomenon in passing. In the Beverley household in 1680,
just after the marriage of the widow Hone and Robert Beverley, we
found Keeble, Hone, and two sorts of Beverley children, conceivably
ranging in age from unmarried children in their early twenties to the
just born. Had we dropped into just about any other household in
Middlesex, we would have found much the same thing—orphans,
half-brothers, stepbrothers and stepsisters, and wards running a
gamut of ages.[28] The father figure in the house might well be an uncle
or a brother, the mother figure an aunt, elder sister, or simply the
father's "now-wife"—to use the wording frequently found in conveyances and wills. Neither the romantic depictions of an Alice Morse
Earle or a Mary Newton Stanard nor the connotations of social science
terminology—the image of the nuclear family with its slowly greying
parents and maturing children—applies. Historians more prone than

Wormeley genealogy in *VMHB*, XXXVI (1928), 287–291. The quotation is from the
printed version, p. 290.

  28. Given the current emphasis on the makeup of the household, it is surprising
that this phenomenon has not been more widely noticed. Michael Anderson, however,
has found it extensively in mid-nineteenth-century Britain. See the revised version of
his "Family, Household, and the Industrial Revolution," in Michael Gordon, ed., *The
American Family in Social-Historical Perspective* (New York, 1973), 59–75. Elizabeth Wirth
Maverick in "Nature versus Nurture: Patterns and Trends in Seventeenth-Century
French Child-Rearing," in deMause, ed., *History of Childhood*, 288–289, suggests much
the same thing, writing that "a high mortality and remarriage rate introduced a
complex kinship relationship into the households." But she inexplicably links her
statement to that of Marc Bloch on the decisive influence of the French grandparent. As
is pointed out below, high mortality vitiates the influence of grandparents.

we to use psychoanalysis can (and perhaps will) make great use of the mass trauma and the disruption of childhood implied.[29] They need only cite the case of Agatha Vause: By the time she was ten she had lost a father, two stepfathers, a mother, and her guardian uncle. But we must accept that what we take for traumatic loss was the norm for these children. To use the symbolism of Johann Sebastian Bach, death was a singing watchman in their world, teaching them from an early age that life was transitory. A planter of nearby Stafford County, referring back to his childhood, put the matter succinctly in a letter to his mother: "Before I was ten years old as I am sure you very well remember, I look'd upon this life here as but going to an Inn, no permanent being."[30] And what we might take for the disruption of childhood involved, conversely, a system for rooting the parentless child within the society.

Kinship and quasi-kinship were the essentials of the system. One can even argue that they were accentuated in the society in large measure in response to the expectation of parental death and parentless children. Even in the earliest days in the area of what would become Middlesex, the county's people linked themselves together. It does not seem simply fortuitous that two separate branches of Robinson family men should settle in the county, or that a third, covert line should be represented by Frances Robinson and her children. Neither does it seem fortuitous that four husbands of Eltonhead sisters should seat themselves within a few miles of each other, or that Henry Corbin, busily establishing himself financially in Northumberland, should move to Middlesex immediately following his marriage to an Eltonhead widow. Brothers-in-law (and their children and stepchildren) would be kin to one's own children, ready at hand to step in when death left children parentless.

In the years to and after 1700 the cementing and recementing of kinship by cousin marriages, the marriages of stepbrothers and stepsisters, of wards and natural children, the extension of kinship through godparentage and by virtue of sequential marriages that made quasi-kin of unrelated children, proceeded at such a pace as to leave the best of genealogists far behind. That such relationships

29. That they are turning in this direction is indicated by William Saffady, "The Effects of Childhood Bereavement and Parental Remarriage in Sixteenth-Century England: The Case of Thomas Moore," *History of Childhood Quarterly*, I (1973), 310–336.

30. William to Mrs. Mary Fitzhugh, June 30, 1698, in Davis, ed., *Fitzhugh and His Chesapeake World*, 358.

were meaningful is attested to by the regularity of bequests to god-children, to sons- and daughters-in-law (the seventeenth century's dual expression for stepsons and daughters as well as for children's spouses), to nephews, nieces, and cousins. And such relationships were called upon when death made children parentless. The Edmonds guardian whom Edwin Conaway challenged in 1654 was the children's mother's first husband's son by a prior marriage. When young Humphrey Jones was orphaned, there was on hand to look after him Randolph Seager: Young Humphrey was his father's son by a third marriage; Seager was the son of Humphrey's father's second wife by a prior marriage; and Seagar's wife was Humphrey's half-sister. Garrett Minor designated two Vivion brothers-in-law and a Montague cousin to serve as trustees for his children. And that Edwin Thacker was the grandson of the sister of Ralph Wormeley's children's grandmother (their first cousin twice removed) was enough to allow Wormeley in 1701 to consider Thacker a "relative" and call upon him to serve as co-overseer of the children's inheritances. For children, stability lay not so much in transitory parents but in the permanent network of relatives and quasi-relatives in which they were imbedded. Instability, for children and for parents contemplating their children's parentless future, lay in being outside the system. James Jordan, new to the county when he wrote his will in 1710, had not even friends to rely upon: "If it Should please God to take my wife whilst my Children [are] younge and Uncapeable of Governing themselves," he wrote, please God "the Worshipfull" county court would "take them under theire tuition and Care and then what Small Estate there may be to be Equally devided Amonst them."[31]

One suspects that in their situation the children of Middlesex matured early. There seems little enough of that emotional content of family life which gives meaning to childhood as we know it—little time for it given the fact of many children and the shortness of life itself. Only in one of the many wills surviving from Middlesex in this period does one catch a hint of that whimsey which proceeds from the love of a parent toward a child, when George Ransom leaves to his daughter Elizabeth a "Jack in the box."[32] The strictures as to education that have been quoted here and there as we proceeded reflect a pragmatic outlook toward a life of work and property: Let the

31. Middlesex County, Will Book B, 1713–1734, p. 42.
32. Middlesex County, Wills, Etc., 1675–1798, Pt. 1, p. 1.

boy learn "to reade, write, and Cast Accots"; let the girl learn the rudiments of "housewifery."[33] And the very fact that children were heirs and heiresses matured them. We catch sight of children in their early teens acting to preserve inheritances—the Thacker children moving against their stepfather Stanard—and of fathers, in their efforts to protect their orphaned children's estates, attempting to push sons into an early legal maturity. As early as 1656 the law allowed orphans at seventeen to control the produce of their own labor, while increasingly in the eighteenth century men attempted to lower the age of majority by testamentary declarations. John Summer, for example, in 1703, specified that his son of sixteen was of age to dispose of his estate with the advice of designated executors, while Thomas Norman, in 1727, declared it to be his will that his seventeen-year-old son Robert "Act and do for himself."[34]

Even when fathers lived to see their sons into maturity—when death did not take the parent and leave the boy fatherless but proper-tied—fathers seem impelled to set sons up independently, as Richard Perrott, Sr., did when he turned property over to his son Richard, Jr., when the latter was twenty-two.[35] (The norm being early parental death and youthful inheritance, it almost seems as if the long-lived father felt obliged to keep his son equal to his peer group.) Authority within the community, too, was shared with the young. Matthew Kemp was sitting on the parish vestry and county court by age twenty-one; young Perrott was named to the vestry and court at twenty-six; so, too, was Robert Dudley. Indeed, the "fathers" of the community—meaning the vestrymen and justices—ranged in age in 1687 from young Kemp to Abraham Weekes and John Mann, the two senior members at fifty-six years of age; over half were under forty. Fifteen years later the same situation prevailed. Half were under forty, with the members ranging in age from William Wormeley at twenty-four to John Wortham at fifty-seven. In this context George Washington's eighteenth-century career does not seem particularly unusual: Born in 1732, losing his father at eleven, raised by various relatives (including his half-brother Lawrence), inheriting Mount

33. Will of Jane Cocke, *ibid.*, 92.

34. Hening, comp., *Statutes at Large*, I, 416–417; Middlesex County, Will Book A, 1698–1713, pp. 146–147; Will Book B, 1713–1734, p. 306.

35. Middlesex County, Deeds, Etc., 1679–1694, No. 2 [1a], p. 15. The many conveyances of this sort have the advantage of providing a date at which a son was established independently; the same phenomenon, but without the date, can be observed in wills where a son is left "the plantation whereon he now lives"—this particular example from the will of Marvell Moseley in Will Book B, 1713–1734, p. 238.

Vernon at age twenty, Washington was a militia lieutenant colonel commanding at Fort Necessity at age twenty-two and a burgess at twenty-six; at twenty-seven he married a widow with two small children, and at forty-three commanded the Revolutionary army.

We cannot help but contrast what we have found in this early Virginia community with what current scholarship is depicting for New England. No direct comparison can be made; New England's scholars have been relatively mute on the subject of parental death and orphanhood. Philip Greven, for example, does not even index "orphans" in his study of Andover, Massachusetts. John Demos has much to say in his study of Plymouth, but while his picture of the testamentary provisions regarding the parentless is very much like that found in Middlesex, his picture is based on limited sources.[36] Moreover, Demos's discussion of orphans, his mortality figures (together with Greven's seventeenth-century figures), and his and Greven's figures for mean age at first marriage offer a conundrum. Demos does not write as if orphanhood was an exceptional circumstance in Plymouth society; yet the mortality figures, arranged to form a table of life expectancies (as in table 2), suggest that the potential for orphanhood was all but nonexistent.[37] In Middlesex, where first-married men and women could expect to die in their late forties and late thirties respectively, parental death and orphanhood were (as we have seen) inherent in the highly idealized median marriage. The mean child could not escape the loss of parents.[38] But in New England, if the figures offered by Demos and Greven are to be accepted, the mean marriage ended with the death of the wife at around sixty-three, the widower dying at around seventy; the eldest child of the marriage would be approximately forty at the time of the mother's death and forty-four when the father died, while the youngest child

36. Greven, *Four Generations*; Demos, *A Little Commonwealth*. Demos relies very heavily on the 1631 will of Mary Ring. He also seems to construe the accommodation of parentless children as servitude (p. 115).

37. The same type of conundrum is offered by the matter-of-fact approach to remarriage by Demos (but not by Greven). If the mortality figures are correct, the potential for remarriage would be minimal, and remarriage exceptional. Greven notes the exceptional nature of remarriage (using it to substantiate his mortality figures); Demos does not.

38. The same is suggested by life expectancies in seventeenth-century Maryland, one sample of which is included in table 2 for comparative purposes. Our gratitude to Lorena S. Walsh and Russell R. Menard for making their data available to us in advance of publication of their "Death in the Chesapeake: Two Life Tables for Men in Early Colonial Maryland," *Maryland Historical Magazine*, LXIX (1974), 211–227. That three independent samples drawn from Chesapeake society are so alike (and so variant from the New England samples) tends to substantiate all three.

TABLE 2. Comparative Life Expectancies: The Seventeenth-Century Chesapeake and New England

Having Achieved Age	One Can Expect to Live Until Age:						
	Middlesex		Maryland	Andover, Mass.		Plymouth Colony	
	Married Males (N = 259)	Married Females (N = 258)	Males (N = 153)	Males (N = 192)	Females (N = 108)	Males (N = 645)	Females
20	48.8	39.8	46.0	64.6	62.1	69.2	62.4
25	48.7	41.3	47.7	—	—	—	—
30	49.4	43.6	50.4	69.3	65.3	70.0	64.7
35	50.8	45.7	53.0	—	—	—	—
40	53.0	48.6	55.6	71.8	68.7	71.2	69.7
45	55.0	54.2	59.5	—	—	—	—
50	57.7	59.3	62.0	73.5	72.1	73.7	73.4
55	62.7	62.7	65.6	—	—	—	—
60	65.8	67.9	69.3	75.6	76.4	76.3	76.8
65	70.0	70.0	74.4	—	—	—	—
70	73.6	73.7	77.0	80.3	81.9	79.9	80.7
75	77.9	80.2	78.5	—	—	—	—
80	—	—	—	86.6	89.6	85.1	86.7
85	—	—	—	—	—	—	—
90	—	—	—	95.0	95.8	—	—
95	—	—	—	—	—	—	—
100	—	—	—	—	105.0	—	—

Sources:
  Middlesex: see Appendixes 1 and 2; Maryland: courtesy of Russell R. Menard and Lorena Walsh—see n. 38; Andover: computed from data in Philip J. Greven, Jr., *Four Generations: Population, Land, and Family in Colonial Andover, Massachusetts* (Ithaca, N.Y., 1970), 27, 108; Plymouth: John Demos, *A Little Commonwealth: Family Life in Plymouth Colony* (New York, 1970), 192. N.B.: Demos's first achieved age is 21 rather than 20. The computation technique has been adopted from George W. Barclay, *Techniques of Population Analysis* (New York, 1958), chap. 4.

would be twenty-three and twenty-seven. Orphanhood was either an exceptional circumstance in New England—and the contrast with Virginia startling, to say the least—or the mortality figures offered are incorrect.[39]

39. Terry L. Anderson and Robert Paul Thomas, "White Population, Labor Force and Extensive Growth of the New England Economy in the Seventeenth Century," *Journal of Economic History*, XXXIII (1973), 634–667, develop their argument in large part

If New England's mortality figures stand, however, together with
the startling contrast, where does that leave us? Certainly it suggests
that we are dealing with two entirely different types of childhood
along the seventeenth-century Anglo-American coast—in New England one lived more in a parental situation; in the Chesapeake area
one lived more in a kinship situation. It suggests, too, an ancillary, but
equally startling, contrast between the societies: that in Virginia we
ought not to expect the generational tension of which the New England scholars have been making so much.[40] When, as in Middlesex,
half of the sons (50.6 percent of our sample) lost their fathers before
reaching legal maturity or marriage—and the tendency with respect
to the others was for fathers to set mature sons up independently in
their early twenties—the potential for tension hardly existed.[41] And

---

by equating a stable population model to Greven's data, specifically the United Nations
model life table Level 45, Female, and Level 65, Male, as presented in United Nations,
Department of Economic and Social Affairs, *Population Studies*, No. 22, *Age and Sex
Patterns of Mortality: Model Life-Tables for Under-Developed Countries* (New York, 1955);
No. 25, *Methods for Population Projections by Sex and Age* (New York, 1956); and No. 39,
*The Concept of a Stable Population: Application to the Study of Populations of Countries with
Incomplete Demographic Statistics* (New York, 1968). As early as 1931 Alfred J. Lotka, the
"father" of stable population theory, sketched a method for assessing the extent of
parental loss from life table data in "Orphanhood in Relation to Demographic Factors:
A Study in Population Analysis," *Metron: Rivista Internazionale di Statistica*, IX (1931),
37–109. Applying Lotka's shorter method (unadjusted for posthumous and puerperal
orphans) to the tables suggested as pertinent by Anderson and Thomas leads to a
crude estimate of 10% of New England's children losing their fathers by age 15, 14%
losing their mothers, and 1.5% losing both. But is the designated model life table (and
the data from which it is extrapolated) appropriate? Linda Auwers Bissell in a study of
"From One Generation to Another: Mobility in Seventeenth-Century Windsor, Connecticut," *William and Mary Quarterly*, 3d Ser., XXXI (1974), 79–110, notes in passing
(p. 93*n*) that of a sample of 99 sons born between 1650 and 1669, 31 received land before
their 16th birthday but after the death of their fathers—31.9% of the sample, a figure
more to be expected in Middlesex than in New England! If the phenomenon of fatherless sons proves so alike it will be hard to understand divergent mortality schedules
and life expectancies. As is pointed out in the appendix, the potential for error
(particularly errors resulting from name confusion) is enormous; Greven and Demos
were working in the "pioneer days" of such research, before that potential was fully
understood—Greven, for example, assuming that "adult deaths were almost always
recorded." (*Four Generations*, 109.) Mortality is so crucial both for understanding New
England society and for comparative purposes, and the works of Demos and Greven
are proving to be such influential studies, that perhaps a retest of the Andover/Plym-
outh data is in order.
    40. See, for example, Sumner Chilton Powell, *Puritan Village: The Formation of a
New England Town* (Middletown, Conn., 1963), chap. 8; Kenneth A. Lockridge and
Alan Kreider, "The Evolution of Massachusetts Town Government, 1640 to 1740,"
WMQ, 3d Ser., XXIII (1966), 567; Greven, *Four Generations*, 279–282; James A. Henretta,
"The Morphology of New England Society in the Colonial Period," *Journal of Interdisci-
plinary History*, II (1971), 388–391, and his *The Evolution of American Society, 1700–1815:
An Interdisciplinary Analysis* (Lexington, Mass., 1973), 36–37.
    41. One can argue that relatively early male mortality and the early independence

it means that we ought not to expect much of tradition in this Virginia society, again in contrast to New England, whose scholars are suggesting the great strength of tradition.[42] For tradition on a folk level tends to pass from a society's elderly to its youth, from grandparents to grandchildren. Few of Middlesex's children ever knew their grandparents.[43]

"In the name of God Amen . . . ," Maximilian Petty wrote—to return to the scene with which we began. A year after Petty's death his widow, Christian, married again, giving young Maximilian and Ann (now eleven and eight and a half respectively) a stepfather. The marriage, to William Briscoe, a former servant of Petty's and his successor as undersheriff of the county, was hardly successful; there were no children, and in 1692 Briscoe was jailed for sexually assaulting Mrs. Margaret Whitaker. In mid-1700 he died, and Christian was free to marry again—her new husband, John Vivion, being a widower twice over with five children. Christian was the "now-wife" to whom Vivion left the use of his land and the care of two of his own minor children when he died in 1705. Of Maximilian, Jr., we know little; presumably he died soon after his mother's remarriage. Ann, however, grew to propertied womanhood. By the time she married Thomas Smith in 1698 (at age eighteen) she was twice an heiress, once by the will of her father and again by the will of her godfather, Augustine Cant. In 1700 her stepfather Briscoe would, in a way, make her an heiress again, leaving his estate to her husband and children (although giving his widow, Christian, its use through her life). Ann's marriage to Smith lasted until her death in 1704. Two children are known to have been born to the marriage, both of them minors when left

---

of sons had an effect upon the Chesapeake labor system as well. The New England scene of a man and one or more sons at work on the family fields—or, given the nature of agricultural labor, lolling in the barn in off-seasons and during inclement weather (a phenomenon that Edmund S. Morgan has rightly observed but perhaps overburdened in "The Labor Problem at Jamestown, 1607–1618," *American Historical Review*, LXXVI [1971], 595–611)—simply could not apply in Virginia. How, then, was labor supplied to the "family farm"? In the context of this question, servants and ultimately slaves—at least on the smaller holdings—might well be construed as substitutes for sons. The problem will be dealt with at length in another place, but see Morgan, "Slavery and Freedom: The American Paradox," *Journal of American History*, LIX (1972), 5–29.

42. Greven, "Historical Demography and Colonial America: A Review Article," *WMQ*, 3d Ser., XXIV (1967), 453; Kenneth A. Lockridge, *A New England Town, The First Hundred Years: Dedham, Massachusetts, 1636–1736* (New York, 1970), *passim*; Darrett B. Rutman, *American Puritanism: Faith and Practice* (Philadelphia, 1970), 47–51.

43. In contrast, note John M. Murrin's aside in an extensive review essay on the New England social history in *History and Theory*, XI (1972), 238, that it may well be that grandparents were a New England invention.

motherless, the younger but a few months old. The next year Smith died, and they were orphaned children.

1. A Note on the Sources and Method

The essential method of our study of Middlesex from its settlement to *circa* 1750—of which this essay is a part—has been to break down all records pertaining to the county (and its parent county, Lancaster, prior to the separation of the two) and reassemble them on a name basis, outlining in effect the lives of as many of the people residing in Middlesex during the period as possible. We hesitate to use the word *reconstitution* to describe the method because of the limited demographic connotation of the word; our biographies include not merely vital events but all available information relative to each person—kinship and quasi-kinship relationships, land patents, conveyances, debts, lawsuits, commercial and farm activities, relationships to church and government, literacy, and so forth. We have made no assumption that any given type of record is complete. For example, we assume serious underregistration of all vital events and feel it requisite to supplement the normal source (the parish register) with any and every other type of record, including the examination of tombstones. Neither do we assume that any published material is inevitably accurate—the published *Parish Register of Christ Church, Middlesex County, Va., from 1653 to 1812* (Richmond, Va., 1897) is rife with error, as any comparison with the original in the Virginia State Library, Richmond, will show.

As an example of the method (with specific reference to the present subject), consider the case of Henry Thacker, Jr.: A variety of records establishes his residence in the county during the last two decades of the seventeenth and first decade of the eighteenth century. From both the parish register and the manuscript Miscellaneous Records of Marriages and Deaths (and Births), 1663–1763, Va. State Lib., we pick up his parentage and date of birth, his wife's first name (Elizabeth), and the names and birth dates of seven children. A Thacker genealogy[44] supplies his wife's maiden name and parentage. That Thacker had an illegitimate daughter by Mrs. Eleanor (Willis) Allden is established by the Middlesex County Order Book, No. 2, 1680–1694, Va. State Lib. (the court's fine of Mrs. Allden; Mrs. Allden's suit against Thacker resulting in a court order to him to maintain the child; and a court-directed indenture of the child). Thacker's death is not in the parish register but can be determined as being between December 15, 1709 (when he wrote his will), and January 2, 1710 (when the will was entered), from the manuscript Will Book A, 1698–1713, Va. State Lib. The death of an Elizabeth Thacker, widow, is recorded in the register, but there is another Mrs. Elizabeth Thacker alive at the time—the wife of Henry's nephew Edwin; the existence

44. P. W. Hiden, "Webb, Thacker, Vivion," *WMQ*, 2d Ser., V (1925), 171–179.

in Will Book B, 1713–1734, of Elizabeth Thacker's will (dated two days before the death and citing Henry's known children) demonstrates conclusively that it was, indeed, Henry's widow whose death was recorded. The lives of Thacker's children are similarly outlined. We know, for example, that all his legitimate children were alive in December 1709 by virtue of their being mentioned in his will, and they are tracked into their own marriages, child-bearing, and death.

Thacker's is a fairly straightforward case. He was, for one thing, conscientious in registering the births of his legitimate children. In the case of Thomas Kidd, Jr., to cite another example, seven children were registered, but three additional children—his first, fifth, and sixth—must be picked up from his will in Will Book B, where they are named as heirs and the order of birth established. Thacker's date of birth is registered. But in other cases we must find it in the records of another county, in English sources, in the attestation of age noted (in the case of minor children arriving as servants) in the Order Books, or in affidavits of various kinds. Thacker's will survived, albeit his death was not registered. Yet in other instances the fact of a man's death is only picked up from the fact of his widow's remarriage as recorded in the register or the records; in still other cases both the death of the husband and remarriage of the widow are known only by virtue of the application (recorded in the Order Books) of a new husband seeking to join in the administration of the estate. For their part, women seldom left wills. Given the underregistration of deaths, their demise can frequently be ascertained only from documentation of the husband's remarriage or from references in his will to his "now-wife" as a different person from the known wife. Tracking women through their various marriages is obviously the most arduous task, requiring close attention in the Order, Deed, and Will Books to the administration of estates, conveyances (both by women and by husbands who had to indicate the approval of their wives to particular sales), and above all the mention in men's wills of their "sons- and daughters-in-law," that is, their "now-wives'" children by prior marriages.

Such prosopography is both painstaking and time-consuming. Shortcuts exist and are tempting; one can "drop into" a community at a sequence of specific dates, or use various enumerations (in Virginia tithe and militia lists, for example), or extract from only one type of record (the parish register). But in our experience the results will be error-ridden. Name confusion will be inevitable. At one point in time we have five coexisting Frances Thackers. Robert Chowning appears on a tithable list of 1668 and a militia list of 1687; he is likely to be taken for one man, but the two names are actually of father and son. Paul Philpots had three wives within ten years, the first and third named Susanna (and with children named John by each Susanna). How easy it would be to pick up his marriage to Susanna and his widow Susanna, presume one marriage, and miss two! And linkages will be consistently missed. From the register alone one might learn that a Jane Cocke married Rice Jones in February 1680 and had two children by him through 1685; that a Jane and John Smith had a son John baptized in 1690. But only by prosopography can one mesh the entries: Jane was in actuality Jane (Cocke) Jones-

Smith; she bore in all seven children—three to Jones, four to Smith—and died by February 1696. For us, the potential for error in the shortcuts seems compelling, and conclusions that do not rest on full prosopography seem suspect. Certainly the phenomenon of parental loss and orphanhood could not have been investigated by us in any other way.

2. The Middlesex Life Table

Because the life table presented in table 2 was only the third generated for the early Chesapeake, and remains unique in encompassing females,[45] it seems incumbent upon us to outline its construction in some detail. The table is based upon 517 cases (259 male, 258 female) drawn from the prosopography described in Appendix 1. Criteria for entry into the sample were our knowledge of a year of birth before 1711 and of, at some point in time, both the subject's marriage and residency in Middlesex. The criterion of marriage clearly imposes a limitation on broad interpretations of the table, although given our interest in parental loss the criterion was mandatory. Since the life spans of the unmarried could not bear on our subject, the table refers only to men and women who both survived to marriageable age and chose at some time in their lives to marry.

From our prosopography we ascertained not only the year of birth but the year of death for 313 cases (183 male, 130 female). For convenience we refer to this as the empirical data and to the male and female life tables generated from it—given in columns 2 and 7 of table A-1—as empirical tables. (These, and all tables, were computed utilizing the technique described in Walsh and Menard, "Death in the Chesapeake," one aspect of which deserves to be underscored: Cases were included in the compilation of person-years-lived only for the years they were residents of Middlesex; in terms of the tables one consequence is that the figures for N represent not survivors from an initial population but participants in the given cohort whose years in Middlesex contributed to the pool of person-years-lived for that cohort.) In historical demography such empirical tables are axiomatically suspect on the basis of possible record bias. The automatic question is: Is there something in the very act of record keeping that tends to bring about a greater probability of a record of death at one age than at another? The suspicion is particularly directed at recorded female deaths. Our own belief is that the prosopography described, and particularly the fact that it is undertaken across a number of record sets rather than on the basis of one set, minimizes the potential for bias. But the absence of bias cannot be conclusively shown; hence we have utilized a standard technique to enter into consideration the 204 cases (76 male, 128 female) for which no record of death has as yet been found. In the first instance we have arbitrarily assumed that the death took place on the day following the last date at which, on the basis of the records, we know the

45. Walsh and Menard, "Death in the Chesapeake," *Md. Hist. Mag.*, LXIX (1974), 211–227, present two male life tables. See also the life table in Daniel Blake Smith, "Mortality and Family in the Colonial Chesapeake," *Jour. Interdiscipl. Hist.*, VIII (1978), 415. This tends to confirm (with regard to males) both our results and those of Walsh and Menard.

TABLE A.1. Years-to-Live under Various Assumptions of Middlesex Married Males and Females Born through 1710

	Males						Females				
Achieved Age	High (1)	Emp. (2)	Low (3)	Md. Pref. (4)	Va. Pref. (5)	Achieved Age	High (6)	Emp. (7)	Low (8)	Md. Pref. (9)	Va. Pref. (10)
15	—	—	—	—	—	15	19.2 (246)	21.8 (125)	30.1 (247)	26.5 (247)	24.9 (246)
20	24.0 (244)	27.3 (177)	30.2 (244)	28.8 (244)	28.8 (244)	20	15.0 (236)	17.0 (125)	24.9 (251)	21.3 (251)	19.8 (249)
25	19.4 (240)	22.1 (180)	25.0 (247)	23.7 (247)	23.7 (247)	25	12.6 (196)	13.5 (114)	20.9 (241)	17.1 (241)	16.3 (230)
30	16.1 (219)	18.1 (171)	20.8 (239)	19.4 (239)	19.4 (239)	30	11.5 (142)	12.2 (85)	18.3 (213)	14.1 (213)	13.6 (198)
35	13.7 (186)	15.0 (153)	17.4 (221)	15.8 (221)	15.8 (221)	35	10.1 (101)	11.1 (61)	15.3 (189)	10.6 (189)	10.7 (167)
40	12.6 (139)	13.2 (123)	14.8 (191)	13.0 (191)	13.0 (191)	40	9.9 (63)	11.5 (39)	12.2 (165)	8.1 (140)	8.6 (121)
45	11.2 (102)	11.8 (92)	12.6 (160)	10.0 (160)	10.0 (160)	45	8.7 (41)	10.1 (26)	10.3 (123)	8.6 (74)	9.2 (65)
50	9.3 (75)	9.7 (69)	8.6 (135)	7.7 (115)	7.7 (115)	50	10.4 (21)	11.1 (15)	9.8 (79)	8.9 (41)	9.3 (38)
55	8.2 (48)	8.5 (46)	7.9 (83)	7.7 (60)	7.7 (60)	55	9.9 (14)	10.8 (10)	8.3 (55)	7.4 (27)	7.7 (26)
60	6.3 (32)	6.3 (32)	5.4 (56)	5.8 (38)	5.8 (38)	60	7.2 (11)	8.0 (8)	7.9 (32)	7.9 (14)	7.9 (14)
65	5.3 (17)	5.3 (17)	4.7 (26)	5.0 (18)	5.0 (18)	65	4.1 (7)	4.7 (6)	4.8 (23)	5.0 (10)	5.0 (10)
70	3.6 (9)	3.6 (9)	2.9 (12)	3.6 (9)	3.6 (9)	70	6.6 (2)	6.6 (2)	7.7 (6)	3.7 (5)	3.7 (5)
75	2.9 (2)	2.9 (2)	2.9 (2)	2.9 (2)	2.9 (2)	75	5.2 (1)	5.2 (1)	5.8 (4)	5.2 (1)	5.2 (1)

Note:
Number of participants in the various cohorts is given in parentheses.

Source:
See text of Appendixes 1 and 2.

subject was alive. This constitutes an assumption of high mortality—columns 1 and 6 of table A-1. In the second instance we assumed that the subject for whom we had no known date of death lived ten years beyond the point at which we know he or she was alive, and then died according to the empirical schedule for the age cohort then achieved. As an example: A hypothetical Alice Smith is last known to be alive at age twenty-three; the assumption considers that she died at age 23 + 10 + 12.2 = 45.2, the last figure added being the empirical table's value for the years of life remaining to a woman achieving the 30–35 cohort. This second constitutes an assumption of low mortality—columns 3 and 8 of table A-1. In theory the high and low mortality assumptions generate extreme boundaries between which the true table values presumably lie, and various devices have been used to approximate these true values. One scheme, for example, is to opt for a mid-point between extremes. Walsh and Menard preferred a scheme by which the unknowns were presumed dead at the age at which they were last recorded alive plus the years-yet-to-live for persons at that age as derived from the empirical tables. (The hypothetical Alice Smith would be assumed dead at age 23 + 17.0 = 40 in this scheme.) To facilitate comparison between the Middlesex and Maryland data we have included in table A-1 life tables based upon this assumption—columns 4 and 9 labeled "Maryland Preferred." For our part the application of any single, uniform scheme seems to violate the nature of the data itself. For of the 128 females whose date of death is unknown, the last entry in the record for 56 (43.75 percent) is the birth of a child. Obviously some of these died in or shortly after childbirth, and while we do not know exactly how many, we do know that the probability of immediate death is something greater for these 56 than for the remaining 72 and considerably greater than for the 76 male unknowns who did not hazard childbirth. But none of the assumptions considered thus far—the high and low mortality assumptions and Walsh and Menard's "Maryland Preferred"—take into account these differing probabilities. The Maryland preferred corrective, for example, in assuming that none of these women died in childbirth, tends both to overestimate the years-yet-to-live for women in their fertile years and underestimate for women beyond childbearing. So too does the low mortality assumption, while the high assumption tends to the opposite. Columns 5 and 10 of table A-1—a "Virginia Preferred" assumption—attempt in a crude fashion to accommodate this variable probability. In column 5, with reference to males, we have simply duplicated column 4, considering that for males the Maryland preferred assumption—namely, that the unknowns died according to the empirical schedule for the age at which they are last recorded as alive—is as good as any and more logical than most. Column 10, with reference to females, assumes that one-half of the females for whom the last record was a childbirth died during or shortly after that birth, while the other half (and all the rest of the unknowns) died according to the empirical schedule for their then-achieved age cohort. This Virginia preferred assumption has been used in the text.

The presentation of the Middlesex female life table—informally before and formally at the Seventeenth-Century Chesapeake conference—evoked considerable surprise and even some consternation. Demographic theory generally tends to suggest—but not without exceptions—that women live longer than men; in the table the reverse is true through the women's fertile years, and only in the later ages does the norm hold. Theoretical considerations, too, would require that, if the life table values are sound and the population is to have any natural growth, fertility in Middlesex be higher than is generally thought. Moreover, the female life table clearly contradicted the impressions

TABLE A.2. Hypothetical Age at Death of Five Couples

| Wife | | Husband | |
Age at Death	Years from Marriage at Age 20	Age at Death	Years from Marriage at Age 24
40	20	65	41
39	19	42	18
38	18	41	17
37	17	40	16
39	19	39	15

of other scholars who, in the absence of hard data on women, had resorted to a variety of indirect approaches to the problem of female vis-à-vis male mortality. One example will suffice. Walsh and Menard surveyed 411 seventeenth-century Maryland marriages and counted wives outliving their husbands by roughly a two-to-one margin. Although they recognized the crudeness of the device, they nevertheless held their results to be firm evidence "that females enjoyed longer lives than males."[46] But consider the following hypothetical sequence of marriages: Alice, at age 18, marries Valentine, age 23; Valentine dies at age 40, and Alice (now 35) marries William (age 41), but dies three years later (at 38); William, now a widower, proceeds to marry Betty (age 37) and dies the next year at age 46; Betty ends the sequence, dying the following year at age 38 while bearing William's posthumous child. In this not improbable scenario the wife has survived the husband in two out of three marriages, but both females died younger than both males. Table A-2 depicts again the potential hazard of counting survivors. In four out of the five hypothetical cases presented the wife survives the husband; yet in no case does the wife live a longer lifespan, and the average age at death for the five women is 38.6 and for the five men, 45.4.

While the Middlesex life table is clearly a better gauge of female vis-à-vis male mortality in the Chesapeake than indirect methods such as those noted, it should be equally clear that we are still in the area of rough approximations. The appearance of precision in such a presentation can be deluding, and the table should be scanned for its broad suggestions rather than read for its precise numerical values. Even at the level of broad suggestions, however, the table—particularly when considered with the Walsh and Menard tables— is provocative. Why the apparent difference between the Chesapeake region and what we think we know about New England, and what consequences follow from the different conditions implied? Are there equally startling intraregional differences within the Chesapeake area awaiting us, differences that are possibly as great as the apparent interregional ones? When, as in figure A-1, the data underlying the table are presented in terms of broadly suggestive age-specific death rates (deaths per cohort divided by person-

46. *Ibid.*, 219.

FIGURE A.1. Mortality: Middlesex Married Males and Females Born
through 1710

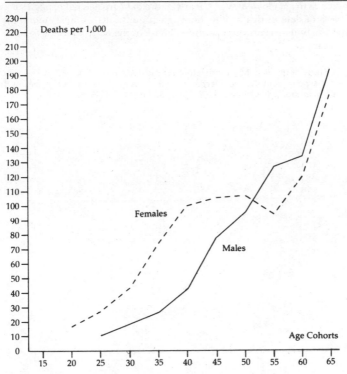

Note:
The data for deaths per 1,000 are smoothed by a three-point running average
procedure.
Sources:
See the text of Appendixes 1 and 2.

years-lived per cohort, utilizing the Virginia preferred assumption with reference to those for whom date of death is unknown), the question of what age-
and sex-specific cause of death is producing the pronounced "bulge" in
female mortality is underlined. The hazards of childbirth is one obvious
answer, but was childbirth more hazardous in the Chesapeake than in New
England? Of the New England scholars only one has suggested such a
childbirth-related bulge; another specifically looked for and failed to find
it.[47] Consideration of cause of death leads to the problem of current versus
generational life tables. The tables presented here are generational—which

47. Maris Vinovskis, "Mortality Rates and Trends in Massachusetts before 1860,"
Jour. Econ. Hist., XXXII (1972), 184–213. Susan Norton, "Population Growth in Colonial

means that because the tables show aggregations of persons born in a particular time frame, the potential variance in the conditions of death at particular times tends to get glossed over. Clearly, more data are needed to aggregate on the basis of date of death. But to cite such questions—a near unending stream occurs to us—is only to cite the richness of the early Chesapeake as a field of research.

America: A Study of Ipswich, Massachusetts," *Population Studies*, XXV (1971), 433–452. We address the point more fully in Darrett B. and Anita H. Rutman, "Of Agues and Fevers: Malaria in the Early Chesapeake," *WMQ*, 3d Ser., XXIII (1976), 31–60.

6

"In dispers'd Country Plantations": Settlement Patterns in Seventeenth-Century Surry County, Virginia

Kevin P. Kelly

When Henry Hartwell and his fellow authors, James Blair and Edward Chilton, wrote their *Present State of Virginia* in 1697, they sadly described Virginia's settlement as "without any Rule or Order." Nor were they alone in their judgment. Robert Beverley, in 1705, joined them in condemning the colony's "unhappy Form of Settlement." The main shortcomings that these critics noted were the region's dispersed plantations and its lack of towns. Not all Virginians saw such flaws in their settlements, but Beverley dismissed this dissent as the ambition of planters seeking to be the lords of vast estates. Hartwell, Blair, and Chilton were harsher, terming opposition as mere "Obstinacy."[1] Although it is now difficult to know which side was more clear-sighted at the time, hindsight indicates that those content with Virginia's geographic arrangements were more correct in their sense of things. In fact, Virginia's settlements were not as haphazardly dispersed as contemporary critics suggested. Rather, Virginia's planters settled in definite patterns, responding to the social and economic conditions of the region.[2]

A valuable way to demonstrate that settlement patterns followed social and economic conditions is to study the process of settlement at

1. Henry Hartwell *et al.*, *The Present State of Virginia, and the College*, ed. Hunter Dickinson Farish (Williamsburg, Va., 1940), 4, 11; Robert Beverley, *The History and Present State of Virginia*, ed. Louis B. Wright (Chapel Hill, N.C., 1947), 57, 118.

2. For an excellent study of a settlement system elsewhere in the Chesapeake, see: Carville V. Earle, *The Evolution of a Tidewater Settlement System: All Hallow's Parish, Maryland, 1650–1783* (Chicago, 1975). For a discussion of Virginia's earliest settlements, see J. Frederick Fausz, "Patterns of Settlement in the James River Basin" (M.A. thesis, The College of William and Mary, 1971).

the local level, where it can be seen in greater detail. For this reason we will examine the pace and pattern of the geographic expansion of Surry County. Situated on the James River across from Jamestown, seventeenth-century Surry extended some twenty miles along the river, bounded on the northwest at Upper Chippokes Creek by Charles City County and on the southwest at Lawnes Creek by Isle of Wight County (see map 1). For most of the century Surry's area of potential settlement, which encompassed some three hundred square miles, stretched only about fifteen miles inland to the Blackwater River. The main James River tributaries, such as Gray's Creek and Lower Chippokes Creek, were short streams extending back from the James only about five miles. At another one to three miles inland, Surry's "upland" crested at approximately one hundred feet. This watershed would prove to be one of the more important geographic features of seventeenth-century Surry, for once it was crossed, Surry's creeks flowed toward the Blackwater River and the Albemarle Sound and away from the main streams of Virginia. As a result it tended to act as a natural constraint on Surry's inland expansion. Nevertheless, Surry attracted planters from the colony's very first days and thus provides a good opportunity to observe settlement patterns throughout most of the seventeenth century.[3] Moreover, enough of the relevant colonial and county records remain to make this examination profitable.

The evidence that establishes when and where people settled in Surry comes primarily from two sources: first, the 398 land patents granted there from the 1620s through the 1690s and, second, the 533 land deeds recorded in the Surry County Court between 1652 and 1700 (see table 1).[4] Prior to 1652, land sales on the "Surry side" of the James River were recorded in James City County and unfortunately have been lost in the subsequent destruction of that county's records.

3. The first known site of English occupation on the "Surry side" of the James was at Smith's Fort in 1608. John B. Boddie, *Colonial Surry* (Richmond, Va., 1948), 14–17.
4. For land grants in Surry prior to 1666 see: Nell Marion Nugent, ed., *Cavaliers and Pioneers: Abstracts of Virginia Land Patents and Grants, 1623–1666* (Richmond, Va., 1934); for those after 1666 see: Virginia State Land Office, Land Patents, Book 6 (1666–1678); Book 7 (1679–1689); Book 8 (1689–1695); Book 9 (1697–1706). Surry's land deeds can be found in Surry County, Virginia, Deeds, Wills, Etc., Book 1 (1652–1672); Book 2 (1671–1684); Book 3 (1684–1687); Book 4 (1687–1694); and Book 5 (1694–1709). Both the land patents and the Surry County records are available on microfilm in the Virginia State Library, Richmond, Virginia.

TABLE 1. Land Transactions

Decade	Grants		Deeds		Adjacent Sales	
	No.	%	No.	%	No.	% of All Sales
1620	5	1	—	—	—	—
1630	79	20	—	—	—	—
1640	45	11	—	—	—	—
1650	42	10	50	9	8	16
1660	57	14	101	19	7	7
1670	40	10	87	16	8	9
1680	100	25	146	27	13	9
1690	30	7	149	28	18	12
Totals	398		533		54	

Sources:
  Surry County, Virginia, Deeds, Wills, Etc., Books 1–5, *passim*; Nell Marion Nugent, ed., *Cavaliers and Pioneers* (Richmond, Va., 1934), I, *passim*; Virginia State Land Office, Land Patents, Books 5–9, *passim*.

One can trace the developing pattern of land acquisition by studying the location of the surviving land transactions. Taking into consideration biases of the data, one can further assume that settlement closely followed the pattern of land acquisition.

One of the problems in using patents as an indicator of settlement is that the actual seating of the land could predate its patent by several years. Michael Nicholls has found that this was a common occurrence in early eighteenth-century Southside Virginia when planters sought to delay paying patenting fees.[5] Similar delays may also have occurred in Surry. In 1699, for example, a commission sent to investigate the land claims in the officially closed frontier south of the Blackwater River found that eighteen of fifty-four claimants had actually seated their lands.[6] In light of this evidence it must be remembered that a patent date only approximates the date of actual settlement.

A second major difficulty is that land patents were often held for speculation rather than for actual settlement. Yet the speculative

5. Michael L. Nicholls, "Origins of the Virginia Southside, 1703–1753: A Social and Economic Study" (Ph.D. diss., The College of William and Mary, 1972), 75–79.

6. Surry County, Virginia, Court Orders, Book 2 (1691–1713); the Commission's deliberations are recorded at the back of the order book.

MAPS 1–8. The first map below shows Surry County, Virginia, in the 1600s, and the seven maps that follow show settlement patterns in the county from 1620 through 1690.

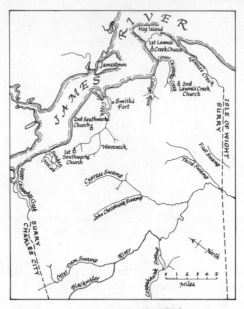

Map 1

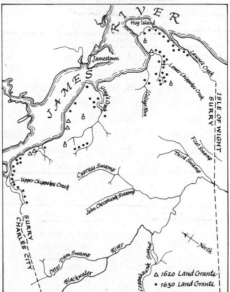

Map 2

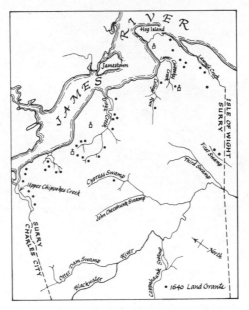

Map 3

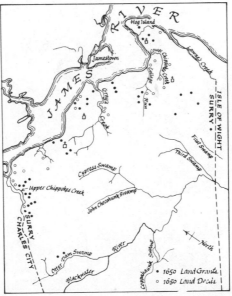

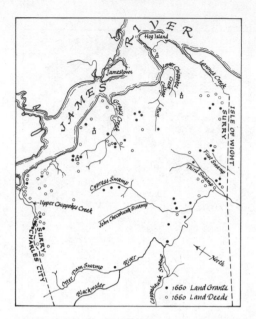

Map 5

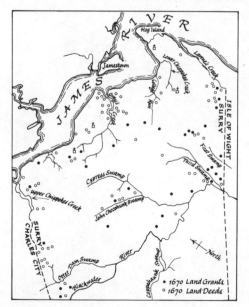

Map 6

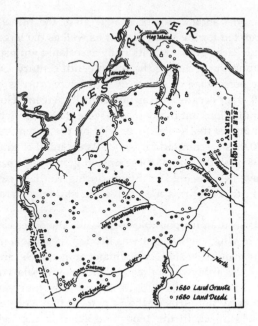

Map 7

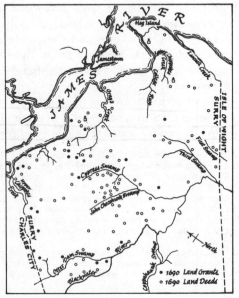

Map 8

purpose of grants should not be exaggerated; the principle of the headright operated for the small planter as well as the large.[7] In fact, few of the truly large grants traditionally associated with speculation were taken up in Surry during the seventeenth century. Only in the 1640s did the percentage of grants over 850 acres run as high as 18 percent; in all other decades it was nearer to 13 percent. However, an even better indication that many grants were meant for actual settlement is the number that were never sold by the patentee. Between 1660 and 1690 these accounted for some 40 percent of all grants. At an average of 433 acres the size of these unsold grants approximated the size of the average freehold in Surry during the late seventeenth century and further confirms the impression that they were meant as plantations.[8]

Even grants secured for possible speculative purposes can point to the direction in which settlement was headed, because a majority of all grants were eventually sold, either intact or in parcels, and because the average interval between their patenting and sale was brief—nine years during the 1660s and 1670s and only four years in the 1680s. This is even more true of the 54 percent that were subdivided rather than sold intact. In the 1660s and again in the 1680s, initial sales occurred quickly at an average of six and three years respectively. Moreover, these subdivided tracts averaged only 233 acres in size, which provides further evidence that they were taken up by planters who actually planned to settle on them. Even those grants sold intact averaged only 430 acres, suggesting that they, too, were meant for actual settlement.[9]

Land sales, on the other hand, are less likely to reflect the speculation of the large planter than original patents and are more likely to show the acquisition of land for actual settlement and plantation use.

7. W. Stitt Robinson, Jr., *Mother Earth: Land Grants in Virginia, 1607–1699*, Jamestown 350th Anniversary Historical Booklets (Williamsburg, Va., 1957), 32.

8. Kevin P. Kelly, "Economic and Social Development of Seventeenth-Century Surry County, Virginia" (Ph.D. diss., University of Washington, 1972), 130–131; the percentage of grants never sold is based on an examination of the subsequent land transactions of nearly 200 land patents in Surry between 1660–1689. The title research was confined only to the lifetime of the patentee and no attempt was made to trace the history of the property to widows and heirs. Undoubtedly some of these grants were eventually broken up and sold.

9. The discussion of the grants sold or subdivided is based only on those deeds where definite references to the earlier grant were made. Fortunately, the number of doubtful cases account for only 11% of all suspected and certain sales.

For example, in the subsequent resale of plantations acquired when large grants were subdivided, 74 percent of those plantations sold were transferred intact. A further suggestion of the nonspeculative nature of most sales was that during the last half of the seventeenth century, only 25 percent of all land sales exceeded the average freehold size.[10] Still the historian must exercise caution in using land deeds to trace settlement patterns. A full 10 percent of sales, for instance, involved the purchase of land adjacent to that already owned by the buyer. The location of land involved in these sales shows not expansion, but rather, the important process of enlarging existing plantations. Also, within the course of a decade the same land might change hands more than once. Despite these problems, patents and deeds, analyzed together, do present a general picture of the geographic distribution of Surry plantations over time.

Surry, like the rest of the Chesapeake, was bound to the outside world by an intricate network of relationships. Judicial, political, and ecclesiastical pressures all worked to overcome the local isolation of the Bay communities. The key force behind social integration, however, was the area's commitment to tobacco production and to a trading network.[11] The economic necessities of the region, which includes Surry, in turn affected local spatial features. In a self-contained and self-sufficient area, as sociologist Amos Hawley points out, the need for a continual interpersonal relationship would predominate. As a result its inhabitants valued residential proximity and thus formed compact settlements.[12] On the other hand, a region ruled by its need to produce a valuable trading commodity would develop differently. There residents would tend to move out of the villages and into the countryside to make more effective use of the land. The geographic characteristics of a region dependent on the outside world would display periodic community centers, dispersed artisans, and scattered plantations.[13] Thus Surry's dependent status

10. Kelly, "Economic and Social Development of Surry County," 128–131.
11. Darrett B. Rutman makes this point in "The Social Web: A Prospectus for the Study of the Early American Community," in William L. O'Neill, ed., *Insights and Parallels: Problems and Issues of American Social History* (Minneapolis, Minn., 1973), 83–85.
12. Amos H. Hawley, *Human Ecology: A Theory of Community Structure* (New York, 1950), 223–225, 239–245.
13. *Ibid.*, 225–230, 239–245, 269–270.

and the geographic implications of that status suggest that an explanation for the timing, pace, and pattern of Surry's expansion will be found in the context of Virginia's economy and overall growth. The full story of this relationship is complex and is only part of the total development of Surry's society. But the highlights of this relationship, as they relate to Surry's settlement, can be outlined here.

The successful development and effective marketing of tobacco in Virginia by 1617 produced a boom during the 1620s that brought immigrants to the colony scrambling after quick riches. Although this boom soon collapsed and the easy times were gone by 1630, their effects remained. People still flocked to Virginia, settling along its navigable waterways.[14] Aided by a price recovery in the mid-1630s, the "Surry side" benefited during this expansion as did all the area south of the James.[15] The initial surge of grants in Surry, which occurred before 1640, set the basic pattern of Surry's early settlement. These grants were confined primarily to the James River frontage and to the mouths of the two boundary creeks, Lawnes Creek and the Upper Chippokes. The only inland patents were on Gray's Creek and along Lower Chippokes, well within the James River drainage (see map 2).[16] By the early 1640s Surry's newly settled residents optimistically established their own parishes and were soon petitioning for a complete separation from James City County.[17]

14. This account of Virginia's early growth is drawn from Edmund S. Morgan, *American Slavery, American Freedom: The Ordeal of Colonial Virginia* (New York, 1975), 90, 108–158.

15. Information on Virginia's early tobacco prices comes from the data assembled by Russell R. Menard, "A Note on Chesapeake Tobacco Prices, 1618–1600," *Virginia Magazine of History and Biography*, LXXXIV (1976), 401–410. Between 1634 and 1644 the counties south of the James grew at a rate of 14% annually, while those on the lower James-York peninsula actually lost population at a yearly rate of .6%. Morgan, *American Slavery, American Freedom*, 412–413.

16. It must be noted that it was not possible to fix the location of the land grants and deeds with exact precision. Although the art of survey improved in Surry during the seventeenth century, it remained one of metes and bounds. This is a most imprecise type of survey because it relies on physical features of an area to mark the boundary and these markers could easily disappear. Moreover they give no hint to their exact location, particularly to the historian who is trying to reconstruct settlement patterns 300 years after the fact. Fortunately, in 50% and 70% of the deeds and grants respectively the descriptions of their location included references to recognizable streams, creeks, and swamps. It is from such references and other directional information such as "southeast of the westernmost branch . . . " that the maps were constructed. However, because of the vague nature of even the best description, the plots of the grants and deeds on the maps must be taken as only approximate. For a discussion of similar problems with surveys, see Earle, *Evolution of a Tidewater Settlement System*, 182–188.

17. In 1652, two parishes existed in the area that became Surry County. Lawnes

The price of tobacco continued to fall during the 1640s and 1650s, and soon population growth south of the James slowed.[18] By 1653 it had ceased altogether in Surry. Consequently the pace of settlement slackened, and there was little change in the basic pattern of extension along the James River and up its main tributaries (see maps 3 and 4). In the 1640s more grants were given out on Gray's Creek and some farther inland along the smaller streams that flowed into the James. Only three grants can be identified on the swamps that flowed into the interior of Surry and emptied into the Blackwater River. In the 1650s settlement moved along Surry's northwestern boundary to the head of Upper Chippokes Creek. The larger-sized grants there and at the headwaters of Lawnes Creek suggest that these regions drew the attention of early speculators (see table 2). While the decade of the 1650s saw the continued patenting of land near the Blackwater at the 1640 rate, the land deeds reveal that no one was yet willing to buy land there.

The curtailment of Surry's expansion during these years was the predictable result of low tobacco prices coupled with the generally poor quality of tobacco grown in the county.[19] Surry, which had to compete for settlers with the richer lands still available in the Middle Peninsula and the Northern Neck, was placed at a severe disadvantage. Few planters attracted to Surry could afford to suffer the higher transportation costs of a move inland across the county's watershed. As a result, while Virginia's more fertile areas grew at better than 7 percent annually, Surry actually lost population during the 1650s and 1660s.[20]

Moreover, the real threat of Indian attack provided added incentive

Creek Parish, established in 1640, ran from Lawnes Creek to College Run and extended inland indefinitely. Southwarke Parish, created in 1647, included the area between College Run and Upper Chippokes Creek. The boundaries of the two parishes remained unchanged until 1738. George Carrington Mason, "The Colonial Churches of Surry and Sussex Counties, Virginia," *William and Mary Quarterly*, 2d Ser., XX (1940), 286–287.

18. Morgan, *American Slavery, American Freedom*, 412–413. Between 1644 and 1653 the rate of tithable increase of the Southside counties fell to 4.6% annually.

19. There is no direct evidence concerning the quality of Surry's tobacco in the seventeenth century. However, the recorded selling price of each county's tobacco, received in payment of quitrents in 1702, 1703, and 1704, reveals that only the tobacco of the Eastern Shore and the counties south of the lower James brought a consistently lower price than Surry's. C.O. 5/1313, 196–197; C.O. 5/1314, 437–438, Public Record Office.

20. Surry's tithable population fell from 518 in 1653 to only 383 in 1674. The estimated total population of the counties of the Middle Peninsula and the Northern Neck rose during the same years by 7.7% annually. Morgan, *American Slavery, American Freedom*, 404, 412–413.

TABLE 2. Regional Average Size of Land Grant and Land Deed by Decade

	James River				Blackwater River				Heads of the Upper Chippokes & Lawnes Creek			
Decade	No. of Observ.	Patent	No. of Observ.	Deed	No. of Observ.	Patent	No. of Observ.	Deed	No. of Observ.	Patent	No. of Observ.	Deed
1620	6	290	–	–	–	–	–	–	–	–	–	–
1630	68	491	–	–	–	–	–	–	4	525	–	–
1640	39	685	–	–	3	375	–	–	7	1,250	–	–
1650	36	454	21	404	7	612	–	–	7	791	1	600
1660	23	487	38	215	24	419	9	224	7	474	8	251
1670	17	500	25	212	21	726	15	280	2	575	12	273
1680	22	617	31	164	56	463	64	212	4	278	6	189
1690	11	387	34	176	10	578	53	182	4	181	1	80

Sources:
Surry County, Virginia, Wills, Deeds, Etc., Books 1–5, *passim*; Nell Marion Nugent, ed., *Cavaliers and Pioneers* (Richmond, Va., 1934), I, *passim*; Virginia State Land Office, Land Patents, Books 5–9, *passim*.

to the planters of Surry to huddle near the James. All of Virginia was severely hurt by the attack of 1622 in which some 350 people were killed, 64 of whom were "Surry side" inhabitants.[21] The memory of this event was not quickly forgotten. In 1644 Virginia was again subjected to an all-out Indian attack, with the settlers living at the fall line of the main Virginia rivers and on the south side of the upper James bearing the brunt of it. Whether the planters of Surry were actually involved is not clear, but the main Indian tribe of the area, the Warrasqueoc, were members of the attacking Powhatan confederation.[22] Tensions were not relieved until the 1660s, when treaties negotiated with the still formidable Indians living south of the James established the Blackwater as the boundary between them and the English.[23] Not surprisingly, it was only in that decade that land grants on the branches of the Blackwater began in any real numbers.

Thus, after more than thirty years of settlement a combination of impediments worked to hold Surry's planters in a crescent-shaped pattern extending from the head of Upper Chippokes along the James and up Lawnes Creek. Except for plantations along the boundary creeks, the population had moved little more than three to five miles inland. Within this crescent, as Surry became a separate county in 1652, land transactions were heavily concentrated in three distinct areas, with the population tending to cluster at the mouth of Upper Chippokes, in the area between Lawnes Creek and Lower Chippokes, and along Gray's Creek. None of these neighborhoods was able to become truly dominant. The county courthouse was placed at Wareneck on Gray's Creek simply because it was the most central location.

In the decades of the 1660s and the 1670s, when population once again began to grow and the pressure for expansion was renewed, Surry's settlement was forced to take its first slow steps in breaking out of this pattern (see maps 5 and 6). In the 1660s the area around what was called the First Swamp, near the Surry-Isle of Wight boundary on the southeast, saw the most growth. A few planters also took up grants in the area of Cypress Swamp and the Blackwater itself.

21. Richard L. Morton, *Colonial Virginia* (Chapel Hill, N.C., 1960), I, 77–85; John C. Hotten, ed., *The Original Lists of Persons of Quality . . . and Others Who Went from Great Britain to the American Plantations, 1600–1700* (London, 1874), 201–265.
22. Morton, *Colonial Virginia*, I, 153.
23. *Ibid.*, I, 229; Morgan, *American Slavery, American Freedom*, 230.

Despite an increasing number of land purchases in the areas near the Blackwater, the majority of land sales still transpired in the James River crescent in the 1660s and 1670s. Moreover, the boundary creek headwaters lost their speculative appeal as interest in the interior grew. But even so these first steps were hesitant ones, for at the end of the 1670s only the additional area of settlement around First and Third Swamps in Lawnes Creek Parish disturbed Surry's characteristic crescent arrangement.

In the following ten years, however, that configuration drastically changed. Steadily through the 1680s, Surry's population continued the growth begun in the mid-1670s, not peaking until the mid-1690s. And significantly, the number of households increased at a faster rate in the 1680s than in the 1670s or the 1690s.[24] With this growth the pace of land transactions quickened to new highs as both land grants and land sales were predominantly located upon the main tributaries of the Blackwater (see map 7). Although the Third Swamp region of Lawnes Creek Parish continued to be an active area of land acquisition, most settlement took place in the region of the Cypress and John Checohunk swamps. The region between Upper Chippokes and Otterdam Swamp also experienced increased attention from planters. As the 1680s ended, the interior of Surry was nearly completely settled. A large number of planters then lived more than ten miles from the James, and having crossed Surry's watershed, they were not even nominally connected to it by the creeks and streams that ran past their plantations. Most of the land transferred in the 1690s was located in the area opened in the 1680s, reinforcing the movement inland and the breakup of the population clusters that had characterized Surry just twenty years earlier (see map 8). Although a few planters were even beginning to venture south of the Blackwater it was not until that area was officially opened in the early eighteenth century that Surry would again experience an expansion on the scale of the 1680s.

This dramatic change in Surry's settlement pattern was a result of

24. Kelly, "Economic and Social Development of Surry County," 19. Surry's households increased by 38% from 236 in 1680 to 325 in 1690 compared to only a 17% increase between 1670 and 1680 and a 12% increase between 1690 and 1700. In the only two other counties where a comparison can be made, Accomack County's households increased by 16% during the 1680s and in Lancaster County they increased by 30% between 1679 and 1691. See the Accomack and Lancaster county records of the Virginia State Library.

TABLE 3. Regional Land Prices
(Decade average price per acre in pounds of tobacco)

| | | *Area* | | |
| | *James River* | | *Blackwater River* | |
Decade	*Price*	*% of Total Sales*	*Price*	*% of Total Sales*
1670	44.8	48	9.8	29
1680	26.2	31	15.9	63
1690	51.1	39	16.9	60

Sources:
    Surry County, Virginia, Wills, Deeds, Etc., Books 1–5, *passim*.

the collapse of the tobacco economy during the 1680s. One of the longest depressions of the century, the collapse began with the fall of tobacco prices in the late 1670s, and except for a brief respite in the mid-1680s, it gripped Virginia well into the 1690s.[25] At the onset of the depression, growth in the Middle Peninsula and the Northern Neck was arrested. Almost without exception the tithable population of those areas declined in the early 1680s, and, in contrast to Surry, the formation of new households there slowed. While the affluent areas of tidewater Virginia retrenched, the counties of Surry, Henrico, and Charles City grew steadily and continually throughout the depression.[26] The common attraction of each of these counties for the hard-hit planter was the lure of their open frontiers. That Surry had remained confined to a narrow crescent now worked to its advantage.

Specifically, the key to Surry's attraction was that its available interior land was inexpensive. As table 3 shows, land in the newly settled districts was always cheaper than land in the older areas of

25. No good Virginia tobacco price series exists for the period after 1660. However, Russell Menard has constructed an excellent farm price series for Maryland during the last half of the seventeenth century. Although the absolute level of the price may have differed, and the timing may have varied slightly, it is likely that Virginia's prices followed the same general trend. Russell R. Menard, "Farm Prices of Maryland Tobacco, 1659–1710," *Maryland Historical Magazine*, LXVIII (1973), 80–85.

26. This observation is based on the number of tithables per county, available at the Virginia State Library, Richmond, Virginia. Henrico's tithables increased from 436 in 1680 to 712 by 1690; Charles City grew from 714 in 1682 to 814 in 1685 and to 1,052 by 1698. Surry grew from 383 in 1674, to 413 in 1678, to 626 in 1690, finally peaking at 641 in 1692. Most of Virginia's other counties lost tithables during the first half of the 1680s before beginning to grow by 1690.

Surry, reflecting its lack of improvements and distance from the James. In the 1670s land near the James sold for better than four times as much as land inland. Even in the 1680s, when demand drove up the price of land near the Blackwater and lessening demand lowered it along the James, the former still sold for 60 percent less. The lower price of interior land was doubly important to the planter seeking the opportunity to acquire a plantation in Surry during the depression years of the 1680s. First, the lower price overcame one of the major disadvantages to the county's inland settlement by balancing off the increased cost of transporting tobacco to the James. Second, it provided the planter the opportunity of acquiring a plantation equal in size to those in Surry's older areas with a smaller initial investment. In fact, from the 1670s until the end of the century, the Blackwater region recorded the largest average land sale size, if only by a small margin. Thus it is quite natural, given the unpleasant conditions elsewhere in Virginia, that Surry's interior no longer appeared inhospitable to prospective settlers.

Moreover, Surry's depression-era growth and expansion offer concrete confirmation of Edmund Morgan's suggestion that ex-servants unable to make it in the affluent areas of Virginia found their opportunity in a frontier region like Surry.[27] In Lawnes Creek Parish, where differences in household composition between newly settled and well-established areas can be glimpsed in the 1680s, the small householder—the younger man, the newly freed servant, and the poor planter—led the vanguard of actual settlers inland.

Social differences between the various regions within Surry reflected by tithable household size are difficult to check. Each year the court divided the county into precincts to facilitate the tabulation of the taxable population. With little regard for recognizable neighborhoods, these precincts simply ran perpendicular to the James River and extended back as far as the Blackwater. As a result they included newly settled areas as well as old ones. In 1681 and 1683, and again in 1688 and 1689, in Lawnes Creek Parish the commissioners departed from their normal routine and counted the settlers around the First and Third swamps separately and called the area the Blackwater precinct.[28] While land was first acquired there in the 1660s and 1670s,

27. Morgan, *American Slavery, American Freedom*, 420.
28. Surry Co., Va., Deeds, Wills, Etc., Book 2, 292–294.

it too participated in the expansion of the 1680s. One of the oldest sections of the parish was also counted separately in 1681 and 1683. Known as Chippokes precinct, it included the planters living around Lower Chippokes Creek. This area was some thirty to forty years older than the Blackwater precinct, having been settled in the 1630s and 1640s. Comparison of the tithe lists of the two areas reveals the significant differences in the social and economic composition of Surry's interior.

One can see immediately that the mean tithable household in 1681 and 1683 was smaller by one full member in the Blackwater precinct, despite the fact that both regions contained approximately the same number of households (see table 4). Two factors account for the lower mean in the Blackwater precinct. First, the proportion of households containing only a single tithable was significantly higher in Blackwater. There it ranged between 67 percent and 73 percent in the two years; whereas, in Chippokes the percentage decreased from 53 percent to 48 percent. In addition, the percentage of large tithable households was greater in Chippokes precinct. In Blackwater in 1681, no household included more than three tithables; in contrast, 31 percent of all the households in Chippokes did. By 1683 the percentage in Blackwater of those listing three or more had increased to 5 percent, while the proportion decreased in Chippokes, but was still 12 percent higher. Black slaves were also more numerous in the Chippokes precinct. In 1681 there were only two in Blackwater, and they were living on the quarter of a nonresident planter. There were nine in Chippokes. However, by 1683 the difference in this regard diminished somewhat. The number of blacks in Blackwater increased to six, while the number of blacks in Chippokes remained unchanged.

The picture of the Blackwater precinct at the end of the 1680s was much the same. The mean household size had increased only slightly, while the percentage of single tithable households remained constant at approximately 70 percent. The proportion of large households had increased over the early years of the decade, but still none contained more than seven tithables. There were more blacks by 1688 and 1689, but the majority of them were listed on the quarters of larger planters and not among the smaller ones. Unfortunately, no comparison with Chippokes can be made during this period because by the end of the 1680s it was included in the lower precinct of Lawnes Creek. Never-

TABLE 4.   Variation in Tithable Household Size, Lawnes Creek, 1681–1689

1681 Precinct

No. Tithable per Household	Blackwater No.	%	Chippokes No.	%	Lawnes Creek No.	%
1	14	67	10	53	27	43
2	6	29	2	11	24	38
3	1	5	1	5	6	9
4	—	—	3	16	2	3
5	—	—	1	5	2	3
6	—	—	1	5	—	—
7	—	—	—	—	2	3
8	—	—	—	—	—	—
9	—	—	—	—	—	—
10	—	—	—	—	—	—
11	—	—	1	5	—	—
12	—	—	—	—	—	—
Totals	21		19		63	
Mean household size	1.38		2.68		2.04	

1683 Precinct

No. Tithable per Household	Blackwater No.	%	Chippokes No.	%	Lawnes Creek No.	%
1	16	73	11	48	41	61
2	5	23	7	30	16	24
3	—	—	1	4	5	7
4	—	—	—	—	3	4
5	1	5	1	4	—	—
6	—	—	2	9	—	—
7	—	—	—	—	1	1
8	—	—	—	—	—	—
9	—	—	—	—	—	—
10	—	—	1	4	1	1
11	—	—	—	—	—	—
12	—	—	—	—	—	—
Totals	22		23		67	
Mean household size	1.40		2.39		1.74	

1688 Precinct

No. Tithable per Household	Blackwater No.	%	Lower Precinct, Lawnes Creek No.	%
1	29	74	55	57
2	7	18	23	24
3	1	3	7	7
4	—	—	4	4
5	1	3	3	3
6	—	—	—	—
7	1	3	1	1
8	—	—	—	—
9	—	—	2	2
10	—	—	—	—
11	—	—	—	—
12	—	—	1	1
Totals	39		96	
Mean household size	1.48		1.97	

1689 Precinct

No. Tithable per Household	Blackwater No.	%	Lower Precinct, Lawnes Creek No.	%
1	32	71	70	71
2	8	18	18	18
3	3	7	4	4
4	—	—	1	1
5	1	2	—	—
6	1	2	2	2
7	—	—	1	1
8	—	—	—	—
9	—	—	2	2
10	—	—	—	—
11	—	—	—	—
12	—	—	1	1
Totals	45		99	
Mean household size	1.52		1.68	

Sources:
"Tithable lists, 1681, 1683, 1688, and 1689," Surry County, Virginia, Deeds, Wills, Etc., Book 2, pp. 294, 335; Book 4, pp. 66, 71, 121–122.

theless, it was only in 1689 that the distribution of tithables in Blackwater resembled the distribution of tithables within the rest of the
parish. This resulted not from any changes in Blackwater but from
an increase in the ranks of the small planters caused by economic
retrenchment elsewhere in the parish.[29]

It is clear from the presence of large numbers of small householders
and the near absence of slaves and servants in Blackwater that the
county's inland regions did not appeal to Surry's larger and well-
established planters. For them the main advantage still rested in the
older areas near the James. The interior was recognized simply for its
future potential. Yet the differences between new and old sections
should not be exaggerated. As a whole, Surry was one of Virginia's
poorer counties. With its overall high percentage of single tithable
households and its lack of truly grand and wealthy planters, the
regional differences inside Surry may have been more in degree than
in substance.[30]

As a result of the expansion of the 1680s, Surry ended the seventeenth century fixed in a geographically dispersed settlement pattern.
Although land transactions were still more highly concentrated in
some sections of the county than in others, the relatively uniform size
of land sales in all areas worked to keep planters living far apart. In
addition, Surry's planters began almost immediately to consolidate
their holdings. As mentioned earlier nearly 10 percent of all sales,
averaging approximately one hundred acres, were involved in this
process. While such consolidation eased a planter's daily movement
back and forth to his several tobacco fields, it also worked to maintain
distance between neighbors.[31]

The inland spread of population also meant that there still was no
dominant geographic center in Surry. Wareneck, with its ordinary,
gristmill, and court buildings, remained the judicial center of the
county, but became the focus of activity for only a few days every two
to three months. The one attempt to legislate a "town" for Surry

29. For a discussion of the effects of the depression on Surry planters, particularly
on the retrenchment of the small slave owners, see Kevin P. Kelly, "The Structure of
Household Labor in Late Seventeenth-Century Virginia: Surry County, a Case Study"
(paper presented to the Annual Meeting of the Southern Historical Association, Dallas,
Texas, Nov. 9, 1972), 7–17.

30. Kelly, "Economic and Social Development of Surry County," 132–158, 186–196.
A good comparison of Surry County with several other counties in Virginia can be
found in Morgan, *American Slavery, American Freedom*, 221–222, 226, 228–229, 419.

failed. In 1691, under considerable pressure from colonial officials, the county commissioners finally bought fifty acres at the mouth of Gray's Creek and ordered that the area be subdivided into half-acre town lots.[32] However, due to a lack of interest, not one lot was sold during the remainder of the seventeenth century. In the absence of urban centers, artisans lived among the planters they served. Millers, for example, could be found at the Third Swamp, at the head of Upper Chippokes, and at Sunken Marsh, as well as near Lawnes Creek.[33] The deeds also reveal that tailors, shoemakers, coopers, and blacksmiths could be found scattered throughout the county.

Isolation can be an inherent problem in an area of dispersed settlements. When Surry was still bound to the James, this was less of a problem. The distances between neighbors were short and easily covered by foot. Moreover, access to the James and its tributaries made water transportation possible.[34] The spread of settlement inland in the 1680s and 1690s altered the situation. Surry's residents were then living far removed from one another. As the line of settlement crossed over into the Blackwater watershed, many of Surry's planters had moved out of touch with the James and away from easy access to the main trading routes of the Chesapeake. Rather than give in to the problems that resulted from expansion, Surry's inhabitants worked hard to overcome them by building a network of roads that linked themselves together and Surry's backcountry to the James. While the earliest known road in Surry connected the inhabitants of Hog Island Main to a river landing and a store in the 1630s, it was only in the last twenty years of the century that the construction of

31. A similar process with a similar result occurred in All Hallow's Parish, Maryland. See Earle, *Evolution of a Tidewater Settlement System,* 220.

32. Surry Co., Va., Deeds, Wills, Etc., Book 4, 223. Also see A. W. Bohannan, *Old Surry: Thumb Nail Sketches of Places of Historic Interest in Surry County, Virginia* (Petersburg, Va., 1927), 55.

33. For various references to Surry's mills see: Surry Co., Va., Deeds, Wills, Etc., Book 1, 148, 298, 310, 319; Book 2, 253; Book 4, 10; Orders, Book 1, 298. For a similar pattern of dispersed artisans in All Hallow's Parish, Maryland, see Earle, *Evolution of a Tidewater Settlement System,* 78–91.

34. The loss of the "Surry side" records, coupled with only scattered inventories before the 1670s, makes it impossible to know precisely how important water transportation was to Surry's early settlers, but there are hints. For example, prior to the establishment of the area's own parishes in the 1640s, Surry side planters were expected to cross the James River to attend services; in 1658 a group of runaway servants had lined up two boats to aid in their flight; and finally, during Bacon's Rebellion, the rebels attempted to confiscate a local boat. Boddie, *Colonial Surry,* 148; Surry Co., Va., Deeds, Wills, Etc., Book 1, 119–123; Book 2, 130.

highways became a major concern.[35] To insure that planters would provide the necessary labor to build and care for them, men of recognized prestige and authority were appointed surveyors of the highways. Grand juries also began to include the failure to maintain roads in the presentments. The planters themselves, whenever they felt that the court had ignored their needs, petitioned it to create new highways or reroute old ones.[36] Finally, to take advantage of road travel Surry's planters increased the number of horses they owned.[37] While Surry's settlements may have been scattered as the century ended, it was a rare plantation that remained truly isolated from either its neighbors or the outside world.

A slow, and at times almost moribund, growth followed by an explosive expansion marked the course of Surry's seventeenth-century settlement. In both periods Surry's experience was the natural outcome of its response to Virginia's overall growth. It was, after all, a change in the attitudes of prospective settlers toward Surry, and not a change in the conditions within the county—its geography, its unproductive soil, its relative lack of affluence—that affected its settlement. Surry was viewed as an unattractive backwater prior to 1680. But as the depression of the 1680s closed off economic opportunity in large areas of Virginia, the need to find it elsewhere overcame the earlier reluctance to settle in Surry. Although the details of Surry's experience may parallel only frontier areas, the explanation of that experience carries importance for the rest of Virginia. The dependence of Surry's settlement on outside forces supports the argument that no area of Virginia was settled independently of the larger social and economic needs of the colony. Furthermore, Surry's experience sug-

35. Robert Caufield, in his petition to the court in 1686, complained that the road to his store had been illegally closed. To support his claim that it should be reopened, he added that it had been a public road for over fifty years. Surry Co., Va., Orders, Book 1, 55.

36. For examples of petitions concerning roads and Grand Jury presentments see: Surry Co., Va., Orders, Book 1, 728, 458; Book 2, 50, 54; and Deeds, Wills, Etc., Book 3, 84. A discussion of the prestige of the highway surveyors can be found in Kevin P. Kelly, "Political Order in Surry County, Virginia, 1682–1703" (paper presented at the 32nd Conference in Early American History: The Seventeenth-Century Chesapeake, College Park, Maryland, Nov. 1–2, 1974).

37. The percentage of horses owned by Surry's decedents rose from 25% in the 1660s to 69% in the 1690s. Carville Earle found a similar increase in All Hallow's, from 47% in the 1670s to 81% in the 1680s. Earle, Evolution of a Tidewater Settlement System, 142–157.

gests that a relationship between settlement and society exists within an area as well. Surry's expansion of the 1680s, for example, not only dispersed its settlement, but also reinforced the small-planter nature of Surry's society. Thus, as our knowledge of the intricacies of the settlement process increases, not only will we be able to answer questions of how the various regions in the colony were actually settled, but also we will begin to see how the settlement patterns themselves affected the social development of Virginia.

7

Immigration and Opportunity:
The Freedman in Early Colonial Maryland

Lois Green Carr
and Russell R. Menard

Over the seventeenth century the pace of immigration and the character of the immigrant group had a continuing impact on the shape of Chesapeake society. Unlike New England, where substantial immigration lasted only a decade, Virginia and Maryland received a continuing influx of Europeans—mostly Englishmen—that had a profound effect on population growth and social structure in the region. The opportunities available to new settlers and the ability of Chesapeake society to assimilate immigrants into a New World community are central themes in the history of the tobacco coast.[1]

Most immigrants arrived as servants.[2] If they lived to complete

1. For recent discussions of immigration to the Chesapeake, see Mildred Campbell, "Social Origins of Some Early Americans," in James Morton Smith, ed., *Seventeenth-Century America: Essays in Colonial History* (Chapel Hill, N.C., 1959); Wesley Frank Craven, *White, Red, and Black: The Seventeenth-Century Virginian* (Charlottesville, Va., 1971), 1–37; Russell R. Menard, "Immigrants and Their Increase: The Process of Population Growth in Early Colonial Maryland," in Aubrey C. Land, Lois Green Carr, and Edward C. Papenfuse, eds., *Law, Society, and Politics in Early Maryland* (Baltimore, 1977), 88–110; Menard, "Immigration to the Chesapeake Colonies in the Seventeenth Century: A Review Essay," *Maryland Historical Magazine*, LXVIII (1973), 323–329; Menard, "Economy and Society in Early Colonial Maryland" (Ph.D. diss., University of Iowa, 1975), 153–224, 396–422; David W. Galenson, "'Middling People' or 'Common Sort'?: The Social Origins of Some Early Americans Reexamined," *William and Mary Quarterly*, 3d Ser., XXXV (1978), 499–524; David Souden, "'Rogues, whores and vagabonds': Indentured Servant Emigrants to North America, and the Case of Mid-Seventeenth Century Bristol," *Social History*, III (1978), 23–41. See also the essay by James Horn in this volume.

2. A study of the status of immigrants from headright entries concludes that 70% of the colonists who came to Maryland between 1634 and 1681 arrived as indentured servants. The majority of free immigrants arrived between 1646 and 1652 and between 1658 and 1667, both periods of substantial migration from Virginia to Maryland. Since many of the settlers from Virginia had arrived as servants and completed their terms before crossing the Potomac, the figure of 70% doubtless understates the proportion of servants in the immigrant group. Before 1646, in the mid-1650s, and after 1667, when there is less evidence of internal migration, more than 85% of the immigrants in the

their terms they entered Chesapeake society without any belongings except their "freedom dues," which in Maryland consisted of clothing, an axe and a hoe, and three barrels of corn, all due from the former master—and until 1681 a 50-acre land warrant obtainable on demand from the proprietor. In all, these dues were worth six to seven hundred pounds of tobacco.[3] With this start, the freedman, as ex-servants often were called, began a new life.

What kind of life would he lead? What work would he do? What kind of property might he acquire? How good were his chances to become a planter, to marry and raise children, to participate in community decision making—in short, to be fully integrated into Chesapeake society? These are basic questions. A study of freedmen, particularly those who had completed servitude but had not yet established households or acquired land, is a study not only of free men at the bottom of this immigrant society but of a stage in the careers of large numbers of inhabitants of the seventeenth-century Chesapeake. An evaluation of freedmen's prospects is a study of opportunity for the great majority of men who immigrated.

Several aspects of life in the Chesapeake colonies affected all who came, servants or free. First, the pattern of growth in the tobacco industry shaped the fortunes of incoming Englishmen. For nearly seventy years after the beginnings of successful commercial tobacco cultivation in Virginia the industry expanded, although at a steadily decelerating pace, as productivity gains permitted colonial planters to sell their crop for less and English merchants brought Chesapeake tobacco to the major ports of Europe. Exports of tobacco grew from a mere twenty-five hundred pounds in 1616 to fifteen million pounds by the late 1660s. Growth continued for another fifteen years, although at a much slower rate: tobacco exports passed twenty-one million pounds in the early 1680s and twenty-eight million pounds by the end of the decade. But the inability of planters to achieve further cost

---

headright sample came as servants, a figure that may more closely represent the composition of the European immigrant group to the entire Chesapeake during the 17th century. Menard, "Economy and Society," 162.

3. In 1677 a Maryland inventory itemized and valued freedom corn, clothes, and tools at 500 pounds of tobacco. Inventories and Accounts, IV, 384, MS, Hall of Records, Annapolis. Unless otherwise noted, all manuscript sources cited are at the Hall of Records. The 50-acre land warrant was probably worth at most 120 pounds of tobacco, the price established for a Maryland warrant in 1681, when the headright system ended there. Freedom dues may have had a somewhat greater value at mid-century when prices for food and clothing were higher.

reductions, a sharp increase in British customs, and the disruption of trade by the turn-of-the-century wars ended this long, expansive phase of Chesapeake economic history. For nearly thirty years beginning in the 1680s, the Chesapeake tobacco industry suffered stagnation and depressed prices interrupted only by a short boom in 1685 and 1686 and a somewhat longer period of peace and prosperity around 1700.[4]

Demographic conditions also shaped Chesapeake society during the seventeenth century. For one thing, life was short. A substantial number of immigrants died soon after they arrived, victims of a now vague complex of diseases that contemporaries called "seasoning." How many failed to live through the first year is unknown, but the figure was high enough to provoke frequent comment. And, although the chances of survival increased as the seventeenth century progressed, the Chesapeake colonies were considered dangerous to new arrivals as late as 1700, particularly during late summer.[5] Many of the servants who survived seasoning, furthermore, did not live to complete their terms. Altogether, perhaps 40 percent of those who

4. Russell R. Menard, "The Tobacco Industry in the Chesapeake Colonies, 1617–1730: An Interpretation," *Research in Economic History,* V (1979); Jacob M. Price, "The Economic Growth of the Chesapeake and the European Market, 1697–1775," *Journal of Economic History,* XXIV (1964), 496–511.

5. For evidence that the seasoning rate declined in the middle decades of the 17th century, see Thomas J. Wertenbaker, *The Planters of Colonial Virginia* (Princeton, N.J., 1922), 39–40; Edmund S. Morgan, *American Slavery, American Freedom: The Ordeal of Colonial Virginia* (New York, 1975), 180–184; Wyndham B. Blanton, *Medicine in Virginia in the Seventeenth Century* (Richmond, Va., 1930), 37–41. According to William Berkeley, writing in 1671, "There is not often unseasoned hands (as wee terme them) that die Whereas heretofore not one of Five scaped the first yeare," C.O. 1/26, fol. 198, Public Record Office. Berkeley's assertion should not be accepted without question, for there is some evidence of high seasoning rates in the last third of the 17th century. In 1670, for example, reports attribute a shortage of servants in the colonies to high mortality. William Wakeman to Joseph Williamson, Apr. 22, 1670, S.P. 29/274, no. 213; Anthony Thorold to James Hickes, June 11, 1670, S.P. 29/276, no. 115. The mortality rate among soldiers sent to Virginia in the wake of Bacon's Rebellion was very high. According to one report more than half died less than a year after arrival. John Gibbons to Joseph Williamson, Nov. 6, 1676, S.P. 29/386, no. 206; Richard Watts to Williamson, May 6, 1677, S.P. 29/393, no. 121; same to same, S.P. 29/394, no. 69. In 1702 concern over heavy mortality among crew members affected decisions as to when the Virginia fleet would set sail. Gov. Nicholson to Board of Trade, Mar. 13, 1703, C.O. 5/1313, no. 16i; Petitions of Merchants, trading to Virginia and Maryland . . . , Oct. 23, 1702, C.O. 5/1313, no. 4i. As late as 1720, John Hart reported that the Maryland "climate is unhealthy, especially to strangers." Hart to Board of Trade, Aug. 25, 1720, *Md. Hist. Mag.*, XXIX (1934), 252. It is possible that the rate of seasoning mortality declined across the middle decades of the 17th century and then increased as Africans introduced *falciparum* malaria to the Chesapeake colonies. See Darrett B. and Anita H. Rutman, "Of Agues and Fevers: Malaria in the Early Chesapeake," *WMQ*, 3d Ser., XXXIII (1976), 31–60.

immigrated under indentures during the middle decades of the century died before they finished their terms, an annual death rate of about 10 percent.[6] Even those who survived their terms could not expect a long life. In Maryland around mid-century immigrant males who reached age twenty-two could expect to die in their early forties, and 70 percent failed to reach their fiftieth birthday.[7]

In addition, there was a severe shortage of women. Men outnumbered women by six to one among immigrants who left London for the Chesapeake in the middle 1630s. The proportion of women among immigrants doubled by the 1650s and continued to increase slowly thereafter, but men still outnumbered women by about two and a half to one among new arrivals at the end of the century.[8] The shortage of women prevented many men from marrying and forced others to delay marriage until late in their lives.

These demographic facts had a profound impact on the history of the Chesapeake colonies. High mortality and sexual imbalance, along with a late age at first marriage for immigrant females, prevented reproductive population increase until near the end of the seventeenth century, postponed the emergence of a native-born majority, and kept the society sensitive to changes in the character of the immigrant group and the opportunities offered new arrivals.[9] Moreover, delayed marriage created a disproportionately large group of bachelors, most of whom did not form households until they could find a wife. Even the most successful former servants, men who eventually gained moderate prosperity and full membership in the New World community as husbands, fathers, heads of households, and participants in government, often spent part of their lives after leaving servitude without a family or a fixed residence.

Little is known about these unmarried men who had left servitude behind but who were still inmates in the households of others.

6. Lorena S. Walsh, "Servitude and Opportunity in Charles County, Maryland, 1658–1705," in Land, Carr, and Papenfuse, eds., *Law, Society, and Politics*, 130; Menard, "Economy and Society," 226, 236.

7. Lorena S. Walsh and Russell R. Menard, "Death in the Chesapeake: Two Life Tables for Men in Early Colonial Maryland," *Md. Hist. Mag.*, LXIX (1974), 211–227.

8. Menard, "Immigrants and Their Increase," in Land, Carr, and Papenfuse, eds., *Law, Society, and Politics*, 96. See also Craven, *White, Red, and Black*, 25–28; Irene W. D. Hecht, "The Virginia Muster of 1624/5 as a Source for Demographic History," *WMQ*, 3d Ser., XXX (1973), 65–92; Herbert Moller, "Sex Composition and Correlated Culture Patterns of Colonial America," *ibid.*, II (1945), 117–118.

9. Menard, "Immigrants and Their Increase," in Land, Carr, and Papenfuse, eds., *Law, Society, and Politics*, 88–110.

Indeed, before Edmund Morgan's recent work historians barely ac-knowledged their existence.[10] How many were there? What work did they do? What was their status in Chesapeake society? And what were their prospects for exchanging that status for one further up the hierarchy? Their proportion in the population is impossible to esti-mate with any precision. Morgan quotes statements suggesting that by the 1670s as many as a fourth, perhaps even a third, of the able-bodied men in Virginia fell into this category, but the statements are casual and of uncertain quality.[11] Tax lists remain for some counties, but they do not distinguish free inmates from indentured servants. Maryland and Virginia censuses also fail to make the distinction. What the tax lists and censuses do make clear is that there were very large numbers of men who lived in the households of others. Many such inmates must have been servants or ex-servants.

Recently freed servants who had yet to acquire a family leave only faint tracks in most surviving records. Fortunately, the probate rec-ords of Maryland for the second half of the seventeenth century offer an exceptional opportunity to study this group. The most rewarding of these records are the inventories of estates, which list all of a man's moveable property from his servants and slaves and pots and pans to his yard goods for sale and credits due from his debtors. When administration accounts accompany the inventories, these show debts payable and the final balance of the estate. Since life was short, many of those whose estates were subject to probate were unmarried freed-men inmates.

A sizable sample group of freedmen inmates is available from a study, undertaken by the St. Mary's City Commission, of all such inventories and accounts for four Maryland counties—St. Mary's, Calvert, Charles, and Prince George's—from 1658 to 1705.[12] The four counties are contiguous, occupying more than sixteen hundred square miles on the lower Western Shore of Maryland, and include some of the best tobacco land along the Chesapeake. The records are com-plete, and the reporting, at least of inventories, is surprisingly full.[13]

10. Morgan, *American Slavery, American Freedom*.
11. Edmund S. Morgan, "Slavery and Freedom: The American Paradox," *Journal of American History*, LIX (1972), 20.
12. The National Science Foundation has supported this project, "Social Stratifica-tion in Maryland, 1658–1705" (GS-32272).
13. For the reporting rate, see Russell R. Menard, P.M.G. Harris, and Lois Green Carr, "Opportunity and Inequality: The Distribution of Wealth on the Lower Western Shore of Maryland, 1638–1705," *Md. Hist. Mag.*, LXIX (1974), 175–176; 1,735 decedents left inventories.

The inventories themselves offer much of the evidence, and accompanying probate records, along with a variety of other sources, supply the rest.

The simplest way to identify freedmen inmates among all those whose estates were inventoried is to establish first who were unmarried; second, who among the unmarrieds were not the heads of households; and finally, who among these had indeed immigrated into the colony as servants. The first two steps presented no problems. Of the 1,672 male decedents inventoried in the four counties over the forty-eight years surveyed, 1,161 were married or had been married, the marital status of 62 could not be determined, and 452 (26 percent) were bachelors. Of the bachelors, the presence or absence in the inventories of housekeeping goods suggested that 150 kept house. Thus, 302 individuals are known to have been unmarried inmates in the households of others.

The last, and more difficult, step was to determine which of the 302 individuals identified from the initial survey as bachelor inmates had arrived in the colony as servants. First excluded were those known to have been born in Maryland or Virginia (31) or to have come as free immigrants (16), in all about 15 percent. Ninety-three more were eliminated because evidence indicated that they had paid their own way to the colonies. Of this group, 69, or 21 percent of all bachelor inmates, were dropped because, as merchants or professional men, they seem likely to have had sufficient capital or education to have financed their own passage to the New World. Twenty-two men (7 percent of all bachelor inmates) were dropped for miscellaneous reasons. This group included those who, on their first appearance in the records, were identified by the title of mister or gentleman or whose assets included such signs of gentle status as silverheaded swords.[14]

Remaining, then, are 162 men: all immigrants, all unmarried, all members of other men's households, and none with signs of social origins that would suggest they had come as free immigrants. Of these, 70 certainly came as servants and it is probable that the remaining 92 did also. Since the 70 known servants were somewhat wealthier than the others, it is unlikely that the 92 men of uncertain origin in-

14. Only one man's status was ambiguous by the standards applied: "Mr. Alexander Winsor" arrived as a servant but was a schoolmaster. William Hand Browne *et al.*, eds., *Archives of Maryland . . .* (Baltimore, 1883–), LXVII, 154–155, hereafter cited as *Md. Archives*; Patents, XVIII, 387; Inventories and Accounts, III, 6, V, 117.

clude many free immigrants who started their New World careers with capital.[15] These 162 men can be studied as a group.

In an economy built upon the production and marketing of tobacco, most freedmen inmates must have worked in agriculture or crafts. Their inventories bolster this supposition, for 58 percent (94) show either hoes, tobacco crop, or credits, which in estates of this kind usually represented payment for labor. Other men had craftsmen's tools, or the probate records otherwise designated them as craftsmen. Only four had trading goods in amounts sufficient to suggest they were peddlers. Twenty-five men left no clues to their occupations, but there is no reason to suppose that they did not earn their livings as the others did.

The great majority of freedmen inmates were agricultural workers and there was a steady demand for their labor. Tobacco was a labor-intensive crop, but one which required no special skills. Moreover, even a small planter who did not yet have the resources to purchase a servant could improve his position by sharecropping with an efficient freedman. There is some evidence that two men could produce more than double the crop of one, making an extra hand worth having even if he would not work for less than a full crop share.[16] Probably more important, an additional laborer contributed to more than the size of the commercial crop; he could clear land, build fencing to protect orchards and crops, assist in constructing houses and out-buildings, help at slaughter time, and so on. Thus the steady need for unskilled labor provided plenty of work at good wages.

There were three kinds of working arrangements in common use. The freedman might agree to labor for a year in exchange for either wages or a share of the crop; he might lease land for his own use; or he might work for wages by the day. Contracts found in court and probate records show a variety of agreements by the year. Somerset County on Maryland's lower Eastern Shore, first inhabited by English-men in the early 1660s, provides some instructive examples of the contracts available on the Chesapeake frontier. In 1669 Thomas Willis contracted to serve James Mills for a year in return for lodging, diet, payment of taxes, and 2,800 pounds of tobacco and cask. Three years

15. In both groups, 41% had less than £10 of inventoried property; but 29% of men with known origins had £10–19 and 30% had £20–59; whereas among those of unknown origin, the figures are 36% and 23% respectively.

16. Unpublished research of Paul Clemens, Rutgers University.

later Daniel Clawson made a similar arrangement with Ambrose White, except that 2,500 pounds of tobacco and cask was the agreed upon sum.[17] These were very generous contracts, given that 2,000 to 2,500 pounds of tobacco was the maximum that a man could raise under favorable conditions.[18] Such agreements indicate that laborers were needed for more than the cash crop they could raise. They also reflect the very high ratio of land to labor in the Chesapeake colonies in the seventeenth century. Abundant natural resources and a perennial scarcity of labor allowed workers to bargain from a position of strength and kept wages high, so high that they often approached and sometimes exceeded what the worker could produce.[19]

Contracts as lucrative as those negotiated by Willis and Clawson were unusual and perhaps obtainable only in newly settled regions where the large supply of nearly free land and the pressing need for help with the arduous task of carving out new farms intensified competition for workers. Probably more typical of the arrangements in older and more densely populated areas was Edward Fulser's contract made with Robert Long of Charles County in 1667: Fulser was to live with Long for a year and "use truly and faithfully his utmost Care and Endeavours in Every business Employments or affairs that Shall from the Said Long be appointed or Comitted to his Charge" in return for payment of his taxes, 1,400 pounds of tobacco, cask, and a young sow with pigs by her side. Unlike Willis and Clawson, Fulser evidently was expected to pay for his room and board.[20] Other kinds of contracts called for crop sharing. Francis Graile of St. Mary's County, "a freeman that lived on the plantation" of his former master, Thomas Pierce, made a crop with Pierce's servants in 1674. Graile's share was 2,359 pounds of tobacco. He evidently received room and board as well, perhaps for supervising other workers. Men like Conyers Barbiers and James Marran, both of whom worked for shares in Calvert County in the mid-1670s, paid for their accommodations and poll taxes.[21]

The overseer, who supervised other labor, was usually able to

17. Somerset County Judicial Records, DT#7, 69; AZ#8, 269–270.
18. For crop sizes, see Menard, "Economy and Society," Appendix VI, 490. The largest crop share found in a freedman's inventory was 2,520 pounds of tobacco.
19. Evsey D. Domar, "The Causes of Slavery or Serfdom: A Hypothesis," *Jour. Econ. Hist.*, XXX (1970), 18–32.
20. *Md. Archives*, LX, 306.
21. Inventories and Accounts, IV, 229, 402 (quotation), 480–481.

make a more favorable contract than other freedmen. If he worked for wages, they were worth more than a share; if he took a share of the crop, he received additional pay or was allowed lodging, diet, washing, and his poll tax. Contracts could have elaborate provisions for determining which resources the planter guaranteed and which the freedman would supply. Overseers might bring livestock with them to be pastured with the planter's and share proportionately in the increase of the herds thus pooled. Sometimes overseers had wives; such men, by definition excluded from this study, probably had been or were about to become planters.[22]

Some men who clearly were not householders worked for neither wages nor a share of the crop but rather leased ground and tobacco housing from a planter. No contract of this kind has been found, but administration accounts occasionally show payments for "ground howsing and diat" or "acco of house ground Leavy & Casque." In these instances, crop, if it appears in the inventory, is not described as a-share. It was the freedman's own crop.[23]

Finally, some men worked for day wages rather than contracting their full time for a season. Short-term wages were high—fifteen to twenty pounds of tobacco a day was usual over the second half of the seventeenth century—but no planter would hire labor at such prices for more than a short time. These freedmen would be in demand when tobacco plants were transplanted in late spring and during the cutting season in late summer. Otherwise employment opportunities must have been sporadic. But the high rate of pay may have brought in income as great as a more secure agreement would provide.[24]

Doubtless there were combinations of these various arrangements. Men who leased house and ground were not necessarily bound by contract to work only for one master. Small debts receivable in their inventories suggest that they also worked as day laborers, even

22. See, for example, *Md. Archives*, XLIX, 326–327; Inventories and Accounts, V, 430, VI, 635; Charles County Court and Land Records, L#1, 201–202; P#1, 70–71; Provincial Court Judgments, DS#A, 421–423.

23. Inventories and Accounts, III, 73, IV, 340, VIII, 80, XIIIA, 259–260, XVI, 30, 38–39, XXIII, 90. Since this essay was written, two suits for breach of contract for lease of house and ground have been found. *Md. Archives*, LX, 305; Charles County Court and Land Records, R#1, 107.

24. Manfred Jonas, "Wages in Early Colonial Maryland," *Md. Hist. Mag.*, LI (1956), 27–38; Lois Green Carr, "County Government in Maryland, 1689–1709" (Ph.D. diss., Harvard University, 1968), text, 593. Carr has revised her view, expressed here, that there were not large numbers of laborers.

though the greatest demand would come at times when their own crop required attention. Or a man in this position might agree to work for his landlord at a lower rate when he had free time. Possibly sharecroppers or long-term wage laborers were allowed a bit of moonlighting during slack times, but this seems less likely. Men on yearly contracts were not far removed in status from indentured servitude. They usually could not be sold and they could sometimes insist that they not be put to "beating [corn] at the mortar & grinding at the mill," evidently among the most unpleasant and laborious of tasks, but their time belonged to their masters.[25]

What kind of agreement most benefited the freedman without a household? Perhaps the inmate who leased ground for his own crop was in the best position. He might not always make as much tobacco as he could under sharecropping arrangements—often amounts found in the instances when such arrangements can be proved were low—but he could augment his income by highly paid day labor and he had more freedom than men who farmed shares or worked under long-term wage contracts. In a good crop year, crop sharing was possibly preferable to wages; in a bad year, a fixed payment might offer a better hedge. Of course the terms of a long-term wage contract and the capacity to insist on a crop share depended on the ability of the freedman to bargain.

Nonhouseholders may have found that no arrangement for agricultural labor offered as great an opportunity to accumulate wealth as did the practice of a skill, at least as the tobacco industry began to stagnate after 1680. Before that date inventories of craftsmen and agricultural laborers reveal only a slight difference in wealth (see table 1). Once tobacco production ceased to expand and planters attempted to diversify the economy by developing other staples and a greater degree of local self-sufficiency, the wealth of men with skills increased and that of farm workers fell.[26] Perhaps diversification enhanced the opportunities of craftsmen, a gain furthered by increased population density, which permitted the support of a greater variety of occupa-

25. E.g., Somerset County Judicial Records, DT#7, 69.
26. Unpublished findings from the project "Social Stratification in Maryland" are similar to those of Carville V. Earle, *The Evolution of Tidewater Settlement: All Hallow's Parish, Maryland, 1650–1783*, The University of Chicago Department of Geography Research Paper No. 170 (Chicago, 1975), table 27, 122–123. Sheep raising, yarn spinning, and wheat culture increased markedly over the years 1680 to 1710, and shoemakers and tailors began to appear.

TABLE 1. Mean Wealth of Craftsmen and Agricultural Laborers, 1658–1705

Date	Craftsmen		Agricultural Laborers	
	N	Mean	N	Mean
1658–1670	3	£ 9.36 sterling	12	£ 14.83 sterling
1671–1680	11	19.82	31	21.34
1681–1687	10	20.48	16	13.78
1688–1696	5	14.99	15	14.93
1697–1705	10	24.99	20	13.18
Total	39	19.89	94	16.29
1658–1680	14	17.58	43	19.52
1681–1705	25	21.18	51	13.56

tions. At the same time the decline in tobacco restricted the progress of men forced to earn a living by working for others in the fields. The proportion of freedmen inmates who left evidence that they practiced a skill increased after 1680, suggesting that they responded to this shift in opportunities.

Of those inmates who were craftsmen about two-thirds (26) were coopers or carpenters. Eight were tailors, two were shoemakers, two were millers, one was a plasterer. The skills represented served the basic needs of the tobacco economy. Since plows and carts were still unusual even by the end of the period, there was little need for blacksmiths or wheelwrights—clothing and housing for people and cask for the crop were the main requirements. Milling corn was a future convenience. In most seventeenth-century households someone had the exhausting task of pounding corn with mortar and pestle.

Whether or not he was skilled, the laborer in this society could always find work that would house and feed him. The surviving Maryland court records of the seventeenth century show little concern with the "settlement" of paupers and none for warning out vagrants, a few women of loose morals excepted. Only the truly impotent needed assistance. The Board of Trade of the 1690s and early eighteenth century suggested construction of workhouses, but the assembly dismissed the idea. "The Province wants workman," it averred, "workeman want not work."[27]

Despite the ready availability of work at good wages, freedmen

27. Carr, "County Government in Maryland," text, 359–364; *Md. Archives*, XXII, 381 (quotation), XXVI, 117–118.

who died as inmates accumulated little wealth. Of the 162 who left inventories, only a handful had land and none had moveable assets worth as much as £60. The inventories show the kinds of moveable property they had and allow comparison with the property of others.

In analyzing inventories it is useful to divide capital and noncapital goods, defining as capital any property capable of producing income. Livestock, tobacco crop, tools, trading goods, cash, and debts receivable are subcategories of capital goods. Corn in excess of three barrels is included in capital, since three barrels of corn per man per year was the standard seventeenth-century allowance for consumption. Weapons, including guns and fishing gear, are defined as noncapital, nothing suggesting that men fished or shot game for commercial use.

In many respects estates of freedmen inmates resembled those of other men. Only a handful had no capital assets, and nearly all had more than half of their estate in capital. Such assets included livestock, tobacco crop, credits, and tools, although tools, worth little, were a major part of only very small estates. Only ten estates had cash, always a rarity, and although many men put surplus income into cloth, which could be traded, such investment was usually small. These characteristics are common to the estates of most people regardless of economic position.

Examined in greater detail, however, the capital assets of freedmen inmates are distinguishable from those of householders, including tenant farmers with similar amounts of moveable wealth. Among all decedents, 151 worth less than £60 were clearly tenant farmers. Like freedmen inmates, they had no land and usually owned no bound labor. But in other respects the estates of freedmen show differences. Tenant householders were less likely than freedmen to have credits, since they worked mostly for themselves. They also were more likely to have livestock (see table 2), and the character of their livestock was different. Usually included were cattle and hogs for butter, cheese, bacon, and hides. The great majority of nonhouseholding freedmen, by contrast, either had no livestock or had only horses for purposes of transportation (see table 3).

The noncapital assets of freedmen inmates consisted primarily of clothing, cloth, often a chest, and sometimes guns or other weapons (see table 4). Occasionally a man had his own bed. Some bachelors did not neglect their personal appearance. Looking glasses, combs,

TABLE 2. Assets of Freedmen Compared to Assets of Tenant Farmers with Movable Wealth Valued at Less than £60

	Tenants (N = 151) Inventories with Asset		Freedmen (N = 162) Inventories with Asset	
Asset	N	% Total N	N	% Total N
Livestock	138	91.4	102	62.9
Credits	64	42.4	93	57.4
Labor	12	7.9	2	1.2
Land	0	0.0	5	3.1

TABLE 3. Livestock Holdings of Freedmen without Households, 1658–1705 (in Percentages)

Holdings	1658–1670 (N = 17)	1671–1680 (N = 51)	1681–1693 (N = 41)	1694–1705 (N = 53)	Total (N = 162)
No livestock	58.8%	43.1%	31.7%	28.3%	37.0%
Horses only	0.0%	25.5%	41.6%	43.4%	32.7%
Cattle only	29.4%	13.7%	7.3%	0.0%	9.3%
Hogs only	5.9%	0.0%	0.0%	3.8%	1.8%
Two livestock types	0.0%	9.8%	14.6%	20.8%	13.6%

TABLE 4. Personal Property in the Inventories of Freedmen without Households, 1658–1705

	Number of Estates with Item	
Item	N	%
Clothing	121	74.7
Chest	68	42.0
Cloth	60	37.0
Bed	25	15.4
Gun	25	15.4
Razor	16	9.9
Comb	14	8.6
Books	13	8.0
Looking Glass	9	5.6
Pistol	8	4.9
Sword	8	4.9
Violin	3	1.8

and razors appear, and investment in clothing could be considerable. Abraham Addams, a carpenter worth £55, had five suits of apparel valued at £9.[28] Three men had violins, and thirteen had books. A variety of odds and ends appeared across all wealth levels—a pewter bottle, a thimble, a "barber's old case," a parcel of "lumberment." Compared to property of householders, of course, the variety of noncapital goods was small. Inmates are identified by the absence of utensils for the kitchen and dairy and other household goods.

"Wareing cloathes," a chest, crop, or a credit, and by late century a horse, were the typical assets of freedmen inmates, although one or more might be missing from any particular estate. While the pattern differed from that of householders with similar amounts of wealth, these differences should not be exaggerated. When a man decided to establish his own farm he could convert credits, or even horses, into cattle and hogs and a few household goods, provided his debts were not overwhelming. A freedman inmate with cattle or hogs may have hoped to soon form a household. If so, about a quarter of those under study were preparing for such a move when death intervened (see table 3).

Although freedmen without households were poor, they were by no means the only poor. Among all decedents, 57.6 percent (999) had inventories worth less than £60 and freedmen inmates were only 12.8 percent of this group. Table 5A, furthermore, shows that they dominated no wealth level, not even the lowest. Of course, land is excluded from these calculations and in consequence the figures somewhat distort reality. Table 5B shows that among the landless decedents—tenants plus landless bachelor inmates—freedmen without households constituted more than half of men worth less than £13, and in the living population they were undoubtedly a greater proportion of poor landless men. On the other hand they may have had more to enjoy than most householders—including those with land—at similar levels of moveable wealth. A man with a wife and children needed several times the amount of goods of a bachelor to achieve the equivalent per capita wealth in moveables.

Nevertheless, freedmen inmates may have held a position less favorable than that of householders for moving up the scale of wealth. Four-fifths of these inmates had estates worth less than £23, whereas among decedents overall more than three-quarters of those worth

28. Inventories and Accounts, XX, 41.

TABLE 5. Landholding and Householding Characteristics of Decedents, 1658–1705

Wealth in £ Sterling	Part A					
	All Decedents	All Householders	All Known Tenants	All Tenants[a]	All Bachelor Inmates[b]	All Freedmen Inmates
0–4	52	20	10	13.33	32	18
5–12	173	85	28	45.28	85	69
13–22	244	157	40	60.97	79	41
23–29	139	115	25	31.94	23	12
30 +	1,127	1,038	74	86.20	83	22
Totals	1,735	1,415	177	237.34	302	162

	Part B				
	All Landless Men			Freedmen Inmates without Land	
Wealth in £ Sterling	Tenants	Bachelor Inmates	Total	N	% of Landless Men
0–12	58.61	103	161.61	86	53.2
13–22	60.97	65	125.97	38	30.2
23–29	31.94	18	49.94	12	24.0
30 +	86.20	64	150.20	21	14.0
Totals	237.34	250	487.72	157	32.2

Notes:
[a]If unknowns, these are distributed according to knowns.
[b]Of the inmates, 7 were women, and 11 were married or widowed men. These are not counted.

more than £22 had left inmate status behind them. Such a difference suggests that formation of a household was an important step in the accumulation of property. However, this proposition requires careful testing. Perhaps instead most men simply preferred to be house-holders once they had acquired sufficient capital. Even unmarried men were often masters of households. A preference for household-ing may distort the wealth structure of men who lived as inmates. To settle this question requires further comparison of freedmen inmates' wealth with that of other groups and a look at the degree to which various assets could be used to hasten the accumulation of wealth.

A crude measure of the prospects of freedmen inmates may be derived from a comparison of their inventoried property with that of other freedmen decedents. While no inmate had acquired as much as

£60, the record for unmarried freedmen householders, 70 of whom could be identified, was considerably better.[29] Nearly three-fifths (40) had £23 or more, whereas only one-fifth of those without householas had this amount of property. Ten householders had £60 or more and the wealthiest was worth £171. Only 5 of the 162 inmates had land at death and only 2 had bound labor, the two prime income-producing assets in this economy; but among those who had formed households before they died at least two-fifths and probably half had land and 21 percent had servants. Furthermore, the group who headed households and whose time of arrival is known (38) left more wealth for each year they had been in Maryland than did men who remained in the house of another: £1.75 per year for housekeepers, but only £1.42 for inmates. Information about married freedmen decedents whose time of arrival is known (196) is less detailed, but they clearly resembled decedents overall more than freedmen without households. A handful accumulated extraordinary fortunes and 57.1 percent died worth £60 or more.

However, these contrasts do not account for the fact that inmate decedents were likely to be younger than householders, a fact that necessarily had limited their opportunities to accumulate wealth. A better way to measure the prospects of those living is to compare the wealth of freedmen inmates inventoried at various times with that of all decedents in the same age groups. Among decedents overall—79 percent of whom were householders—wealth increased until late middle age, but not among freedmen inmates.[30] The number of years a freedman had been in Maryland is used as a surrogate for age in table 6A, which shows that mean years in the colony doubled after 1696 without a corresponding increase in mean wealth. Apparently most men who did not form households and establish their own farms were unable to improve their position even after years of labor. A look at all the freedmen inmates who had been in Maryland for more than fifteen years bolsters this proposition. Longevity made little difference to prosperity. Mean wealth for men who had lived fifteen or more years in Maryland (17) was £17.36, whereas for all

29. Of 150 bachelor householders, 36 were sons, 11 were free immigrants, 13 were merchants, and 9 were eliminated for miscellaneous reasons as men unlikely to have arrived as servants, leaving 70.

30. Menard, Harris, and Carr, "Opportunity and Inequality," *Md. Hist. Mag.*, LXIX (1974), 176–178.

TABLE 6. Longevity and Accumulation for Freedmen, 1658–1705

Date	Number of Freedmen	Mean Years in Colony	Mean Wealth Accumulated	Mean Wealth per Mean Year
Part A				
1662–1664	4	11.25	£13.08 sterling	£1.16 sterling
1665–1670	2	7.00	17.96	2.56
1671–1674	5	9.33	22.21	2.39
1675–1677	17	11.10	20.64	1.86
1678–1680	2	14.00	10.04	.73
1681–1684	5	11.40	15.85	1.39
1685–1687	8	12.90	14.52	1.13
1688–1693	5	17.80	8.26	1.06
1694–1696	2	12.50	7.20	.58
1697–1699	3	21.33	12.84	.60
1700–1702	2	19.50	32.46	1.71
1703–1705	2	24.00	16.43	.68
Part B				
1662–1677	28	9.67	18.47	1.91
1678–1705	29	15.43	14.70	.95

whose date of arrival is known (57) it was £16.80. Men on the rise left the group to become householding farmers; those who remained were no better off than younger laborers.

The position of freedmen without households, furthermore, deteriorated toward the end of the seventeenth century. True, the long run movement of mean wealth for this group—as shown by the linear least squares calculation in figure 1—suggests considerable stability; but the falling trend line of the median indicates that the majority were losing ground. The good fortune of a few kept the mean from falling, but most decedent freedmen inmates grew poorer as the eighteenth century approached.

The relationship between the length of time a man had been in Maryland and his wealth at death indicates that this deterioration began in the late 1670s (see table 6A). The ratio of men whose date of arrival is known to the mean number of years these decedents had lived in the colony measures the amount of wealth per year accumulated and allows comparison across time. The ratio drops sharply in the years 1678 to 1680, and except for the years 1700–1702, remains low for the rest of the period. The number of estates in most groups is

FIGURE 1. Mean and Median Wealth of Freedmen without Households, 1658–1705, by Grouped Years

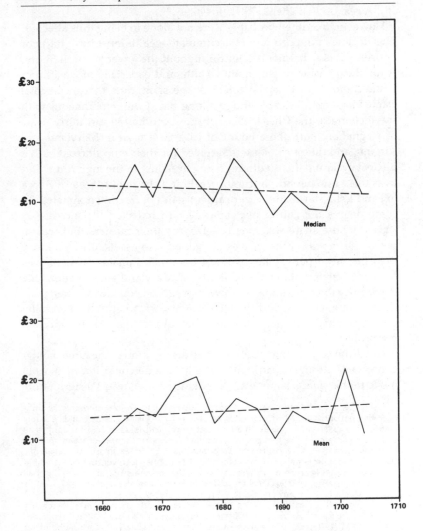

small, but the pattern is strong and is even stronger when the groups are further collapsed into those who died before and after 1678 (table 6B). A real decline after 1678 seems likely.[31]

However, freedmen probably were not alone in being thus affected. This decline in opportunity to accumulate wealth must have hit poor householders as hard or harder throughout the lower Western Shore. A rapid expansion of per capita wealth, and especially of wealth per white capita, ended in the 1680s, at the same time that mean total estate value for all estates ended a long rise. Contemporaneous with these changes, the Chesapeake tobacco economy began thirty years of stagnation; both the amount of tobacco grown in Maryland and Virginia and the price planters received for their crop fluctuated in a distinct cyclical pattern without rising or falling in the long run.[32] But over this same period per capita wealth on the lower Western Shore fell and fell faster than the per capita wealth of freedmen inmates. To some degree this fall in per capita wealth reflected the increase in slaves, whose share was mostly seized by their masters. But wealth per white capita, even if slaves are added into assets, also fell faster than the mean per capita wealth of freedmen inmates.[33] As natives replaced immigrants in the majority of Maryland's population, life expectancy improved, the sex ratio approached equality, women married at younger ages, and the birthrate rose.[34] A naturally increasing population had to share an income from tobacco that was not increasing proportionately.

Nevertheless, among wealthholders the position of the householder was clearly stronger than that of the man who could not or did not move to this status. Among all decedents on the lower Western Shore

31. After 1696 the ratio may be distorted but not enough to undermine the findings. By then only men who had been in Maryland for 15 years or more could be surely identified as ex-servants because the termination of headrights in 1681 brought to an end the records most likely to prove servitude. The mean number of years spent in Maryland therefore rises sharply after 1696, but this rise is at least partly the result of a change in the sources rather than a change in the society. However, the movement of the ratio of mean years to mean wealth follows the movement of mean wealth of all freedmen inmates after 1696. Thus the distortion is probably minimal.

32. Menard, "Economy and Society," figs. VI–1, VI–2, VI–3.

33. For preliminary discussions of per capita wealth changes in 17th-century Maryland, see Russell R. Menard, "Comment on Paper by Ball and Walton," *Jour. Econ. Hist.*, XXXVI (1976), 123–125, and Menard, Harris, and Carr, "Opportunity and Inequality," *Md. Hist. Mag.*, LXIX (1974), 183–184. We intend a more detailed discussion in the near future.

34. Menard, "Immigrants and Their Increase," in Land, Carr, and Papenfuse, eds., *Law, Society, and Politics*.

mean wealth adjusted for age did not fall across the period of stagnation, despite an increase in the number of wealthholders as children
matured and moved away from home. But among freedmen without
households this decline appears once wealth is adjusted for length of
time in the colony (see table 6).[35] Evidently men who had households
and farms were more likely than inmates to accumulate physical
assets that in turn produced increased wealth.

Householders, for example, could more easily pasture and otherwise care for livestock, the poor man's major growth asset. An inmate
might arrange with his landlord for pasturage or even penning, but
he had to pay for these accommodations. He would find housing and
care of servants even more expensive. Lodging, diet, and washing
ran at least eight hundred to one thousand pounds of tobacco a year,
more than the rent of a farm. The inmate paid more for himself alone
than he would pay in rent as a householder.[36] Clearly men found it
advantageous to become householders before making major investments in livestock or labor.

Furthermore, inmate status may not have encouraged saving. This
proposition is difficult to test, but a comparison of final balances of
freedmen inmates with those of tenant farmers at similar wealth
levels is suggestive. Half the freedmen inmates accounted for had in-
sufficient assets to pay their debts. But among tenant farmers worth
less than £60 nearly half again as many (73.6 percent) possessed
solvent estates and could pay all their debts (see tables 7A and 7B).
Since wealth levels were the same, the differences must lie in kinds of

35. Since this essay was written, P.M.G. Harris has pointed out that date of
settlement affects wealth patterns and has identified three regions on the lower Western
Shore that reflect these effects. His disaggregation of mean total estate value by these
regions shows that mean total estate value stayed level or rose over all three regions,
1680 to 1705. Harris, "Integrating Interpretations of Local and Regionwide Change in
the Study of Economic Development and Demographic Growth in the Colonial Chesapeake, 1630–1775," in *Working Papers from the Regional Economic History Research Center*,
I, no. 3 (1978), 35–71 and fig. 1, p. 50. Further disaggregation by householding and
landowning categories does show some decline for householders not proved to have
land, but only in Charles County was the decline on the same order as that for
freedmen. Of decedents in this category, 28% were in Charles County. Unpublished
research of P.M.G. Harris.

36. Rents found in contracts at mid-century and about 1700 were 300 to 500
pounds of tobacco. Russell R. Menard, "From Servant to Freeholder: Status Mobility
and Property Accumulation in Seventeenth-Century Maryland," *WMQ*, 3d Ser., XXX
(1973), 53; Prince George's County Court Record A, 264, C, 42–42a. Inmate expenses
are found in administration accounts and judgments for debts, e.g., *ibid.*, A, 243;
Charles County Court and Land Record K#1, 61; P#1, 181; V#1, 18; Inventories and
Accounts, I, 9–10, IV, 340, VIII, 80, XIV, 30–39.

TABLE 7. Solvency of Freedmen Inmates and Tenant Farmers, 1658–1705

Total Estate Value	Number of Estates	Estates Accounted		Accounted Estates Solvent	
		N	% Estates	N	% Estates Accounted
		Part A. Freedmen Inmates			
£0–£22	128	51	39.8	24	47.0
£23–£59	34	17	50.0	10	58.8
Totals	162	68	42.0	34	50.0
		Part B. Tenant Farmers			
£0–£22	78	39	50.0	24	61.5
£23–£59	73	48	65.7	40	83.3
Totals	151	87	57.6	64	73.6
		Part C. Married and Bachelor Tenant Farmers			
Married		73		54	74.0
Bachelor		14		10	71.4

property owned and the kinds of obligations incurred, but also in the incentive or necessity to spend. While a planter with a household might not raise a larger tobacco crop than a laborer, his orchard, kitchen garden, cattle, and hogs could produce food and drink for his family, who were a source of labor for the production and preparation of these necessities. Although the tenant farmer paid rent, it was less than the laborer paid for diet and lodging. But perhaps more important, the tenant evidently was more careful of what he had. The family man, especially, had incentive to keep ahead of his debts, lest he leave a widow and young children without means of support. Before debts were paid, per capita wealth of the tenant family was clearly less than that of the freedmen inmates of the same wealth level.[37] But the evidence from the final balances provides clear indication that tenant householders, including men with families (table 7C), maintained a stronger position than did freedmen who lived as inmates.

All told, then, men without households were at a disadvantage even though their services in a labor-short society were in demand. A man who wanted to move out of the bottom quartile of holders of moveable wealth usually needed more than the profits of his labor; he

37. Per capita here includes credits, cash, and bound labor.

needed to save and save in capital investments that could also produce wealth. Formation of a household increased his opportunities to make and benefit from such investments.

The evidence so far presented has revealed much about the economic position of freedmen inmates but has shed little light on their personal lives and social status. Clues to this side of their history suggest experiences less bleak than might be supposed but a status that was not improving.

Wills offer revealing personal statements otherwise unavailable from a society in which communication was largely oral. Forty of the 162 freedmen inmates left wills that tell us something of their personal feelings and relationships. Only three mentioned family in England.[38] The others did not look back to an old life; rather they left their livestock or clothing or tobacco to "loving friends" encountered in the New World. Several may have hoped to marry women they made their "well-beloved" executrixes.[39] Others named the householders with whom they lived as their executors and chief legatees. Jonathan Pearce in 1685 left his estate to his friend James Moore "for the care and trouble he hath been about me and too littel for his trouble." Morgan Pranch left most of his estate to his executor Thomas Guyther "for good will and respect I bare to him."[40] Several men left legacies to children in the families with whom they lived.[41] Some were still living with their former masters.[42] Clearly these men were not alienated outsiders but identified themselves with the household. The cold records of the probate court often described freedmen as having "dyed Childless and Unmarried and without relations for ought ever appeared in this province," but they were not necessarily without homes and friends.[43]

Such personal relationships were possible in part because the social distance between freedmen and employer often was not great. Indeed, for much of the seventeenth century masters shared a common experience with their laborers, bound as well as free. Masters were almost invariably immigrants, often former servants. Even those who

38. Wills, V, 118, 321, IX, 9.
39. *Ibid.*, IV, 111, V, 37; Testamentary Proceedings, XVIILB, 10.
40. Wills, VI, 37, 69.
41. *Ibid.*, II, 225, 358, 409, V, 321, IV, 259, I, 620, VII, 349; Testamentary Proceedings, IF, 28–29, VII, 205–206.
42. Wills, II, 409, V, 389, IV, 259; Patents, XIII, 121; *Md. Archives*, LX, 188; Inventories and Accounts, IV, 320, 398, 402, IX, 353–354, X, 97, 163, XII, 21, 22, 67.
43. Testamentary Proceedings, VIII, 112, 335.

had arrived as free men usually came from English families of middling status, as did many who had come under indentures.[44] Most
masters, furthermore, did not have great wealth. Before 1670 servants
or slaves appear in estates of 50 percent of the planters on Maryland's
lower Western Shore who left personalty worth £30 to £50 sterling,
and more than half of all servants in inventories appeared in estates
appraised at less than £200.[45] Men of low or middling wealth levels
also hired freedmen labor. Among the seventy freedmen in this study
who left certain evidence of being ex-servants, forty-one surely died
in the houses of their employers or chief creditors, and the property
and status at death of twenty-three of these employers are known.
All were landowners, but half had moveable property worth less than
£150 and five had less than £70. Two had only £24. Tenant farmers,
furthermore, also hired or sharecropped with free labor, as payments
found in their probate records prove.[46]

Laborers, bound or free, who worked for small or middling planters
were seldom isolated from the master's family. Such planters could
not afford to maintain separate servants' quarters detached from their
homes. Often servants and free laborers must have been fully integrated into family life, sharing meals, sleeping under the same roof,
being treated like poor relations or at times like sons or daughters.
Nor could most planters afford to exempt themselves or members of
their families from the hard work of farming. Masters and laborers
working side by side in the fields must have been a frequent sight in
the Chesapeake before the last quarter of the century. Shared social
experience as well as common social origins must have diminished
differences in status between freedmen and their employers.

Some freedmen without households even achieved sufficient status

44. For the middling status of indentured servants at mid-century, see Campbell,
"Social Origins," in Smith, ed., *Seventeenth-Century America*; for a modification of the
argument, see Galenson, "'Middling People' or 'Common Sort'?" *WMQ*, 3d Ser.,
XXXV (1978). Men appointed to major office were more likely than others to have
gentle origins, but Menard has found that among Maryland justices of the peace, most
did not style themselves even "Mr." upon arrival. Menard File, Hall of Records. For
example, of the 135 justices appointed in Charles, Talbot, and Kent counties, 1660–1692,
61 did not style themselves "Mr."; 34 had this title or one higher. Information is lacking
for 40, but it is unlikely that enough had titles to make this group a majority. Even by
the early 18th century successful immigrants were not usually men born gentlemen.
Between 1696 and 1709, 15 immigrants became justices of Prince George's County. Five
may have been gentlemen on arrival. Carr, "County Government in Maryland," text,
618.

45. Menard, "Economy and Society," 347, 352.

46. Inventories and Accounts, IV, 408, VI, 293.

in the community to be appointed to local office. At least six of those studied—all proved ex-servants—had served on juries and one had been an undersheriff. Probably similar service would be found for others were not court records destroyed for two of the counties represented. Such opportunities were probably most widespread while the population was small and participation in local government was necessarily broad. Of the six office-holding freedmen, the two with very small estates had served in the 1660s. All the others were among the wealthiest of the freedmen group. Edward Abbot and Robert Cooper were tailors, in effect entrepreneurs, and Giles Cole, with a £41 estate, leased land for his crop from neighbors but made his home with Henry Hawkins, a justice of the peace. Cole was probably considered a planter.[47] As population increased, participation of non-householders in local government probably became confined to those who were well known in the area and had visible resources sufficient to establish households if they chose.

Freedmen were not outcasts, then, and most planters had once been freedmen. Nevertheless, men who lived as inmates in other men's households had an ambiguous status in a society organized around "masters of families." In 1677, for example, a Talbot County judgment described John Cooke as "a Freeman *belonging* to Richard Bayley," and in 1699 a Baltimore County tax list showed "George Smith Junior and *his* freeman."[48] It was usual for the head of the household to pay the freedman's taxes and be reimbursed from his labor. Even Giles Cole owed his landlord for his levies as well as for ground, housing, and cask for his crop. Doubtless this arrangement was a convenience to the freedman as well as to the sheriff who collected the tax, yet it was also a sign of uneasy status. In the eighteenth century the law would require a laboring man without a household to find a householder to guarantee his tax; until one was found such a man could be imprisoned.[49]

This ambiguous status was in part the result of the physical mobility of freedmen. Virginia tax lists for Northampton and Surry coun-

47. *Md. Archives*, LVII, 598, XLIX, 259, 409, LX, 559, LIII, 363, LI, 285, 477; Inventories and Accounts, III, 37, 108, II, 133, IV, 340–345, VIII, 57, 117, 228–231, IX, 194, 461.

48. Talbot County Judgments, 1675–1682, 109; Baltimore County List of Taxables, 1699–1706, 1, MS, Maryland Historical Society, Baltimore. Italics in this quotation are added by the authors.

49. Acts 1719, c. 12, Thomas Bacon, ed., *Laws of Maryland at Large* . . . (Annapolis, Md., 1765).

ties indicate that freedmen changed households frequently, and lists for Baltimore County, Maryland, for the first six years of the eighteenth century suggest that tax collectors had difficulty pinning freedmen down.[50] It is possible, furthermore, that freedmen's mobility increased as the seventeenth century progressed. They may have become less settled, less identified with a neighborhood as more acquired horses that enabled them to travel easily.

Toward the end of the seventeenth century, the social status of freedmen, like their economic position, deteriorated. First of all, social distance between servants and ex-servants and their masters or landlords increased. A change in the social origins of servants and freedmen was in part responsible. Mildred Campbell's study of indentured servants who sailed from Bristol in the middle of the century and from London in the early 1680s indicates that many were from middling English families.[51] There are indications, however, that after 1680 men of this status became a smaller proportion of immigrants. The number of Irish servants who came to Maryland rose sharply in the mid-1680s and by the turn of the century enough had arrived to arouse fears of popery in the more paranoid English colonial officials.[52] The decline in age observable among servants recorded in immigrant lists and among servants without indentures whose times of service are recorded in the county courts also suggests a fall in social status. Parents presumably would be reluctant to send young children to the New World unless there was difficulty in providing for them at home. Frequent references in the lists to servants sixteen years old and under as poor, friendless, or orphaned support this conclusion.[53]

Another indication of increasing social distance lies in the rising wealth of masters. By 1700 more than half the servants in inventories appeared in estates appraised at £700 or more.[54] Many freedmen

50. Morgan, *American Slavery, American Freedom*, 430; Robert A. Wheeler, "Geographic Mobility in Surry County, Virginia" (paper, Stonybrook Conference in Early American History, 1974); Baltimore County List of Taxables, 1699–1706.

51. See citations in n. 44.

52. See Francis Nicholson to Board of Trade, Aug. 20, 1698, *Md. Archives*, XXIII, 498; Thomas Lawrence to Board of Trade, Oct. 25, 1703, W. Noel Sainsbury *et al.*, eds., *Calendar of State Papers, Colonial Series* (London, 1860–), *America and West Indies, 1703*, no. 1190. Beginning in the mid-1680s there is a sharp increase in the proportion of servants brought into Charles County Court to have their service period determined who had distinctively Irish names. See Charles County Court and Land Records.

53. This argument is elaborated and documented in Menard, "Economy and Society," 414–417.

54. *Ibid.*, 347.

may have continued to work with small planters; but in the last decades of the century doubtless ex-servants were integrated into their master's family with less frequency, more often ate and slept in separate quarters, and labored beside other servants or slaves rather than beside the master and his family. In addition the growth of slavery and the growing identification of blacks with fieldwork may have led to a debasement of all labor and laborers.

As population grew, furthermore, the probability of participation in community service diminished. Edward Abbot, who sat on a Provincial Court jury in 1680, was the last among those studied to perform such service. By the early eighteenth century all local officeholding was becoming closely tied to ownership of land, and the laws, although not always enforced, required that jurors be freeholders.[55] Freedmen without households were probably the first to suffer from diminishing opportunity to share the privileges—and the burdens— of full membership in the community.

One form of service, on the other hand, was asked primarily of freedmen without households and families: service on military expeditions. At least nine freedmen inmates served in the war against the Susquehannocks in 1675 and at least five of them lost their lives. Another died at the garrison established near the falls of the Potomac in 1696. Only four other men among all decedents left evidence of being called to such service. All able-bodied men theoretically served in the militia, but, except among officers, men with farms and families were far more likely than were laborers to be spared service that risked their lives or took them from their crops. The laborer was more expendable.

Clearly the establishment of a household was a critical step in achieving an improved position, both social and economic. Men did so at very low wealth levels. Some of the very poorest inventoried decedents, men worth hardly a pound, had left the status of freedmen to become householders. No doubt the opportunity to marry often determined a man's decision, and as sex ratios improved the number of poor men's households increased. Before 1671, the point at which householders were a majority of inventoried decedents was reached at £15 to £19 of moveable wealth; by the early 1680s this point had fallen to £10 to £14. At this level 90 percent of all inventoried decedents were more likely than not to be householders.

55. Carr, "County Government in Maryland," text, 487–488, 601–608.

Some men formed households without waiting to marry; among inventoried freedmen, as we have seen, seventy fell into this category. Without a wife to provide companionship and assistance such a move presented difficulties which freedmen occasionally solved by joining forces with other bachelors. Two or more men would lease or even buy a tract together, pool their livestock, and share household goods. At least four of the bachelors under study and perhaps as many as twenty died while living with a partner. Walter Gifford—worth £18 —wrote a revealing letter on his deathbed at the Susquehannock fort.

Loving Mate—My Love remembered to you and all the rest of my friends. I desire You to be carefull of what we have and if it should please God I should dye I give all in Generall to you do not want anything that is necessary for you mind the Cooper and hasten him, no more at present but my love to you. I rest your loving ffriend and Mate.[56]

But with or without a partner, the bachelor householder shared in the advantages of householding. He was likely to accumulate more property than those who did not or could not make this choice, and there was no ambiguity in his status. He had a place in the community and paid his own taxes.[57] The census takers of the early eighteenth century recognized his position as one of the "masters of families."[58]

In finally judging the position of the freedman, then, we must look at his opportunities to establish a farm, perhaps acquire land, and become a master of a family. The data presented so far does not allow a direct test of freedmen's opportunities since by definition the group so far studied includes only unmarried men who for the most part had failed to acquire property, power, and position when they died. However, recent studies of servants in Maryland during the seventeenth and early eighteenth centuries, based on the careers of roughly 1,700 individuals, record changes in opportunities with some precision and allow a direct evaluation of life chances across the early colonial period. Much work remains, particularly on the issues of regional variations and the exact timing of change, but it is possible to offer a tentative generalization. The evidence is presented elsewhere and only the pattern need be described here.[59]

56. Wills, II, 360.
57. Of the 70 housekeepers, 12 (17%) were jurors or had military commissions as opposed to 6 of the 162 men without households.
58. *Md. Archives*, XXV, 256, 258–259.
59. The evidence is presented in Menard, "Economy and Society," 236–239, 246–

Most servants who migrated to Maryland from the 1630s through the 1650s, if they escaped early death, achieved considerable property and status and were fully integrated into the community as small planters, masters of families, and participants in local government. A substantial proportion of the early arrivals went well beyond such modest accomplishments to acquire sizable fortunes and membership in the emerging Chesapeake gentry. Opportunities began to decline after 1660 and did so progressively for two decades. However, the extent of the decline should not be exaggerated. Servants who arrived in the newly settled regions of Maryland in the 1660s and 1670s, although they were not as successful as those who arrived earlier and seldom attained prominence, often became small, independent planters and minor officials in local government. Further, there is evidence that some servants from the older regions of the province where the decline was most sharply felt were able to move to the Chesapeake frontier and build successful careers. And even in the older counties on Maryland's lower Western Shore, ex-servants often gained a foothold in society as tenant farmers, while those who lived long enough to see their children grow into adults (a rare achievement in the seventeenth century) usually acquired plantations of their own.[60]

By the end of the seventeenth century, however, freedmen's opportunities had clearly become slim. The decline, which began in the 1660s in the oldest areas, became severe after 1680, when it apparently affected all regions of the province without regard to date of settlement. The careers of most servants who came to Maryland between 1680 and 1710 can be summarized briefly. The majority entered the Chesapeake during two short periods of prosperity, 1685 to 1686 and

248, 419–420; Menard, "From Servant to Freeholder," *WMQ*, 3d Ser., XXX (1973), 37–64; Walsh, "Servitude and Opportunity in Charles County." See also Wertenbaker, *Planters*.

These discussions of opportunity consider only men for two related reasons. First, women who completed their terms usually married immediately, thus changing their names, and, in the absence of marriage registers, making it nearly impossible to follow their careers. Second, the only opportunity open to most women was marriage. See Campbell, "Social Origins," in Smith, ed., *Seventeenth-Century America*, 73–74; Moller, "Sex Composition and Culture Patterns," *WMQ*, 3d Ser., II (1946), 129–131, 139; Lois Green Carr and Lorena S. Walsh, "The Planter's Wife: The Experience of White Women in Seventeenth-Century Maryland," *ibid.*, XXXIV (1977), 542–571. Given the sex ratio, the opportunity to marry remained high for women throughout the 17th century.

60. All but one of the 72 men who died on the lower Western Shore between 1658 and 1684 leaving inventories and adult children were landowners. The proportion of landowners then declined, but, even if all the uncertains are classified as tenants, the percentage remained above 70.

1698 to 1702. When they completed their terms they found themselves free men with no capital and little credit in a depressed economy
that offered little chance of advancement. After a few years as hired
hands or sharecroppers, or perhaps a brief attempt at tenant farming,
they left the tobacco coast for more promising regions. Some scattered
evidence, hardly conclusive, suggests that the pattern established in
these years persisted for the remainder of the colonial period.[61]

These biographical studies of indentured servants suggest that
long-term trends in opportunity were directly related to the rate of
expansion of the Chesapeake tobacco industry. While the industry
was vigorous and growing it created demands for goods, services,
and labor and generated credit upon which poor men could capitalize
in order to make the transition from servant to freeholder. Rapid
expansion of the tobacco industry made Maryland a good poor man's
country in the early and middle decades of the seventeenth century.
But as the rate of growth slowed and eventually approached zero,
opportunities first declined—although less sharply on the frontiers of
settlement than in the older regions of the province—and later disappeared.

The disappearance of opportunity paralleled and reinforced the
decline in the status of servants and freedmen inmates. Earlier, despite important differences in the legal position of masters and servants, the social distance between them was often narrow. And,
given the extent of opportunity around mid-century, it was a gap a
servant could expect to cross once out of his time. By the 1690s the
increased distance between the master's wealth and the poor man's
prospects had made it more difficult for a servant even to aspire to his
master's station.

The emergence about 1700 of a predominantly creole white society
further hastened the disappearance of opportunities for ex-servants.
The native-born had intrinsic advantages. Even sons of poor men
usually inherited a cow or a few household goods that gave them a
headstart over immigrants just completing service, and natives could

61. This suggestion is based on Menard's preliminary investigation of population
growth and opportunity in 18th-century Somerset County. See also Edward C. Papenfuse and Gregory A. Stiverson, "General Smallwood's Recruits: The Peacetime Career
of the Revolutionary War Private," *WMQ*, 3d Ser., XXX (1973), 117–132; Paul G. E.
Clemens, "Economy and Society on Maryland's Eastern Shore, 1689–1733," in Land,
Carr, and Papenfuse, eds., *Law, Society, and Politics*, 153–170; Allan Kulikoff, "Tobacco
and Slaves: Population, Economy, and Society in Eighteenth-Century Prince George's
County, Maryland" (Ph.D. diss., Brandeis University, 1976), chap. 5.

start working for themselves at an earlier age. Nor was the native born's advantage necessarily only economic. Whether creoles felt a social preference for fellow natives is an issue not yet much explored. But a recent study of jury selection in Charles County, Maryland, suggests that discrimination was practiced against immigrants once a sufficient pool of natives was available.[62] If such discrimination extended to marriage patterns, the mobility by marriage that assisted many a seventeenth-century career also became more limited for immigrants.

Thus a society which once promised indentured servants eventual integration into the community they served had become one that offered newly freed workers a choice between poverty or emigration. Over time, servitude in the Chesapeake colonies had become less like English apprenticeship, less a means of preparing for full membership in a New World community, and more a kind of short-term slavery.

Edmund Morgan has contended that freedmen grew disillusioned with their chances in Virginia as early as the 1660s and thereafter became frustrated, dangerous men.[63] Since such men left little direct testimony of how they regarded their prospects, the first part of this proposition is difficult to evaluate. Nevertheless, several of the conclusions to this essay, which depict a longer persistence and a slower decline of opportunity, suggest that this picture of the freedman requires modification.

Before 1680, while the Chesapeake still offered freedmen some opportunities to become planters, it is unlikely that they thought their prospects bleak. Those who died on the lower Western Shore of Maryland were still young men who had not long been free, and they were surrounded by freedmen who had become farmers.[64] They were surely not yet despairing of their chances. Indeed, if we are right in believing that freedmen's estates were usually reported to the probate court, then most ex-servants who had died by 1680 had at least

---

62. Unpublished research of Lorena S. Walsh, St. Mary's City Commission, Annapolis, Maryland.

63. Morgan, "Slavery and Freedom," *JAH*, LIX (1972), 22–27.

64. Date of arrival is known for 29 of 67 men who died before 1680. None had been in Maryland for as much as 20 years and only 4 had been there as long as 15 years. Mean time in the colony was 11 years. Five to six years would have been spent in service. Across the whole period, date of arrival is known for 57 of 162 men. Seven had been in Maryland more than 20 years and 17 for 15 years or more. Mean length of time in the colony was 12 years and only about half that time was spent as a freedman.

made the transition to householder on the lower Western Shore or had moved to an area where they could.

After 1680, as opportunities severely contracted, freedmen evidently emigrated to newer colonies. Reports of emigration appear as early as 1681 and by the 1690s the outmigration had reached epidemic proportions. In the mid-1690s and again during the severe depression that accompanied Queen Anne's War, there were numerous complaints that lack of opportunity was driving former servants to Pennsylvania, the Carolinas, and the Jerseys.[65] Demographic data indicate that the complaints were justified. Taxable figures for both Maryland and Virginia show a slight decline from the late 1680s to the mid-1690s, and an examination of Maryland census figures demonstrates that at least one thousand men left that colony between 1704 and 1712.[66] Former servants, this suggests, when faced with disappearing opportunities, did not stay in the tobacco coast and vent their rage against the social order, but left the region in search of better prospects elsewhere.

The evidence of heavy emigration does suggest that by the turn of the century poor men had a low opinion of their chances: the freedman testified with his feet. Was outmigration rooted in despair, or was it a more hopeful choice? Firm answers to such questions are impossible, but what we have learned about the lives of freedmen does not suggest that most were alienated and bitter. Even toward the end of the century they could see well-established men who had begun careers in the Chesapeake as servants and this example perhaps inspired hope of eventual success. The occasional insight into personal relationships provided by wills, furthermore, suggests that many freedmen, even if they failed to form families or accumulate property, built close friendships and affectionate ties to other members of their community. And, although their chances of joining the ranks of small planters were slight, they could still find work at good wages, suggesting that those who emigrated may have done so less

65. Francis Nicholson to Board of Trade, Mar. 27, 1697, *Md. Archives*, XXIII, 87–88; Nicholson to duke of Shrewsbury, June 14, 1695, *Cal. S. P. Col., 1693–1696*, no. 1891; Thomas Lawrence to Board of Trade, June 25, 1695, *ibid.*, no. 1916; *Md. Archives*, XIX, 225–226, 237, 250, 258, 539–540, XX, 279, 328, 329, XXIII, 84; John Seymour to Board of Trade, June 23, 1708, CO V/716/pt. III; Edward Lloyd and others to Board of Trade, Nov. 4, 1710, *ibid.*, V/717/pt. II; Petition of the President, Council and Assembly of Maryland to Board of Trade, Nov. 10, 1713, *ibid.*, V/717/pt. IV. PRO Transcripts, Library of Congress. Wertenbaker, *Planters*, 145–146, 177, 179.

66. Menard, "Economy and Society," 417–418.

out of a sense of despair than because they thought they could do better in the more recently settled and more rapidly growing American colonies.

Were freedmen, then, a source of social disruption and political instability, feared by their social superiors? Much of the evidence which suggests that they were comes from letters written by supporters of Governor Berkeley during Bacon's Rebellion, evidence perhaps more than a little tainted by hysteria and self-interest. Supporters of the other side countered with assertions that the rebels were men of property and standing.[67] Unmarried landless laborers were a potentially disruptive force in Chesapeake society, but it would be easy to exaggerate their importance. Freedmen perhaps made an appeal to violence easier to organize, but the struggle for power among those at or near the top seems the much more important source of violent conflict. A study of the Revolution of 1689 in Maryland concludes that freedmen had little importance in that upheaval, while examinations of Chesapeake politics earlier in the century suggest that disputes between Lord Baltimore, London tobacco merchants, and prominent planters in both Maryland and Virginia were by far the most important source of turmoil.[68]

Several comments about inmates made by colonial officials in periods of relative stability survive; they contain little of the fear found in the letters written during Bacon's Rebellion. In 1666, for example, the Maryland lower house opposed a cessation of tobacco production in part because it would force the "young Freemen"—and it is clear they meant men who were not heads of households—who were, they argued, ". . . the greatest strength of this Province," to leave the colony for want of employment.[69] The year 1666, it should be noted,

67. See the letter of Mrs. William Byrd, quoted in Richard L. Morton, *Colonial Virginia* (Chapel Hill, N.C., 1960), I, 239.

68. Morgan suggests that New Kent men were poor but that most were planters. *American Slavery, American Freedom*, 265. Perhaps the men of New Kent as described there were like those of Talbot County, Maryland, in 1689, whom Peter Sayer called "silly mobile" who needed reminding that they were risking their estates. *Md. Archives*, VIII, 158. For freedmen in the Maryland Revolution of 1689, see Lois Green Carr and David William Jordan, *Maryland's Revolution of Government, 1689–1692* (Ithaca, N.Y., 1974), 192–193. On earlier conflicts, see Robert P. Brenner, "Commercial Change and Political Conflict: The Merchant Community of Civil War London" (Ph.D. diss., Princeton University, 1970); Menard, "Economy and Society," 111–152; Bernard Bailyn, "Politics and Social Structure in Virginia," in Smith, ed., *Seventeenth-Century America*, 90–118.

69. *Md. Archives*, II, 44. The Upper House disagreed with this assessment. *Ibid.*, 46–47.

came at the bottom of a severe depression, when one would expect Morgan's "wild young men" to be at their most discontented and dangerous. The massive exodus of former servants in the mid-1690s and again in the early eighteenth century, both periods of depression, was duly noted and universally deplored by officials in Maryland and Virginia. Governor Nicholson even suggested that enticing such men away from the tobacco coast be made a criminal offense.[70] If the men at the top despised and feared the freedman, would they not have encouraged and applauded his departure and breathed a sigh of relief once he had gone?

As servants and freedmen found their prospects declining in the Chesapeake toward the end of the seventeenth century, demographic changes altered the role of ex-servants in the society of Maryland and Virginia. The growth of slavery and the rise of a native-born majority in the white population diminished both the importance and the visibility of the freedman.

The growth of slavery can be understood as the product of an interaction between Old World supplies and New World demands for labor. The widespread availability of cheap land, because it kept wages high, encouraged the use of unfree labor in the Chesapeake colonies. For a time, however, indentured servants—young men drawn largely from the middling groups of English society—supplied tobacco planters with sufficient workers. Through the middle decades of the seventeenth century, the supply of servants to Maryland and Virginia grew more rapidly than the number of households, permitting planters to meet their needs for labor without resort to slaves. Planters, however, depended on a steady increase in the number of young Englishmen willing to seek their fortunes in tobacco, a situation in turn dependent upon the high birthrate and secular decline in real wages that characterized English society before 1650. Just prior to mid-century, the birthrate fell and England's population stopped growing, or at least grew at a slower pace. Chesapeake planters felt the impact of the fall in the early 1660s when a decline in the number of young men entering the work force and a rise in real wages led to a growing reluctance on the part of Englishmen to try their luck in the colonies. Tobacco planters faced a labor shortage, a shortage aggravated by growing colonial demands as the Chesapeake continued to expand and rapid development began in the middle colonies and the

70. See above, n. 65.

Carolinas. A dwindling supply of middling Englishmen forced planters to draw more heavily upon other groups—women, American Indians, Irishmen, the poor, convicts, and, most important, Africans —to meet their needs for labor.[71] The consequences were soon visible on Maryland's lower Western Shore. Despite broader recruitment in Britain, slaves outnumbered servants among unfree workers by 1690 and, in some Maryland counties, slaves dominated the total labor force as early as 1710.[72]

At the same time that slaves began to outnumber servants, native-born white men began to enter the labor force in rapidly increasing numbers. By the first decade of the eighteenth century the adult white population of both Maryland and Virginia was predominantly creole.[73] This transformation was the result, in part, of an increase in the rate of reproductive population growth and in part of the slowdown in the rate of British migration to the Chesapeake.[74] The growing supply of native-born workers probably did not push out immigrant laborers. Labor shortages were too severe. But immigrant servants and ex-servants were no longer the backbone of even the white labor supply.

The declining proportion of freedmen inmates can be followed among inventoried decedents. Before 1690 in St. Mary's County freedmen inmates were 11 percent of all decedents, but during the last decade of the century they dropped to 6 percent. Despite the great influx of servants from 1698 through 1702, the drop continued over the next three decades until it reached nearly 2 percent (see table 8).

71. The argument of this paragraph is developed more fully in Russell R. Menard, "From Servants to Slaves: The Transformation of the Chesapeake Labor System," *Southern Studies*, XVI (1977), 355–390.

72. In the early 1660s estates showed a mean of 1.7 servants per household. By about 1720 the mean had dropped to .53 servants per household. Menard, "Economy and Society," fig. VII-I. Slaves first outnumbered servants in 1690 and continued to do so thereafter with the exception of the years 1698 to 1702, when a heavy importation of servants caused servants to slightly outnumber slaves once more. *Ibid.*, 337. The census of 1710 shows slaves as more than 50% of taxables in Calvert and Prince George's counties. *Md. Archives*, XXV, 258.

73. David W. Jordan, "The Royal Period of Colonial Maryland, 1698–1715" (Ph.D. diss., Princeton University, 1966); Martin Quitt, "The House of Burgesses after Bacon's Rebellion" (paper, Southern Historical Association, 1973). Even the leadership of the Maryland frontier county of Prince George's showed the change. Carr, "County Government in Maryland," text, 696. For a detailed study of the beginnings of natural increase in Maryland, see Menard, "Immigrants and Their Increase," in Land, Carr, and Papenfuse, eds., *Law, Society, and Politics*.

74. Menard, "Immigrants and Their Increase," in Land, Carr, and Papenfuse, eds., *Law, Society, and Politics*.

TABLE 8. Freedmen as a Percentage of All Male Decedents

| | St. Mary's County | | Prince George's County | |
	All Male Decedents	% Freedmen	All Male Decedents	% Freedmen
1658–1670	83	10.8		
1671–1680	169	10.7		
1681–1690	131	10.7		
1691–1700	145	6.2	46[a]	13.0[a]
1701–1710	191	5.2	103	5.8
1711–1720	321	4.4	216	8.8
1721–1730	374	2.4		

Note:
[a]Figures are for the year 1696–1700. The county was established in 1696.

Sources:
"Social Stratification in Maryland, 1658–1705" (data through 1705); "The Making of Plantation Society in Maryland," National Endowment for the Humanities Grant RO-10585-74-267 (St. Mary's County data, 1706–1730); Carr Inventory File (Prince George's County, 1706–1720).

This decline in the proportion of freedmen in older counties such as St. Mary's was accelerated by emigration to newer areas, including the Maryland frontier. In Prince George's County, established in 1696, the percentage of all decedents who were freedmen inmates was higher than in St. Mary's, despite a lower reporting of dead men's estates.[75] But freedmen's chances for success even here were not improving: of 116 servants brought into the county between 1696 and 1705, only 5 to 8 appeared as heads of households on a nearly complete tax list of 1719.[76] Since the tax list names only the "house-keepers," the number of these ex-servants who actually left the county cannot be estimated, but it seems likely that immigrants without capital were moving on.

75. In 1704 there were 1,356 adult white males in St. Mary's and in 1710 there were 1,088. In Prince George's the figures are 880 and 845 respectively. An unknown proportion of these men were indentured servants. From 1706 to 1710, 105 men left inventories in St. Mary's County, but only 36 did so in Prince George's. From 1711 to 1720, 321 men left inventories in St. Mary's, but only 216 in Prince George's. Supposing the proportion of indentured servants was the same in both counties, in 1704 St. Mary's had 35% more adult free white males than had Prince George's and in 1710, 22% more. But St. Mary's had 66% more reported estates of free white males over the years 1706 to 1710 and 33% more over the years 1711 to 1720. The decline of white taxables in both counties suggests emigration from both; nevertheless, more freedmen may have remained on the frontier than in the older counties.

76. Menard, "Economy and Society," 419–420.

Certainly freedmen inmates diminished greatly as a proportion of the Prince George's labor force after the early eighteenth century. In a census taken in 1704, men who were not housekeepers or sons living in their parents' households comprised 32 percent of the Prince George's County taxables and slaves constituted 34 percent.[77] On a tax list of 1733 such white men were not more than 14 percent of the taxable population, and some of these were surely native-born, while slaves had risen to 51 percent.[78] That same year, in the older tobacco county of Calvert, white laborers—excluding sons living at home— were at most only 11 percent of the taxable population and slaves were nearly 60 percent (see table 9).[79]

Thus by the 1730s and probably much earlier, immigrant former servants without households were of minor importance in the society of Maryland's tobacco coast. Over most of the seventeenth century they had been a principal source of labor and had constituted the pool from which planters were recruited. By the eighteenth century slaves were the majority of laborers and native-born whites were the planters. Servants and freedmen did not disappear, but they were no longer basic elements in the social fabric. The transformation rendered negligible whatever social problems a discontented class of freedmen had posed. The new problems that slavery presented now challenged Maryland society.

77. *Md. Archives*, XXV, 256, 258. Total white males, not heads of households, were 35% of all white males, but 10% have been subtracted as an allowance for sons of the head of the household. The percentage is a mean of those found on Baltimore County List of Taxables, 1699–1706. However, only men with the same surnames as the household head were counted as sons. Identification of other kin would increase the percent of relations and lower that of hired or indentured laborers. No allowance has been made here for professionals or other kinds of inmates who were not farm laborers.

78. The Black Books, II, nos. 113–123, MS. Again the figures for hired or indentured white labor are an upper bound. Stepsons or other kin may be included and no allowance has been made for professionals, etc.

79. White laborers remained more numerous in some areas where tobacco had less importance. Servants continued to be imported into Talbot County, an area less able to command adequate supplies of slaves. In 1733, 26% of the taxable population consisted of white nonhouseholders who were not sons living at home. Only 32% of the taxables were slaves. In 1704 the proportions had been 38% and 23% respectively. Md. State Papers, Series Z, Scharf Collection, Box 118; *Md. Archives*, XXV, 256; Talbot County Judgments, 1703–1704, proceedings at end of Nov. 1704 Court (volume is unpaged). The proportion of white inmates had decreased since the early 18th century but far less than on the lower Western Shore. Nevertheless, the character of this inmate population had changed, for many must have been born in Maryland. In 1704 immigrant servants or freedmen must have been the great majority of inmates. But by 1733 they may well have been a minority.

TABLE 9. Analysis of Taxables, 1704 and 1733, for Calvert and Prince George's Counties

	Total Taxables[a]	Total White Taxables	Taxed Heads of Households[b]	White Male Inmates	Sons of Householders[b]	White Inmates Less Sons	Taxable Slaves
	N	N	% taxables	% taxables	% taxables	% taxables	% taxables
1704							
Calvert	(1,613)	928	19	38	2	36	(42)[c]
Prince George's	1,299	880	32	36	3	32	34
1733							
Calvert	1,967	814	24	17	5	11	59
Prince George's	3,759	1,851	30	19	5	14	51

Notes:

[a]The figure for total taxables in Prince George's in 1704 is from Prince George's County Court Record B, 340. The figure for Calvert was adjusted from the figures for white taxables and slaves given in the census of 1704. Since slave children are counted with taxable slaves, taxable slaves have been estimated by subtracting the proportion of children found in lower Western Shore inventories, 1701–1710. See Russell R. Menard, "Economy and Society in Early Colonial Maryland" (Ph.D. diss., University of Iowa, 1975), 403.

[b]For 1704, sons are estimated as 10% of heads of households, the mean ratio found on Baltimore County lists of taxables, 1699–1706. For 1733 they are conted from county taxable lists.

[c]Adjustments for this figure are explained in n. 1, above.

Sources:

Except as noted, figures for 1704 are from a census printed in *Md. Archives*, XXV, 256. Those for 1733 are from the Black Books, II, nos. 113–123 (Prince George's); Charles M. Stein, *The History of Calvert County* (Baltimore, 1960), 375–381 (Calvert).

8

Political Stability and the Emergence of a Native Elite in Maryland

David W. Jordan

The seventeenth century was an era of marked instability in southern politics. Recurrent turmoil and unrest interrupted the administration of provincial government in both Maryland and her sister colony of Virginia. The instability was more pervasive, however, than is demonstrated by the overt disruptions and rebellions, numerous though they were. Even in times of relative peace, the primary institutions of provincial government—the council, assembly, and provincial court—suffered considerable discontinuity in membership and effective service. Tenures were brief, experience a rare commodity, and a qualified and sustained political leadership practically nonexistent. Not until the closing years of the century did continuity and a knowledgeable leadership become characteristic of the membership of these institutions, and not until the end of the first decade of the eighteenth century did an established, second-generation ruling group become dominant in Maryland's provincial politics. A comparable elite had emerged only slightly earlier in Virginia.

This slow evolution of political stability and social order contrasted sharply with developments several hundred miles to the north in colonies also founded by the 1630s. The New England settlements suffered far less violence and unrest and attained rather mature and stable governing institutions within a few years of their founding. Political leadership resided in a respected ruling elite that enjoyed a remarkable continuity of service and that transferred its power quite successfully to its sons and grandsons. In Massachusetts as early as the 1670s second-generation colonists sat in the General Court in significant numbers, and in the 1680s they predominated in the legis-

An earlier version of this essay was presented at the Southern Historical Association Convention, November 10, 1973.

The author wishes especially to thank David Ammerman, John Murrin, Alison Olson, and Thad Tate for their most helpful criticisms.

lature. By 1691 the Massachusetts council was "composed mainly of second and third generation New England merchants." At the end of the century in one New England town after another, the situation resembled that of Windsor, Connecticut, where all of the major political officials were sons or grandsons of the distinguished early settlers. Yankee descendants of Puritan immigrants, often representing the third generation of their families in America, governed New England colonies just fifty to sixty years after their founding.[1]

Chesapeake colonial politics remained considerably less mature, less predictable, and less stable throughout the seventeenth century. Stability in this sense is not defined as complete harmony or the absence of factions and dissension, but rather as a people's ability to express and resolve differences within existing institutions without undue resort to violence, rebellion, and intrigue. This political sophistication requires a certain maturity of governing institutions and widespread public acceptance of the men elected or appointed to them. Through most of the century, both Maryland and Virginia lacked sufficient social stability for these critical developments. Such social cohesion did not arrive in the Old Dominion until two decades after Bacon's Rebellion and not until the turn of the century in Maryland. Some pockets of settlement did achieve these conditions earlier, and local governing institutions there often reflected a degree of stability and responsibility not yet present in provincial politics.[2]

The political history of colonial America has all too frequently been

1. Timothy H. Breen and Stephen Foster, "The Puritans' Greatest Achievement: A Study of Social Cohesion in Seventeenth-Century Massachusetts," *Journal of American History*, LX (1973), 5–22; Robert Emmet Wall, Jr., "The Membership of the Massachusetts General Court, 1634–1686" (Ph.D. diss., Yale University, 1965), 70; Bernard Bailyn, *The New England Merchants in the Seventeenth Century* (Cambridge, Mass., 1955), 176–177; Richard L. Bushman, *From Puritan to Yankee: Character and the Social Order in Connecticut, 1690–1765* (New York, 1967), 11. See also Richard S. Dunn, *Puritans and Yankees: The Winthrop Dynasty of New England, 1630–1717* (Princeton, N.J., 1962); John J. Waters, "Hingham, Massachusetts, 1631–1661: An East Anglian Oligarchy in the New World," *Journal of Social History*, I (1968), 351–370; and Bruce C. Daniels, "Democracy and Oligarchy in Connecticut Towns: General Assembly Officeholding, 1701–1790," *Social Science Quarterly*, LVI (1975), 460–475.

2. For a stimulating discussion of the ingredients of political stability and a study of contemporary English politics, see J. H. Plumb, *The Growth of Political Stability in England, 1675–1725* (London, 1967). Lois Green Carr and David William Jordan, *Maryland's Revolution of Government, 1689–1692* (Ithaca, N.Y., 1974), describe the society of that colony in the late 17th century and argue for the presence of significant stability in some local government as early as the 1680s. For Virginia, see Bernard Bailyn, "Politics and Social Structure in Virginia," in James Morton Smith, ed., *Seventeenth-Century America: Essays in Colonial History* (Chapel Hill, N.C., 1959), 90–115; John C. Rainbolt, "The Alteration in the Relationship between Leadership and Constituents in Virginia, 1660 to 1720," *William and Mary Quarterly*, 3d Ser., XXVII (1970), 411–434; T. H. Breen,

divorced from the study of society. Especially in examining the seventeenth century, historians have focused too narrowly upon constitutional precedents, specific institutional changes, and those highly dramatic struggles and revolts preserved in official legislative and executive records. Social analyses have traditionally relied on impressionistic literary evidence or conclusions drawn from intensive examinations of specific conflicts within a limited period of time. Such approaches generally fail to explain satisfactorily the social dynamics of politics or the gradual evolution of institutions.[3] A systematic study of officeholders and the political process over a more extended period of time, buttressed by findings from recent demographic research, promises to reduce those shortcomings and to illuminate much about the heretofore dark paths that most colonies followed to political maturity. Prosopographical analysis of seventeenth-century provincial officeholders in Maryland, a colony often neglected in scholars' concentration on Virginia, suggests a profitable model for exploring the emergence of stable politics in other southern colonies. These biographies furnish important insights into the uncertainty and ineffectiveness that characterized politics in Maryland in that first century of settlement and demonstrate unquestionably the absence of an established governing elite before 1700.[4]

"A Changing Labor Force and Race Relations in Virginia, 1660–1710," *Jour. Soc. Hist.*, VII (1973), 3–25; and Martin H. Quitt, "The House of Burgesses after Bacon's Rebellion" (paper presented at the Southern Historical Association meeting, 1973).

3. The historiography of colonial politics is well discussed in Jack P. Greene, "Changing Interpretations of Early American Politics," in Ray Allen Billington, ed., *Reinterpretation of Early American History: Essays in Honor of John Edwin Pomfret* (New York, 1968) and Bernard Bailyn, *The Origins of American Politics* (New York, 1968), but one should consult also Paul Lucas, "A Note on the Comparative Study of the Structure of Politics in Mid-Eighteenth-Century Britain and Its American Colonies," *WMQ*, 3d Ser., XXVIII (1971), 301–309. The enormity of the research task has until quite recently discouraged many scholars from extended sociopolitical analyses. Jack Greene originally intended to include greater consideration of the social structure of politics in *The Quest for Power: The Lower Houses of Assembly in the Southern Royal Colonies, 1689–1776* (Chapel Hill, N.C., 1963), but the "task proved much too large" and the eventual volume was a narrower constitutional study (see Greene's preface). Greene's essay, "Foundations of Political Power in the Virginia House of Burgesses, 1720–1776," *WMQ*, 3d Ser., XVI (1959), 485–506, is a good example of what can and should be done on a more extended basis, and more important, for the 17th century. Such scholarship for the southern colonies in the 1600s is very meager, particularly when one observes such other fruitful work for 18th-century Virginia as David Alan Williams, "Political Alignments in Colonial Virginia Politics, 1698–1750" (Ph.D. diss., Northwestern University, 1959); Jackson T. Main, "The One Hundred," *WMQ*, 3d Ser., XI (1954), 354–384; and Robert and B. Katherine Brown, *Virginia 1705–1786: Democracy or Aristocracy?* (East Lansing, Mich., 1964), among many relevant works.

4. The arguments of this paper rest especially upon biographies of the 424 men

A continuing progression of relatively young men, almost exclusively first-generation settlers in the colony, presided briefly in turn over Maryland's provincial politics for at least seventy years after Cecil Calvert established this haven for Catholics on the shores of the Chesapeake Bay. This prolonged ascendancy of immigrants constitutes the most striking feature of the colony's political life in the seventeenth century. It did not arise from the refusal of early adventurers to transfer the reins of political power to a younger generation. Indeed, there was a dearth of the aging patriarchs and their descendants whom one often encounters in New England political life. Any successful explanation of the phenomenon of continued immigrant control must begin with a consideration of the critical demographic profile of the society from which the officeholders emerged.

Throughout the 1600s a steady flow of new settlers from across the Atlantic remained vital to the very existence of both Maryland and Virginia. An extraordinarily high death rate and an unusually low proportion of women among the immigrants combined to restrict severely any natural growth of the population and to postpone the appearance of many native-born English colonists. Although at least 23,500 persons, not including Negroes, migrated to Maryland between 1634 and 1681, the colony's population did not exceed approximately 19,000 in 1681. Not until the 1690s did Maryland show evidence of any significant increase by natural growth, and it was not until some time in the ensuing twenty years that persons born in the colony first constituted a majority of the population. Virginia had reached a comparable stage just slightly ahead of Maryland. The total population of the Old Dominion in 1699 was probably 62,800, although immigration to the colony during the century had probably approached 100,000.[5]

---

who were members of the council, provincial court, or assembly from 1660 to 1715, and less directly upon those men who were provincial officeholders in the three previous decades. Such a prosopographical study would be impossible without the voluminous court and local records that have survived for 17th-century Maryland. Only a portion of these materials have been published in William Hand Browne *et al.*, eds., *Archives of Maryland . . .* (Baltimore, 1883–), hereafter cited as *Md. Archives*; the unpublished manuscript sources are available at the Maryland Hall of Records, Annapolis.

Comparisons with Virginia throughout this paper draw primarily on Martin Quitt's "Virginia House of Burgesses 1660–1706: The Social, Educational and Economic Bases of Political Power" (Ph.D. diss., Washington University, 1970). Quitt examines 301 men who sat between 1677 and 1706, but he admits this is not a complete list. His research, depending primarily on the provincial records, did not exhaust the county-level manuscripts upon which my list of officeholders draws heavily for its completeness.

5. Russell R. Menard, "Immigrants and Their Increase: The Process of Population

Undoubtedly the harsh realities of sheer survival in these two tidewater colonies, with their low life expectancy and reproduction rates, significantly influenced the development of political institutions and the evolution of political stability. While New Englanders at this time apparently enjoyed remarkable life-spans, a male who migrated to Maryland at age twenty could expect to live only to his early forties, and a second-generation male colonist could anticipate only an additional four years of life. Death often abruptly terminated a promising political career. Again unlike New England, the family unit was not common among early settlers, and with the scarcity of women opportunities for marriage and procreation were sharply reduced. At least 70 percent and perhaps as many as 80 to 85 percent of the male decedents during the century succumbed without sons or with sons not of age.[6] Consequently a man seldom lived long enough to establish a firm place in this frontier society or to assist his sons as they came of age.

It became important for the eventual composition of Maryland's elite that so few of the early provincial officeholders had surviving sons who were of an age to capitalize on their fathers' brief successes. Of the fifty-six councillors who sat from the colony's founding to 1689, only seven had sons who ever attained provincial office, and only two of those seven ever acquired a council commission.[7] Dur-

---

Growth in Early Colonial Maryland," in Aubrey C. Land, Lois Green Carr, and Edward C. Papenfuse, eds., *Law, Society, and Politics in Early Maryland* (Baltimore, 1977), 88–110; Arthur E. Karinen, "Maryland Population, 1631–1730: Numerical and Distributional Aspects," *Maryland Historical Magazine*, LIV (1959), 365–407; and, on Virginia, Wesley Frank Craven, *White, Red, and Black: The Seventeenth-Century Virginian* (Charlottesville, Va., 1971), esp. p. 25; and Edmund S. Morgan, *American Slavery, American Freedom: The Ordeal of Colonial Virginia* (New York, 1975), 395–423.

6. I am grateful to Lois Green Carr for sharing with me the early findings of the St. Mary's City Commission's study, "Social Stratification in Maryland, 1658–1705," which she is conducting with P.M.G. Harris and Russell R. Menard. See also Lorena S. Walsh and Russell R. Menard, "Death in the Chesapeake: Two Life Tables for Men in Early Colonial Maryland," *Md. Hist. Mag.*, LXIX (1974), 211–227. In Plymouth Colony, a man reaching adulthood (age 21) could expect to live to age 70. John Demos, "Notes on Life in Plymouth Colony," *WMQ*, 3d Ser., XXII (1965), 271–272. First-generation male settlers of Andover, Massachusetts, enjoyed an average life-span of 71.8 years, while the second generation averaged 65.2 years. Philip J. Greven, Jr., "Family Structure in Seventeenth-Century Andover, Massachusetts," *ibid.*, XXIII (1966), 239–240.

7. The two second-generation councillors were Baker Brooke (1658–1679) and Nicholas Sewall (1683–1689), sons of Robert Brooke (1649–1653) and Henry Sewall (1661–1665). The five assemblymen and their councillor fathers were: Leonard (1682–1684) and Thomas Greene (1644–1650); John (1678–1682, 1686–1692) and William Stone (1656–1660); Philemon (1671–1684) and Edward Lloyd (1658–1668); Joseph (1686–1688) and John Pile (1648); and Henry (1704–1706) and Henry Coursey (1660–1670, 1676–1684). William Calvert, son of Gov. Leonard Calvert (1633–1647), sat in the

ing the next decade, the 1690s, another fifteen resident Marylanders served as councillors. Of these, six died without male heirs, and three others had only very young sons at the time of their deaths. In only four instances would members of the next generation of these fifteen families successfully follow their fathers in achieving this high appointive office.[8] The absence or youthfulness of heirs plagued assembly members as well. As a consequence, new immigrants arriving quite late in the century still enjoyed extraordinary political opportunity. These later settlers could and often did experience a political mobility undreamed of for newcomers in most older colonies.

The nature and pattern of immigration asserted a pervasive influence in still other ways. During the colony's first four decades ships arrived primarily with indentured servants. Upon completion of their terms, these young men, with no appreciable wealth or education, constituted the backbone of the free population upon whom depended the smooth functioning of government. Offices of necessity descended upon individuals who could never ordinarily entertain realistic expectations of holding local, much less provincial, positions of power. Immigrants of wealth and education were rare in the early decades, and those who did come were usually Catholic in religious persuasion. Their religion was at first no bar to officeholding. But a substantial influx of more affluent Protestant immigrants in the 1660s, 1670s, and 1680s altered dramatically the profile of the assembly and council, by sharply curtailing access to high office for both second-generation Catholics and less well-to-do settlers. Like a similar group who settled in Virginia about mid-century, this later wave of immigrants included a number of younger sons of English gentry and merchants who bore established social and political credentials and who usually brought sufficient capital to secure large estates quite rapidly. The pressures exerted by these wealthier and better-educated late arrivals contributed to the social instability of that "time of troubles" that particularly plagued both colonies in the last quarter of the century.[9]

---

assembly (1663–1664, 1666) and on the council (1669–1682). At least 23 of the councillors died without surviving sons.

8. Those four successful fathers and sons were: John (1691–1705/06) and Thomas Addison (1708–1727); Nicholas (1691–1697) and Charles Greenberry (1708–1713); Thomas (1698–1700) and Benjamin Tasker (1723–1768); Thomas Lawrence, Sr. (1691–1698) and Jr. (1700–1701). The Lawrences were royal placemen who never considered themselves as permanent residents of the colony. It became more common after 1689 for sons of councillors to serve at least in the assembly.

9. See elsewhere in this volume, Lois Green Carr and Russell R. Menard, "Im-

The political upheavals themselves, both actual rebellions and aborted ones, had their own special impact on the evolution of offices and access to them. Ingle's Rebellion, the Puritan struggles of the Commonwealth period, and Fendall's Rebellion earlier in the century had each left political casualties, men whose allegiance to the losing side had resulted in their temporary or permanent banishment from political offices. But the consequences were both more pervasive and more permanent after the successful revolt of the Protestant Associators in 1689, Maryland's "Glorious Revolution." That climactic struggle effectively eliminated Catholics and Quakers from political officeholding until the American Revolution, almost a century later.[10]

Adherents of these now excluded faiths had held an extraordinary percentage of the provincial offices prior to the revolution, and several families among them represented whatever embryonic elite may be said to have existed in Maryland at that time. While Catholics and Quakers together probably accounted for no more than 25 percent of the colony's population, they constituted a far higher proportion of the residents who qualified economically for the important political offices at the end of the century. Catholics had always served in heavily disproportionate numbers in the council, provincial court, and assembly. Although the number of Catholics elected to the lower house of the assembly had declined somewhat after mid-century, their control of the two more powerful appointive bodies had increased. Religious affiliations are known for 118 of the 156 assemblymen elected during the years 1660–1689. Of these 118, 23 were Quakers and 20 were Catholics. At least 19 and probably 21 of the 32 councillors serving between 1660 and 1689 were Catholics, and Lord Baltimore's council in 1689 included only one Protestant, William Digges, who had married the proprietor's stepdaughter. Since ac-

migration and Opportunity: The Freedman in Early Colonial Maryland"; also, Menard, "The Growth of Population in Early Colonial Maryland, 1631–1712," manuscript prepared for the St. Mary's City Commission, on file at Hall of Records, Annapolis. Bernard Bailyn first suggested the significance of different waves of migration upon southern politics in his essay, "Politics and Social Structure in Virginia," in Smith, ed., *Seventeenth-Century America,* 90–115.

10. Carr and Jordan, *Maryland's Revolution of Government.* The standard accounts of Maryland's early political history, particularly the rebellions, include: John E. Pomfret with Floyd M. Shumway, *Founding the American Colonies, 1583–1660* (New York, 1970), 75–100; Charles M. Andrews, *The Colonial Period of American History,* II (New Haven, Conn., 1936), 274–379; Wesley Frank Craven, *The Southern Colonies in the Seventeenth Century, 1607–1689* (Baton Rouge, La., 1949), vol. I of Wendell Holmes Stephenson and E. Merton Coulter, eds., *A History of the South;* and Bernard C. Steiner, *Maryland during the English Civil Wars* (Baltimore, 1906–1907) and Steiner, *Maryland under the Commonwealth: A Chronicle of the Years 1649–1658* (Baltimore, 1911).

ceding to the proprietorship in 1676, Charles Calvert had deliberately reserved council and court appointments for fellow Catholics and relatives of the Calvert family. One of the few Protestant councillors had been Quaker Samuel Chew.[11]

After the revolution, only abandonment of former religious convictions would enable these Catholics and Quakers, or their descendants, to subscribe to the test oath or oath of abhorrency, now required of all provincial officeholders. There are very few examples of such conversions or continued family activity in public office.[12] This discrimination against religious minorities delayed for over another decade the likelihood of more than incidental numbers of second-generation officeholders. The exclusion of so large a pool of otherwise qualified men broadened, at least temporarily, political opportunity for many more Protestants, especially recent immigrants or less affluent older settlers.[13] The new royal council appointed in 1691, for example, was composed almost entirely of men from the later wave of immigrants. Only one of the twelve men had any family ties to the councillors of the previous thirty years. A few years later, royal governor Francis Nicholson voiced concern over the serious consequences of Catholic and Quaker exclusion. He found it frustratingly difficult to fill appointive positions with men of talent, experience, and wealth, and he despaired of the quality of assemblymen, especially their lack of

11. Carr and Jordan, *Maryland's Revolution of Government*, 37–45, 194–200, 211–215, discuss the political roles and attitudes of Catholics and Quakers during these years. For a more extended study of the council, see my "Maryland's Privy Council, 1637–1715," in Land, Carr, and Papenfuse, eds., *Law, Society, and Politics*.

12. The political influence of Quakers and Catholics continued through their economic weight, lobbying, their use of the ballot, and often through Protestant in-laws. Freeholders on occasion elected Quakers, but the assembly refused to seat them. *Md. Archives*, XIII, 352, 358, 366, XIX, 29. Among the several known examples of continued family officeholding, Thomas Brooke, son of an assemblyman and both nephew and grandson of councillors, had converted to the Anglican faith sometime prior to his own appointment to the council in 1691; three of Brooke's brothers were Jesuits. Christopher Johnston, "The Brooke Family," *Md. Hist. Mag.*, I (1906), 66–73, 184–188, 284–289. Elisha and Benjamin Hall, sons of Quaker delegate Richard Hall, each served briefly in the lower house in the 1690s before Elisha declared himself a Quaker and Benjamin, who married Thomas Brooke's sister Mary, became a Catholic. See Christopher Johnston, "Hall Family of Calvert County," *ibid.*, VIII (1913), 291–301. Two Anglican brothers-in-law of the Halls, Walter Smith and John Smith, were delegates in the next decade. Wills 6, fols. 13–15, Maryland Hall of Recs., Annapolis.

13. This special opportunity is discussed in greater detail below. The exclusion also meant, significantly, a more rapid return to public office of those non-Quaker Protestants who had actively opposed the revolution and supported Lord Baltimore. For example, by the mid-1690s 5 of the 11 Provincial Court justices were former proprietary adherents, and some of them had been rabidly so. Gov. Francis Nicholson particularly promoted their return to office. *Md. Archives*, XX, 137, VIII, 132, 136, 181–182, 285.

education. He lamented to his English superiors that many of the "ablest men for estates and Parts in this Country are Quakers, Some are Papists, others disaffected Protestants."[14]

A low life expectancy, a dearth of indisputably qualified people, and the repercussions of political upheavals combined to ensure immigrants an unusually prolonged ascendancy in Maryland's politics. Table 1 presents the geographical origins and conditions of entry into the colony of the 424 individuals who held provincial office from 1660 to 1715.[15] At least 77.7 percent and probably as many as 81.7 percent of those men who served in the assembly, council, or provincial court between 1660 and 1689 had come to Maryland as adults. Another 15.4 percent had either been transported as children or young adults from Europe by some older relative or friend or had come to Maryland from birthplaces elsewhere in the New World.

Only three colonists who can be definitely identified as native-born held provincial office prior to 1689. The first, Ignatius Causine, won election to the lower house in 1671, while Leonard Greene became a delegate in 1682. Each of these men was Catholic, and each served only one term. Richard Gardiner, also Catholic, probably served in the assembly in 1681 and was definitely a delegate from 1686 until his death the following year.[16] Two other delegates may have been

14. Thomas Brooke, a late appointment apparently made to mollify Lord Baltimore, was the nephew of Baker Brooke and stepson of Henry Darnall, a Catholic cousin of Lord Baltimore and councillor from 1679 to 1689. Johnston, "Brooke Family," *Md. Hist. Mag.*, I (1906), 71, 185. John Courts was also an exception to the immigrant status, but his father, a former servant, had held no public office. Carr and Jordan, *Maryland's Revolution of Government*, 249–250. For Nicholson's concern, see his letter to Lords of Trade, Nov. 15, 1694, C.O. 5/713, 111, No. 114, Public Record Office.

15. During this period, freeholders chose 400 men to serve in the lower house, the only elective office in the provincial government. A total of 69 men held commissions to the council, but 45 of them are also included in the assembly membership. Finally, 84 individuals officiated as Provincial Court justices; all of them also served either in the assembly or on the council. The court and council memberships were almost identical prior to 1694, when the two were separated and the court enlarged to provide geographical representation from each county. This practice continued until Gov. John Seymour's judicial reforms in 1707 reduced the court to four justices. By 1715, however, there was again significant overlapping with the council membership. Records of these three institutions are available in *Md. Archives*, except for the court proceedings after 1683, for which manuscript volumes are on deposit at the Hall of Records. All other manuscript sources used in this paper, unless otherwise noted, are also to be found at the Hall of Records.

16. *Ibid.*, LX, 350, establishes Causine's nativity. He lived another 20 years after his one term in the legislature. Wills 7, fol. 53. Thomas Greene, Leonard's father, was one of the colony's earliest settlers; he immigrated in 1634. Patents 1, fols. 17, 41, 42; *ibid.* 2, fol. 346. Leonard Greene died in 1688. Wills 4, fol. 313. Gardiner was the son of Burgess Luke Gardiner. Wills 1, fol. 631; Patents ABH, fol. 77.

TABLE 1. Origins of Provincial Officeholders, 1660–1715

	Serving 1660–1689	First Elected or Appointed 1689–1699	First Elected or Appointed 1700–1715
Free immigrants originally from Europe	122 (69.7%)	48 (42.9%)	23 (16.8%)
Indentured servants	14 (8.0%)	13 (11.6%)	3 (2.2%)
Free children or young adults transported by others originally from Europe	13 (7.4%)	4 (3.6%)	6 (4.4%)
Known natives of Maryland	3 (1.7%)	22 (19.6%)	71 (51.8%)
Probably natives of Maryland	2 (1.1%)	3 (2.7%)	9 (6.6%)
Known natives of other colonies	10 (5.7%)	8 (7.1%)	5 (3.6%)
Probably natives of other colonies	4 (2.3%)	1 (0.9%)	1 (0.7%)
Unknown origins, probably free immigrants	7 (4.0%)	13 (11.6%)	19 (13.9%)
Total	175	112	137

natives, but the evidence is incomplete and doubtful. Ten others were born in the New World and later moved to Maryland.[17] Even generously counting young adult immigrants like Baker Brooke, who was twenty-two when he migrated with his father, no more than twenty-eight delegates prior to 1689 can qualify for second-generation

17. Joseph Pile, who served one term from 1686 to 1688, was almost certainly native-born. His parents, John and Sarah Pile, had immigrated by 1643/44. Patents 2, fol. 508; *Md. Archives*, IV, 250. Another probable, although less certain, native was John Stevens, who served one term, 1676 to 1682. He was the son of a William Stevens who immigrated in 1651. Elias Jones, *History of Dorchester County Maryland* (Baltimore, 1902), 388. Nine known New World natives, all born in Virginia, were Richard Bennett, Samuel Chew, John Vanhack, John Hynson, Philemon Lloyd, Thomas Marsh, John

status.[18] The council and provincial court were even more exclusively the domain of immigrants. Before 1691, neither body had included a native of the colony; one member had been a possible native of the New World, and another had come to Maryland as a child.[19]

The decade following the revolution constituted an important transitional period. Immigrants still dominated the membership of provincial institutions and comprised a majority of the 112 men who first served between 1689 and the turn of the century, but the percentage of immigrants was declining. The council acquired its first native members in 1691 with the appointments of John Courts and Thomas Brooke, while another twenty men born in the colony first gained seats in the lower house during the decade. Three additional delegates were probably natives, and eight assemblymen were born in other New World colonies. Although still a minority—at least 58.1 percent and perhaps as many as 69.7 percent of the new officeholders were not natives of the New World—the second generation of colonists was gradually acquiring an important voice in the provincial government. Fellow "creoles" to the south in Virginia were but a few years ahead of their Maryland counterparts in assuming a prominent role in politics.[20]

Stone, and George and Nathaniel Utie. James Browne was born in Massachusetts. Probable natives of Virginia were Luke Gardiner, Cornelius Howard, and George Wells and possibly William Digges (see n. 19).

18. Johnston, "Brooke Family," *Md. Hist. Mag.*, I (1906), 69. Probably at least four or five others were of adult status when they migrated with parents. Second-generation status would normally be accorded only to native-born and those individuals who came to the colony before their mid-teen years.

19. William Digges was either a young infant when his father, Edward Digges, came to Virginia in 1650 or he was born soon thereafter. The father served on the Virginia council. William was a justice of the peace by 1671, which suggests an English birth. He moved to Maryland in 1679 when he married Elizabeth Sewall, the proprietor's stepdaughter, and was immediately appointed to the council and court. Lyon G. Tyler, "Pedigree of a Representative Virginia Planter," *WMQ*, 1st Ser., I (1893), 83–84. Digges's brother-in-law, Nicholas Sewall, had migrated at about age six with his father, Henry Sewall, in 1661. Patents 5, fol. 251. He joined the council and court in 1683.

20. Immigrants had also clearly dominated the Virginia assembly until the end of the century. Of those burgesses who served in the period 1677 to 1706, 60% had arrived in 1660 or later or were descended from individuals who arrived after 1660. The percentage of native-born delegates increased from about 20% of the members of the Long Assembly (1662–1676) to 36% of the 285 men who first sat after 1676. Nearly 10% of the delegates between 1677 and 1706 can be classified as second generation. Quitt, "Virginia House of Burgesses," 9–12. The last assembly elected in Virginia in the 1690s had only 9 immigrants out of 42 burgesses whose place of birth has been determined. Rainbolt, "Relationship Between Leadership and Constituents in Virginia," *WMQ*, 3d Ser., XXVII (1970), 430. Rainbolt's stimulating essay focuses upon somewhat different aspects of the maturing political process in the Chesapeake colonies. He postulates

Native Marylanders clearly captured control of the assembly and council in the early 1700s. At least seventy-one men born in the colony successfully entered provincial politics in the first fifteen years of the new century, and an additional nine were probably natives. Together with native-born members from the previous decade, they collectively altered the profile of the typical officeholder. The assembly of 1704–1707 was the first legislative body in the colony's history in which a majority of the members were either native-born or had immigrated to Maryland as children.[21] By the close of the royal period, in the assemblies of 1712–1714 and 1715, immigrants, even counting every unknown possibility, comprised no more than 29 percent of the total membership of either assembly. Many of these immigrants were now residents of lengthy duration, like Matthias Vanderheyden, who had been in Maryland at least thirty-three years.[22] The council experienced the same change. By 1710 natives also constituted a majority of that body. When the Calverts regained the province in 1715, the councillors included seven natives of Maryland and two natives of Virginia who had migrated as very young children. Of the three remaining councillors one was a known immigrant and two were men whose origins are uncertain, but the three had been residents of Maryland for at least forty, thirty, and twenty-seven years respectively.[23] Two of the five justices of the provincial court in 1715 were native-born, and the other three had each been in Maryland at least twenty-eight years and probably much longer.

---

the emergence of "a new style of politics . . . which involved a familiar relationship between authority and constituents." *Ibid.*, 418. Edmund S. Morgan has recently amplified upon this change "toward populism," as he interprets the new relationship. See *American Slavery, American Freedom*, esp. 338–362.

21. Of the 46 original members of this assembly, 4 were third-generation Marylanders, and 24 qualify as second-generation colonists. Nineteen of these 28 men were native-born. By-elections returned 6 other members, 3 of whom were natives.

22. On Vanderheyden, see *Md. Archives*, XIII, 245. The assembly of 1712–1714 had 58 members, of whom only 12 were definitely adult immigrants while 5 others may have been. The assembly elected in 1715 had 50 members, with 9 known adult immigrants and only 2 other possibilities, several of whom are very doubtful. Most of these known or possible immigrants had won their first elections much earlier.

23. The council in Virginia had attained a majority of native-born members by 1692, almost two decades before the Maryland council. Bacon's Rebellion had also been less influential in its effect on Virginia's ruling elite than had been the 1689 revolt in Maryland. For example, the Virginia council in 1660 had eight members representing five families; three of those families would be represented at the last council meeting in 1775 when almost all of the councillors were related somehow to the 1660 members. James LaVerne Anderson, "The Governors' Councils of Colonial America, A Study of Pennsylvania and Virginia, 1660–1776" (Ph.D. diss., University of Virginia, 1967), 2–9.

The preponderance of recent immigrants among the Maryland officeholders of the seventeenth century had a profound impact on the development of important political issues. The proprietary efforts to promote religious toleration and full political participation by members of all Christian sects failed because of the continual arrival in Maryland and the election to office of Protestants unaccustomed to such toleration, which was actually illegal in England. Little opportunity and few means were present to educate the new immigrants in local practices and customs, which meant a constant challenge to the status quo.[24] Furthermore, freeholders seldom had the extensive acquaintance with political candidates one might find in an English or New England constituency. The widely scattered plantation settlements operated against development of much familiarity with one's fellow colonists, especially those who had not resided long in the province, as most settlers had not. In such circumstances, the freeholders were not alone in making mistakes of judgment; on several occasions, the proprietor or his governor appointed presumably honorable, qualified men to high office, only to discover soon after that they were unfit for public trust.[25]

It was not only the flagrant reprobate who served a brief tenure in office. Short careers, with commissions or mandates often quickly terminated, characterized most provincial officeholders in the 1600s. Consequently, the assembly, council, and court experienced very little continuity or longevity of service. The first decade of the eighteenth century again becomes the critical turning point when one measures the tenure of given individuals in office.

Freeholders chose four hundred different delegates for nineteen separately elected assemblies that convened between 1660 and 1715. There were five assemblies in the 1660s, usually of just one year's duration each, but thereafter elections became less frequent and multiple sessions of each assembly more common. After 1694, royal governors summoned a new assembly only every three years, according to English practice, or upon the beginning of a new royal or gubernatorial tenure.

The overwhelming majority of the delegates, fully two-thirds, received endorsement from the electorate no more than twice, with one-term assemblymen accounting for 46.3 percent of all men elected

24. Carr and Jordan, *Maryland's Revolution of Government*, 226–227.
25. For the most notorious such appointment, that of William Mitchell in 1649, and its consequences, see Steiner, *Maryland under the Commonwealth*, 38–42.

during the fifty-five year period.[26] Although the lower house rarely
enjoyed the luxury of many experienced legislators, the return of
previously elected delegates increased noticeably, if slowly, as the
period progressed. Table 2 shows that the assemblymen with longer
tenures served mainly after 1700. The revolution of 1689 was unde-
niably influential in restricting continuity through its exclusion of
Catholics and Quakers, but there is little evidence even among Angli-
cans and other Protestants of recurring terms in the assembly or even
extended service on the appointed council or court in the seventeenth
century. Only twenty-three delegates among the four hundred legislators won election six or more times in their political careers, and
only five of these twenty-three first sat prior to 1689.[27] An additional
five first appeared in the lower house in the subsequent decade,
while the clear majority, thirteen delegates, won their first elections in
the fifteen years between 1700 and 1715.[28]

Table 3, breaking down membership by assembly, illustrates in
another manner the discontinuities of service by showing the number
and percentage of newcomers and those delegates returned from the

26. In Virginia, longevity in office was also a rare occurrence. Only 15 men, or 5%
of the burgesses elected between 1677 and 1706, served for six or more terms. Some
45% were elected but once, and the two colonies shared an almost identical figure of
66% of the members being elected to two assemblies or less. Quitt, "Virginia House of
Burgesses," 192.

27. Richard Preston of Calvert County, a Quaker and one of the wealthiest men
in the colony, served eight terms between 1654 and his death in 1669. None of his
descendants held provincial office. Thomas Allen Glenn, *Preston at Patuxent* (Philadelphia, 1900). Joseph Wickes of Kent, an Anglican, won the endorsement of his
constituents on seven occasions despite being barred from public office for seven years
in the 1660s for his role in Fendall's Rebellion. He had served in three assemblies in the
1650s and returned to office in 1669; he was apparently inactive in politics from 1684
until his death in late 1692. None of his three sons held provincial office. Percy G.
Skirven, "Seven Pioneers of the Colonial Eastern Shore," *Md. Hist. Mag.*, XV (1920),
236–241. Richard Woolman of Talbot, a Puritan immigrant from Virginia in 1650, served
six terms between 1659 and his death in 1681. His son held no office. Finally, Kenelm
Cheseldyne and John Coode, each a son-in-law of former councillor Thomas Gerard,
had both been elected twice from St. Mary's City or County before 1689, and each won
four subsequent elections in the royal period. Cheseldyne's son served one term in the
assembly in 1712–1714, while none of Coode's sons held office above the county level.
See Carr and Jordan, *Maryland's Revolution of Government*, 242–243, 245–248.

28. The five men first elected between 1689 and 1700 and their respective number
of terms were James Maxwell (9); James Smallwood (8); and Thomas Smithson, William
Whittington, and James Phillips (6 each). The remaining thirteen in decreasing order
of longevity were John Mackall (14); John Ward (9); Robert Tyler, Thomas Trueman
Greenfield, E. A. Herman, and Joseph Hill (8 each); Richard Colegate, Robert Ungle,
and Daniel Mariartee (7 each); and Thomas Bordley, James Harris, Matthias Vanderheyden, and Roger Woolford (6 each). The second-generation officeholders were
Greenfield, Hill, Herman, Harris, and Woolford.

TABLE 2. Number of Terms Elected, 400 Delegates, 1660–1715

	Serving 1660–1689	First Elected 1689–1699	First Elected 1700–1715	Total
Elected once, never sat^a	0	7 (6.4%)	3 (2.2%)	10 (2.5%)
One term	74 (47.4%)	47 (42.7%)	54 (40.3%)	175 (43.8%)
Two terms	35 (22.4%)	19 (17.3%)	26 (19.4%)	80 (20.0%)
Three terms	20 (12.8%)	21 (19.1%)	19 (14.2%)	60 (15.0%)
Four terms	8 (5.1%)	7 (6.4%)	14 (10.4%)	29 (7.3%)
Five terms	14 (9.0%)	4 (3.6%)	5 (3.7%)	23 (5.8%)
Six terms	3 (1.9%)	3^b (2.7%)	4 (2.9%)	10 (2.5%)
Seven terms	1 (0.6%)	0	3 (2.2%)	4 (1.0%)
Eight terms	1 (0.6%)	1 (.9%)	4 (2.9%)	6 (1.5%)
Nine terms	0	1^c (.9%)	1 (0.7%)	2 (0.5%)
Fourteen terms	0	0	1 (0.7%)	1 (0.3%)

Notes:
^aThese men were declared unduly elected, found ineligible for office, or died before the assembly convened.
^bTwo of these three delegates were initially elected at the end of the decade.
^cJames Maxwell served only one term prior to 1704.

immediately preceding assembly. First-term legislators constituted 48 percent or more of the membership of ten of the nineteen assemblies, but only two of these ten convened after 1693. Conversely, returning members exceeded 30 percent of the membership in only four of the nine assemblies that met between 1660 and 1689, but after that year the incumbents never comprised less than 30 percent and numbered 40 percent or more in five of the ten assemblies.

The increase in the collective experience of the assemblies, especially after 1700, is demonstrated still further in table 4. Taking account of legislative experience in other than the immediately preceding assembly, this table presents the cumulative longevity of all delegates sitting in those assemblies that met in each approximate decade. After the 1660s, which had assemblies of somewhat greater experience,[29] the collective assemblies of the next three decades had only 6.6 percent to 8.1 percent of their members serving four or more terms and

29. The five assemblies of the 1660s had collectively almost twice the percentage of delegates of either four or more terms of service or three or more terms. Shorter assemblies and more frequent elections enabled some men to accumulate more terms if not necessarily more years of service. Potential opposition to several men had also been eliminated by the seven-year ban on officeholding placed on some participants in Fendall's Rebellion in 1660. Finally, the proprietor's reduction of representation for each county from four to two delegates in the 1670s restricted opportunity for reelection.

TABLE 3. Reelected Delegates and Newcomers by Assembly

Assembly	Total Number of Delegates	Number and % of Returning Members	Number and % of First-Term Members
1661	16	4 (25.0%)ᵃ	10 (62.5%)
1662	17	7 (41.2%)	5 (29.4%)
1663–1664	20	4 (20.0%)	11 (55.0%)
1666	21	5 (23.8%)	8 (38.0%)
1669	27	8 (29.6%)	13 (48.1%)
1671–1674/75	45 (12)	10 (30.3%)	29 (64.4%)
1676–1682	58 (16)	14 (33.3%)	40 (70.1%)
1682–1684	24 (1)	15 (62.5%)	7 (26.6%)
1686–1688	26 (4)	5 (22.7%)ᵇ	13 (50.0%)
1689–1692	43 (5)	13 (34.2%)	28 (65.1%)
1692–1693	49 (7)	13 (30.9%)ᵇ	32 (65.3%)
1694–1697	61 (19)	16 (38.1%)	29 (47.5%)
1697/98–1700	58 (12)	26 (56.5%)	25 (43.1%)
1700–1704	51 (5)	25 (54.3%)	19 (37.2%)
1704–1707	52 (6)	15 (32.6%)	27 (51.9%)
1708A	50	20 (40.0%)	22 (44.0%)
1708B–1711	59 (9)	42 (84.0%)	15 (25.4%)
1712–1714	58 (8)	19 (38.0%)	30 (51.7%)
1715	50	21 (42.0%)	18 (36.0%)

Notes:

Total number of delegates: The initial figure represents original members and those delegates later returned in by-elections, with the specific number of added delegates stated in parentheses.

Returning members: The percentages are based on the proportion of original members only.

First-term members: These numbers and percentages include both original and added members of each assembly.

ᵃOne returning member had never actually attended meetings of the previous assembly.

ᵇOne returning delegate in each of these assemblies never took his seat.

12.7 percent to 24.4 percent serving three or more terms. The three assemblies of 1701–1708, however, had 14.3 percent of their members serving four or more terms and 32.4 percent three or more, while the comparable figures for the next three assemblies, from 1708 to 1715, were 22.4 percent and 34.5 percent respectively. These percentages reflect a continuity remarkable for any legislative body.

Moreover, freeholders were not blindly returning any incumbents who stood for reelection, nor do longer life-spans of assemblymen account for this increased continuity. This continuity represents, instead, the presence in Maryland of more men of a clearly recognized

TABLE 4. Longevity of Service for Assembly Delegates by Approximate Decades

Terms of Service	1661–1669	1671–1682	1682–1689	1689–1700	1701–1708	1708–1715
One term	31 (47.6%)	60 (68.9%)	19 (42.2%)	73 (54.1%)	42 (40.0%)	49 (42.2%)
Two terms	19 (29.0%)	16 (18.4%)	16 (35.6%)	29 (21.5%)	29 (27.6%)	27 (23.2%)
Three terms	6 (9.2%)	4 (4.6%)	7 (15.6%)	24 (17.8%)	19 (18.1%)	14 (12.1%)
Four terms	7 (10.7%)	4 (4.6%)	0	5 (3.7%)	8 (7.6%)	13 (11.2%)
Five terms	1 (1.5%)	1 (1.2%)	2 (4.4%)	4 (2.9%)	5 (4.8%)	9 (7.8%)
Six terms	0	2 (2.3%)	0	0	2 (1.9%)	3 (2.6%)
Seven terms	0	0	1 (2.2%)	0	0	0
Eight terms	1 (1.5%)	0	0	0	0	1 (0.8%)

Note:
Individuals are not included who were elected but were either never allowed to take their seats or died before the assembly convened. Dates represent the beginning and end of groups of assemblies, arranged approximately by decade.

ability and social standing that earned them reelection as long as their legislative actions satisfied the freeholders. For example, the incidence of illiteracy among delegates declines significantly over these years, and there is evidence of increasing voter sophistication and a reluctance to return men unresponsive to the electorate's wishes or too beholden to the governor. As early as 1671, Charles Calvert had found it necessary to establish representation for St. Mary's City, a mere cluster of buildings with scarcely any population, in order to guarantee seats in the lower house for two strong proprietary spokesmen who were no longer certain of election in the county at large. Other governors subsequently found it increasingly difficult to muster support for unpopular bills and they complained repeatedly of feisty assemblies. After 1692, especially, the evidence multiplies of representatives consulting their constituents on certain issues before enacting legislation. Freeholders also increasingly used their ballots discriminatingly to elect or defeat candidates on the basis of their views on a variety of critical issues: establishment of the Anglican Church in the 1690s; the role of Catholics in the public life of the colony; the distribution of power between local and provincial organs of government; regulation of the tobacco trade; patronage; or almost any attempt by the executive to reform or alter colonial practices.[30]

The most dramatic illustration of this heightened voter sophistication came in the two assembly elections of 1708. Governor John Seymour had attempted unsuccessfully to obtain from the 1704–1707 assembly a thorough reform of the judicial system of the colony. Frustrated by their resistance, Seymour had proceeded on his own to alter substantially the structure of the Provincial Court and to dismiss numerous provincial and county justices who opposed his reforms.

30. For Calvert's motives in 1671, see *The Calvert Papers, Number One*, Maryland Historical Society, *Fund Publication No. 28* (Baltimore, 1889), 265–266. By the late 1680s the proprietor could no longer control even these seats. Records of the county courts and of the Committee of Elections and Privileges, which functioned sporadically in the 1670s and 1680s but regularly after 1692, suggest an increase in the number of contested and challenged elections late in the century and especially after 1700. For examples of some contested elections in one county, see Kent County Court Proceedings, I, fol. 877; ID No. 2, fol. 57; GL I, fol. 378; 1707–1709, fols. 150, 157; JS No. W, fols. 28–29, 51–52, 122–124. On consultation of constituents, see *Md. Archives*, VII, 369, 424, XIII, 176, XIX, 577, XXIII, 372–373. Gov. Nicholson commented especially on the impact of issues on the elections of the 1690s in his letter to Lords of Trade, Nov. 17, 1697, C.O. 5/714/II, No. 47iv. David W. Jordan, "The Royal Period of Colonial Maryland, 1689–1715" (Ph.D. diss., Princeton University, 1966), has the most complete discussion of politics during this period; on elections, see esp. 82–86, 147–148, 186–188, 212–220.

In the summer of 1708, freeholders elected an assembly firmly resolved to resist the governor. The delegates fought Seymour on every imaginable issue for a week, before he angrily dissolved them and called for new elections. Forty-one of the fifty dismissed delegates were promptly reelected and the nine new members represented no gain of support for the governor. Seymour's strategy of using patronage to punish opponents and to curry support backfired disastrously: among the few members not reelected to these two assemblies were the delegates who had cooperated with the governor. Seymour's frustrations compare interestingly with those of Governor Alexander Spotswood in Virginia six years later. Spotswood found voters similarly disturbed over his efforts to reform the tobacco inspection system and his use of patronage to obtain necessary votes for passage of the required legislation. At the next election, the freeholders wreaked vengeance on the governor and his cohorts by not returning twenty-seven of the twenty-nine burgesses who had accepted Spotswood's bribery.[31]

Governors encountered fewer obstacles in controlling the membership of the council, which was appointed with no fixed terms. Even so, the executives could rarely rely on loyal service for an extended period. Again, greater continuity and longevity of service did not come until the end of the century (see table 5). The average tenure of the thirty-two Maryland councillors sitting between 1660 and 1689 barely exceeded seven years, with only six men serving for more than ten years.[32] For the seventeen men appointed between the revolution and 1700, the average tenure increased slightly to nine years. Thereafter, substantially longer tenures became the rule; the twenty individuals who first received a council commission between 1700 and 1715 served for an average of thirteen years, and the council of eleven men sitting in 1715 would enjoy an average tenure of nineteen and a half years. Service on the provincial court prior to 1694 had closely paralleled that of the council. From the clear division of the two

31. Jordan, "Royal Period of Colonial Maryland," 249–260; *Md. Archives*, XXVII, 179–374, contains the journals of these two assemblies. Morgan, *American Slavery, American Freedom*, 359–361, discusses Spotswood and the Virginia election.
32. Very erratic attendance patterns of councillors further limited continuity. The most remarkable tenure for this period was the 26 years on the council (1656–1682) served by Philip Calvert, uncle of the third Lord Baltimore. Philip Calvert's death, coming just shortly before circumstances required his nephew to return to England, was a critical loss for the proprietor.

TABLE 5. Longevity of Service for Councillors

	Serving 1660–1689	First Appointed 1691–1699	First Appointed 1700–1715
2 years or less	6 (18.8%)	2 (11.8%)	4 (20.0%)
3 to 5 years	11 (34.4%)	0	2 (10.0%)
6 to 10 years	9 (28.1%)	9 (52.9%)	4 (20.0%)
11 to 15 years	2 (6.2%)	4 (23.5%)	4 (20.0%)
16 to 20 years	3 (9.4%)	2 (11.8%)	1 (5.0%)
Over 20 years	1 (3.1%)	0	5 (25.0%)

bodies that year until 1707, tenures on the bench averaged four years, but after 1707 the court's membership too became considerably more stable.

Longer service within these three bodies meant an important accumulation of experience with greater knowledge of procedures, organization, precedents, and greater skill in achieving objectives. A number of the earliest legislators with lengthier tenures were well-educated men whose knowledge and experience vastly exceeded that of most other colonists, and these factors were particularly important to political stability. These men, although relatively few in number, held influential positions as speakers of the house or as chairmen of the embryonic committee system that falteringly emerged in the 1670s but flourished in the 1690s. They were undoubtedly instrumental in the very evolution of these positions of importance within the assembly. Significantly, many of them were lawyers by profession, and as such were among the very few in the colony with formal legal training. Men like Thomas Notley, Philemon Lloyd, Robert Carvile, Kenelm Cheseldyne, and Robert Smith understood the issues and their implications, appreciated the importance of how laws were phrased, and brought a new sophistication and stability to provincial politics.

Thomas Smithson's career is illustrative of the influence and impact such men could and did have toward the end of the century. Familiar with English law and previously a justice of the Talbot County bench, Smithson in 1694 began the first of his six successive terms in the assembly. He quickly demonstrated his impressive abilities and in his first term received appointment to the Committee of Grievances and the Committee of Laws, the two committees rapidly emerging as the most important agencies of the legislature. In 1698 Smithson became speaker of the lower house, and from that time until he ended his legislative service in 1711, he was always either speaker or chairman of the Committee of Laws. He played an important role in the compilation of the colony's laws in 1700. Concurrently with most of his tenure in the assembly, Smithson also sat as a justice of the Provincial Court, and he was chief justice for eight of his eleven years on that bench. His services were so valuable in that capacity that the assembly voted him a special gratuity to discourage his retirement. The colony and its officials were well aware of the special caliber of men like Smithson who were a rare phenomenon in Maryland's first century of settlement.[33]

As Smithson and other burgesses increasingly gained reelection to their seats, accessibility to the assembly and to other provincial offices became much more difficult. Two accompanying developments, closely related to this continuity, also helped to restrict the political opportunities of the average colonist or newcomer to Maryland. Officeholders increasingly possessed greater wealth and were related to other officeholders. Both poorer men and recent immigrants of wealth often found it almost essential to be related by blood or marriage to certain families to attain office themselves.

Recent studies have drawn a helpful outline of the social and economic structure of the colony in the late seventeenth century. Possession of 1,000 or more acres of land characterized one as a "great planter," and a personal estate worth at least £500 sterling ranked one among the wealthiest 4 percent of the population.[34] Men of less

33. On Smithson, see *Md. Archives*, XIX, 173, 335, XXIII, 438, XXIV, 83, 198, 288, 327, XXVI, 109, 122, 392, 597, XXVII, 62, 181, 269, 412, 519, XXIX, 35, 109, 299; Provincial Court Judgments, WT No. 3, fols. 1–3, 612–614; TB No. 3, fols. 258–259; TB no. 2, fols. 65–67; PL No. 1, fol. 233; TP No. 2, fol. 330. Of the 48 professional lawyers who practiced in Maryland during this period, 20 of them, or 41%, served in the assembly and they were usually among the most active members. Alan F. Day, "Lawyers in Colonial Maryland, 1660–1715," *American Journal of Legal History*, XVII (1973), 145–165.

34. A study of Maryland inventories for the decade 1690–1699 has shown that only 1.5% of the personal estates appraised in those years exceeded £1,000 in value and that only an additional 2.2% of the estates were worth between £500 and £1,000. Aubrey C. Land, "Economic Base and Social Structure: The Northern Chesapeake in the Eighteenth Century," *Journal of Economic History*, XXV (1965), 639–654, and Land, "Economic Behavior in a Planting Society: The Eighteenth-Century Chesapeake," *Journal of Southern History*, XXXIII (1967), 469–485. A comparable picture of wealth concentration emerges from Russell R. Menard, P.M.G. Harris, and Lois Green Carr, "Opportunity and Inequality: The Distribution of Wealth on the Lower Western Shore of Maryland, 1638–1705," *Md. Hist. Mag.*, LXIX (1974), 169–184; Robert G. Schonfeld and Spencer Wilson, "The Value of Personal Estates in Maryland, 1700–1710," *ibid.*,

affluence were frequently among the provincial officeholders of the seventeenth century. In the assemblies of the 1660s and 1670s, as many as 45 percent of the delegates owned less than 1,000 acres and 75 percent had personal estates at death valued at under £500.[35] The relative absence of great differences between the officeholders and the general populace seriously disturbed Cecil Calvert. Alarmed that the colonists might not accord proper deference to the political leaders, in 1665 the proprietor had even considered "the wearing of habbits medals or otherwise" so that "some visible distinction or Distinctions might be drawn."[36]

Calvert's concern, solved partially by bestowing large grants of land and much profitable patronage upon his preferred officers, became less acute with the heavy influx of more prosperous immigrants. The wealth of assemblymen began to increase noticeably in the 1680s, when at least 75 to 85 percent of the delegates of both assemblies possessed a minimum of 1,000 acres, while about 50 percent had personalty worth at least £500.[37] The revolution of 1689 momentarily gave some less affluent Protestants an opportunity to achieve provincial office by an early declaration of allegiance to the rebel cause, but rarely were these men able to maintain their positions and continue in office beyond the mid-1690s.[38] Thereafter, it became quite unusual for a provincial officeholder to own less than 1,000 acres, and almost never below 500 acres, unless he was a wealthy merchant or heir-at-law. Personal estates only rarely fell below £500 and were often considerably higher, especially as merchants became more predominant in the colony's political life. When men with smaller estates gained office, they usually came from newly settled frontier areas where fewer persons possessed great wealth. Even so, only two of

LVIII (1963), 333–343. See also Carr and Jordan, *Maryland's Revolution of Government*, 180–186.

35. I am indebted to Russell Menard for use of his notes on the wealth of assemblymen prior to 1689.

36. *Md. Archives*, XV, 16.

37. Similar wealth began to characterize even local officeholders, sheriffs and justices particularly. See Russell R. Menard, "Major Officeholders in Charles, Somerset and Talbot Counties, 1676–1689," MS on file, Hall of Records.

38. For example, relatively poorer delegates John Campbell, Thomas Staley, Thomas Davis, William Blankenstein, William Hopkins, James Keech, John Thomas, Henry Mitchell, and Samuel Hopkins all won election to the rebel assembly in 1689. Six served only one term, while Campbell and Mitchell won election twice and Staley served in three assemblies. Only in the instance of the Samuel Hopkins family did members of the next generation hold provincial office. Samuel, Jr., served in two assemblies (1715, 1716–1718) while his brother Nathaniel sat for one term (1722–1724).

TABLE 6. Wealth of Councillors, 1660–1715

	1660–1689		1691–1699		1700–1715	
Number of councillors	32		15[a]		18[b]	
Landholdings unknown	3	(9.3%)	1	(6.6%)	0	
Own less than 1,000 acres	2	(6.2%)	1	(6.6%)	1	(5.5%)
Own less than 2,000 acres	5	(15.6%)	5	(33.3%)	4	(22.2%)
Own 2,000–5,000 acres	11	(34.3%)	6	(40.0%)	9	(50.0%)
Own over 5,000 acres	13	(40.6%)	3	(20.0%)	5	(27.7%)
Estate unknown	11	(34.3%)	1	(6.6%)	5[c]	(27.7%)
Estate less than £500	6	(18.7%)	0		1	(5.5%)
Estate less than £1,000	12	(37.5%)	2	(13.3%)	4	(22.2%)
Estate £1,000–2,000	5	(15.6%)	10	(66.6%)	4	(22.2%)
Estate over £2,000	4	(12.5%)	2	(13.3%)	5	(27.7%)
Both less than 1,000 acres and £1,000	1	(3.1%)	0		0	
Both over 2,000 acres and £1,000	7	(21.8%)	8	(53.3%)	8[c]	(44.4%)

Notes:

[a]Does not include Thomas Lawrence, Sr., or Edward Randolph, two royal placemen with commissions to sit on the council. They never considered themselves permanent residents of the colony.

[b]Does not include Thomas Lawrence, Jr., or Robert Quarry, also royal placemen who were not regular residents.

[c]Among the unknown estates are those of four councillors of undisputably great wealth. These four men almost assuredly had estates worth over £2,000, and since they all owned over 2,000 acres, the percentage of councillors (1700–1715) with over 2,000 acres and £1,000 should probably be 66.6%.

the sixteen delegates who represented Prince George's County, from its establishment on the western frontier in 1695 to the end of the royal period, owned less than 1,000 acres at the time of election, and both had sizable personal estates acquired by active engagement in mercantile affairs.[39] Councillors were generally even wealthier than assemblymen. The four Prince George's men who held commissions, for example, each owned in excess of 2,000 acres and three had over 6,000.[40] Table 6 shows that while councillors were always among the wealthier members of the society, they became decidedly more affluent with the passage of time, particularly with respect to their personal estates.

39. Lois Green Carr, "County Government in Maryland, 1689–1709" (Ph.D. diss., Harvard University, 1968), text, 562–698, analyzes the officeholders from Prince George's County and provides full biographical information. Virginia burgesses were similarly drawn increasingly from the wealthiest families in the colony. Quitt, "Virginia House of Burgesses," 159–179.

40. Carr, "County Government in Maryland," 562–698.

Higher standards of wealth placed men of lower social origins at a great disadvantage, for mobility and the acquisition of large fortunes were becoming progressively more difficult. Earlier in the century the opportunities even for former indentured servants had been quite remarkable. Thirteen of the 275 servants who had entered Maryland by 1642 eventually held high political offices and two of them even gained appointment to the council.[41] During the 1660s, six former servants sat as delegates (see table 1). Thereafter, examples of such mobility became less common, a result of the declining profitability of the tobacco trade as well as the presence in Maryland of more men of talent and wealth.[42] For the few former servants who did overcome disadvantageous odds, climbing the political ladder required more years and more connections. Of the 137 provincial officeholders first serving between 1700 and 1715, only three men are known to have enjoyed that success. Philip Lynes had meandered through a check- ered career of thirty-three years in Maryland before his election in 1701 to one term in the lower house. Marriage a few years later to the sister of Governor Seymour brought Lynes's appointment to the council, where he served briefly before his death. Francis Dollahyde, resident of a frontier county, had been in Maryland twenty-four years before his election to the first of four terms in 1704. Finally, Solomon Wright, also representing a frontier county, sat for four terms begin- ning with a by-election victory in 1700. Twenty-six years had elapsed since his arrival in Maryland under indenture. Wright's son Charles became something of an exception himself when he won election as a delegate in 1712: he was one of only a very few sons of former servants to acquire high office.[43] Even with such restricted oppor-

41. Russell R. Menard, "From Servant to Freeholder: Status Mobility and Property Accumulation in Seventeenth-Century Maryland," *WMQ*, 3d Ser., XXX (1973), 37–64, esp. 44–47.

42. *Ibid.*, 57–64. These economic and social circumstances, as well as the reduced number of assembly seats and the proprietor's discriminatory patronage policies, affected the mobility of others besides servants. The length of time between migration and first provincial office increased noticeably, although access to local offices still came rather rapidly for the more affluent settler.

43. Patents 16, fol. 411; WC#2, fol. 363; 17, fol. 611 document the earlier servitude of these men, and Wills 14, fols. 330–331 establish the relationship of the Wrights. Most of the servants who eventually gained political office after the 1660s, like the famous example of Daniel Dulaney in the 18th century, were redemptioners or possessed some special skill or education. For example, James Cranford worked in the law office of his master, George Parker, and later became a prosperous attorney himself. Patents 15, fol. 515; Provincial Court Judgments, TL No. 1, fol. 9. Special circumstances attended the servitude of others. Ninian Beale was a political prisoner captured by Cromwell's

TABLE 7. Second, Third, and Fourth Generations to Hold Provincial Office, 1660–1715

	Before 1660	1660– 1669	1670– 1679	1680– 1689	1689– 1699	1700– 1709	1710– 1715
Second generation of family to hold provincial office	2 (2)[a]	3 (1)	7	5 (1)	9	17	20
Third generation of family to hold provincial office	0	0	0	1[b]	2	3	3
Fourth generation of family to hold provincial office	0	0	0	0	0	0	1

Notes:

This table records the first election or appointment of an officeholder.

[a]The numbers in parentheses indicate individuals whose fathers held provincial office in another colony (in all the above cases, Virginia).

[b]Richard Gardiner was only a second-generation elected or appointed provincial office-holder; however, his grandfather, also a Richard Gardiner, had been present at three unelected assemblies held in the colony's first decade of existence.

tunities, former servants or their descendants enjoyed a greater likelihood of political success in Maryland than in Virginia.[44]

Accessibility to high office after 1700 depended increasingly upon one's family name and connections as well as upon high economic status. Such factors had been less important earlier, as few men were successful in transferring or bequeathing power to the next generation of their families (see table 7). The Calverts had been the notable

forces in 1650 and sent to America as a servant. A man of ability, he reestablished himself economically and politically after completing his service. Hans Hanson was born in New Sweden, but at the death of his father was apprenticed to Joseph Wickes of Maryland. Within a decade of completing his service, Hanson had bought a large plantation and contracted a marriage with a wealthy widow. Carr and Jordan, *Maryland's Revolution of Government*, 234–235, 256. For those former servants sitting from 1660 to 1680, an average of 16 years elapsed between arrival under indenture and election to the assembly; after 1680, it required an average of 23 years, with only four men accomplishing the feat in less than 14 years. On declining opportunities for former servants, see also Lorena S. Walsh, "Servitude and Opportunity in Charles County, Maryland, 1658–1705," in Land, Carr, and Papenfuse, eds., *Law, Society, and Politics*.

44. Quitt states that no servant arriving after 1640 served as a burgess between 1660 and 1706 and that no burgess during these years had descended from a former servant. "Virginia House of Burgesses," 274. The dismal prospects for freedmen in Virginia constitute a central theme of Edmund Morgan's recent study, *American Slavery, American Freedom*.

exceptions: controllers of extensive land and patronage, they could always find positions for sons, nephews, or cousins who came to America. Otherwise, no significant multigenerational officeholding emerged under the proprietors, although in-law relationships were often of importance. Excepting the Calverts, only fifteen individuals became the second generation of their respective families to hold provincial office before 1689, and only Richard Gardiner could lay any claim to being a third-generation officeholder (his grandfather had been present at three early unelected assemblies). Eight of these sixteen men were Catholics and one was a Quaker, with the descendants of councillor Robert Brooke constituting certainly the most successful family, and the only one to continue service into the next generation.[45] The remaining seven Protestants represented seven different families, only three of which would have additional members of the same or later generations to attain provincial office. The Lloyds, Hynsons, and Stones are the only examples of families thus clearly establishing themselves before 1689.[46] The other four men either had no sons or their heirs did not succeed in politics.[47]

The first decade of royal government brought little additional gain in the number of successful descendants. Nine sons of former provin-

45. Baker Brooke, an assemblyman on special writ in 1658 with appointment to the council immediately thereafter, was the first second-generation officeholder in the colony. His brothers, Thomas and Charles, also sat in the assembly. The other second-generation officeholders were Luke Gardiner, Leonard Greene, Joseph Pile, and Nicholas Sewall, all Catholics. William Berry was the Quaker.

46. Edward Lloyd I was a delegate in 1654 and 1658 and a councillor from 1658 to 1669 when he returned to England. His son Philemon served three terms in the assembly prior to his death in 1685 and was speaker of the lower house. His three sons were each a delegate and councillor. See discussion below and Christopher Johnston, "Lloyd Family," *Md. Hist. Mag.*, VII (1912), 221–222, 423–426. Thomas Hynson sat in two assemblies (1654, 1659/60) before his role in Fendall's Rebellion barred him from office for seven years; he died in 1667. His son John sat in three assemblies (1681–1682, 1694–1697, 1701–1704) and another son, Charles, served for one year in 1700. A grandson, John, was elected in 1708 but died before the assembly convened. Other Hynsons served steadily throughout the 18th century. Johnston, "Hynson and Smith Families," *ibid.*, XVIII (1923), 186–192. William Stone was proprietary governor (1648–Mar. 1652; June 1652–1654) and councillor (1656–1660). His son, John, was a delegate for three terms (1678–1682, 1686–1688, 1689–1692), but was lukewarm in response to the revolution and did not sit again during the royal period. Two members of the next generation, Thomas and William Stone, sat in the assembly. Harry Wright Newman, *The Stones of Poynton Manor* (Washington, D.C., 1937).

47. They were George Wells, William Hatton, John Brooke, and Thomas Marsh. Hatton was the nephew, not the son, of Thomas Hatton, who raised him in Maryland. Four additional men were sons of provincial officeholders in Virginia, but none of the four had heirs who held office. They were George and Nathaniel Utie, Richard Bennett, and William Digges.

cial officeholders first won election or appointment, while Thomas Brooke, an Anglican convert from Catholicism, and Edward Lloyd became only the second and third third-generation officeholders, and the first to serve for any appreciable length of time. Only three of the eight new second-generation families would continue their prominence into another generation—the Dents, the Smiths of Calvert County, and the Ennalls.[48]

In the fifteen years after 1700 a constellation of new families would assume their places in a rapidly emerging oligarchy. Thirty-seven second-generation officeholders, six third-generation politicians, and even one fourth-generation officeholder entered the provincial government, substantially more than the total of all such men in the previous history of the colony. Important new families included the Hammonds, Frisbys, Addisons, Dashiels, Harrises, Pearces, Taskers, Trippes, Wards, and a few others. Sons of these families were soon following the familiar pattern so engagingly described for mid-eighteenth-century Virginia by Charles Sydnor. From management of plantations and businesses, these sons would selectively gain election or appointment to county judicial, political, military, or religious offices, and then posts in the provincial government would come as almost a natural right.[49]

These families further concentrated their new power by extensive intermarriage. Some of the unions, assisted by the passage of time, brought to an end political rivalries that had divided men since the late proprietary years.[50] Elaborate kinship networks, extending through sons- and brothers-in-law, characterized the membership of assembly, council, and court. The council and court by 1715 again resembled the closely related family enclaves of Lord Baltimore's council and court in the 1680s, but this time it was a more broadly based Protestant elite whose power would continue for many generations.

48. For these three prominent families, see Harry Wright Newman, *The Maryland Dents* (Richmond, Va., 1963); Christopher Johnston, "Smith Family of Calvert County," *Md. Hist. Mag.*, III (1908), 1, 66–70; Jones, *History of Dorchester County Maryland*, 288–292.

49. Charles S. Sydnor, *Gentlemen Freeholders: Political Practices in Washington's Virginia* (Chapel Hill, N.C., 1952).

50. For example, Thomas Addison, son of Councillor John Addison who owed his success in provincial politics to his active role in the revolution of 1689, married Elinor Smith, whose father, Walter, was a principal opponent of that uprising and whose uncle, Richard Smith, was even imprisoned for his opposition to the rebels. King George's Parish Register 1701–1801, fol. 243; Wills 13, fols. 244–248; Johnston, "Smith Family of Calvert County," *Md. Hist. Mag.*, III (1908), 68–70.

Two different families, the Lloyds and the Addisons, possessed the greatest political power. Edward Lloyd of Talbot County reached the council in 1701; his appointment marked the beginning of the consolidation of power within the council with a shift from the county by county representation that had primarily influenced appointments since the revolution. Lloyd's brothers Philemon and James would receive council commissions in 1710 and 1722 respectively after serving in the lower house. Brother-in-law Richard Tilghman, a burgess by age twenty-five, joined the council in 1710. He and Philemon Lloyd were two of the five Provincial Court justices in 1715. Matthew Tilghman Ward, another brother-in-law, was also a nominee for the council, eventually receiving his commission in 1719; meanwhile, he sat in the assembly where he became speaker of the house in 1716. Further marriage ties bound the Lloyd interest only slightly less directly with other Eastern Shore delegates.[51]

Thomas Addison of Prince George's followed his deceased father on the council in 1708 at age twenty-nine without even serving previously in the assembly. He soon became a Provincial Court justice as well. Addison's half-sister was married to Councillor Thomas Brooke, whose own son-in-law, Philip Lee of the Virginia Lees, would sit on the Maryland council shortly after 1715. Commissions would also go then to Addison's brother-in-law Benjamin Tasker and his son-in-law James Bowles. Before their appointments, these men represented lower Western Shore counties in the assembly, as did the Dents and Smiths of Charles and Calvert counties, who were also closely related to Addison.[52]

Similar family networks, though somewhat less extensive and powerful, prevailed in other counties. Political leadership, earlier diffuse and unstable, was now coalescing in this native-born elite, men of similar wealth, experience, and background. Prior service and family ties bound these gentlemen with county government more extensively than ever before. Royal governors started to complain bitterly of the troublesome "native" or "country" party. The astute Francis Nicholson had perceived the emerging problem as early as

    51. Johnston, "Lloyd Family," *Md. Hist. Mag.*, VII (1912), 424–426; Johnston, "Tilghman Family," *ibid.*, I (1906), 281–282; *Md. Archives*, XXXIII, 297, XXV, 395; Wills 15, fols. 80–83.
    52. Jordan, "Royal Period of Colonial Maryland," 215–218; *Md. Archives*, XXV, 327, XXXIV, 121, 485, XXXV, 195.

1699 when he observed in his concluding report as governor that the interests of the mother country and colony were rapidly diverging. With the increasingly local orientation of the assembly, he noted, it was absolutely necessary that any governor "be esteemed by the people, or at least the major part of them, to be a lover of them and their Country, and not that he be Sent, or comes to make or retrieve a fortune." He further remarked that councils, as well as elected assemblies, "By Nature and Self Interest" would promote legislation considered to be "for the good of their Country," even when these acts might be "very prejudicial to his Majesty's Interest and Service." Nicholson applied these same observations to Virginia, where he became governor upon leaving Maryland.[53]

The Maryland assembly had not yet completed its "quest for power," but it was winning more and more initiative and privilege from reluctant executives. These were the critical years when the lower house established the right to select its own officers and evolved more elaborate internal organization. The assembly began to acquire more control over patronage and finances, largely through the shrewd phrasing of statutes and an unwillingness to pass legislation governing important matters for more than a year or two at a time. These advances clearly owed much to the stability and heightened caliber of representatives, however much royal governors might disparage them as ignorant, backward, and low born.

This ruling group was quick to protect itself against new men, especially "outsiders" who appeared unwilling or hesitant to settle permanently in Maryland. In 1704 the assembly reenacted a lapsed statute of 1694 "for the Incouragement of Learning and Advancement of the Natives of this Province." Directed against new immigrants and particularly fortune seekers, the law sought in part to prevent absentee officeholding, and it required a three-year residence in the colony before one's eligibility to hold "any office of Trust or Profitt," except by immediate commission from the crown. This legislation, in its tone and objectives, was characteristic of many other

53. Nicholson to Lords of Trade, July 1, 1699, C.O. 5/1310, 2. Over the next two decades, the correspondence of Govs. Nicholson, Seymour, and Spotswood hammered at these changes in Chesapeake politics. For examples from the latter two, see Seymour to Lords of Trade, June 10, 1707, and Mar. 10, 1708/09; *Md. Archives*, XXV, 262–267, 267–270; and R. A. Brock, ed., *The Official Letters of Alexander Spotswood, Lieutenant-Governor of the Colony of Virginia, 1710–1722* (Virginia Historical Society, *Collections*, N.S., I–II [Richmond, Va., 1882–1885]), *passim*.

statutes the delegates were now promoting, largely in retaliation against Sir Thomas Lawrence, secretary of the colony. No issue concerned the Maryland assembly more during the royal period than the powers and profits of this placeman who never deigned to consider himself a Marylander and who came to epitomize an outside, alien threat to local interests.[54]

John Seymour, governor of the colony from 1704 to 1709, had to defend the unpopular Lawrence, a fellow officer of the crown, and to uphold the royal prerogative against vigorous assaults from assemblymen prepared to battle over other issues of economy, defense, and institutional reforms. It was an unenviable assignment, usually fought in vain as he repeatedly accused the assembly of an unwise separation of "the true Interest and service of your Country from that of the Crown of England." Obstinacy and belligerence failed to sway the delegates, nor was Seymour's strategy of circumventing opposition through patronage any more successful. Of necessity after the defeats of 1708, Seymour was becoming more amenable to local concerns in the months immediately prior to his death in 1709.[55]

Maryland went without a resident governor for the next five years (1709–1714), a critical period during which the leading families actively worked to secure their positions. During this time, the council under the presidency of Edward Lloyd supervised the colony's affairs with persistent pressure from the assembly. A comparable situation prevailed in Virginia, as the council without a resident governor was enjoying a resurgence of power but with greater attentiveness to the wishes of the lower house. The political developments in both colonies gravely disturbed Robert Quarry, a customs collector and the highest ranking royal placeman then in the Chesapeake area. He urged the rapid dispatch of new governors and pointedly advised the Lords of Trade that in the future it would be wisest not to give councils the power to pass acts after the death of a governor: "The generallity of the Councills being Gentlemen of the Country are wholly in the Interest of the Assembly and as ready to lessen the Prerogative in all things as they [the assembly] are and therefore it requires care in the

54. *Md. Archives*, XIX, 100–101, XXVI, 429–430; Jordan, "Royal Period of Colonial Maryland," 231–242.
55. *Md. Archives*, XXVI, 373. Seymour told the assembly in Apr. of 1706, "I have neither Lands nor House to loose here on any Suddaine fatall insult, as you Gentlemen Freeholders have; yet my Reputation, which is dearer to me than anything in this World, lyes at stake." *Ibid.*, 524.

choice of them and those that are steady to the Queen's interest ought to be Supported and Encouraged. I could mention many wrong Stepps that have been taken by some Governors in their Recommending to your Honourable board persons fitt to be of the Council."[56]

Not even resident governors, as John Hart and Alexander Spotswood would soon discover, could completely restrain this new power in Maryland's and Virginia's provincial politics. Henceforth, the supreme authority, whether the crown or once again the proprietor in Maryland after 1715, would have to confront an entrenched elite, occasionally augmented by the admission of new men. Some success would come in marrying portions of that ruling elite to a "court" party, but no longer would executives have so free a hand in governing the colonies. The First Families of Maryland, like their counterparts in Virginia, had clearly emerged and assumed their places, and in spite of continuing factionalism, they would dominate provincial affairs in the eighteenth century's golden age of deferential politics.[57]

56. Quarry to [David Pulteney, Lord of Trade], Dec. 2, 1709, C.O. 323/7, 1. On Virginia, see also Morgan, *American Slavery, American Freedom*, 356–359.

57. On politics in Maryland from 1715 to the American Revolution, see Charles Albro Barker, *The Background of the Revolution in Maryland* (New Haven, Conn., 1940); Aubrey C. Land, *The Dulanys of Maryland: A Biographical Study of Daniel Dulany, the Elder (1685–1753) and Daniel Dulany the Younger (1722–1797)* (Baltimore, 1955); Ronald Hoffman, *A Spirit of Dissension: Economics, Politics and the Revolution in Maryland* (Baltimore, 1973); and David Curtis Skaggs, *Roots of Maryland Democracy, 1753–1776* (Westport, Conn., 1973). For Virginia, see n. 3.

9

English-Born and Creole Elites
in Turn-of-the-Century Virginia

Carole Shammas

American colonial historians have always been more concerned with the American than with the colonial. It has been the Englishman in the process of becoming an American, not the Englishman in the process of becoming a colonial, that has preoccupied most scholars. Admittedly, certain problems arise when one attempts to discuss the effects of colonialism on whites in America. In the colonizer versus colonized framework of Third World historical literature, Anglo-Americans clearly fall into the colonizer category,[1] and research during the last fifteen years or so, first on blacks and more recently on Indians, has brought out some of the ramifications of that role. There is, however, another side to consider. Having practically destroyed the aboriginal population and enslaved the Africans, the white inhabitants of English America began to conceive of themselves as the victims, not the agents, of Old World colonialism. Although expressed most strongly at the time of the Revolution, this consciousness of colonial status had actually evolved slowly over the generations.

In tracing the evolution of this colonial consciousness, the point at which English settlements became controlled by native-born inhabitants appears to be of some significance. The available studies on the emergence of a creole ruling class in the various colonies have been concerned primarily with the relationship of that emergence to social mobility, but scholars are beginning to note as well other dimensions of this change from immigrant to native. For example, John Rainbolt has suggested that the rise of a creole elite in Virginia was an important cause of what he perceived as an alteration in the political style of the colony's leaders between 1660 and 1720. I would like to pursue

I would like to thank Reginald Horsman, John M. Murrin, and Alison G. Olson for their comments and criticisms.

1. For an example of how these terms are used in Third World literature, see Albert Memmi, *The Colonizer and the Colonized* (Boston, 1967).

this line of inquiry a bit further and compare the general experiences and responses of the English-born generation that still controlled Virginia in the 1680s with those of the native group that came to power at the end of the century.[2]

Although Virginia was founded in 1607, Englishmen tended to think of it as a colony of Old World emigrants—and properly so—until almost the end of the seventeenth century. Their view of those emigrants was not particularly flattering. Emigration to Virginia connoted social inferiority: at best it meant one could not compete in English society and had to leave the country to be a success; at worst it meant one had to leave the country—period. Believing the colony to be the habitat of convicts, whores, poorhouse veterans, and bankrupt citizens, people at home considered it especially fitting that such base creatures chose to cultivate a base crop like tobacco. The passage of years and the establishment of a viable economy produced only one discernible change in attitude. Instead of conceiving of the emigrants as worthless idlers, Englishmen characterized them as worthless moneygrubbers who neglected societal amenities and thought only of trade. Far from excepting the colony's leadership from this general indictment, English critics often heaped special abuse on those in places of authority and laughed at their social pretensions.[3]

2. On dating the rise of native elites and on the relationship of that rise to social mobility see Martin Herbert Quitt, "The Virginia House of Burgesses, 1660–1706: The Social, Educational and Economic Bases of Political Power" (Ph.D. diss., Washington University, 1970), and David Jordan, "Political Stability and the Emergence of a Native Elite in Maryland" in this volume. Rainbolt's article, "The Alteration in the Relationship between Leadership and Constituents in Virginia, 1660 to 1720," appeared in the *William and Mary Quarterly*, 3d Ser., XXVII (1970), 411–434. See also John C. Rainbolt, *From Prescription to Persuasion: Manipulation of the Seventeenth Century Virginia Economy* (Port Washington, N.Y., 1974); Bernard Bailyn, "Politics and Social Structure in Virginia," in James Morton Smith, ed., *Seventeenth-Century America: Essays in Colonial History* (Chapel Hill, N.C., 1959), 90–115; and David Alan Williams, "Anglo-Virginia Politics, 1690–1735," in Alison Gilbert Olson and Richard Maxwell Brown, eds., *Anglo-American Political Relations, 1675–1775* (New Brunswick, N.J., 1970), 79–91. Works that have dealt with some aspects of the problems of being an English colonial in America include John Clive and Bernard Bailyn, "England's Cultural Provinces: Scotland and America," *WMQ*, 3d Ser., XI (1954), 200–213; Jack P. Greene, "Search for Identity: An Interpretation of the Meaning of Selected Patterns of Social Response in Eighteenth-Century America," *Journal of Social History*, III (1969–1970), 189–220; Kenneth Lynn, *Mark Twain and the Southwestern Humor* (Boston, 1959), 3–22; and Ronald Syme, *Colonial Elites: Rome, Spain, and the Americas* (London, 1958), 54–64. There is no study on the cultural maturation of the white colonial population comparable to that of Gerald W. Mullin's *Flight and Rebellion: Slave Resistance in Eighteenth-Century Virginia* (New York, 1972) for Afro-Americans.

3. Morgan Godwin, *The Negro's and Indian's Advocate, suing for their Admission into*

The rather curious treatment Bacon's Rebellion received in the
Restoration press well illustrates the persistence and depth of these
assumptions about the Virginian social order. Considering that in
post-Civil War England armed rebels generally ranked just above the
plague in popularity, the sympathy accorded Virginia's disturber of
the peace was rather remarkable. The newsletter written about the
event devoted more space to a description of Bacon's "extraordinary
parts" than to a condemnation of the uprising. It told of his good
family background, put the best construction possible on his reasons
for emigrating to Virginia, and then described those accomplishments
that had immediately singled him out for a council seat when he
arrived in the colony. Whatever the writer's intentions might have
been, the pamphlet left the distinct impression that Bacon, though
misdirected, was a giant among pygmies and that Virginia simply
could not absorb a man of his high birth, superior abilities, and "large
soul."[4]

Several years later, Aphra Behn, an English playwright with Tory
leanings, decided Bacon's Rebellion furnished proper material for a
play demonstrating the Stuart principle that the public interest was
sometimes best served by those who dispensed with legal niceties.
Although Behn had spent some time in English Surinam, there is no
indication that she had any special knowledge or interest in the
colony of Virginia; she seems rather to have derived her information
about the plantation from the streets of Restoration London. Going
much further than the newsletter account, her play *The Widdow Ranter,
or, the History of Bacon in Virginia* presented the rebel as a genuine hero
and the leaders of the colony as rogues whose low social origins

the Church . . . (London, 1680), 98–99, 168, and Morgan Godwin, *Trade Preferr'd before
Religion, and Christ made to give place to Mammon* . . . (London, 1685), 6. Virginia's
vestries according to Godwin were "Plebian Juntos." Promotional tracts such as John
Hammond's "Leah and Rachel, or, the Two Fruitfull Sisters Virginia and Mary-land
[1656]," in Clayton Colman Hall, ed., *Narratives of Early Maryland, 1633–1684* (New
York, 1910), 281–308, which sought to correct the impression that Virginia was still
populated by the dregs of society, appear to have made little impact.
   4. *Strange News from Virginia; Being a Full and True Account of the Life and Death of
Nathanael Bacon* . . . (London, 1677), in Harry Finestone, ed., *Bacon's Rebellion: The
Contemporary News Sheets* (Williamsburg, Va., 1956), 5–18. Another news sheet followed, *More News from Virginia* (London, 1677), which reported the fate of those
involved in the rebellion, and it is also reprinted in Finestone. Bertha Monica Stearns,
"The Literary Treatment of Bacon's Rebellion in Virginia," *Virginia Magazine of History
and Biography*, LII (1944), 163–179, discusses the newsletters and fictional pieces written
on Bacon's Rebellion from 1677 to modern times.

rendered them unfit for office.[5] Behn's council was made up of former criminals and "broken" tradesmen who had migrated to Virginia and acquired large estates. While they put on gentlemanly airs, their illiteracy, ignorance of the law, and cowardice bubbled to the surface when they had to administer justice or to defend the colony from its enemies. Furthermore, they lacked all sense of their own inadequacy and imagined themselves to be better governors than the statesmen of England. Bacon, an "honest gentleman," possessed certain high ideals about service to the country that the base councillors could not begin to comprehend, and thus when he went to fight the Indians without a commission, they attempted to destroy him. In the final act Behn rewrote history. Bacon committed suicide, but his forces prevailed. The buffoonish councillors, finally admitting they had no talent for governance, retired, as one put it, "to bask under the shade of my own Tobacco, and drink my punch in Peace." The rest of the colony looked ahead to the arrival of the new governor from England and a hoped-for reformation in their affairs.

This tendency to sympathize with Bacon stemmed from deep skepticism about the legitimacy of the Virginia elite.[6] The idea of emigrants growing rich and then passing themselves off as gentlemen and governors seemed to offend Englishmen's hierarchical sensibilities. Behn's low-life councillors, even allowing for the distortions produced by parody, bore little resemblance to the solid sorts with good middling class backgrounds who held office in Virginia in the 1670s. Nevertheless, Englishmen, certain that the colonials would not have left if they

5. Aphra Behn, "The Widow Ranter," Montague Summers, ed., *The Works of Aphra Behn*, IV (New York, 1915), 215–310. For information on Behn's life and a summary of the plays see Frederick M. Link, *Aphra Behn* (New York, 1968).

6. Even the report issued by the commissioners sent to investigate the rebellion for the crown, "A True Narrative of the Rise, Progresse, and Cessation of the Late Rebellion in Virginia," in Charles M. Andrews, ed., *Narratives of the Insurrections 1675–1690* (New York, 1915), 105–141, while condemnatory of the uprising, noted Bacon's good family background and lashed out at the "Cowardize and Basenesse of the Generality of Sir William Berkeley's Party," 110–135. Wilcomb E. Washburn, *The Governor and the Rebel: A History of Bacon's Rebellion in Virginia* (Chapel Hill, N.C., 1957), 2–3, attributes the commissioners' unfavorable comments about the colony's leadership to their postrebellion conflicts with Berkeley. Their criticisms are, however, not so much directed at the governor personally as at the colonists in general. Bacon, William Byrd I, and the other alleged coconspirators, according to the report, had been drinking when they decided to strike out against the Indians, and their followers, "freemen but lately crept out of the condition of Servants," also became stirred up through the use of liquor. *Ibid.*, 110–113. On the other hand, Berkeley's supporters, as quoted above, were considered base and cowardly. The commissioners' assessment of the level of politics in Virginia at that time bears a striking resemblance to Behn's.

could have become leaders at home, stubbornly persisted in presenting the most extreme examples of colonial social mobility as the
norm.[7] Regardless of what might transpire in the New World, the
social status of the colonial, in English eyes, remained what it was
before migration. Even promotional tracts, the most sanguine writings
on the colonies, tacitly recognized this fact. Such pamphlets promised
land, economic security, and even riches, but never gentility.

Bernard Bailyn has described the actual immigrants who dominated
Virginia in the Rebellion era. Frequently the younger sons of merchant
families, they came to the colony in mid-century just at the time
when the appallingly high mortality rate for Englishmen in the colony
was probably beginning its decline. Through commercial and political
connections as well as by marriages with widows and heiresses of
dead planters, these immigrants managed to obtain large estates and
to supplant the previous ruling group. If their letters and papers—a
meager output to be sure—are any indication, then these men understood quite well that the benefits of the New World were primarily
economic. The attraction of Virginia was not climate, high culture,
political glory, or military conquest. In the middle of the seventeenth
century, Virginia was not even the first choice among the plantation
colonies; rather it had the reputation of being the place to go if you
did not have the resources to set up a West Indies sugar establishment.
Virginia no longer had a boom-town atmosphere, but ambitious
immigrants still married eleven-year-old girls or forty-five-year-old
women for their pigs, cows, and household furnishings, competed
vigorously with fellow planters for a share of the labor supply, and
sought out troublesome offices that would aid in the building of their
fortunes.[8]

7. Behn, "Widow Ranter," 254, has one of the councillors declare: "Well gad zoors,
'tis a fine thing to be a good Statesman"—to which a newly arrived planter replies,
"Ay Cornet, which you had never been had you staid in Old England."
    8. Bailyn, "Politics and Social Structure," in Smith, ed., Seventeenth-Century Ameri-
ca, 98–102. Also see Edmund S. Morgan, American Slavery, American Freedom: The Ordeal
of Colonial Virginia (New York, 1975), 180–184. Colonel [Henry] Norwood, "A Voyage to
Virginia (1649)," in Peter Force, comp., Tracts and other papers relating principally to the
origin, settlement, and progress of the Colonies in North America, from the discovery of the
country to the year 1776, III (Washington, D.C., 1844), 4, notes the contemporary
attitudes about the West Indies and Virginia. The two best sources for information on
the preoccupation of this generation remain Richard Beale Davis, ed., William Fitzhugh
and His Chesapeake World, 1676–1701 (Chapel Hill, N.C., 1963) and the William Byrd I
letterbooks published in the VMHB, XXIV–XXVIII (1916–1920). The Ludwell Papers in
the Virginia Historical Society in Richmond mainly pertain to the next generation,

The low opinion of Virginia at "home" and the motives behind most planters' migration seemed to militate against the majority of the immigrant elite taking the colony's institutions, honors, or anything besides their own estates too seriously. The general attitude toward colonial offices is revealed in the terms these men used to refer to them: "public business," "profitable employments," and "share of the government."[9] Colonists sought offices primarily to protect their interests. Of course, they must have enjoyed being set above the crowd. But no one really pursued a political career as such. Moreover, it was the English public world that mattered. Significantly, Virginia's first political organization, the Loyal Society, was formed not for any colonial cause but to defend James II. The society even used London nativity as the basis for membership. (While the governor, Lord Howard of Effingham, had encouraged the group, his request that the English authorities at home publish a sermon delivered to the society and send back copies so that "they may see I have formed theyr desire" indicates considerable grassroots enthusiasm.[10]) In this period when one might well imagine that the alignments provoked by Bacon's Rebellion would still inform the structure of politics, the colonists instead were flinging the epithets of "Whig" and "Papist" at one another and using these mother country labels to define their own local disputes.[11]

The general attitude of the immigrant elite toward their colony's inadequacies can best be described as stoic, with lapses. When the time arrived to write a will, Nicholas Spencer, a mid-century immigrant whose kinship ties to the Culpeper family enabled him to become secretary of the colony, could not resist taking a few parting shots at the society he had helped govern for almost thirty years. He

although there are some interesting letters on Philip Ludwell's retirement in England. Almost all the rest of the correspondence for these years is between colonists and crown officials.

9. William Byrd I to Warham Horsmanden, July 25, 1690, *VMHB*, XXVI (1918), 128; William Fitzhugh to Lord Culpeper, Jan. 8, 1682/83, Davis, ed., *Fitzhugh*, 134; Fitzhugh to Robert Fitzhugh, Jan. 30, 1686/87, *ibid.*, 200.

10. Lord Howard of Effingham to William Blathwayt, May 10, 1686, Blathwayt Papers, XIV, Colonial Williamsburg, Williamsburg, Va. [microfilm in the State Historical Society of Wisconsin]. The sermon was printed with an introduction by Richard Beale Davis. See Deuel Pead, "A Sermon Preached at James City in Virginia," *WMQ*, 3d Ser., XVII (1960), 371–394. Davis quotes from the Effingham letter but leaves out the last lines, which referred to the printing arrangements.

11. See Nicholas Spencer to William Blathwayt, Apr. 27, 1689, Blathwayt Papers, XVI, and Davis, ed., *Fitzhugh*, 37–38, 296–299.

opened the document with the request that his body "be buried simply according to the Church's use, and without the indecencies of funerals in this country," and closed it with the order that his debts be paid in money and not in commodities, as the "unequal and dishonourable law of Virginia" permitted. William Fitzhugh was less sharp but still far from sentimental about his adopted home. In 1686, about a decade and a half after his own arrival, he invited his sister to come to Virginia, but only "if she cannot otherwise better her self." Virginia was a "fertile country," he told another correspondent, which unfortunately had poor religious and educational facilities and where good society was "seldom to come at except in books."[12] What is most revealing about these immigrant critiques is their brevity: no tortured analyses of Virginia's cultural shortcomings or clever satires designed to disassociate elite members from colonial provincialism, such as those later composed by native sons; they were instead passing remarks uttered by men who apparently considered promotional tracts the proper vehicle, and superior economic opportunities the proper grounds, for any apologia that might be made for the colony.[13]

As with past generations, this immigrant elite still looked almost entirely to England for solutions to the two basic problems of colonials —the dependence of their estates on what they called "contingencies" and the primitiveness of their surroundings. European wars that cut off trade and threatened to bring foreign fleets to their shores, fluctua-

12. Will of Nicholas Spencer signed Apr. 25, 1688, and probated in London, Jan. 15, 1698/99, Virginia Colonial Records Project Survey Report 5021, typescript copy in the Virginia State Library, Richmond; Fitzhugh to Henry Fitzhugh, Apr. 22, 1686, Davis, ed., *Fitzhugh*, 171; and Fitzhugh to Nicholas Hayward, Jan. 30, 1686/87, *ibid.*, 203.

13. Fitzhugh prepared a short summary discourse of Virginia and a digest of its laws, but it is no longer extant. His approach to such a work, however, is revealed in a letter he wrote to Nicholas Hayward on May 13, 1687, stating his intentions: "Sr., I have had it in my thoughts to write a small treatise, or History of Virginia, describing its Scituation, Temperature, and fertility, nature of present inhabitants, with their method and manner of living, the plenty of Iron Mines, almost everywhere in the Country, and probable conjectures of the Discovery of others . . . together with the prodigious quantity of wood to manage the same, the plenty of all sorts of provision the easie and profitable living of the people therein. It's regular easie and even Government in its severall Courts of Justice, together with their respective powers and methods of proceeding, with divers other heads too many to be enumerated. . . . I have only mentioned this to you Sir to desire your opinion, whether a business of this nature might be of any advantage for the persuading Inhabitants hither, and might not be prejudicial to me in my particular Concerns. . . . " *Ibid.*, 224.

tions in tobacco prices, governmental changes in England, and the political and economic intrusions of a new court favorite into the colony's business kept most planters in a constant state of anxiety. Seldom, however, did they respond collectively to these threats through their local institutions or unite to present a common front. Instead each man preferred to work through individuals in England whom he felt could produce beneficial results, and when completely frustrated, he sometimes resorted to violence. Probably the early experience of these men in the colony, when kinship with a governor or proprietor gave them immediate access to places, made them believe that direct appeal to some "person of quality" in England was the only effective way to proceed, even when, as was usually the case, their contacts were neither highly placed nor effective. Despite continual setbacks, they retained the belief that magical things might happen—new offices be created or policies reversed—if only one could whisper in the right ear or cross the right palm with silver. Every man or family tended to act alone and trusted English correspondents before their fellow colonials, who often were sending rival petitions. In the late 1680s Philip Ludwell went to England to try to oust Governor Effingham from office. Effingham had pursued policies on quitrents and on the setting of fees that hurt almost every interest in the colony; yet, while Ludwell managed to get a petition of support from the Burgesses, most of the substantial planters, anxious to keep on Effingham's good side and suspicious of Ludwell's motives, chose to keep out of the fray. William Fitzhugh carefully instructed his brother-in-law, then in London, to be sure to let Effingham know that, even though Ludwell had stayed at his house for some time, he knew nothing about "his affairs." William Byrd made the same disclaimers and considered the mission to be "his [Ludwell's] cause." Byrd told his contacts in England that Ludwell might use his London visit to take from Byrd a lucrative office to which the latter lacked a clear title. When Ludwell assured him that he had no such design, Byrd began to suspect that Ludwell's son-in-law, Daniel Parke, Jr., might go after the position. These colonial leaders showed little responsiveness not only to "the people" but to one another as well. "Friends at court" would settle all their difficulties. In situations where influence failed or seemed inappropriate, the large planter turned rebel, using the dissatisfaction of Virginia's large unpropertied class for his own ends.

Citing uprisings such as Bacon's Rebellion and the plant-cutting riots as examples, Edmund Morgan has labeled the Virginia of this period "the volatile society."[14]

Whenever this generation felt the need for certain commodities—clothing, furniture, books—or skilled persons, such as apprentices or ministers—they ordered it from England. One of Nicholas Spencer's letters demonstrates the degree to which these later seventeenth-century immigrants still relied on English goods and services. Having felt ill for some time, Spencer carefully described his symptoms to his brother who was living in England, and then asked him to consult a physician and to write back the diagnosis.[15] Some items, of course, could not be relayed in a letter or packaged and sent. A constant stream of colonial consumers flowed into the mother country seeking to satisfy their wants.

The ultimate solution to the problem of colonial primitiveness was to return permanently to England, and there are indications that this very solution was not infrequently attempted. Of the twenty male correspondents in William Fitzhugh's letterbook who at one time resided in Virginia and whose later history can be ascertained, one fifth re-emigrated, and several others had sons or fathers who went back while the correspondents stayed and managed the family estate.[16] Colonists who tried to make their Virginia holdings support a gentleman's life in the English countryside ran into many problems. Liquidating the estate and simply moving to England were almost out of

14. H. R. McIlwaine, ed., *Executive Journals of the Council of Colonial Virginia* (Richmond, Va., 1925), I, 472–473; Fitzhugh to Roger Jones, May 18, 1685, Davis, ed., *Fitzhugh*, 168–169; Fitzhugh to George Luke, Oct. 27, 1690, *ibid.*, 287; and Byrd letters in *VMHB*, XXV (1917), 263, XXVI (1918), 252–253, 255, 390. H. R. McIlwaine, ed., *Legislative Journals of the Council of Colonial Virginia* (Richmond, Va., 1918), I, 147. John Rainbolt, "Leadership and Constituents in Virginia," *WMQ*, 3d Ser., XXVII (1970), 412, discusses the lack of responsiveness to popular desires. William Berkeley's plan for commercial development in Virginia and the way it was handled is another outstanding illustration of this tendency to look to England. See Sister Joan de Lourdes Leonard, "Operation Checkmate: The Birth and Death of a Virginia Blueprint for Progress 1660–1676," *WMQ*, 3d Ser., XXIV (1967), 44–74. Morgan, *American Slavery*, 213–292.

15. Nicholas Spencer to Brother Spencer, June 13, 1672, Sloane Manuscripts, 3511, fol. 134, British Library [Museum].

16. The returnees were Henry Hartwell, Thomas Mathews, Lord Culpeper, and Roger Jones. Nicholas Spencer's son William returned to England as did William Hardidge's father. The father of William Lee and Richard Lee II, Richard Lee I, tried to reestablish the family in England, but his early death made it impossible to retain his English estate. The information is in Ludwell Lee Montague, "Richard Lee, the Emigrant 1613(?)–1664," *VMHB*, LXII (1954), 3–49, although the author gives a different interpretation to the re-emigration than I have here.

the question due to the poor prices received for Virginia acreage. Efforts to trade plantations for land in the British Isles seldom succeeded. In the 1680s William Fitzhugh thought he might be able to find a disgruntled English Whig who would be interested in such an exchange, but the Glorious Revolution came and went without any offers. Next, he informed his English agent that he would even be willing to accept an estate in Ireland or Scotland if no trade could be made with an Englishman, but still there were no takers. In the early eighteenth century, Lord Fairfax, heir to the enormous Northern Neck proprietary, attempted to barter his Virginia estate for crown lands in Derby. Despite Fairfax's attestations that the quitrents for the Northern Neck amounted to almost £500 per annum and that the revenues from the Derby lands provided little more than £150, the queen would agree only to a lease, not a sale, of her holdings. Unable to accept such a disadvantageous proposal, Fairfax eventually emigrated to Virginia.[17] The few planters who did return permanently to England usually retained ownership of their land and left kin in charge of management. Hired overseers seldom worked out. This arrangement, of course, required a substantial estate and competent, healthy relatives. Even then, as Philip Ludwell (who returned to England at the end of the seventeenth century) discovered, there were innumerable problems involved in being separated from close family members and in trying to live off bills of exchange from Virginia tobacco shipments.[18]

Finding reintegration into the home society and identification with Virginia equally difficult, this immigrant elite in their New World society seemed to derive their main pleasure from their estates. In letters home these founders of family fortunes reported with an air of great satisfaction the construction of buildings and the acquisition of acreage and luxury items. They compared their current circumstances with what they had in the beginning. Although the "extraordinary

17. Davis, ed., *Fitzhugh*, 175–176, 178, 189–190, 203–204, 218, 270. On the Fairfax exchange see Fairfax Memorial and Blathwayt Report, Mar. 12, 1708/09 and Jan. 22, 1708/09, Brock Collection, Box 227, Huntington Library, San Marino, Cal., and Blathwayt Journal, T. 64/89, 401–405, Public Record Office. Gov. Francis Nicholson noted in 1699 that "when the Virginia Estates come to be appraised or sold, it is not so much above half the value." C.O. 5/1310, 17, P.R.O.

18. See for example Philip Ludwell I to Philip Ludwell II, Dec. 20, 1707, and Stephen Fouace to Philip Ludwell II, Apr. 22, 1711, Lee-Ludwell Papers, Virginia Historical Society, Richmond; and Stephen Fouace to Philip Ludwell II, Aug. 8, 1710, *VMHB*, V (1897–1898), 44–45.

Ambition to be *thought well of"* in England, which one contemporary observer noted as characteristic of these planters, might not always be realized, their colonial accomplishments did enable them to give handouts and advice on how to make one's way in the world to their less prosperous English kin.[19] Their culture had told them one migrated to Virginia primarily for material advancement. By becoming great planters, they had achieved as much success as was thought possible in a colonial environment.

Creole consciousness did not surface in America until almost the end of the century. Beginning in the 1680s English officials, foreign visitors, and even immigrant colonists started to take special note of those inhabitants born in the New World, calling them "natives," "creoles," "countrie-born" or using the name of their colony —"Bermudians," "Barbadians," and so forth.[20] In Virginia, where these distinctions did not become common before the 1690s, the appellations "native" and "Virginians" were most often bestowed upon the American-born. Yet these terms continued to cause some confusion because they had originally been used to describe the Indians. "Creole" appeared occasionally in reference to both native whites and blacks.[21] It is no coincidence that this singling out of natives as a group occurred at about the time they began to outnumber

19. M. G. [Morgan Godwin], *A Supplement to the Negro's and Indian's Advocate . . .* (London, 1681), 8. There are many instances in both the Byrd and Fitzhugh letters of pride in material achievements. "I have a long time in a strange land, struggled hard with fortune's adverse hand, but thank God in the end, by God Almighty's blessing upon my mean endeavours, (having no friend or relation to lend a supporting hand) have overcome, and I praise God live very contentedly and well." So wrote Fitzhugh to one relative and made similar statements to other kin. Davis, ed., *Fitzhugh*, 169–174. Both Byrd and Fitzhugh stressed that they were well fixed but not vastly wealthy, *ibid.*, 200 and 361; and William Byrd to Warham Horsmanden, July 25, 1690, *VMHB*, XXVI (1918), 128. On aid and advice to English kin see William Byrd I to Thomas Byrd, Apr. 16, 1688, *ibid.*, XXV (1917), 254; and Davis, ed., *Fitzhugh*, 186–187, 219.

20. W. Noel Sainsbury *et al.*, eds., *Calendar of State Papers, Colonial Series* (London, 1860–), XI (*America and West Indies, 1681–1685*), no. 1093, XII (*1685–1688*), nos. 396, 552, 617, 852, XIII (*1689–1692*), nos. 1484, 2787 (*1702–1703*), nos. 200, 230, 737, XXIII (*1706–1708*), no. 975, hereafter cited as *Cal. State Papers, Col.* Governor William Beeston to William Blathwayt, Aug. 26, 1694, Blathwayt Papers, XXI.

21. John Clayton notes the mix-up in terms in 1687. See Edmund Berkeley and Dorothy Smith Berkeley, eds., *The Reverend John Clayton. A Parson with a Scientific Mind: His Scientific Writings and Other Related Papers* (Charlottesville, Va., 1965), 21. For use of terms "native" and "Virginia" to refer to those born in the colony see Berkeley, *John Clayton*, 25 (1687); Memorial, Blathwayt Journal, [July] 1692, T. 64/88, 360, P.R.O.; Governor Edmund Andros to William Blathwayt, Mar. 3, 1692/93, Blathwayt Papers; Henry Hartwell, James Blair, and Edward Chilton, *The Present State of Virginia and the College*, ed. Hunter Dickinson Farish (Charlottesville, Va., 1940), 14; H. R. McIlwaine, ed., *Journals of the House of Burgesses, 1695–1702* (Richmond, Va., 1913), 131; C.O.

the English-born in the House of Burgesses and to take over more and more Council positions.[22]

What made the native-born colonist appear distinctive? First, Englishmen noted the biological differences between themselves and the creoles. Evidently some in the mother country had assumed that the conditions of the New World would severely alter those born there; commentators thought it necessary to state that white native settlers had flaxen hair and "delicate parts" just like people at home. Still, these observers believed the native-born were biologically different in the sense that they, like the Indians, allegedly lived shorter lives and suffered from certain types of diseases. The clergyman John Clayton described to a fellow of the Royal Society a number of maladies he had observed in Virginia, listing them under the heading "distempers among the English-Natives" as though they were peculiar to creoles. The belief also sprang up that those born in the New World reacted more violently to smallpox and consequently took their lives in their hands when they journeyed back to England.[23]

Second, Englishmen found white natives of America, including the elite, culturally inferior. In this period they did not yet attribute their deficiencies to environmental degeneration, but rather to isolation

---

5/1310, fol. 17; C.O. 5/1312, nos. 19, 21. Thomas Reade, an English visitor, referred to them as "American Brittains," "The Life of Tho. Reade Rector of Moreton, In the County of Dorset Written by His Hand," 1692, 27, Alderman Library, University of Virginia, Charlottesville. For "creole" see C.O. 5/1318, fol. 286V, and Journal of William Hugh Grove, 1692–1732, item 3850, 115, Alderman Library, University of Virginia, Charlottesville. The only instance I have found of a native Virginian using the term creole is William Byrd II, and he used it in an ironic manner. Offering unsolicited advice on foreign affairs to Sir Charles Wager, he wrote, "You will pardon me Sir for presuming to obtrude my Creolean Notions in Affairs so high above my humble sphere . . . ," Feb. 17, 1740/41, Byrd Letterbook, VI, 240, Virginia Historical Society.

22. Martin Quitt, "Virginia House of Burgesses," has numbers in ten-year blocks for native-born and immigrant Burgesses from 1676. For the years 1697–1706, he notes that 48 natives and 47 immigrants entered the House. This is compared to 39 natives and 58 immigrants in 1688–1696 and 29 natives and 64 immigrants in 1677–1686.

23. Edmund Berkeley and Dorothy S. Berkeley, "Another 'Account of Virginia' by the Reverend John Clayton," *VMHB*, LXXVI (1968), 434; "The Life of Tho. Reade," 27; Stanley Pargellis, "An Account of the Indians in Virginia [1689]," *WMQ*, 3d Ser., XVI (1959), 230; Berkeley and Berkeley, eds., *John Clayton*, 25–27, 39; and Wm. J. Hinke, trans. and ed., "Report of the Journey of Francis Louis Michel from Berne, Switzerland to Virginia, October 2, 1701–December 1, 1702," *VMHB*, XXIV (1916), 26. West Indian creoles also were assumed to have a shorter life-span due to a more rapid rate of physical degeneration. Richard S. Dunn, *Sugar and Slaves: The Rise of the Planter Class in the English West Indies* (Chapel Hill, N.C., 1972), 332–333. Historical demographers working on the Chesapeake have found the changeover to a native population brought significant changes in mortality and fertility. See Russell Menard, "The Demography of Somerset County Maryland: Preliminary Report" (paper presented to the Stony Brook Conference on Social History, June 1975).

and lack of education.[24] Visitors commented upon the ignorance of
Virginians in practical arts and good husbandry, while the colony's
royal officials, like their counterparts in other colonies, questioned
the ability of the natives to manage public affairs and to act respon-
sibly.[25] In 1693 Governor Edmund Andros blamed the inclination of
the Burgesses "to effect popularity" on the "new members and Virginians." His successor, Francis Nicholson, felt that concrete measures
should be taken to deal with the emerging creole problem. Because
native leaders were too "self-interested," practice should become
policy, and only men sent from England should occupy the positions
of governor and lieutenant governor. After the colonists refused to
obey a royal request that they send military aid to New York, Nicholson grew more sharply critical. "The country consists now mostly of
Natives," he wrote to the Board of Trade, "few of which either have
read much or been abroad in the world, so that they cannot form to
themselves any Idea or Notion of those things," meaning defense of
the empire. "Tho in point of Trade and of Plantation Affairs," he
added drily, "they are knowing." He then requested an attorney
general from England because the natives lacked the necessary quali-
fications for this office. As officials became more conscious of creoles,
the formerly maligned English-born colonists acquired new virtues.
Nicholson admitted that during the Civil War "several Gentlemen of
Quality had emigrated and others of good parts," but no more would
come because all the best land and "widows or maids of any good
fortune" had been co-opted by the natives. When Nicholson sent an
emissary back to the mother country to correct any erroneous notions
about affairs in Virginia that the home authorities might have picked
up from colonial agent William Byrd II, the governor emphasized that
his courier was an "old Englander" and thus could be trusted.[26]

24. For 18th-century theories about degeneration, see Antonello Gerbi, *The Dispute
of the New World: The History of a Polemic, 1750–1900*, trans. Jeremy Moyle (Pittsburgh,
Pa., 1973); Henry Steele Commager and Elmo Giordanetti, *Was America a Mistake?: An
Eighteenth-Century Controversy* (New York, 1967).

25. On ignorance of Virginians see Joseph Ewan and Nesta Ewan, *John Banister and
His Natural History of Virginia* (Urbana, Ill., 1970), 361 and other citations in note 26
below. As the 17th century was coming to a close, governors in the West Indies and
Bermuda complained constantly that the natives' biases, ignorance, and loose morals
made them unsuitable for office. Sainsbury *et al.*, eds., *Cal. State Papers, Col.*, XI
(*1681–1685*), no. 357; Headlam, ed., *ibid.* (1702), nos. 294, 872; and Governor William
Beeston to William Blathwayt, Aug. 26, 1694, Blathwayt Papers, XXI.

26. Governor Edmund Andros to William Blathwayt, Mar. 3, 1692/93, Blathwayt
Papers, III; C.O. 5/1310, fols. 17–19, C.O. 5/1312, nos. 19, 21.

Though perhaps less antagonistic toward creoles than Nicholson, English-born inhabitants of Virginia assessed the situation similarly. In their report on the colony to the Board of Trade in 1697, Henry Hartwell, James Blair, and Edward Chilton blamed the lack of towns on the native majority in the House of Burgesses, whom they believed never had seen one and, therefore, could not imagine the advantages of urban development. In their view the level of administration had been higher "while the first Stock of *Virginia* Gentlemen lasted, who having had their Education in *England*, were a great deal better accomplish'd in the Law, and Knowledge of the World, that [sic] their Children and Grand-children who have been born in *Virginia*, and have had generally no Opportunity of Improvement by good Education, further than that they learned to read, write, and cast Accompts, and that but very indifferently."[27] The tone was gentler but the message just as damaging.

English society had questioned the social origins of the immigrant elite; in the case of the native elite they questioned its Englishness. The aspersions cast on native abilities, however, did not automatically create a uniform body of patriotic Virginians. Some wealthy young creoles had ambivalent feelings about being so permanently identified with their colony. Unlike the immigrants, they had not chosen colonial status; rather, it had been thrust upon them. Thus they sometimes spoke with bitterness of "this country where fortune hast cast my lot" and of being "condemned to Virginia." Kenneth Lynn has described the way in which William Byrd II, who had spent most of his childhood and youth in England, continued throughout his life to play to an English audience and tried to disassociate himself from ordinary American inhabitants.[28] Nevertheless, no matter how exasperated creoles might become with conditions in Virginia, they naturally refused to recognize the view of outsiders, and of some English-born colonists, that American nativity made them culturally inferior. Instead they gave other, sometimes critical, but definitely more palatable, explanations for what appeared to be colonial shortcomings. In doing so they did not single out creoles but spoke of the inhabitants in general. The coldly objective air of the immigrant leaders toward

27. Hartwell *et al.*, *Present State of Virginia*, ed. Farish, 14, 45 (quoted).
28. William Byrd II to Sir Hans Sloane, Apr. 20, 1706, *WMQ*, 2d Ser., I (1921), 186; Ruth Bourne, "John Evelyn, the Diarist, and his Cousin Daniel Parke II," *VMHB*, LXXVIII (1970), 18; and Lynn, *Mark Twain*, 3–22.

the advantages and disadvantages of colonial life slowly disappeared
and was replaced by the necessarily more committed stance of the
natives.

One method of protecting the colony and themselves was to attack
the English way of life. From Massachusetts to Georgia, the standard
colonial defense against the greater sophistication of the mother country was praise for "the virtues of simplicity." Virginians' first use of
this argument appeared in 1699, when they endeavored to drum up
support for the College of William and Mary. A speaker at an event
promoting the school contended that after journeying to England for
an education, the colonial child might return filled with more of "the
Luxury then with the Learning of England" and not know how "to
brook our more simple and Less Costly way of Living in Virginia."
Allegations about the debilitating effects of the mother country's
refined habits were a way of countering charges that a colony and its
inhabitants lacked civility.[29]

Natives seemed to recognize, however, that the cultural weaknesses
of a plantation society could not be entirely explained away in this
manner. They too bemoaned some features of colonial life and even
reproached themselves for Virginia's primitiveness, but they chose
different grounds than those of their detractors. One historian has
noted that in the early eighteenth century Virginians like William
Byrd II and Robert Beverley II constantly harped on the laziness of
themselves and their fellow colonials. He has pointed out that what
made these men perceive laziness as a problem was the absence of
the traditional signposts of industry, such as towns, in the colony.
One might go on to say that laziness also provided Virginians with a
line of defense, for it was certainly better to be thought lazy than just
plain inferior; better to be thought too lazy to erect towns than to be
thought too ignorant to know what one was; and better to be thought
too lazy to follow the principles of good husbandry or to compose
great literature than to admit that one's colonial backwardness prevented achievements of this kind. Laziness was not an attractive

29. "Speeches of Students of the College of William and Mary Delivered May 1,
1699," *WMQ*, 2d Ser., X (1930), 328. Earlier, one finds individuals of native birth
claiming their simple upbringing in Virginia made them less disingenuous than those
who had been exposed to a more cosmopolitan milieu; see "Defense of Col. Edward
Hill," *VMHB*, III (1895–1896), 240. But to the best of my knowledge the "virtues of
simplicity" argument was first employed in defense of the colony as a whole in the
college speech.

quality, but it was preferable to English explanations for colonial deficiencies.[30]

Native Virginians had to come to terms with the circumstances of their birth in another respect as well. Social mobility in the colony was limited, and the natives who became leaders usually were the sons of immigrant elite members. Their ample patrimonies placed them in a different position from their fathers, who had been founders of the family fortune. They could not derive the same satisfaction from strictly material achievements. But what new goals were available to privileged natives? The English ruling class could not absorb them. Creoles found it no easier than those before them to remove permanently to England. Immigrant fathers lacked the clout to obtain places for enterprising sons, even in the plantation office, and adult colonials who left America for an extended period of time risked losing their Virginia posts. Englishmen alone could be absentee officials. Out of one whole generation of native-born Virginians, only the adventive Daniel Parke II (1669–1710) managed to enter the English political arena, and he bequeathed a heavily mortgaged estate to his heirs as proof.[31] On the other hand, colonial offices and perquisites stayed open to Englishmen; indeed governorships were literally reserved for them. As long as the colony continued to be dominated by the English-born, it seemed normal enough that the governor should be sent from England also. But when natives whose fathers' wealth had provided them with the education, leisure time, and money needed to purchase an office found themselves continually

30. David Bertelson, *The Lazy South* (New York, 1967), 61–84. Bertelson gives numerous examples of cases in which Virginians blamed their failures on laziness and lack of direction.

31. After many humble entreaties to William Blathwayt, Nicholas Spencer finally managed to obtain a place for his son, but William Byrd I was not as lucky. Blathwayt wrote the latter that it was "not in my power to find a suitable Employmt" for his heir, William Byrd II. See Byrd I to Blathwayt, Nov. 1, 1692 and Blathwayt to Byrd I, Feb. 20, 1692/93, Blathwayt Papers, XIII; Spencer to Blathwayt, May 9, 1686, *ibid.*, XIV, and Dec. 22, 1686, Mar. 29, 1687, and Feb. 15, 1687/88, *ibid.*, XVI. On extended absence from the colony counting as grounds for removal from Council, see W. L. Grant and James Munro, eds., *Acts of the Privy Council of England, Colonial Series, 1680–1720* (London, 1910), II, 762–763, which deals with Governor Spotswood's attempt to get rid of Byrd II because the latter had been in England for three years. On Parke see Bourne, "Evelyn and Parke," *VMHB*, LXXVIII (1970), 3–33. The story of Parke's encumbered estate is a long one, but it seems that his debts began to mount after he went to England, bought property, ran for Parliament, and went to the wars with Marlborough. The Custis Papers and several other collections in the Virginia Historical Society, Richmond, have a number of items pertaining to the problems with which his heirs, the Byrds and the Custises, were plagued.

passed over in favor of old English soldiers whose backgrounds were no more glorious than their own, then the second-class status of colonials could not be denied nor could the fact that the English patronage system benefited them even less than it had their predecessors.[32]

It is not surprising, therefore, that as the creoles came to dominate Virginia society, they exhibited a new receptivity toward building up colonial institutions and a decreasing dependence on English ones. Although this receptivity became more pronounced as the eighteenth century progressed, it manifested itself in several ways almost immediately.

Sometime in 1699 an anonymous Virginian sat down and composed a rather sophisticated and knowledgeable essay on the government of the English colonies. Despite the subject and the author's identification of himself as "An American," the tract did not exude intercolonial goodwill. It attacked the favorable picture of the northern colonies, particularly Pennsylvania, contained in a recent book by Charles Davenant, the English political economist, and defended Virginia against certain criticisms leveled in the same work. Although the essay cannot be taken as evidence of incipient nationalism, neither was it a thinly disguised promotional tract or simply a special plea from the tobacco interest. "The Design of these Papers is not to treat of the Trade, but the Government of the Plantations," declared the author, "not how to make them great, and rich, by an open free Traffick, but happy, by a Just and Equal Government; that they may enjoy their Obscurity, and the poor way of living which Nature is pleased to afford them out of the Earth, in Peace, and be protected in the Possession thereof, by their lawful Mother England."[33] The sug-

---

32. Louis B. Wright and Marion Tinling, eds., *The Secret Diary of William Byrd of Westover, 1709–1712* (Richmond, Va., 1941), 84–85, 159, records Byrd's efforts to obtain the governorships of Maryland and Virginia. He was told Marlborough had declared "that no one but soldiers should have the government of a plantation." Earlier, Byrd II and William Spencer, the son of Nicholas, had both lost out to Edmund Jennings, an English-born colonial, for the secretaryship of the colony. Jennings, one of the few non-natives on the Council in the early 18th century, was highly unpopular. Philip Ludwell II connived to displace him in 1710 but was unsuccessful. Nathaniel Blakiston to Philip Ludwell II, July 20, 1710 and Stephen Fouace to Nathaniel Blakiston, Apr. 22, 1711, Lee-Ludwell Papers.

33. Louis B. Wright, ed., *An Essay Upon the Government of the English Plantations on the Continent of America [1701]* (San Marino, Cal., 1945), 15–16. I have identified the author as Benjamin Harrison III. See Carole Shammas, "Benjamin Harrison III and the Authorship of 'An Essay upon the Government,'" *VMHB*, LXXXIV (1976), but also see Wright's introduction to *Essay Upon the Government*, and Virginia White Fitz, "Ralph Wormeley: Anonymous Essayist," *WMQ*, 3d Ser., XXVI (1969), 586–595.

gestions he went on to make for the achievement of this modest goal, however, would, if implemented, have resulted in anything but obscurity for the colonies and their inhabitants. For one thing, the author wanted the king to define clearly the limits of his powers and those of the colonial governing bodies. Then, taking up on an idea of Davenant's, but making his own improvements to insure that England's "eldest" and most "profitable" colony received more representation, he advocated a general assembly for all the provinces. Not only would colonial representatives attend, but "the better sort of People would look upon it as a piece of Gentile Education, to let their Sons go in Company of the Deputies of the Province to these conventions," which would be held in a different colony each time. Finally, he suggested that a commissioner be appointed to travel from plantation to plantation and make reports to the English government that could be compared with the accounts of governors, colonial agents, and assemblies. In short, the author, perhaps inspired by the English nation in 1689, called for a "Regular Settlement" in the colonies.[34]

Among other things, this slim volume represented an effort on the part of Virginians to endow their institutions and themselves with a new dignity beyond that of just tobacco producers. The comparatively broad nature of the essay and the elaborate plans contained in it for mechanisms and structures to be added to the system marked a new commitment to colonial politics that was echoed in the actions of the planter elite. The so-called rise of the Council beginning in the 1690s, the emergence of the assembly two decades later, and the growing responsiveness of the elite to their constituents reflected this new interest in creating a richer public life in Virginia.[35] Native-born colonials owed their places more to inheritance than to English connections. When they tried to gain favors through patrons in the mother country, their efforts were seldom successful. Consequently the elite resorted more and more to internal institutions to achieve their ends and jealously guarded their prerogatives. Hostility toward "strangers" grew as the assembly passed bills against non-inhabitants

.34. Wright, ed., *Essay Upon the Government*, 24, 48, 49.
35. Jack P. Greene, *The Quest for Power: The Lower Houses of Assembly in the Southern Royal Colonies, 1689–1776* (Chapel Hill, N.C., 1963), 21–31; and Rainbolt, "Leadership and Constituents in Virginia," *WMQ*, 3d Ser., XXVII (1970), 411–434. My chronology differs somewhat from Rainbolt's. He dates the emergence of a new political style from the early 1680s when Robert Beverley I led the agitation for a one-year cessation of tobacco planting. I consider Beverley's rather desperate actions more typical of the old politics than the new.

holding colonial offices and as leaders complained that the crown was using the plantation to solve the Scottish patronage problem.[36] In contrast to the previous period, councillors now presented a fairly unified front when a governor challenged their authority or the integrity of their institutions. It was with sins of this type, rather than with any direct threat to their estates, that the mainly native council charged Francis Nicholson in 1703. The complaints they made against him essentially pertained to assaults on their honor and to attempts "to render the Council [an] insignificant Cypher." At the same time, leaders assiduously courted the people at election time and tried to use them to bolster their own positions.[37] Gradually the native elite abandoned the tactics of armed rebels and took on the trappings of professional politicians.

The 1690s also witnessed, after a series of false starts dating back to the days of the Virginia Company, the successful establishment of a college in the colony. The contributions of the crown to the project helped considerably, but the school could not have prospered without support from the inhabitants. The speeches given at the aforementioned 1699 fête for William and Mary not only defended colonial institutions but also stressed the importance of developing them. According to the student speakers, Virginia should not "be beholding to foreign parts for a thing of soe great Importance." Subsequently the school, if anything, suffered from too much internal attention. Virginians fought with royal officials, the school's Scottish president, James Blair, and among themselves over appropriations, salaries, and policy. As with other institutions, the elite became quite possessive and refused to allow newcomers to sit on the board of governors. Moreover, the planters sent their sons to the college. Figures on the educational backgrounds of later generations of colonial leaders indi-

36. On exclusionism see Byrd I to Ludwell I, June 8, 1691, *VMHB*, XXVIII (1920), 15–16; C.O. 5/1362, fols. 275–278; and McIlwaine, ed., *Journal of Burgesses, 1702–1712*, 281. On anti-Scottish feeling see Nicholas Moreau to Bishop of Litchfield and Coventry, Apr. 12, 1697, Fulham Palace Papers, XIV, nos. 59, 187, Lambeth Palace Library, London.

37. "Charges Against Governor Nicholson," *VMHB*, III (1895–1896), 375. Nicholson thought it significant that of the six councillors who had signed a memorial against him "only Coll. Lightfoot was born in England . . . ," C.O. 5/1314, no. 43 iii g. Relations between Nicholson and the Council had taken a turn for the worse after he had failed in his efforts to marry into the Burwell family. Polly Cary Legg, "The Governor's 'Extacy of Trouble,'" *WMQ*, 2d Ser., XXII (1942), 389–398. On use of the electorate see Rainbolt, "Leadership and Constituents in Virginia," *WMQ*, 3d Ser., XXVII (1970), 418–422; and Quitt, "Virginia House of Burgesses," 278.

cate it succeeded in replacing English schools as the primary dispenser of higher learning to Virginians.[38]

There is no better indicator of the strong sentiments for institutional development during this period than the renewed efforts in the last years of the seventeenth and the first years of the eighteenth century to build towns in the colony. Previous discussions concerning cohabitation had generally been prompted by a desire for tobacco regulation and had come to nothing.[39] Behind the 1691 act for the erection of towns, however, was, as John Rainbolt has noted, a new motive— self-sufficiency. Increasingly Virginians expressed resentment over being at the mercy of imperial commercial policy and what they perceived as the avarice of London merchants. Towns, it was believed, would encourage cloth manufacture and other industries and relieve Virginia's heavy dependence on English products then rendered highly expensive by the reduction in tobacco prices. Opposition to this act came not from ignorant white natives who allegedly did not know what a town was but from crown officials and English merchants who considered colonial manufacturing a threat to the economy of the mother country and who caused the legislation to be suspended. Towns on the scale and of the quantity envisioned by the 1691 law did not materialize, but neither was this century-end push for urban centers the total failure it has sometimes been portrayed as. What became the Tidewater's three most important colonial towns— Norfolk, Yorktown, and Williamsburg—were all developed at this time. Norfolk was nothing more than a few houses until the mid-nineties, when a substantial number of lots were sold and a church, courthouse, and jail were erected. The creation of Yorktown was a direct consequence of the 1691 act. Plans for Williamsburg began in 1699 after the Burgesses passed the necessary legislation in response to Governor Nicholson's desire for a new capital. Virginians had begun to require a level of community interaction above and beyond that afforded by the crossroads pub and the plantation wharf.[40]

38. "Speeches of Students," *WMQ*, 2d Ser., X (1930), 327; Wright and Tinling, eds., *Byrd Diary, 1709–1712*, 335; and Jack P. Greene, "Foundations of Political Power in the Virginia House of Burgesses, 1720–1776," *WMQ*, 3d Ser., XVI (1959), 490. Parke Rouse, Jr., *James Blair of Virginia* (Chapel Hill, N.C., 1971), details the battles over the college.

39. Leonard, "Operation Checkmate," *WMQ*, 3d Ser., XXIV (1967), 44–74; and Nicholas Spencer to Secretary Coventry, Dec. 9, 1680, *VMHB*, XXV (1917), 147.

40. John Rainbolt, "The Absence of Towns in Seventeenth-Century Virginia," *Journal of Southern History*, XXXV (1969), 343–360; C.O. 5/1313, no. 16; Louis Wright,

In 1705 Virginia acquired a history, and in any society that development is always one of significance. Before the appearance of Robert
Beverley's *History and Present State of Virginia*, there had been writings
about Virginia called "histories," composed by Englishmen or English-
born colonists, but they had been tales of personal adventure, promotional tracts, or discussions of particular problems within the colony.
Beverley's book, while including the latter two elements, also featured
at the beginning an extensive, rather Whiggish, account of political
events from 1607 to the present. It was the type of history that was
written about nation-states, but in this narrative Virginia governors
took the place of kings. That Beverley thought the tale of Virginia's
past struggles with English officials and activities of its former colonial
leaders worth researching and putting into printed form, though
such information had no immediate utilitarian purpose, indicated a
new interest in the colony's institutions and traditions. Moreover,
Beverley was not alone in his desire to record the colony's past. At
about the same time, William Byrd II composed an account that is no
longer extant, and Benjamin Harrison III announced his plans to
write a history based on the colony's documents and papers. Unfortunately Harrison died a few years later, and his work never appeared.[41] Colonials, because they were colonials, never completely
internalized their settlement's past or took it as their entire history.
Even the pamphlets of the Revolutionary generation relied heavily on
examples from English rather than colonial history to illustrate political heroism or the effects of tyranny and to argue the rightness of
their cause.[42] Nonetheless, by setting down the major events in
Virginia's past, Beverley gave a sense of permanence and legitimacy
to the society that it had never before possessed.

Creole dominance in Virginia made a difference. Englishmen, like
the plantation's inhabitants, made few distinctions between those

---

"William Byrd's Opposition to Governor Francis Nicholson," *Journal of Southern History*,
XI (1945), 77; Beverley's letter and narrative, Feb. 12, 1703/04 in McIlwaine, ed.,
Executive Journals of the Council, II, 392–393; and, especially, John W. Reps, *Tidewater
Towns: City Planning in Colonial Virginia and Maryland* (Charlottesville, Va., 1972), 65–91,
141–193.

41. Robert Beverley, *The History and Present State of Virginia*, ed. Louis B. Wright
(Chapel Hill, N.C., 1947); John Oldmixon, *The British Empire in America* (London, 1741),
x–xi; and McIlwaine, ed., *Executive Journals of the Council*, III, 149.

42. Note for example the allusions and historical examples in the tracts collected by
Bernard Bailyn, ed., *Pamphlets of the American Revolution, 1750–1776*, I (Cambridge,
Mass., 1965).

born in the Old World and those born in the New until natives began to take control of the colony. When the home culture started to perceive the Virginia creoles as an extra-English group, this New World elite was encouraged to reassess its colonial situation. The material achievements of their fathers, which allowed them to direct their attention to other concerns, tended to promote such a reassessment. Consequently, at the end of the century there emerged new kinds of responses to the problems that arose from living far from the national center of authority and of culture. Virginia's leaders grew more concerned about their colony's deficiencies and more committed to the development of indigenous social institutions. This consciousness was demonstrated by their interest in political activity, education, economic self-sufficiency, and the colony's past. The model for politics, colleges, history, and so forth, however, emanated from the mother country. Thus the founding of new institutions, although it eventually might facilitate political independence, did not make Virginia more American, if by that one means different from England. The process was actually one of replication, and as such it signified an acknowledgment of colonial status rather than an enunciation of American identity.[43]

It remains a matter of conjecture, of course, how significant the emergence of a native elite was in the psychological and institutional development of other colonies. New England began its existence estranged from the mainstream of English life and, therefore, possessed an element of alienation and a strong impulse for institutional development long before natives came to power. In the West Indies, as in the Third World generally, fear of the aboriginal or pseudo-aboriginal (black) population probably retarded or even stifled white creole identification with the colonial environment. Indeed, if slaves had become an overwhelming majority in Virginia or if, on the other hand, the mass of the white population had remained bound servants, the situation undoubtedly would have been different.[44] Finally,

43. On the replication theme see John M. Murrin, "The Legal Transformation: The Bench and Bar of Eighteenth-Century Massachusetts," in Stanley N. Katz, ed., *Colonial America: Essays in Politics and Social Development* (Boston, 1971), 415–449; and Jack P. Greene, "Political Mimesis: A Consideration of the Historical and Cultural Roots of Legislative Behavior in the British Colonies in the Eighteenth Century," *American Historical Review*, LXXV (1969–1970), 337–360.

44. See Morgan, *American Slavery*, 338–362; T. H. Breen, "A Changing Labor Force and Race Relations in Virginia, 1660–1710," *Journal of Social History*, VII (1973–1974), 3–25; and Rainbolt, "Leadership and Constituents in Virginia," *WMQ*, 3d Ser., XXVII (1970), 428–429.

settlements founded after 1660 quite possibly did not experience the transition from immigrant to native in the way discussed here since so many of their inhabitants came not from England but from other colonies. We do know, however, that English officials in a number of older colonies began singling out creoles for special comment during the late seventeenth and early eighteenth centuries, that colonists themselves referred to the creole phenomenon, and that the demographic characteristics of the English and the native-born varied considerably.[45] Consequently it seems likely that the transition to native dominance in other colonies brought with it significant changes, although the changes might not have been exactly the same as those in Virginia.

45. See note 20; Cotton Mather, *Magnalia Christi Americana: or, the ecclesiastical history of New-England, from its first planting in the year 1620, unto the year of Our Lord, 1698* (Hartford, Conn., 1853–1855; reprinted New York, 1967 [orig. publ. London, 1702]), I, 13 and 25; Bernard Bailyn, *Education in the Forming of American Society: Needs and Opportunities for Study* (Chapel Hill, N.C., 1960), 79; and Menard, "Demography of Somerset County."

Index

compiled by
David L. Ammerman

Molina, 112
Moller, Herbert, 17–18
Monacans, 114
Monmouth, 68
Monmouth's Rebellion, 65
Mook, Maurice, 30
Mooney, James, 30
Moore, James, 227
Morgan, Edmund S., 40, 47, 129, 198, 210, 235, 282
Morpeth, 83
Mortality, 46, 64, 208, 209, 246; "starving time" and, 46, 108–110; causes of in Virginia, 96–125; hunger and in Virginia, 97, 98, 99, 108, 109, 110; declining rate of in Virginia, 97, 113, 114, 120, 121, 122; rate of in Virginia, 101, 106–123; "seasoning" and, 104, 113, 120; seasonal fluctuations in, 104–105; Indian warfare and, 116, 117; in Plymouth Colony, 128; sex ratios of, 128; in New England, 128, 171–174, 247; in Maryland, 128, 247; of children, 142; decline of in Maryland, 150, 151; of parents in Virginia, 153–182; attitude toward, 168
Morton, Richard L., 22
Mount Vernon, 170–171

N
Native-born, 49, 127–128, 150, 151, 209, 224, 234–235, 238; early predominance of in New England, 127, 243–244; alleged characteristics of, 288; antagonism toward in Virginia, 286–287; emphasize virtues of simplicity, 288; hostility of toward strangers, 291–292. *See also* Native-born elite
Native-born elite: in Maryland, 49, 243–273; in Virginia, 49, 50, 274–296
Neill, Edward Duffield, 6, 11
Neroche, 82
New England, 22, 32; compared with Chesapeake, 51, 68, 126, 127, 128, 129, 133, 171, 172, 173, 206, 243–244, 246, 247; family life in, 126–127, 247; marriage in, 127; mortality in, 171, 172, 173–247; orphans in, 171–173; stability of government in, 243, 244, 246
Newport, Capt. Christopher, 97, 99
Nicholls, Michael, 185
Nicholson, Francis, 238, 250, 270, 286, 292, 293
Nonhouseholders. *See* Freedmen inmates
Norfolk, 293
Norman, Robert, 170

Norman, Thomas, 170
North, Roger, 87
Northampton County, 41, 229
Northern Neck, 193, 197
Northumberland, England, 83
Northumberland County, Virginia, 154
North Wales, 66
Notley, Thomas, 262
"Now-wife" (defined), 167

O
O'Daniell, Margaret, 144
Opportunity: in Maryland, 206–241 *passim*
Orphans, 131, 135; in Maryland, 141–151 *passim*; in Virginia, 153–177; county courts and, 134, 144–146, 161, 162, 165–166, 169; provided for by will, 136, 137, 162–167 *passim*, 169; community responsibility for, 141, 146, 151, 162; percentage of, 143, 162; mistreatment of, 143–146; bound as servants, 144–146, 159, 161; education of, 145, 162, 164, 170; clothing for, 145–146; property of, 164–167; in New England, 171
"Orphans' Court," 165
Osborne, Mary, 163
Osgood, Herbert L., 11
Otterdam Swamp, 196
Out-migration, 236, 237, 239, 240
Overseers, 213–214
Owen, Kimbrough, 27
Owens, Humphrey, 165
Owings, Donnell, 20

P
Pamunkey River, 114
Parents: in England, 126; in New England, 126; control of over children, 131–137, 147, 148, 151; early death of, 134, 147; early death of in Virginia, 153–182. *See also* Children
Parke, Daniel, Jr., 281, 289
Patents. *See* Land patents
Patten, John, 72, 74
Paupers, 216
Pearce, Jonathan, 227
Percy, George, 26, 97, 98, 99, 101, 102–103
Perrott, Richard, Sr., 170
Perrott, Richard, Jr., 154, 156, 170
Petty, Ann, 153
Petty, Christian, 153
Petty, Maximilian, 153
Petty, Maximilian, Jr., 153
Phippard, Mary, 139, 140

Notes on the Contributors

DAVID L. AMMERMAN, Professor of History at The Florida State University, is the author of *In the Common Cause: American Response to the Coercive Acts of 1774*. In 1975–1976 and 1978–1979 he was Visiting Editor of Publications at the Institute of Early American History and Culture.

LOIS GREEN CARR, Historian at the St. Mary's City Commission in Annapolis, Maryland, is the co-author of *Maryland's Revolution of Government, 1689–1692*.

CARVILLE V. EARLE, Associate Professor of Geography at the University of Maryland, Baltimore County, is the author of *The Evolution of a Tidewater Settlement System: All Hallow's Parish, 1650–1783*, and various articles on early American history.

JAMES P. P. HORN, doctoral candidate in American Studies at the University of Sussex, is working on a comparative study of local society in England and the Chesapeake during the seventeenth century. In 1976–1977 he was a Visiting Fellow at The Johns Hopkins University.

DAVID W. JORDAN, Professor of History at Grinnell College, is the co-author of *Maryland's Revolution of Government, 1689–1692*, and the co-editor of *A Biographical Dictionary of the Maryland Legislature, 1635–1789*. He is completing a study of the evolution of representative government in Maryland.

KEVIN P. KELLY, Research Associate with the Colonial Williamsburg Foundation, is now completing a study of Surry County, Virginia, and has begun a similar examination of the urban and rural societies of colonial York County, Virginia.

RUSSELL R. MENARD, Associate Professor of History at the University of Minnesota, was formerly a Fellow at the Institute of Early American History and Culture and a Research Associate at the St. Mary's City Commission in Annapolis, Maryland.

ANITA H. RUTMAN of Durham, New Hampshire, is a lecturer on paleography and a bibliographer. She is co-compiler (with Lucy Clark) of *The Barrett Library: Oliver Wendell Holmes: A Checklist of Printed and Manuscript Works of Oliver Wendell Holmes in the Library of the University of Virginia*.

DARRETT B. RUTMAN, Professor of History at the University of New Hampshire, is the author of (among others) *Winthrop's Boston: Portrait of a Puritan Town, 1630–1649*.

CAROLE SHAMMAS, Associate Professor of History at the University of Wisconsin-Milwaukee, is currently doing research on early modern consumer demand.

THAD W. TATE, Director of the Institute of Early American History and Culture, is also Professor of History at The College of William and Mary. The author of *The Negro in Eighteenth-Century Williamsburg*, he was editor of the *William and Mary Quarterly* from 1967 to 1971.

LORENA WALSH, Research Associate at the St. Mary's City Commission in Annapolis, Maryland, is continuing her research on the social history of the colonial Chesapeake.